Folklore in the Modern World

World Anthropology

General Editor

SOL TAX

Patrons

CLAUDE LÉVI-STRAUSS
MARGARET MEAD
LAILA SHUKRY HAMAMSY
M. N. SRINIVAS

MOUTON PUBLISHERS · THE HAGUE · PARIS

Folklore in the Modern World

Editor

RICHARD M. DORSON

MOUTON PUBLISHERS · THE HAGUE · PARIS

ISBN 90–279–7740–2 (Mouton)
0–202–90060–6 (AVC Inc.)
Jacket photo by J. Calder
By permission of ABC Press, Amsterdam
Cover and jacket design by Jurriaan Schrofer
Indexes by Society of Indexers, Great Britain
Phototypeset in V.I.P. Times by
Western Printing Services Ltd, Bristol
Printed in Great Britain

General Editor's Preface

Although everybody knows the difference between traditional and modern or between folk and urban, as they do between prose and poetry, it is an act of high scholarship to recognize and analyze the obvious and to bring it as "a new paradigm" into the scientific purview. The virtue of this process necessarily carries with it the vice of leaving out the middle. The distinctions are not at all clear in the real world; and as soon as they are made, tensions are established which lead eventually to a new paradigm. The present book is a large step toward resolution, as scholars from all parts of the world gathered to discuss the variety of situations in which lies something called folklore. It is not surprising that the smaller gathering was inspired by a uniquely heterogeneous Congress.

Like most contemporary sciences, anthropology is a product of the European tradition. Some argue that it is a product of colonialism, with one small and self-interested part of the species dominating the study of the whole. If we are to understand the species, our science needs substantial input from scholars who represent a variety of the world's cultures. It was a deliberate purpose of the IXth International Congress of Anthropological and Ethnological Sciences to provide impetus in this direction. The World Anthropology volumes, therefore, offer a first glimpse of a human science in which members from all societies have played an active role. Each of the books is designed to be self-contained; each is an attempt to update its particular sector of scientific knowlege and is written by specialists from all parts of the world. Each volume should be read and reviewed individually as a separate volume on its own given subject. The set as a whole will indicate what changes are in store for anthropology as scholars from the developing countries join in studying the species of which we are all a part.

The IXth Congress was planned from the beginning not only to include as many of the scholars from every part of the world as possible, but also with a view toward the eventual publication of the papers in high-quality volumes. At previous Congresses scholars were invited to bring papers which were then read out loud. They were necessarily limited in length; many were only summarized; there was little time for discussion; and the sparse discussion could only be in one language. The IXth Congress was an experiment aimed at changing this. Papers were written with the intention of exchanging them before the Congress, particularly in extensive pre-Congress sessions; they were not intended to be read aloud at the Congress, that time being devoted to discussions—discussions which were simultaneously and professionally translated into five languages. The method for eliciting the papers was structured to make as representative a sample as was allowable when scholarly creativity—hence self-selection—was critically important. Scholars were asked both to propose papers of their own to suggest topics for sessions of the Congress which they might edit into volumes. All were then informed of the suggestions and encouraged to re-think their own papers and the topics. The process, therefore, was a continuous one of feedback and exchange and it has continued to be so even after the Congress. The some two thousand papers comprising *World Anthropology* certainly then offer a substantial sample of world anthropology. It has been said that anthropology is at a turning point; if this is so, these volumes will be the historical direction-markers.

As might have been foreseen in the first post-colonial generation, the large majority of the Congress papers (82 percent) are the work of scholars identified with the industrialized world which fathered our traditional discipline and the institution of the Congress itself: Eastern Europe (15 percent); Western Europe (16 percent); North America (47 percent); Japan, South Africa, Australia, and New Zealand (4 percent). Only 18 percent of the papers are from developing areas: Africa (4 percent); Asia-Oceania (9 percent); Latin America (5 percent). Aside from the substantial representation from the U.S.S.R. and the nations of Eastern Europe, a significant difference between this corpus of written material and that of other Congresses is the addition of the large proportion of contributions from Africa, Asia, and Latin America. "Only 18 percent" is two to four times as great a proportion as that of other Congresses; moreover, 18 percent of 2,000 papers is 360 papers, 10 times the number of "Third World" papers presented at previous Congresses. In fact, these 360 papers are more than the total of *all* papers published after the last International Congress of Anthropological and Ethnological Sciences which was held in the United States (Philadelphia, 1956).

The significance of the increase is not simply quantitative. The input of scholars from areas which have until recently been no more than subject matter for anthropology represents both feedback and also long-awaited theoretical contributions from the perspectives of very different cultural, social, and historical traditions. Many who attended the IXth Congress were convinced that anthropology would not be the same in the future. The fact that the next Congress (India, 1978) will be our first in the "Third World" may be symbolic of the change. Meanwhile, sober consideration of the present set of books will show how much, and just where and how, our discipline is being revolutionized.

Readers of this book are likely to be interested in many others in this series, not only those on folklore and the arts—descriptively in all parts of the world, and methodologically—but also the many which deal with urbanization, ethnicity, migration, and the varied cultural responses to a rapidly changing world.

Chicago, Illinois   SOL TAX
August 4, 1978

Acknowledgments

First, I wish to express my appreciation to the National Endowment for the Humanities for a grant of $15,000 to defray travel expenses of participants to the Conference on Folklore in the Modern World. A supplementary grant for local and organizational expenses from the office of Dr. George M. Wilson, then Dean of International Studies at Indiana University, assisted with our budgetary needs. Marsha Siefert held a Folklore Institute assistantship during 1972–1973 to aid me with the planning details for the conference and contributed energetically, efficiently, and unflaggingly to their execution. Inta Carpenter has labored many long hours with me over the editing of the conference papers for publication in the present volume. Sol Tax gave generously of his counsel and enthusiasm in support of the folklore pre-Congress conference. I also thank Harvard University Press for permission to reprint the essay "Folklore in the modern world" from my book *Folklore and fakelore.*

RICHARD M. DORSON

Table of Contents

PART ONE

Introduction

RICHARD M. DORSON

The editor of this volume organized a pre-Congress conference on the topic "Folklore in the Modern World" at the Bloomington campus of Indiana University from August 28–30, 1973. Folklorists from thirty-one countries and four continents attended and presented papers, from which I have selected those reproduced here. Part One contains my keynote address, "Folklore in the modern world," which suggests four fresh lines of inquiry for the folklorist, together with papers falling under those rubrics: folklore and the city, folklore and ideology, folklore and industrialism, and folklore and mass media. Papers whose emphases lie outside those themes are assembled in Part Two, but they still reflect the general conference viewpoint of considering the content and the processes of folklore in a postindustrial world. It should be noted that the conference participants wrote their papers before hearing the keynote presentation, although likely topics had been suggested to them in advance.

A sense of convergence and consensus emerged among the international fraternity of folklorists at the conference sessions on the need to modernize the strategy of their discipline. At the same time they often disagreed sharply, in spirited panel discussions, on the proper strategy to adopt. The conference format called for an eight-minute summary of each paper, followed by comments on the papers from appointed panel critics, after which the discussion was thrown open to the floor. From the taped transcripts of the panel and floor commentaries I shall remark briefly on certain observations that seem especially pertinent.

Commenting on folklore in the city, several panelists challenged the formal presentations. Most of the speakers, asserted Barbara Kirshenblatt-Gimblett, were studying imported urban folk traditions rather than indigenous matter, in the fashion of the discredited survivalists. They did so because folklorists could readily identify immigrant-ethnic groups in the city and knew how to deal with them. Kirshenblatt-Gimblett identified three trends in the study of imported urban folklore: (1) an interest in the mere persistence of the old traditions as memory culture — for example, the retention of Polish folksongs in Detroit; (2) an interest in the urban-induced changes of the old traditions, such as Czech harvest festivals being adapted to the city or water witches being dowsed within city limits; and (3) the urban revitalization and renaissance of old folk forms, in terms of nationality parades and renewed interest in costume and cuisine. But for the folklore created in and about the life of the city, she felt that few of the conference authors had much to say. A start had been made by Imre Katona, in commenting on mass songs sung by city dwellers; and by Gyula Ortutay, in alluding to a special subgenre of urban jokelore.

Robert A. Georges underscored the new problems to be encountered in studying folklore in urban environments, because the greater number, nature, variety, and intensity of stimuli in the city than in the country induced a greater range and complexity of responses. Since people's perceptions and conceptions supply the basis for their expressive behavior, that is, their traditions and folklore, the task of the folklorist in the city in analyzing that expressive behavior was intensified.

Indra Deva raised the question: What is a city? He pointed out that Asian cities existed in preindustrial, premodern societies, and that in such cities folklore and the folk way of life predominated. Elite culture was confined to a tiny minority, and even among this elite the royal ladies might speak the language of the folk. So "folklore in the city" should not be correlated with "folklore in the modern world." With industrialization the folklore changed but did not die out; industries possess informal (human) as well as formal (economic) structures.

Daniel P. Biebuyck underscored Deva's point with respect to African cities and warned against the mistakes made by scholars a couple of decades earlier in studying problems of African life in terms of polarities and discontinuities between the rural and the urban. In 1959, at a conference in Kampala sponsored by UNESCO and the International African Institute, a group of social scientists came to the conclusion that even in black Africa there are many types of cities, some extremely old, that reveal an almost complete continuity with rural phenomena in matters of neighborhood communities, formation of interacting groups, and probably the corresponding folklore (Southall 1961).

Influences from modern cities in turn radiated out to the countryside as a reverse phenomenon, Biebuyck added. Rural narrators increasingly were taking models from written literature, and rural historians were incorporating travelers' accounts into their oral histories.

Bringing to a boil the implications in some of the commentators' critiques, Dan Ben-Amos flatly stated: "I feel we are involved in some kinds of self-deception....We are still in the middle of the nineteenth century looking at survivals." The panelists were changing the situation in which they looked at folklore but not the basic premises of their discipline. Modern living encompasses both urban and rural life, and to separate them arbitrarily sets up a false dichotomy. "We have to look at folklore in the modern world, and also we have to look at folklore in modern terms. We have to lift up folklore as an academic discipline and face modern issues and modern frameworks that deal with these problems."

Linda Dégh responded by declaring that theoreticians should not theorize without knowing their materials, in this case without having engaged in fieldwork in cities. The folklore of the city is what is expressed and believed in by people in the city; it is the reality and the present of city life, which does indeed contain old, archaic motifs — survivals if you will. But if folklorists do not know the old and rural and the preindustrial folklore, how can they judge the changed traditions in the modern city?

Ben-Amos countered that he considered himself an urban folklorist as a result of his fieldwork in Benin City. A Dutch visitor to Benin in the fifteenth century said that its streets were wider than the streets of Amsterdam. It was the Benin experience that had shaped Ben-Amos' ideas.

A secondary theme in the floor discussion centered on ethnicity. Francisco R. Demetrio, speaking of the Philippine situation, remarked on a process unfolding in cities of emerging countries that was opposite to that evidenced in the United States. In the underdeveloped nations, the new-found ethnicity linking rural emigrants to metropolises led to disunion and atomization. Sayyid Hurreiz's paper had illustrated just this tendency among resettled Nubian nomads. Carla Bianco responded that ethnicity unified as well as disunified and cited the formation of Sicilian and Neopolitan clubs among southern Italian workers in Swiss and German factories during the past decade. Such clubs helped overcome the culture shock experienced by workers cut off from their families and in a country with whose language and customs they were unfamiliar. These clubs enabled the workers to identify with speakers of their own dialect. Mona Fikry wondered if the problems of ethnicity should not be considered as problems of social classes rather than of ethnic groupings. She observed that "ethnic groups have class situations in the social structure whether it is in the United States, Europe, Africa, or Asia, and usually class lines are stratified along ethnic colorations." Ethnic custom serves as a crutch to bring pride denied a population group by the social structure.

Roger D. Abrahams capped this exchange with the comment that the folklorist should not and could not either encourage or discourage ethnic persistence. His role was simply that of the analytical observer attempting to comprehend the dynamics through which ethnicity was maintained. An example, comparable to Bianco's factory clubs, was the "home-boy" allegiances in Johannesburg and other South African cities among first- and second-generation migrants from tribal areas who sought out each other in social organizations to assert their "home-boy" ties. The folklorist should not take sides in the debate over melting-pot versus cultural pluralism ideologies.

The issues brought to the surface in the discussions of folklore in the city necessarily extended to the related conference topics on the agenda. Urbanism involved industrialism, which in turn led into the mass media, which at times served as an instrument of nationalism. One unexpected by-product of the industrialization theme was the recognition, noted in the paper of Demetrios Loukatos, of the effects on folklore of the tourist industry — an industry embracing transportation by air, rail, ship, and car, the hostelry of hotels, motels, and restaurants, extensive advertising involving fantasies and daydreams, and the manufacture of an endless variety of objects calculated to inspire sentiments of romantic legendary associations with the places visited. These modern, mass-produced artifacts helped create, as William Hugh Jansen observed, not a "fake-lore," but a popular lore, a *Folklorismus*, as the symposium in the *Zeitschrift für Volkskunde* (1969) labeled this industrial renewal of old traditions.

Commentators on folklore and the mass media pointed out their several relationships. Wilhelm Loots noted that in South Africa mass media had to a large extent taken the place of the oral transmission of folklore elements on one level of communication but had complemented and supplemented the still-continuing oral transmission on another level. For example, a cycle of jokes centering on the character *Funamarina* — the most common surname in Afrikaans, corresponding to *Smith* or *Jones* in English — in which the Afrikaners poked fun at themselves, had been traveling in the press, on the radio, and among the people. In addition to the interacting effects of mass media on folklore, and folklore on the media, several speakers drew attention to the role of the folklorists in utilizing television and radio for the collection, presentation, and discussion of folklore. Bai T. Moore recounted the initiation of his radio program in 1963, "Legends and Songs of Liberia," which in the course of four years brought in from listeners some 500 folktales, legends, parables, pithy sayings, farming songs, and other lore, along with historical traditions about fighting between Liberian tribesmen with bows and arrows and French soldiers with carbines. A legend of a warrior's footprint in a rock led Moore to dig on the site and uncover pottery fragments and new information on the history of Ivory Coast potters. A biographical song sung by a woman in Monrovia provided Moore with clues to reconstruct the life history of a prominent educator who began his career working as a steward boy for the Germans and came to Monrovia in 1902 to establish a local school.

In the Hawaiian Islands, Katherine Luomala reported, television and radio had utilized folklore materials both for instruction and entertainment. Faculty members from different departments of the University of Hawaii had collaborated on a general series of television talks about the folklore, mythology, geology, culture, ethnic groups, and industries on the islands. Skilled narrators from particular islands had retold folktales on radio programs, and these tales had reentered the oral tradition.

Barbara Babcock emphasized similarities between oral folk traditions and mass media, similarities not only of structure and pattern but also of communicative and expressive function. A daytime soap opera might be fulfilling the same function as a night-time storytelling session.

The session "Folklore and nationalism, politics, ideology" aroused the highest degree of emotionalism. In their papers on the rallying songs and symbols of the nationalist movement in Bangladesh, Mazharul Islam and Zahurul Haque gave personal testimony to the close interrelationship of a revolutionary cause with orally circulated ballads and tales that, while carrying immediate topical associations, followed traditional forms. From his extensive research in the Finnish folklore archives, William A. Wilson summarized the ideological shifts of Kalevala studies through the nineteenth and twentieth centuries that followed prevalent political philosophies. Wande Abimbola spoke of the potentialities of the media in Liberia turning from Western models and fashions to indigenous styles based on folklore themes. Paulo de Carvalho-Neto (in his paper and from the floor) offered examples of the racist deprecation of blacks in the oral poetry and narratives of Latin America. Together the panelists and commentators stressed the centrality of folklore and folk attitudes in the political thought of the general population. As Felix Oinas pointed out, the socialist countries in particular had always directed their collecting and research toward songs, tales, and sayings that were ideologically proper.

REFERENCES

Folklorismus
   1969   Folklorismus *Zeitschrift für Volkskunde* 65.
SOUTHALL, AIDAN, *editor*
   1961   *Social change in modern Africa*. London and New York: Oxford University Press for the International African Institute.

APPENDIX: PARTICIPANTS
FOLKLORE IN THE MODERN WORLD:

An International Conference

Abimbola, Wande (Nigeria-S)
Abrahams, Roger (University of Texas-S)
Acipayamli, Oran (Turkey-S)
Andrzewski, B. W. (Britain-P)
Araki, Hiroyuki (Japan-S)
Babcock, Barbara (University of Texas-D)
Baghban, Hafizullah (Afghanistan-S)
Ben-Ami, I. (Israel-D)
Ben-Amos, Dan (University of Pennsylvania-S; D)
Biebuyck, Daniel (University of Delaware-D)
Bianco, Carla (Italy-S; D)
Brednich, Rolf (Germany-S)
Bromley, Julian (U.S.S.R.)
Chaudhuri, Dulal (India-P)
Cortazar, Augusto R. (Argentina-P)
Dannemann, Manuel (Chile-S)
de Carvalho-Neto, Paulo (Brazil-S)
Dégh, Linda (Indiana University-S)
Demetrio, Francisco (Philippines-D)
Deva, Indra (India-D; S)
Dömötör, Tekla (Hungary-D; S)
Dorson, Richard M. (Indiana University)
Dundes, Alan (University of California-S)
El-Shamy, Hasan (Egypt-S)
Falassi, Alessandro (Italy-S)
Fernandez, James (Dartmouth-D; S)
Fikry, Mona (Libya-S; D)
Fortun, Julia Elena (Bolivia-S)
Gavazzi, Milovan (Yugoslavia-P)
Georges, Robert (UCLA-D; S)
Gopalan, Venkatachara (Indiana State-D)
Goswami, Praphulladatta (India-P)
Greverus, Ina-Maria (Germany-S)
Haque, Zahurul (Alcorn University-S)
Heilfurth, Gerhard (Germany-P)
Henderson, M. Carole (Canada-S)
Hurreiz, Sayyid (Sudan-S)
Islam, Mazharul (Bangladesh-S; D)
Jansen, Wm. Hugh (University of Kentucky-S)
Katona, Imre (Hungary-S)
Kirshenblatt-Gimblett, B. (Columbia University-D)
Klymasz, Robert (Canada-S)
Kosova, Maria (Czechoslovakia-S)
Lee, Du Hyun (Korea-S)
Lison-Tolsana, Carmelo (Spain-S)
Loots, Wilhelm (South Africa-D)
Loukatos, Demetrios (Greece-S)

Luomala, Katherine (University of Hawaii-S)
Mabuchi, Toichi (Japan-P)
Maranda, Elli Köngäs (Canada-S; D)
Meserve, Walter (Indiana University-S)
Moore, Bai T. (Liberia-S)
Morsy, Ahmed (Egypt-P)
Newall, Venetia (Britain-S; D)
Nha-Trang, (Thailand-S)
Oinas, Felix (Indiana University)
Okoreaffia, C. O. (Nigeria-P)
Ortutay, Gyula (Hungary-S; D)
Pentikäinen, Juha (Finland-D; S)
Rihtman-Augustin, Dunja (Yugoslavia-P)
Saleh, Ahmed (Egypt-S)
Sen Gupta, Sankar (India-S)
Sklowdoska-Antonowicz, K. (Poland-S)
Spyridakis, Georgios (Greece-P)
Tavares de Lima, Rossini (Brazil-P)
Ting, Nai-Tung (Northern Illinois University-S)
Vázsonyi, Andrew (Indiana University-S)
Voigt, Vilmos (Hungary-S)
Wildhaber, Robert (Switzerland-S)
Wilson, William A. (Brigham Young University-S)
Younis, Abdel (Egypt-P)

Key: S = speaker
       D = discussant
       P = paper of nonattendant

Folklore in the Modern World*

RICHARD M. DORSON

THE TRADITIONAL CONCEPT

From its initial conceptualization folklore has suggested the outlines of a hidden, forgotten, and backward culture. This culture of the folk was hidden in two ways: deep in remote time, in a prehistoric past, when early man perceived the world animistically, or at least in the pre-Christian era, when pagan man indulged in barbarous rites; and far off in places, away from the busy centers of civilization, in the peasant villages of the countryside and mountain ridges. Among the rural folk, old ways, customs, and beliefs, once vital and central in their epoch, lingered on as outmoded survivals — so ran the formula. In the minds of different folklore scholars the past took varying forms. It might be visualized as the dawn of man in a savage state or a high ancient culture before its erosion, but in any event folklore was past-minded and past-begotten, the shards and shreds, leftovers and relics of a departed age.

Synonyms of folklore in the nineteenth century plainly indicate this conception: bygones, popular antiquities, survivals. Coupled with this notion of folklore were pejorative terms, such as superstitious, illiterate, backward, primitive, which were applied to the people who possessed this culture. But another set of terms — simple, unspoiled, pastoral, close to nature — viewed them in a nobler light. Whether admired or despised, the folk represented a world different from the centers of power, wealth, progress, industry, and intellectual and political activity in the metropolises. This first formulation of folklore can be presented as a set of almost Lévi-Straussian polarities between traditional and modern cultures:

---

* This address has appeared in: Richard M. Dorson, *Folklore and fakelore* (Cambridge: Harvard University Press, 1976), 33–73.

folk vs. elite
rural vs. urban
agricultural vs. industrial
peasant vs. factory worker
illiterate vs. literate
handicrafts vs. machines

word of mouth vs. mass communications
backward vs. modern
superstitious vs. rational
magical vs. scientific
marginal vs. central

These explicitly stated contrasts intrigued the pioneers of folklore studies and aroused them to investigate the newly discovered, unknown, and unsuspected folk culture eclipsed by the high civilization. This theorem of folklore can be readily documented by statements and actions of the great names in the history of folkloristics.

Germany

In the late eighteenth century Johann Gottfried Herder, philosopher and poet, expounded a persuasive theory of literary nationalism based on the oral poetry of the common people who transmitted the soul of the Germanic tradition from its medieval springs, before Renaissance influences had imparted an artificial veneer to German literature. He called for volunteers to collect "songs of the people .. in the unlearned glee-parties of the peasant-folk, songs which often do not scan and which rhyme badly" (Gillies 1945:45). Jacob and Wilhelm Grimm heard his call and went out to collect tales rather than songs, although they considered all oral literature, prose and verse, of the peasantry as *Naturpoesie*. They described their *Kinder- und Hausmärchen* as a "great treasure of antiquity indispensable for research" and believed they could reconstruct the old Germanic pantheon from village traditions. In the *Deutsche Mythologie* which in 1835 elaborated his system, Jacob Grimm called attention to the scholarly values for the cultural historian in such oral sources as a supplement to documentary records: "If these numerous written memorials have only left us sundry bones and joints, as it were, of our old mythology, its living breath still falls upon us from a vast number of stories and customs, handed down throughout lengthened periods from father to son" (Dorson 1966c: viii). The example and concepts of the Grimms inspired nascent folklorists in one European country after another to emulate their mode of collecting and interpreting folk traditions as emblems of a people's proud antiquities.

Great Britain

The influence of the Grimms's investigations of *Märchen*, *Sagen*, and

Germanic mythology immediately struck a responsive chord in England, where seventeenth- and eighteenth-century antiquaries had already prepared the way for the recognition of folklore as a word and as a concept. In 1777 John Brand titled his miscellany of notions, customs, and practices culled from printed sources *Observations on popular antiquities* and emphasized their pastness. "The *prime* Origin of the superstitious Notions and Ceremonies of the People is absolutely unattainable; we despair of every being able to reach the Fountain Head of Streams which have been running and increasing from the Beginning of Time" (Dorson 1968b:1). By 1846 another antiquary, William John Thoms, perceived in Brand's accumulated mass of materials the subject matter of a separate branch of learning which he proposed to call "Folk-lore, — *the lore of the people*" as a deliberate substitute for "popular antiquities" (Dorson 1968b:7). Fully as much as its replacement, the new term stressed the past: "No one who has made the manners, customs, observances, superstitions, ballads, proverbs, &c., of the olden time his study, but must have arrived at two conclusions: — the first, how much that is curious and interesting in these matters is now entirely lost — the second, how much may yet be rescued by timely exertion" (Dorson 1968b:53).

Here, in the baptismal rite of folklore, appears the classic cliché of the folkloric enterprise: the old traditions and rites are disappearing; hurry up and collect them as fast as you can. For the next century and more collectors would be motivated by this premise. In a follow-up statement a week later in *The Athenaeum* Thoms correlated folklore with a pastoral, anti-industrial setting by quoting from his contemporary, Thomas Keightley, author of *The fairy mythology*, who opined "that the belief in Fairies is by no means extinct in England, —and that in districts, if there be any such, where steam-engines, cotton mills, mail coaches, and similar exorcists have not yet penetrated, numerous legends might be collected" (Dorson 1968b:55–56). The sequence is plainly stated: the advent of modern technology and communications drives out the old supernatural beliefs. In an appended note Thoms observes that what Chaucer said of elves disappearing may now, in 1846, be applied to Keightley's 1838 comment: "But now can no man see non *mails* mo." Even communications have speeded up, as horses gave way to trains. But John Aubrey, the seventeenth-century antiquary, had already mourned the elimination of olden lore by modern contrivances: "Before Printing, Old-wives Tales were ingeniose . . . Now-a-dayes Bookes are common, and most of the poor people understand letters; and the many good Bookes, and variety of Turnes of Affaires, have putt all the old Fables out of doors: and the divine art of Printing and Gunpowder have frighted away Robin-goodfellow and the Fayries" (Dorson 1968a:5–6).

Each new generation of folklorists would echo the refrain that modern ways spelled the death of folklore. Max Müller constructed his system of solar mythology around the concept of a "disease of language" in the mythopoeic age of the Aryan race, during which men forgot the original meanings of words and used them metaphorically; "good morning" is a solar myth. Accepting Müller's theory without challenge, Edward B. Tylor directed his attention to an earlier stage of mankind, the savage state of animistic thought, to formulate his doctrine of survivals: the folklore of today represents the survivals of animistic ways of thinking. Under the spell of this persuasive argument, the "great team" of anthropological folklorists explored collections of peasant folklore and stimulated the local vicar to collect such folklore for the purpose of identifying survivals. That was the great quest, the exciting hunt, to pin down the memorial of a prehistoric rite or custom or myth in its fossilized form as a peasant observance or utterance. Each of the Great Team restated the definition and methodology of folklore in terms of its past-ness, backwardness, and peasantness:

Andrew Lang: "There is a form of study, Folklore, which collects and compares the similar but immaterial relics of old races, the surviving superstitions and stories, the ideas which are in our time but not of it . . . The student of folklore is thus led to examine the usages, myths and ideas of savages, which are still retained, in rude enough shape, by the European peasantry" (Dorson 1968b:219).

Edwin Sidney Hartland: "Let me try to tell you what folklore is. . . . It is now well established that the most civilized races have all fought their way slowly upwards from a condition of savagery. Now, savages can neither read nor write; yet they manage to collect and store up a considerable amount of knowledge of a certain kind. . . . The knowledge, organization, and rules thus gathered and formulated are preserved in the memory, and communicated by word of mouth and by actions of various kinds. To this mode of preservation and communication, as well as to the things thus preserved and communicated, the name of Tradition is given; and Folklore is the science of Tradition" (Dorson 1968b:231).

Alfred Nutt: "The folk whose lore we collect and study is essentially the portion of mankind which has ever remained in closest contact with Mother Earth, the class upon whose shoulders has been laid the task of making the soil yield food, and of doing the drudgery, the dirty work of humanity. . . . In telling you what folklore is I have emphasized . . . certain features that differentiate it sharply from our modern *civilization*. That is, as the word indicates, a product of town-life, folklore is a product of the countryside" (Dorson 1968b:261).

These were no lip-service definitions. The Great Team devoted their major energies to researches in peasant customs and savage myths based on Tylor's doctrine of survivals. In his encyclopedic three-volume treatise on *The legend of Perseus*, Hartland (1894–1896) traced savage elements coalescing in the familiar narratives of classical Greece. George Laurence

Gomme developed his thesis of the mingling of Aryan and non-Aryan layers of ethnic tradition in extant folklore in several books, from *Folk-Lore relics of early village life*, in 1883 to *Folklore as an historical science* in 1908. Edward Clodd pursued the primitive idea of magic attached to names in an examination of one well-known English Märchen, *Tom Tit Tot; an essay on savage philosophy in folk-tale* (1898), and he alarmed some members of the Folk-Lore Society by his presidential address of 1896 with illustrations of savage folk beliefs and rituals surviving in Christian sacraments.

Collectors of folklore followed the lines marked out by the theorists and sought survivals among country folk in Britain and backward races throughout the empire. Robert Hunt in Cornwall, Charlotte Burne in Shropshire, Ella Leather in Herefordshire set the tone for the ample county collection of supernatural local legends pointing back to savage times. Thus, the legend of "The Man with the Hatchet" preserved in an almshouse carving in Leominster, Herefordshire, of a fellow with an axe, above this inscription,

He that gives away all before he is dead,
Let 'em take this hatchet and knock him on ye head

seemed a survival from an age when savages killed the elderly with a mallet. The greatest feats of collecting in Britain took place in the Gaelic-speaking outposts of Scotland and Ireland, where a fading language preserved what Celtic folklorists believed to be the remnants of a poetic pagan mythology. As early as 1860 John Francis Campbell was searching the Highlands and Outer Hebrides for the rich veins of narrative tradition he published as *Popular tales of the West Highlands* (1860–1862). An American of Irish ancestry, Jeremiah Curtin, visited Ireland between 1871 and 1893 to capture oral myths told in the western counties by Gaelic-speaking peasants living in wretched poverty in thatched huts. Other notable field collections to support the survivalist theories came from British colonial administrators and their wives and daughters interrogating peasants in India and tribesmen in Africa.

Scandinavia

In the history of folkloristics the Scandinavian — or Nordic, to include the Finns — scholars have formed an influential bloc, which too has shared the assumptions that folklore belongs to the past and the peasantry. The prime figure in the illustrious record of the Finns, Elias Lönnrot, journeyed to East Karelia in the 1830's to meet singers of ancient Finnish poetry, from whose runes he stitched together the *Kalevala*. As the historian of Finnish folklore research, Jouko Hautala, has written, "the

Kalevala opened up dazzling vistas to the few but nevertheless ardent guardians of Finnish culture; it lifted up to the general view a heroic, magnificent past, of which there had been no previous knowledge" (Hautala 1969:25). So artistic, eloquent, and informative were these oral poems that Lönnrot wondered "how they could have been composed by peasants" (Haavio 1971:3). Julius and Kaarle Krohn used the national epic as a point of departure for their theoretical formulations. "It is my belief that most of the *Kalevala* material is borrowed from neighboring peoples," asserted Julius (Pentikäinen 1971:15). Kaarle Krohn wrote his first major work on the history of the Kalevala runes. His fieldwork, primarily to collect tales, took him to outlying areas in Ostrobotnia, Russian and Northern Karelia, the Forest Finnish districts of Varmland. The historical-geographical method he devised and taught to his students at the University of Helsinki considered the migration routes of tales, runes, and other folklore as they traveled in past centuries from one peasant bard to another. Ultimately the employers of the Finnish method hoped to ascertain the date and place of origin of the tale or ballad type; and if they did not push origins back to the dawn of man, as did the evolutionists, still they looked back in historic time.

In Norway the pioneer collectors Peter Christen Asbjörnsen and Jörgen Moe followed the example of the Grimms in conducting field trips to outlying villages in quest of folktales. As Reidar Christiansen has written, "both were intimately acquainted with the people of the countryside" (Christiansen 1964:xli). Jorgen's son Moltke continued the practice, engaging in his first field foray at nineteen and concentrating on the conservative district of Telemark. In the interests of promoting Norwegian nationalism against Danish dominance, Asbjörnsen and the Moes hoped to recover an ancient Norse mythology discernible in peasant traditions. Magic wishing objects in the *eventyr* appeared to hark back to the Norse god Odin, or "Wish."

The eclectic Swedish folklorist Gunnar Olof Hyltén-Cavallius, who helped lay the foundations for folklore research in Sweden, made capital from his rearing in an old peasant district of Värend in the forests of Småland, although his career took him to Stockholm and Rio de Janeiro. On holidays he collected in Småland; and, as a biographer has written, he "carried his native district with him in his heart and in his suitcase wherever he went" (Bringéus 1971:90). The celebrated theorist of Swedish folklore, Carl Wilhelm von Sydow, also grew up in a rural environment in Småland and enjoyed close contact with servants and cottagers. Though emphasizing the role played by individual bearers of tradition, von Sydow followed Tylor and Lang in ascribing an ancient common inheritance of magic tales to Indo-European speaking peoples.

Similar emphases appear among Danish folklorists. In 1843 Svend Gruntvig made a ringing appeal to his countrymen to send him all known examples of Danish heroic ballads still surviving among the "humblest strata of the population" as a means of recovering the national folk-poetry of the Middle Ages. His writings on Danish mythical ballads stress "their great age, their purely heathen character." Becoming aware well on in his career of the Swedish equivalent of the English "popular antiquities," *folkeminder*, he employed it in the title of his encyclopedic enterprise of 1861, *Popular Antiquities in the Mouth Of the People: Folktales, Ballads, Legends, and other Relics of the Poetry and Belief of the Past, As They Are Still Alive in the Memory of the Danish People* (Piø 1971:193, 207, 214). The tireless Danish collector Evald Tang Kristensen, who published seventy-two books and left a wealth of tale texts unpublished, indulged in little theory about the pastness of folklore but plainly expressed in acts and words his conviction that folklore abounds among the wretched of the earth.

Folklore is mostly in the keeping of poor people; it is as though the comforts of life displace the cultural traditions. It is most reasonable, then, that it is to be found in the poorer moor districts in the middle of Jutland, and it is very seldom . . . that you will meet with rare and well-disseminated folklore in Eastern Jutland, or in the prosperous districts of Western Jutland. . . . As cleanliness and furnishings in the houses of the moor districts ten or twenty years ago [this manuscript is dated 1929, the year of Kristensen's death] left much to be desired . . . I have never come home from a journey without being infested with vermin (Holbek and Knudsen 1971:249).

Kristensen adds little vignettes about the impoverished country folk lacking in the world's goods but rich in songs and tales.

Grundtvig's equally famous student, Axel Olrik, is best known internationally for his theory of epic laws which governed the composition of traditional narrative. This theory derived from his own researches in Scandinavian mythology, medieval heroic poetry, medieval ballads, and magical tales descended from ancient myths. In short, the productions of bards and folk narrators along predetermined lines — direct action, the opposition of two active characters, the final resolution of conflict — are shaped by aesthetic principles of oral literature in operation since the myth-creating age.

Russia

The leading theoretical and field-minded folklorists in nineteenth-century Russia shared the assumptions of their European colleagues. Alexander Nikolayevich Afanasyev examined folktales, proverbs, and folksongs from the perspective of the mythological school, which explained the symbolic meanings of folkloric texts through long-forgotten beliefs about the heavens congealed in metaphors — Max Müller's "disease of language": "The greater part of the mythical concepts of the Indo-European peoples goes back to the remote time of the Aryans. . . . Hence it can be understood why the popular traditions, superstitions, and other fragments of antiquity must be studied comparatively. . . . The comparative method provides the means for restoring the original form of the traditions" (Sokolov 1950:72). This method of comparative mythology looking back to an early Aryan age Afanasyev applied throughout the three volumes of his celebrated work, *The poetic attitudes of the Slavs on nature: An essay in the comparative study of Slavonic traditions and beliefs in connection with the mythical legends of other related peoples (1865–1869)*.

Other interpretations shelved the mythological theory, and Vsevolod Fyodorovich Miller in the 1890's established the "historical school" which, while still pointing backward, aimed its sights at nearer periods of Russian history in the attempt to decipher Russian oral poetry. Disavowing the diffusionist or migrationist theory as to what routes were traveled by the subject elements that entered the *byliny* (epic ballads) from the outside, Miller concentrated squarely on the *byliny* as growths on Russian soil. "I occupy myself more with the history of the *byliny* and the reflection of history in them, beginning the first of these studies, not from prehistoric times, not from the bottom, but from the top. These upper strata of the *bylina* . . . can give, not a conjectural, but a more or less exact representation of a period in the life of the *bylina* which is nearer to us" (Sokolov, 1950:112–113). Miller and other members of the historical school then debated each other as to the precise period and area in which a particular *bylina* was composed. Their speculations ranged widely, from Tartar times down to the sixteenth century. But all agreed that the *byliny* were at least several centuries old.

The theoretical interest of Tsarist folklorists in *byliny* was greatly heightened by the uncovering of an active heroic epic singing tradition in the far-off Olonets region of Karelia. P. N. Rybnikov collected and published over two hundred *byliny* in the 1860's, and A. F. Hilferding recorded over three hundred more in 1871, along with detailed biographies of the bards. In the ensuing decades collectors continued the practice of undertaking field trips to remote areas in search of the prized *byliny*. Two talented pupils of V. F. Miller, the twins Boris and Yury Sokolov, journeyed to the Belozersk region in Novgorod province in 1908 and 1909 for the peasant traditions they would publish as *Folktales and Songs of the Belozernsk Region*. Their volume contains vivid impressions of the peasantry whose confidence they painfully sought to win:

We arrive at a village and ask, "Can we stay somewhere around here?" "Well, whose people are you?" is the first question asked of us, which, in the course of our travels, we have had to answer a thousand times, "From far away, ma, from Moscow." "From Moscow?!" repeats some peasant woman distrustfully and somewhat surprised. . . . "So you say, you're looking for songs. What kind of songs do we have? Are you short of songs of your own in Moscow? Our songs aren't any good. Everyone knows — they're just village songs. We're backcountry people!" (Sokolov and Sokolov 1975:14).

Suspicious, puzzled, distrustful, the villagers conjectured that the Moscow strangers were secret police, politicians, insurgents, even Japanese spies. "Well, they say out there that you were sent for a purpose: to find out where people sing about the tsar and to put those people in jail." The phonograph fascinated the peasants, who considered it an instrument of the devil, and so did the vision of Moscow, which they imagined as a big village.

Japan

Japanese folklore studies evolved in relative isolation, but they too emphasize the past and the peasant. The theoretical preoccupation of Kunio Yanagita, founder of folklore science in Japan, and his school has been the historical reconstruction of pre-Buddhist folk religion. In a tape-recorded interview in 1957, seven years before his death, Yanagita expressed his view succinctly: "Although the uncompromising march of Christianity has all but obliterated traces of ancient faiths in the West, Japan offers scholars an opportunity to observe and study still-vigorous traits of old religious ideologies. Beneath the Buddhism of modern Japan, the folklorist will find vestiges of ancient mountain and ancestor worship" (Dorson 1963:52).

Yanagita acknowledged a debt to George Laurence Gomme's thesis that the folklorist could isolate separate historical ethnic layers in current traditions. From extant rituals, taboos, observances, and legends Japanese folklorists reconstituted the popular deities and the worship accorded them in primeval times. Every essay in *Studies in Japanese Folklore* pursues this goal. Thus, Toshijiro Hirayama perceives in *ta-no-kami* a deity of the rice fields revered by rice farmers in festivals that extend back thousands of years. Nobuhiro Matsumoto analyzes comparative legends of Kogoro the charcoalmaker to conclude that Japanese ironworkers derived their belief system from an ancient immigration of artisans from the Asian mainland. Hiroji Naoe concludes that the family tutelary deity known as *yashiki-gami* is a recent development from an ancient ancestral cult deity of violent disposition, as befits ancestral spirits.

In the fieldwork enterprises he sponsored through the Japanese Folklore Institute, Yanagita set as his targets the small, remote villages of the mountains and seashore. His collecting teams visited hundreds of these villages in compiling the materials presented in *Studies in Mountain Village Life* and *Studies in Fishing Village Life*. These materials cover a spectrum of magico-religious practices and local historical traditions, and apparently support Yanagita's contention that "outside of the big cities, sixty to seventy percent of the population still follow the beliefs and way of life traditional to Japan" (Dorson 1963:51).

United States

In the history of American folklore studies the great catalytic library work and the great catalytic fieldwork belong to Francis James Child and Cecil Sharp. From his study at Harvard, Child corresponded in the 1870's and 1880's with a host of British manuscript holders and European ballad scholars in his hunt for the full roster of *The English and Scottish Popular Ballads*. In classifying his famous canon of 305 ballad types Child stressed the qualifier "popular"; these must be ballads that had lived in the mouths of the people, and consequently ones that had endured for a sufficient length of time to demonstrate their popular currency, presumably from the Middle Ages. Their archaic language and chivalric themes bespoke the past; although there were at hand an abundance of recent topical broadside ballads, Child deliberately dismissed these latecomers as not truly popular and of lesser artistic merit. The old ballads were the best. Child hypothesized that ballad poetry preceded art poetry.

In 1916 Cecil Sharp set out on the trail of the 305 as they were still sung in the southern Appalachians. The Englishman hunting British ballads in America adopted the same premises as the American who had, at long distance, sleuthed traditional ballads in Britain. Sharp went to the backlands where he could recapture the pastoral setting of old in which the ballads flourished. The peasant England of yesteryear, eradicated in the twentieth century by the industrial revolution, survived in mountain pockets of the United States. In the noble mountaineer of North Carolina, Tennessee, Virginia, and Kentucky, Sharp found a replica of the preindustrial English peasant — his very descendant. He describes a scene encountered in the Laurel country of North Carolina:

The region is from its inaccessibility a very secluded one. There are but few roads — most of them little better than mountain tracks — and practically no railroads. Indeed, so remote and shut off from outside influence were, until quite recently, these sequestered mountain valleys that the inhabitants have for a hundred years or more been completely isolated and cut off from all traffic with the rest of the world. Their speech is English, not American, and . . . it is clear that they are talking the language of a past day. . . . The majority live in log-cabins. . . . In their general characteristics they reminded me of the English peasant . . . the majority were illiterate. . . . Although uneducated . . . they possess that elemental wisdom, abundant knowledge, and intuitive understanding which those only who live in constant touch with Nature and face to face with reality seem to be able to acquire (Sharp 1917–1960:xxii–xxiii).

Here are all the stereotypical qualities associated with the carriers of folklore: remoteness, isolation, illiteracy, poverty, and the nobility of heart engendered by a life close to the earth. Sharp did draw some distinctions between mountaineer and peasant, and found a freer, more independent spirit and greater articulateness in the American type. He admired the bearing, the features, the friendly hospitality of these "primitive peoples," whose lack of suspicion contrasts with the fears of the peasants from Belozersk. Aware of the negative image attached to the mountain folk in the eyes of many city people, Sharp countered with assertions that he heard and saw nothing of bloodfeuding and moonshining. In Thoreauvian vein he lauded these cheerful, leisurely residents of Appalachia who enjoyed the graces of life rather than grinding out their lives "making a living." One of these graces was the singing, naturally and spontaneously in the midst of the daily routine, of traditional songs. The folksong inheritance, like the folk themselves, was pure and unsullied by industrial, commercial culture; if a "modern street-song" invaded the mountains, he perceived a cleansing process through which the singers wedded the tawdry text to a traditional tune and reshaped it into the form of a traditional ballad.

In a revealing aside Sharp contrasted the song repertoire of the cowboys, recorded by John Lomax, with that of the highlanders, as two groups similar in their communal isolation. But in spite of their more colorful existence, the cowboys mustered a sorry song fare, in Sharp's judgment, because they had no fund of traditional song, no imaginative past on which to draw, but must compose their ballads and lyrics about their immediate experiences, in the theme of "the cowboy's life is a dreadful life."

Sharp established for American folklore scholarship the guidelines of pastness and physical remoteness which would be followed for the next half century. Subsequent collectors combed Appalachia for further treasures of traditional balladry and published volume after volume with such titles as *Folk-songs from the Southern Highlands, Kentucky Mountain folk-songs, East Tennessee and Western Virginia Mountain ballads*, and *A song catcher in Southern Mountains*. As the scope of folklore collecting widened, the uplands proved also to be a reservoir of traditional tales. Isabel Gordon Carter, Richard Chase, and Leonard Roberts unearthed an exciting cycle of magical Jack tales from the hills of North Carolina, Virginia, and Kentucky. In the Ozark hill country of northern Arkansas and southern Missouri, Vance Randolph amassed all kinds of folkstuff in a region characterized in *The Ozarks; An American survival of primitive society*. One of the best field reports in American folklore, Emelyn E. Gardner's *Folklore from the Schoharie hills, New York* presented a balanced spread of oral traditions from a sequestered German immigrant stock living in mountainous seclusion. She sketched a picture of an ignorant, superstitious people bypassed by time and progress:

As I traveled by stagecoach from prosperous farms and villages of the Schoharie Valley into the hills, where log houses, abandoned grist mills, and long covered bridges still lingered, I realized that I was passing from twentieth-century conditions into those of an earlier period. . . . The customs and beliefs portrayed by Fielding, Smollett, Pepys, and Burns I found to be to a large degree those of the present-day Schoharie hill folk. . . . Of the world outside their immediate environment many of these people know but little. At an election held in Gilboa in 1920, a prospective voter, when asked whether he was born in the United States, earnestly replied: "No, I was born in South Gilboa" (Gardner 1937:2).

Hillfolk in Schoharie County spoke of Pennsylvania, less than fifty miles distant, as "furrin parts" and the Atlantic Ocean as "a big river." One old woman walked a day's journey to see the "steam cars" but ran for her life when she saw a train coming at her round the foot of a mountain. At first suspicious, the Schoharians took Gardner for a "guvment spy," and hid when she tried to take snapshots of them, fearful lest she injure their likenesses and consequently their persons. When she began taking notes on her conversation with a notorious "law character," who customarily "set the law" on her neighbors, the crusty hillwoman snatched away the notebook and pencil and screamed that Gardner was a witch making magic. Following these vivid vignettes, Gardner set forth a banquet of olden lore.

In other American traditions besides those of white mountain folk, field collectors followed similar assumptions. The black population yielded slave songs in 1867 to a trio of northerners, William F. Allen, Charles P. Ware, and Lucy M. Garrison. In 1880 it gave plantation tales to Joel Chandler Harris, whose collections bolstered the thesis that American Negro folklore, originating in black Africa and nurtured in the rural south, reflected primitive superstitions and ecstatic songs and dances of a childlike race. So too the American Indian, whose verbal traditions were carefully recorded by Franz Boas and his anthropologist disciples, appeared to scholars and public alike as the noble savage harking to wild, fanciful myths about beast and bird culture heroes. Boas always sought the oldest strata of precontact mythology recalled by the Indian nations.

THE REVISED CONCEPT

All this is familiar ground, covered when we first succumbed to the fascination of folklore studies, but in the light of my present theme it needs a summary review. Outsiders who regard folklore as an antiquarian, self-indulgent, and frivolous subject — attitudes frequently encountered — conceive of folkloristics as dwelling on a faded past and dealing with picturesque but backward and withered subcultures. Without accepting this value judgment, I concede that folklore studies have been associated from their beginning with antiquities and "primitive" country folk. But another side to the story depicts folklore studies in quite a different light, presents them as contemporary, keyed to the here and now, to urban centers, to the industrial revolution, to the issues and philosophies of the day. In this conception folklore is where the action is, not in some idyllic backwater.

The two views appear so opposed as seemingly to preclude any sutures, and yet they are not irreconcilable. "Folk" need not apply exclusively to country folk, but rather signifies anonymous masses of tradition-oriented people. If country folk move to the city — and in the past decades the metropolises of the world have swelled from the inflow of the rural population — they do not thereby forfeit the interest of the folklorist. Nor do generations born within city limits necessarily fail to qualify as folk groups, for their lives too may be shaped by traditional codes of behavior, dress, cuisine, expression, world view. If we recall the quality in folklore that first attracted the Grimms and the Great Team of Victorians — the sense that its possessors moved in a culture different from that of the intellectuals although living under the same flag — we may redefine folklore to avoid the taint of antiquarianism. If for "popular antiquities" we substitute "oral culture" or "traditional culture" or "unofficial culture" we strike closer to the true concerns of folklorists. "Tradition" too needs reassessment, for traditions are continually being updated. Survivalist Hartland expressed this idea pithily in 1885: "I contend that Tradition is always being created anew, and that traditions of modern origin wherever found are as much within our province as ancient ones" (Hartland 1885:117). The unofficial culture can be contrasted with the high, the visible, the institutional culture of church, state, the universities, the professions, the corporations, the fine arts, the sciences. This unofficial culture finds its own modes of expression in folk religion, folk medicine, folk literature, the folk arts, and folk philosophy. Yet the unofficial culture reflects the mood of its times fully as much as does the official culture, for both are anchored in the same historical period. And an absorbing interest in antiquities may fuel the spirit of nationalism.

This perspective on what might be called the contemporaneity, as opposed to the antiquity, of folklore, is the thesis of a book I have just published entitled *America in legend* (Dorson 1973). This thesis originally evolved in my mind while I was musing over a lecture on "Life styles in American history" for a course on "History of ideas in America." Changing lifestyles being a subject much under discussion, I had conceived an analysis of American history in terms of four major lifestyles: the Religious, from the beginning of colonization to the American Revolution; the Democratic, from the Revolution to the Civil War; the Economic, from the Civil War to the counterculture; and the Humane, emerging in 1964, the date of the Free Speech Movement at Berkeley. In each lifestyle I perceived a common ideal, characterized by the four captions, and permeating the social philosophy, the educational system, the landmark writings, and the culture heroes. Then one day it dawned on me that the folklore of each of the four periods also mirrored the dominant lifestyle. In the religious era the folklore revolved around the providences of God and the sorceries of the Devil and witches as they set snares for men's souls. In the democratic period a gallery of homespun folk heroes sprung from the people, most notably Davy Crockett, captured the nation's fancy. In the economic lifestyle, a bustling folklore of occupations arose around the cowboy, the lumberjack, the miner, the oil driller, the railroad engineer. Finally, within the past decade, the counterculture has produced a teeming body of traditions featuring pill peddlers and draft dodgers as anti-heroes. According to this thesis, the vigorous and vital folklore of each period fades into quiescence or recedes into the hinterland in an ensuing period. Witchcraft beliefs, which permeated society in the seventeenth century, from magistrates and college presidents down to farmers and sailors, still can be heard today, but in the faroff corners of the land. The Davy Crockett who was a living legend in the 1830's and 1840's resurfaced a century later as a Walt Disney boy scout with no folk roots. In our time the cowboy has become a subject for popular films and recordings rather than a dispenser of anecdote and folksong. Meanwhile the youth culture has generated a lively druglore and rock festival scene attuned to the vibrations of the 1960's and 1970's. Many of the themes in this new druglore can be recognized as time-honored in tradition — for instance, the battle of wits between the stupid ogre and the underdog trickster, here represented by the narcs (narcotic agents) and heads (consumers of marijuana and LSD). As Hartland said, tradition is ever being created anew.

This thesis can, I believe, be applied in other places. In his splendid *Religion and the decline of magic* Keith Thomas examined the supernatural belief system in sixteenth- and seventeenth-century England within and without the Anglican Church as a consistent and unitary world view responsive to changing historical conditions. Acceptance of magical ideas declined in the eighteenth century, Thomas concludes, not because technological progress eliminated the need for ritual magic but because society had already moved to new ideas of self-reliance and self-confidence. But when the belief in the efficacy of magical solutions or the dread of witchcraft prevailed, it prevailed throughout the society, and not as a cultural lag among an unlettered peasantry.

For the purposes of this essay I will discuss the contemporaneity and modernity of folklore under four rubrics: the city; industry and technology; the mass media; and nationalism, politics, and ideology.

FOLKLORE IN THE CITY

The more remote and inaccessible the region, the purer and firmer the traditions, the syllogism went, and so folklorists traipsed from their metropolitan homes to *terra incognita*. The hustle and bustle of the modern city, with its factories, department stores, banks, offices, traffic, and tens of thousands of people heaped upon each other in faceless anonymity, seemed to negate all the conditions most suitable for the perpetuation of folklore. With the explosion of urban populations in the nineteenth century, following on the rise of industrialization, the location of factories in cities, and the demand for cheap labor, the character of the city changed. What once had been a market center for the surrounding area now became a teeming industrial community with a large working class. In a provocative essay on the city in American civilization Arthur M. Schlesinger, Sr., countered Frederick Jackson Turner's thesis of the influence of the frontier on American history with a balancing emphasis on the influence of the city, particularly in the past one hundred years. "The new age of the city," he wrote, "rested upon an application of business enterprise to the exploitation of natural resources such as mankind had never known. The city, as insatiable as an octopus, tended to draw all nutriment to itself" (Schlesinger 1949:228). Between 1790 and 1890 the population of the United States grew 16-fold while the number of city dwellers increased 139-fold.

In recent years folklorists have begun to think urban. Although Robert Chambers published *Traditions of Edinburgh*, based on prowls in the old parts of town and interviews with "ancient natives," as early as 1824, he was pursuing antiquities; in any event his book made little impact on folklore science. *South Italian folkways in Europe and America*, written in 1938 by a social worker, Phyllis H. Williams (reprinted in 1969) presented accounts of feast days honoring patron saints and case histories of beliefs in magical practices from Sicilian families in New York and New Haven. Williams intended her study to serve fellow social workers and hospital attendants dealing with Italian slum immigrants, but her investigation showed the potentialities of urban ethnic folklore. In the 1960's two doctoral candidates in folklore, one in the United States at the University of Pennsylvania, the other in England at Leeds University, undertook fieldwork in cities at or near their university bases. Roger D. Abrahams lived for two years in the Camingerley section of Philadelphia and collected the materials that he published in 1964 in a milestone work,

Deep down in the jungle: Negro narrative folklore from the streets of Philadelphia, an interpretive collection containing such explosive obscenities that the first edition (this was before the impact of the Free Speech Movement) had to be sold under the counter. Abrahams disclosed the existence of a powerful black folk expression in northern cities, quite at variance with southern plantation lore. These northern "toasts" (long, often obscene verse narratives), brutal jokes, and games of "playing the dozens" (ritualized exchanges of insults) reflected the new toughness of ghetto street life. Across the Atlantic, Donald McKelvie was conducting field research in Bradford and its environs, a textile manufacturing area, for his dissertation on the folklore of an English urban industrial region. From this work he has published suggestive essays in *Folk Life Studies* (1963) and the *Journal of the Folklore Institute* (1965).

These articles make little effort to introduce texts — although in one McKelvie does append a list of urban proverbs — but concentrate on method and concepts. In directing his attention to industrial cities McKelvie realized that he deals with "living and vigorous tradition," not with "relics and survivals, but with aspects of contemporary custom and social behavior, usage and beliefs — with folklore, in short, as a living activity of a given community, not as a body of knowledge fixed in time, or as a corpus of survivals which does not become folklore until it has reached a certain degree of antiquity" (McKelvie 1963:77–94). He maps out his region to discern within the cement jungle of the city its component human parts, which can be reduced to "a street, a square, or a block of houses." The concept of the neighborhood emerges, as an ingrown community with its own fixed sense of physical boundaries. One informant, asked if she knew of another, said, "Yes, but she comes from White Abbey," a reference to the next street and a house not one hundred and fifty yards away. (When I was doing fieldwork in Jonesport on the Maine coast, a local person, in response to my question whether Pompey Grant was a native, gasped and said, "No indeed, he comes from Columbia Falls" — the next little town, ten miles inland.) Within their neighborhoods many residents live in near isolation, fearful of the traffic and the winter cold, limited by their infirmities, and served in or near their homes by corner stores and traveling vendors and agents. McKelvie investigates the degrees and limits of neighborliness: middle-aged women will bring meals to a sick neighbor but never invite her in to tea or to watch television; their husbands meet friends at a pub, club, football match, at the mill, but never at home. Closely inspecting the physical surroundings of three informants in the Westgate district, he finds that, although all dwelt in very poor circumstances, they revealed considerable differences in their domestic arrangements and social behavior. As the city on nearer scrutiny turns out to be a highly differentiated organism, so does the

apparently homogeneous working-class district dissolve into individual-
ized persons.

Having looked at city folk analytically, McKelvie scans their lore. He
reports little traditional narrative and none of the household tales Sidney
O. Addy had collected in Yorkshire and Derbyshire villages in 1895. But
he did uncover one cycle of scurrilous anecdotes about the Royal Family
— which he does not sample — and another about allegedly true happen-
ings, such as the Death Car sold cheaply because a suicide had left an
ineradicable blood stain on the back seat. Other lore included beliefs in
good and bad luck, expressed through proverbs, amulets, and rituals, and
a corpus of "sub-proverbial sayings" uttered on street corners, in shops,
on buses, across the backyard wall by fatalistic working people who "have
fought a draw with life" and register their resignation with stock epi-
grams: "Yo' don't get owt for nowt." McKelvie excluded from his list
proverbs of national circulation unless they had been reshaped in the
West Riding idiom.

Here we see the folklorist training his sights on the city, rethinking his
orientation, adjusting his categories. McKelvie freely acknowledges the
layers of urban folklife he could not even touch, deposited by successive
ethnic invasions of the Irish, the Slav, the German, the Caribbean, the
Indian, and the Pakistani. His discoveries lie not only in the field but also
in the library. He shrewdly appraises certain well-known authors as urban
folklorists of a kind, particularly Henry Mayhew, the Bohemian journalist who produced between 1851 and 1862 the four volumes of his classic
reportage, *London Labour and the London Poor.*

No folklorist can read Mayhew on, for example, "The Habits, Opinions, Morals
and Religion of Patterers Generally" without being aware that this is the very
stuff of his subject, and that he is in the presence of a collector of the very first
rank. Yet Mayhew was not seeking for survivals: he was recording, for quite other
purposes, the life of the poor of London in his own time; and the results of his
labours is, among many other things, a unique record of some aspects of the
folklore of early Victorian London. He was a folklorist by default perhaps, but
none the less a folklorist (McKelvie 1963:79).

Amen. The very phrase that captions Mayhew's first three volumes
(1968, vol. 1) places its subject matter within the discipline of folklore:
"The London Street-Folk." And they do constitute a folk, these street-
sellers of many commodities, street-finders or collectors of refuse,
chimney-sweepers, street-artists, dock-laborers, watermen, and cab-
drivers. In the fourth volume, a collaborative work, Mayhew and his
associates wrote of prostitutes, thieves, swindlers, and beggars. Observer
and sympathetic interviewer, Mayhew has captured the portraits,
accents, philosophies, and personal histories of the London street-folk in
a manner delectable to the folklorist concerned with traditional life styles.

As an instance of his initiative in field techniques, Mayhew called together a public meeting of "street-sellers, street-performers, and street-labourers" in the National Hall, Holborn, to ascertain "what were the peculiarities and what the privations of a street-life." A thousand persons attended, and a representative from each occupation spoke about his calling. What John Brand called "vulgar Rites and popular Opinions" strew Mayhew's pages. This incident, for instance, involving a "street-Jew" displays a folk prejudice of long standing:

A gentleman of my acquaintance was one evening, about twilight, walking down Brydges-street, Covent-garden, when an elderly Jew was preceding him, apparently on his return from a day's work, as an old clothesman. His bag accidentally touched the bonnet of a dashing woman of the town, who was passing, and she turned round, abused the Jew, and spat on him, saying with an oath: "You old rags humbug! You can't do that!" — an allusion to a vulgar notion that Jews have been unable to do more than *slobber*, since spitting on the Saviour (Mayhew 1968, vol. 2:117).

In the midst of city life Mayhew has caught on the wing an act, and its pithy verbal accompaniment, embodying an esoteric belief, which he glosses. His volumes continually yield such folkloric nuggets.

Another urban study, by an academic scholar, not a folklorist, R. P. Dore's *City life in Japan* (1958), provides evidence of the persistence of living traditional culture in the world's largest metropolis. The magico-religious practices of folk religion, or *minkan shinko*, which the contributors to *Studies in Japanese Folklore* all treated as rural phenomena, adapt surprisingly to urban conditions. *Kami*, the household deities so prominent in village Japan, maintain themselves in Tokyo wards, especially in the kitchen, where 68 out of 255 households in Shitayama-cho reverenced *Kohin-sama*, the kitchen-god. Water-taps and flush toilets did cause attrition among water and lavatory *kami* who guarded the spring-water bamboo pipes and outdoor privies in the country. Still, the whole complex of ancestor-worship, shrine rituals, faith in *fuda*, the wooden or paper tablets carrying the name of the shrine's *kami*, continues in the city. Owners of *fuda* not only place them in the *kamidana*, the household altar to the deity, but at times display them over men's bathhouse locker rooms with their caption "spirit which prevents robbery," or on lightning-rods on roof-tops. Sometimes they paste or nail them to hallways at home to prevent disasters from entering. Worn on the person, *fuda* ward off injury. "Yes, I am sure they have an effect. One day when I had the Narita *fuda* on me, I was at work and fell off a high shelf with a pile of things in my hands. Fortunately the things I was holding fell underneath me and I wasn't hurt. But the *fuda* was broken in two. I was overcome with awed gratitude and burnt the *fuda* and buried the ashes in the earth" (Dore 1958:336). Another *fuda* wearer attributed his survival from a serious train accident entirely to the power of the amulet. Some fuda possessors regarded their potency as spiritual and symbolic rather than magical, in maintaining a link with the *kami* of the shrine.

In recent years folklorists have consciously undertaken urban investigations. Inquiring into industrial folklore, a research group of Hungarian folklorists, led by Linda Dégh, selected as one of its targets the traditions of factory workers in Budapest. After joining the Folklore Institute of Indiana University in 1963, Dégh turned her attention to urban Hungarian immigrants who had come to Gary and East Chicago, Indiana, to work in the steel mills. In one paper published from this research, she describes in depth two Hungarian narrators in Gary, women of eighty-six and of seventy-five, who employ the telephone to exchange personal experiences, obscene anecdotes, jokes, and witch stories. The television set, continually turned on, stirs their memories and imaginations; the serial "Bewitched" led Katie Kis to recall Old Country witch legends. Deprived of their accustomed village audiences and storytelling occasions, Katie Kis and Marge Kovács have discovered in the telephone a substitute channel for their narrative instincts and art, and in their American urban life new sources of gossip and amusement for their memorates. Dégh's article is a model study of how peasant immigrant tale-tellers adapt to American city life (Dégh 1969:71–86).

The work of Dégh and her husband, Andrew Vaszonyi, in these cities of smoke and steel led me there in February 1968, on a brief pilot field trip. My aim was to attempt a *Bloodstoppers and Bearwalkers* of the city: that is, to pursue in Gary and East Chicago the multigroup targets I had aimed at in the Upper Peninsula of Michigan in a remote, rural, and small-town situation. Could a folklorist ply his trade in the city and make contacts and collect among varied ethnic and racial groups in a short space of time? What could he learn about the accommodation of black and ethnic traditions to each other and to their new urban frame? My preliminary answers in an essay (1971), with extracts from a field diary, "Is there a folk in the city?" indicated that the folklorist from the outside can operate within the city as readily as in the southern mountains, and that layer upon layer of folk-cultural traditions lie heaped up in the metropolis. In less than a month it was possible for a folklorist without previous acquaintances to record from southern blacks, southern whites, Greeks, Serbs, Croats, Romanians, Italians, Poles, Czechs, Slovaks, Mexicans, and Puerto Ricans and to obtain intensely dramatic and moving personal histories and experiences.

One of the surprises for the urban folklorist has been the relative paucity of his conventional harvest — tales and songs — and the abundance of saga, as we might call the vivid memoirs of migrants to the city from the countries of eastern and southern Europe and Latin America and from the deep south. Several hypotheses about urban folklore resulted from my trip: the processes of retention and loss of imported folk custom operate at different rates for various nationalities, depending on historical factors (Serbs seemed more culturally conservative and homogeneous than Croats because of their national church and national history); individuals often reveal unexpected deviations from their ethnic bloc; the city is breeding a new lore enveloping its diverse residents. In the case of Gary and East Chicago, elements of this lore derived from traditions of steelworkers, stories of violent crime, and *blason populaire* [ethnic slurs] about the many nationalities and races jostling each other on the city pavements (Dorson 1971:21–52).

American folklorists formally took note of the city in a symposium held at Wayne State University in Detroit in 1968 on The Urban Experience and Folk Tradition. The papers, with prepared comments and taped discussions from the floor, were published two years later in a special issue of the *Journal of American Folklore* and reprinted the following year in book form with a select bibliography. Besides my own paper the symposium included reports on Negro folklore and the city riots of the 1960's, by Roger D. Abrahams; medical beliefs of southern mountain whites as transposed to Detroit, by Ellen Stekert; and the evolving of an urban hillbilly music from country-western music, by D. K. Wilgus. One paper by a nonfolklorist, Morton Leeds, holder of a doctorate in political science, discussed problems of the rural migrant to the city in socioeconomic terms. The prepared comments on each paper and most of the floor comments from the audience were offered by Wayne State University faculty members from several disciplines and from interested Detroit residents, sometimes referred to in the volume as "unidentified black woman." Because of the composition of the discussants, the diversity of the papers, and the concern of some of the speakers and most of the audience with solutions to problems of the urban ghetto, the symposium almost turned into a discussion of applied folklore techniques, and sometimes into defensive postures on behalf of blacks or Mexicans or southern whites, and dealt little with questions of urban folklore theory. As one floor speaker, "second unidentified black woman from Detroit," remarked, "I sit here and listen, and presumably people are trying to solve social problems" (Dorson 1971:63). True, Abrahams' paper analyzing black riots in terms of folk performances on the grand scale and Stekert's reporting on the gulf between folk medicine practiced by southern Appalachian white women and the city medicine of doctors, nurses, and hospitals inevitably invited the questions how can the folklorist help prevent the riots? how can he help build a bridge between doctors and their poor white patients? The very words "folklore in the city" evoke images of the culture of poverty, racial districts, the cement jungle. One discussant, Reverend Hubert Locke, a black theologian, warned against romanticizing the ghetto, and a speaker from the floor reminded the panel of the need to collect from businessmen as well as from ghetto dwellers.

Fieldwork in the city has barely begun. So modest a start has yet been registered toward the tasks of urban folklore and ethnography that any talk of problem solving through folklore is premature and presumptuous. We should regard the cities as teeming laboratories for the folklorist offering almost endless possibilities among ethnic, occupational, socioeconomic, professional groups. From Detroit two ample volumes of Polish folksongs and Armenian wonder tales reveal the retention by first generation immigrants of Old Country traditions. These well-preserved texts elicited by the collectors contain slight traces of their American setting and constitute "memory culture." But the relation of memory culture to New World hyphenated folk culture deserves its own study. In his dissertation on Romanian-American folklore, Ken Thigpen distinguishes between immigrant retentions and new ethnic lore but places them in a continuum. He writes, "What a contrast to the Transylvanian village is an American city like Detroit! What a reorientation must occur in the mind of the budding folklorist whose preparation for fieldwork is anchored in the folklore classics based on rural folk cultures!" (Thigpen 1973:66). In New York City Barbara Kirshenblatt-Gimblett is leading a foray among east European Yiddish folksingers, shortly after completing her folklore doctoral dissertation on folk narrators in the Toronto Jewish community.

One of the most remarkable tradition carriers I ever met resided in Oakland, California, a bearer of Portuguese supernatural lore who had never seen Portugal. Mrs. Florinda Pereira Freitas was born in Honolulu in 1903 to parents from San Michael Island in the Azores who went to Hawaii to work in the pineapple and sugar cane plantations. She moved to Oakland at twenty-one, part of a considerable Portuguese-American migration attracted between 1910 and 1930 by the fruit-packing and textile factories and dairy and fishing industries of the California coast. With eloquence and passion, unlettered Florinda Pereira Freitas recited saint's and biblical legends and accounts of the *feiticeiro* [witch] and the *quebrante* [evil eye]. These were in no way dormant deposits of memory culture but vital experiences. Right in her own home where I recorded her on 26th Street in Oakland in 1968, a suspected *feiticeiro*, also from San Michael Island, came into Florinda's house, to see her new baby, and surreptitiously cut the baby's hair. The baby, Vivian (in 1968 a grown-up daughter), groaned, and Florinda rushed to the bedside, to discover a big piece of hair on the pillow where the feiticeiro had licked the baby with her tongue. "They have sand or some salt and when they lick it's just like a razor blade. They can cut. Sometimes it [the hair] grows or sometimes it never grows in." Florinda rushed around to her mother-in-law, wise in such matters, who took the present the *feiticeiro* had brought — a *camisinha,* baby's blouse — and said, "I'm goin' to fix this so that woman no harm nobody no more. She'll never be no more feiticeiro." And shortly after the *feiticeiro* hastily departed the neighborhood. This happened not in the southern mountains but in the heart of an industrial city.

FOLKLORE AND INDUSTRIALIZATION AND TECHNOLOGY

In the older theory of folklore, Mother Earth and the peasant and pastoral life cradled the seasonal rituals and traditional culture that folklorists studied, not only in oral but also in physical forms. Craftsmen of village and farm, along with oral narrators and bards, transmitted folk skills and products. The industrial revolution silted up the wells of folk energy, so ran the theory, both in terminating the rural rhythms so conducive to storytelling, folksinging, and the persistence of folk belief and in replacing the craftsman by the machine. In common usage "folklore" has meant preindustrial traditions and artifacts. The machine, the factory, the assembly-line method of mass production, and the wholesale distribution and consumption of goods supposedly mark an end to folklore and folklife patterns in the steadily expanding domain of the world they occupy. Have not the old Märchen and Child ballads disappeared in the Westernized, industrialized nations? Urban industrialism has destroyed the old folk community and created in its place a traditionless, faceless labor force, bound to machines.

A body of counter-evidence and counter-theory is beginning to appear. Hermann Bausinger in *Volkskultur in der technischen welt* (1961) challenged the traditional view of tradition. He speaks of a "fundamental new approach in folklore studies:"

For about a century, the field of German Volkskunde studies had seen its principal objective in the attempts to grope back to the era of Germanic antiquities, using clues provided by still living folk traditions. Today, this study of survivals, predominantly mythological in orientation, has by and large been transformed into a historically oriented investigation of contemporary patterns. We no longer believe that industrialization necessarily implies the end of a specific folk culture, but rather we attempt to trace the modifications and mutations undergone by *folk culture in the industrialized and urbanized world* (Bausinger 1968:127).

Bausinger adds that this changed perspective requires a shift in methodology, which has not yet been satisfactorily accomplished, but recent projects clearly demonstrated that the "folklorist brings to the job a set of tools" quite distinct from the tools of the sociologist. Some inquiries of his institute at Tübingen deal with the relation of the tourist industry to folk culture. Examining tourist centers in the Black Forest and the Tyrol, the investigators concluded that the vast influx of visitors into villages catering to tourists did not destroy the old traditions, although the intrusion of alien ways did alter the existing social and economic institutions. Rather, the Tübingen folklorists perceived a complex phenomenon involving processes both of integration and disintegration. This whole question of the conscious commercialization of folk festivals, dances, costumes, and crafts has led to the neologism "Folklorismus" to which the *Zeitschrift für Volkskunde* devoted an issue in 1969. Not only the tourist villages but the whole countryside has responded to the forces of industrialization represented by increased mobility, resulting from the advent of the automobile, the mechanization of agriculture, policies of land reclamation and resettlement, and the spread of small-scale industry into the countryside. Industrialization is seen as a rural as well as an urban development affecting folk traditions. An example Bausinger offers concerns a broadened concept of folk drama to include Christmas plays, local historical performances celebrating anniversaries of an event or a birth- or death-day, and the open-air theater "treating romantic-patriotic themes — which in recent decades has established itself in market squares, parks, stone quarries, and on romantic sites strewn with ruins."

In the Institute for Central European Folk Research at the University of Marburg, directed by Gerhard Heilfurth, a specialist in European miners' folklore, one section is devoted to "Research on Industry and Mining." Projects include "(a) Mining in its key sociocultural position as a link between primitive patterns of production and advanced technology; (b) The vocabulary of mining on the basis of specialized industrial technical terminology; and (c) Forms of industrial life and 'worker's culture'"(Heilfurth 1968:138).

Similarly a team of folklorists in Hungary in the 1950's formed a Group for the Research of Workmen's Folklore, supported by the Hungarian Academy of Sciences, to undertake the "systematic disclosure and study of Hungary's industrial folklore." Directed by Linda Dégh, the group set up such targets as the mode of life, culture, and folklore of skilled iron workers; unskilled workers from the country in the building trades; and apprentices in the new industrial songs of 1860–1945 and the traditional customs and folklore of the agrarian proletariat. This proletariat included such groups as the navvies or seasonal construction workers and the small craftsmen — also remarked on by Bausinger — who shared both agrarian and industrial traditions. In a comparative study of two coal mining villages, Kishártyan and Karancskeszi, the group found preindustrial folklore well preserved among a male population composed almost wholly of miners or factory laborers and much less retained in the other, where 38 percent of the men were agricultural laborers resented by the local authorities and classroom teachers (Dorson 1965).

The redirection of folklore studies in the Soviet Union since 1936 toward Party ideology has strongly stimulated interest in the folklore of factory and mill, not merely in the contemporary period but from earlier times as well. Research in printed sources uncovered songs of workers in foundries and mines in the eighteenth and nineteenth centuries. A characteristic feature, distinguishing workers' from peasants' songs right from the start, lay in the attention to industrial tools and processes:

Oh, you, who bathe us in our own sweat,
The Zmeyevsky foundry!
Sharply, loudly she beats on a board,
And invites people to visit her,
Beside the cord, the side,
There is a trough and a rake,
A poker, a hammer;
We pour a charge into the furnace
Of four hundred poods in weight;
When we have put in the four hundred poods in weight —
In one shift we will burn it all up (Sokolov 1950:577–578).

A pood is approximately seven tons. The song was recovered from an 1865 newspaper.

Another element in this and similar songs stressed the resentment by workmen of their repressive authorities, who are directly named, and the Soviet folklorists also see in these pieces anticipations of the workers' collective, in their spirit of defiance and boldness, as the workers strike back at foremen (often German) and overseers. Yury Sokolov underscores the community of interest between peasant and worker in the early stage of industrialization, when the factory was yet a manufactory with much work done by hand, and the factory workman was usually a transported peasant.

Besides songs and song-poems descriptive of factory life in an earlier day, Soviet folklorists unearthed "secret tales" of Ural workers which related legendary accounts, unknown to the oppressive mill owners and tsarist police, of worker and bandit heroes who conceal treasure in the mountain until the toiling masses inherit the riches of the earth.

After the October revolution the new Soviet folklore, especially the *chastushkas* [short popular rhymes] celebrated not only industrial workers in the city but also country workers on the now mechanized collective farms. The tractor itself becomes a symbol of felicity:

I did not love the tractor driver,
I was not a tractor driver myself.
But when I got behind the wheel myself,
I fell in love with the tractor (Sokolov 1950:649).

Other *chastushkas* hymn the power and efficiency of the tractor, its appeal to girls after their initial shyness, and their romancing of the tractor driver and dreams of some day becoming a tractor driver's wife, or even a driver themselves: "There behind the tractor's wheel / The girl is sitting like a king." With the introduction of machinery and collective management to the farms the successful young workers declared their resentment against the derogatory label "country bumpkins" and composed a *chastushka* leveling all distinctions between city and countryside. Industrialization has thus linked the erstwhile peasant and the city factory worker in a common newfound self-confidence.

A sign of new research in England is Alan Smith's forty-eight-page pamphlet, one-third given over to illustrations, on "Discovering Folklore in Industry" (Smith 1969). Smith provides no references or sources, and his headings — Ships and seafarers, Miners and quarrymen, Apprentices and beginners, Printers and machinery, Unions and factories, The industrial community — promise much more than they deliver. Primarily he deals, as did Sébillot before him in fuller scope, with the curiosa of trades and occupations — the odd belief, saying, or custom, as the rite of "trussing the cooper" or "banging out" the apprentice printer, initiation ceremonies of long standing in which the newly accredited workman is besmeared with soot or ink. Smith's instances of performances by Morris dancers in Cheshire and Lancashire, who wear clogs and who substitute hanks of untwisted cotton rope for the sticks and handkerchiefs they customarily carry, seem small revisions of village observances in an urban, industrial setting. More to the point are the folk beliefs in sterility caused by machinery (such as welding tools), or by service in airplanes at high altitudes; and the legends attached to Ned Ludd, a fictitious apprentice framework knitter of Nottinghamshire, who allegedly smashed his frame with a hammer after being whipped by a magistrate, and so initiated the underground movement of craftsmen against shoddy machinery, or, as others have it, against technological progress. Smith suggests as a preliminary typology survivals of preindustrial traditions in the industrial era, such as Pace Egg plays enacted in factory towns; new growth, for instance, the Londoners' belief in luck brought by chimney sweeps at weddings; and transfers of folk ideas connected with older objects to modern ones, such as the shift from ships to airplanes in the notion that traveling priests or nuns bring bad luck.

In spite of the advanced technology and industrialization of the United States, American folklorists have as yet done little probing into industrial traditions. The chief successes to date are registered by George Korson with anthracite and bituminous coal miners and by Mody Boatright with oil drillers and other oilfield types. Korson brought to the surface an extensive repertoire of miners' songs reflective of underground work, cave-ins and disasters, loyalty to the union, and the ethnic strains among the colliers (Korson 1938, 1943, 1960). Boatright performed a still more difficult feat, since the folklore of the oil industry included little in the way of songs and no folktales of the Märchen variety. But his interviews with oilmen yielded a cycle of tall tales, many highly technical, attributed to the yarn-spinning of Gib Morgan, a Münchausen of the oilfields (Boat-right 1945), and a corpus of legendary anecdotes connected with the location of "black gold," the "Coal Oil Johnnies" who dissipated their sudden fortunes, and the "McCleskeys" who handled theirs frugally. In an ingenious analysis, Boatright identified oilfield types such as the prospector, the driller, the shooter, and the promoter, and associated them with earlier known figures in American folklore, such as the wizard, the ringtailed roarer, and the Yankee trader. He broadened his inquiry to include oral history and so moved from the strict categories of folklore to the related realm of personal reminiscence and experience in the oil-fields. *Folklore of the Oil Industry* (Boatright 1963) demonstrated the continuity of preindustrial and industrial folk themes. The waterwitch slides into the doddle-bugger, the search for buried treasure glides into the quest for liquid gold, the tall tales of hunting and shooting merge with technological whoppers about drilling.

American industrial folklore lies open as a vast, uncharted field. A recent catch-all anthology entitled *Folklore from the working folk of America* concentrates on the older occupations and contains little that can be called industrial (Coffin and Cohen 1973). Two folklore doctoral dissertations at Indiana University are exploring the subject: one by Bruce Nickerson, who has worked in industrial plants, on blue-collar folklore, and another by Betty Messenger on traditions of the linen industry in northern Ireland. In a preview article she samples songs and rhymes circulating in spinning mills:

The yellow belly doffers,
Dirty wipers down,
The nasty, stinking spinning room,
The stink will knock you down (Messenger 1972:18).

Doffers are the young apprentice spinners who replaced the filled bob-bins of yarn with empty ones, and wiped down or cleaned the wet spinning machines while wearing yellow oilskin aprons, hence the "yel-low belly." The doffers sang mill songs, often about themselves.

Meanwhile we await penetration of the steel industry, the entertain-ment industry — a borderland between mass communications and mass manufacturing — the transportation industry (B. A. Botkin and Alvin Harlow's *A treasury of railroad folklore* is primarily a literary compen-dium), the automotive industry, and other industrial giants. Any consideration of industrial folklore should include traditions gravitating to specific machines, such as automobile legends and computer jokes. Two of the great technological symbols of the machine age, the auto-mobile and the computer, have captivated the folk fancy. A series of macabre migratory legends pivots around the auto: the Death Car, the Stolen Grandmother, the Killer in the Back Seat (Drake 1968:92–109),

The Ghostly Hitchhiker (see also Sanderson 1969:241–252). As for the computer, seemingly the most remote and dehumanized of man's modern inventions, it has generated its own stock of terse and elaborate jocular narratives.

FOLKLORE AND THE MASS MEDIA

In the traditional concept of folklore the spoken word is paramount. Oral tradition and oral transmission are supposedly the *sine qua non*, blighted in our time by the printed word and the new electronic channels of communication — radio, cinema, television. Only in hidden pockets of our civilization, deep in mountain hollows, out on scrub country flats, or among extreme orthodox sects like the Amish and the Hasidim, impervious to modern ways, do the undefiled word-of-mouth tradition and face-to-face audience still persist. The enemy of folklore is the media that blankets mass culture: the large circulation newspapers and magazines we read, the movie and television screens we watch, and the recording industry whose discs we listen to. So runs the lament. What is distributed to the millions, after an elaborate, expensive packaging process, does seem the antithesis of the slow drip of invisible tradition.

But there may be linkages between the folk and the mass cultures. Marshall McLuhan has talked about the new oral-aural ambiance of the media which in a way reverts to the early tribal community. The millions share the same spectacles, laugh at the same comedies, idolize the same stars. Some folklorists have already recognized that the mass media transmit, in suitably adapted form, folk items that enjoyed currency in limited circles. Several excellent studies — Charles Keil's *Urban Blues*, Bill Malone's *Country Music U.S.A.*, Archie Green's *Only a Miner* — have examined the complex relation among folksongs, folk music, and folk singers in their natural habitat and the end products of popular hits, studio recording artists, and cabaret performers. A song like "Casey Jones" can coexist in tradition, on the vaudeville stage, as a sheet music best seller, and in obscene parodies — all related in greater or lesser degree. Keil inspects the mechanics and techniques of the recording industry that remold southern Negro blues singers like B. B. King and Bobby Bland into successful entertainers for urban audiences.

As yet few folklorists have ventured into large interpretations of folklore in the mass media, but in 1972 in *Myth and Modern Man* Raphael Patai drew bold analogies between classical myths and expressive formulations in western industrial society. He compares Herakles with Mickey Mouse of Walt Disney's film cartoons:

The basic similarity of the two hero types lies primarily in the power relationship between the hero and his adversary. Whether Mickey or Herakles, the hero in each case faces overwhelming odds. In fact, in the course of the almost ritualized combat sequence, there are invariably one or more junctures at which the hero is quite clearly trapped and defeated . . . A second and equally important similarity between Mickey and Herakles is that both partake of a double character . . . superhuman hero and ridiculous buffoon . . . [Mickey's] very appearance provokes laughter. But then, after sufficient provocation by the Cat, he shows his mettle: underneath the mousey exterior he is, in reality, a great little hero. Inasmuch as he defeats the Cat, he is Superman (Patai 1972:229–230).

So Patai brought a second mass media hero into his equation: Superman of the comic books. In other analogies he likens the magico-mythical qualities of the ambrosia and nectar quaffed by the gods with the Coke sipped by modern mortals, and the smoke and incense rituals of yore with the balm conferred by cigarettes. Madison Avenue advertising in pictures and text underlines the excitement, gaiety, youthful transport, and ecstasy induced by Cokes and Smokes. The ad men also utilize mythical heroes and beasts in advancing the claims of their products through television commercials and magazine ads. The bald, half-naked giant known as Mr. Clean, who magically vanquishes kitchen floor dirt, is a jinni from the *Arabian Nights*. A Green Giant gazes benevolently at dwarfs preparing green peas for market. "Put a Tiger in Your Tank!" advertised the makers of Esso gasoline in the most effective ad ever for an automotive fuel. Posters of the tiger, animated cartoons in TV commercials of the tiger pushing a car, stuffed tigers placed inside cars – all carried further the mythical identification of the automobile with the power of a wild animal.

Magic metamorphosis, according to Patai, characterized much of the advertising for products that can assist the harried housewife in her incessant battle against dirt, odors, and germs. No appliance wins more respect and awe on this score than the washing machine; accordingly ad men stress the "masculine, phallic aspect of this most powerful, active, and aggressive of all major household appliances." In the modern myth of the sexual superman, best characterized by James Bond and known not only through successful films but also from ten miilion copies of books about his adventures, recurs the "archetypal mythical hero," who descends into Hades and wanders like Theseus through a labyrinth of dangers. The man in the street admires and seeks to emulate the virile life style of "007." Although Patai's analogies seem strained, they suggest lines of inquiry that the folklorist more readily than the mythologist might undertake. Patai does touch base with Stith Thompson's *Motif-Index* on one occasion for instances of the mouse in folktales, but for the most part he proceeds by tenuous analogies on supposed myth resemblances.

For the past several years I have assigned graduate students an exercise on culling folklore from the mass media. They clip items from printed sources and note examples from television, radio, and films. Their directions are, first, to identify folkloristic themes; second, to comment on the relation of these themes to oral folk sources; and, third, to interpret the use or purpose to which this mediated folklore is being put. Most students compile intriguing scrapbooks that reveal the wealth of folkstuff encountered in their daily exposure to the media over a period of a couple of months. Some of these reports have been deposited in the Folklore Archives of Indiana University; two have developed theories and typologies original enough to merit publication in the *Folklore Forum*.

Priscilla Denby first catalogues the kinds of media she has combed: "magazines catering to different interests; newspapers; Sunday magazines; plays; television; radio; cartoons; greeting cards; records (pop, folk, classical, rock); illustrations, such as book and record jackets; posters; films; novels; local festivals and customs; children's books and coloring books; advertisements; trademarks; names of places, such as restaurants, inns, and camps; crossword puzzles and games; and various miscellany such as linguistic folklore (puns, dialects, etc.) and a curious chain letter I received in the mail." She then adds potential sources she could not consider at the time, "comic strips, billboards, speeches, cookbooks and recipes, the backs of cereal boxes and other products, pamphlets describing various American tourist attractions and landmarks, recorded tapes for tourists, placemats and matchbook covers from restaurants and gift shops, bumper sticks" (Denby 1971:113–114). This inventory fairly suggests the bombardment of printed, placarded, spoken, sung, screened, and spectacled messages that engulf us all in the age of the media.

To bring order to the folkloric materials gleaned from these diverse sources Denby proposes three large divisions: Folklore qua Folklore; Folklore as Folklure; and Folklore as an Aside. The first category applies to items that deal directly and specifically with folklore, legends, and myths under those terms. "Folklore qua folklore" subsumes more or less informed discussion about our discipline and its processes, and Denby cites as an instance a five-minute segment of an ABC television show on April 6, 1971, explaining the rise of Lieutenant William Calley, accused of the massacre at My Lai, as an American folk hero, and playing the recording of the "Ballad of Lieutenant Calley" that had sold a million copies the previous week. A recording that denounced Calley as un-American was mentioned but not played. Had the ballad simply been played or sung, the rendition might be classified as folk-emulated, but the commentator's attempt to analyze the making of a legendary hero, using the record for documentation, gives the nod to theory, however attenuated, over entertainment. By the neologism "folklure," a happy addition to our terminology, Denby suggests the use of folkloric associations to help sell a product. The film title "Grimms' Fairy Tales" lured moviegoers, including myself, into a skinflick. "Folklore as an Aside" refers to stylistic devices that enhance a topic by giving it a folkloric touch, such as journalistic references to Paul Bunyan feats or objects; and visual devices for the same end, such as the cartoon of an angelic businessman with a magician's wand in his hand and fairy wings clipped to his suit sitting under a large sign reading LOANS.

The other essay, by Tom Burns (1969), concentrated exclusively on television. Burns plunked himself down from the tube at 6:15 A.M. on May 15, 1969, and did not come up for air until 1:30 A.M. the next day. During that time he recorded programs on tape while entering comments on the visual portions in his notebook. To assess his folklore gleanings Burns devised a fourfold test, of text, performance, situation, context. All four elements must be rated "traditional" for the entire item to be considered "true" folklore. A pop artist singing a Child ballad before a studio audience would rate low on the scale because only one element, the text, is met. Burns concluded:

The survey of one day's television programming has revealed that there is a good deal of traditional material (101 items) covering a wide range of genres (twelve) in the television media. There is, however, little "true" folklore. "True" folklore and the material approaching it seem to be present in primarily two areas: (1) in the peripheral regions of the programming on locally produced shows which are directed to a more or less specific subculture audience, and (2) in those programs where the performers on stage can be said to compose a kind of folk group which the mass audience is simply overhearing and viewing (Burns 1969:103).

The least "true" folklore he found to be in advertising. Folk beliefs, especially with supernatural motifs, proved the most prevalent genre, penetrating even prime-time shows but quite divorced from traditional contexts, as in the "kitchen magic" of advertising already remarked on by Patai.

A good example of an in-depth treatment of a single genre is "Folklore in the mass media: head comics," an unpublished paper of John Cicala (n.d.), deposited in the Folklore Archives. Head comics are a countercul-ture mockery of the crime-fighting Superman and the establishment values in newsstand comic books. They appeared in the late 1960's in centers of the youth culture, such as Haight-Ashbury, created, it was reported, by potheads and acidheads while they were stoned. Pictures and text replaced Superman with hippie anti-heroes and savagely carica-tured straight-world character types. Here Cicala describes two protagon-ists:

Two characters one often comes across in Head Comics are Projunior and his teenage companion Honeybunch. Projunior is the prototype of the "freak" revolutionary whose rhetoric is a form of self-lampoon. Usually he doesn't know what is going on around him until it is nearly too late. Honeybunch speaks the clichés of the "teeny-bopper" and has the innocence which gets her into difficult situations, though in some stories about her, she can be a nagging bitch. Both lovers wander in a bleak capitalistic landscape trying to eke out a few pennies in order to exist. This economic necessity often gets them into situations where only their cleverness (as tricksters) or their powers as superlovers can free themselves from "Mr. Man," the personification of capitalistic greed and lust (Cicala n.d.).

In the attached cartoon sequence, Projunior and Honeybunch are out scrounging the streets for pennies when a well-dressed businessman, Mr. Man, passes by. Honeybunch asks him for spare change; he puts his arm around her, expresses his admiration for anti-establishment kids, leads her back to his studio, and gets her stoned; meanwhile Projunior, clad in an animal skin, wanders off musing how to save the world. Suddenly waking from his reverie, Projunior senses through his vibes that an establishment pig is about to seduce Honeybunch and sends her warnings on an astral plane. Honeybunch comes to just in time and lying on her back, spins Mr. Man dizzily around on the heels of her heavy boots, then bounces him off with an epithet, "Take a flying fuck, ya phony liberal fascist fraud!!" But Mr. Man loves it and comes slobbering back for more. Honeybunch defecates in his face; Projunior rushes back into her arms; and the final frame shows them graphically in the sixty-nine position.

For folklore motifs Cicala suggests T41 "Communications of lovers" and F610.0.1 "Extraordinary strong woman," but he finds fewer motifs and folktale analogues for this particular episode than for other of his analyses. The case for folkloric implications can best be made in terms of folk-hero patterns. Projunior conforms to the formulas of the anti-hero in druglore legends about pill-peddlers and draft-dodgers who triumph over police and army officers. He too, with his girl friend, overcomes the evil spokesman for the system, Mr. Man; "the man" in counterculture parlance signifies the enemy, sometimes specifically a narcotics agent.

These few examples indicate the wealth of possibilities for examining folklore in the mass media. The problems of methodology, typology, morphology, aesthetics, cultural analysis are formidable. It is difficult enough to screen the tons of newsprint that engulf the modern world, although, were funds available, a news clipping service clued in to key words (I had great success once with "Paul Bunyan") could salvage a great deal of fleeting folklore. But how to capture folklore on the screen or the air waves? If scholars direct their attention to these questions, they will find answers — for example, in Burns' using one electronic system against another by taping the audio portion of television programs. European folklorists are already actively considering the relation of folklore to mass culture. Hermann Bausinger declares that one of the most pressing questions of folklore research is "whether the basic need for narrative in our time is not now being satisfied by completely different media, such as motion pictures, television, and, above all by certain kinds of reading material which today undoubtedly enjoy a far greater currency than ever before" (Bausinger 1968:131). At the University of Hamburg the folklore institute has sponsored studies on "Radio and Folklore," The Movies — A Subject for Folklore Research," "Folk Literature and Reading Material for the Masses," and "Television and Folk Culture." The Hamburg school of folklorists has revised the older concept of the folk as the "lower orders" in favor of the idea of a community of individuals who form a folk group and share a basic common property (*das Grundständige*). Therefore, *Volkskunst* or folk art must appeal to everybody and be understood by everybody within the larger folk group or people concerned (Havernick 1968:121, fn. 11). No longer is the concept of folk art limited to narrow circles and regions. This train of thought readily leads toward acceptance of a mass culture species of folklore.

FOLKLORE AND NATIONALISM, POLITICS, IDEOLOGY

Far from being an antiquarian hobby, folklore has throughout the history of its study been connected with national issues and concerns. The appearance of folkloristics as a discipline coincided, not by chance, with the heightening of nationalism in a number of countries, since folklore traditions could help reinforce the sense of national identity, once the intellectuals and policymakers become aware of their existence. They faced a paradox in seeking national traits and characteristics in tales, songs, proverbs, and customs found in similar forms in many lands, but the nationalists chose to emphasize seemingly local and indigenous elements. Their quests for a national language, literature, history, mytho-√ logy, and folklore often overlapped, and folklore proved of special use, for it could be embedded in regional dialects, suggest literary themes, and contain remembrances of the mythological and historical past.

Jacob and Wilhelm Grimm clearly associated their work in folklore with the reconstruction of a proud Germanic past. Their researches in philology, legal history, and mythology as well as in folklore proper were directed at reversing the stereotype of wild, savage Teutonic forebears and substituting the vision of an advanced and civilized people, as Jacob forcefully states in the preface to *Teutonic Mythology*. Not a Greek and Roman heritage, but the indigenous Germanic tribes furnished the sources of nineteenth-century German culture. "I do not suppose," observed Jacob drily, "that the old German fancies about beasts crossing one's path, or about the virtues of herbs, were in themselves any poorer than the Roman." Later in the century, in 1858, Wilhelm Riehl developed the nationalist implications of *Volkskunde* in terms of a national folk community, and in the 1930's the Nazi politicians exploited Riehl's thesis. An American scholar has written that under Hitler "the study of folklore was raised to a special place of honor . . . a large part of

Nazi literature designed for children was merely a modernized version of the Grimms' tales, with emphasis upon the idealization of fighting, glorification of power, reckless courage, theft, brigandage, and militarism reinforced with mysticism" (Snyder 1959:219).

The Nazis' use of folklore involved and interwove nationalism, politics, and ideology. As a nationalistic strategy, folklore would restore the old peasant values of community bonds being weakened by urban impersonality; hence political folklorists sought to reverse the trend of migration from country to city. Hitler considered the "preservation of our folkdom" dependent upon the preservation of the peasantry. The Nazi architects followed the Grimms' initiative in exalting the Germanic tribes of old and downgrading the artificial intrusions of Roman civilization which had sapped German folk unity. A new, greater Germany would derive its national purpose and cultural unification from renewal of the pure Nordic-Germanic myths, customs, and rituals. The task of the Nationalist Socialist folklorist was to screen out alien elements. In 1937 Hans Strobel stated, "The aim of folklore is and remains to give an unfalsified representation of that which is true to the *Volk*" (Kamenetsky 1972:223).

In terms of politics, folklore provided practical opportunities for the Nationalist Socialist Party. Otto Schmidt devoted a treatise of 1943 to *Volkstumsarbeit als politische Aufgabe* (The Work of Nationhood as a Political Duty). Professor Hans Strobel inferred the need for political action when he wrote, the same year, "If we want to walk safely into the future, then we will have to walk upon the firm soil of our folklore" (Kamenetsky 1972:226). Party policy produced peasant schools and institutes seeking to revive German folk consciousness through courses on folklore and history and through encouragement of peasant festivals, folk music, and folk dance. The Party's Folk Education Program endeavored to instruct the German people in their role as bearers of Germanic culture (Kamenetsky 1972:221–235). Ideology underscored the special heroic qualities of the fighting German peasant, qualities needed to expand Germany's political boundaries in the drive for "living space." The folk spirit was construed as a martial spirit.

Instances connecting folklore research and the rise of nationalism can be multiplied. That the composition of the Finnish epic *Kalevala* by Elias Lönnrot became a platform and rallying point for the cause of a Finnish language, culture, literature, and mythology is now a commonplace. William A. Wilson is completing a doctoral dissertation in the Folklore Institute at Indiana University exploring the detailed history of the interdependence of folkloristics and nationalistic strivings in Finland. Caught between German and Soviet domination in the twentieth century, and before that submerged by Sweden up to Finland's independence in 1917, Finnish scholars were obliged to shift their philosophical as well as political allegiance between theories of aristocratic and proletarian sources of folk materials. In a paper delivered before the American Folklore Society in November 1972 on "Folklore and National Consciousness in Pre-Nineteenth Century Finland," Wilson traces the story back before Lönnrot to seventeenth- and eighteenth-century figures, such as Daniel Juslenius and Henrik Gabriel Porthan, who exalted the Finnish heritage through the study of antiquities and folk poetry. He states:

In the careful, scholarly work of Porthan we see folklore used as a mirror for Finnish culture, as a means of gaining insight into the mind of the people. In the searing, patriotic writing of Juslenius, we see the tendency in periods of national stress to turn to an imagined heroic past for strength to face the future, and also the tendency to shape the cultural mirror of folklore to reflect the political predispositions of the man holding the mirror. Both these approaches have persisted in Finnish folklore study to the present (Wilson 1976:9).

In Norway, as Oscar J. Falnes has shown in *National Romanticism in Norway*, the movement for Norwegian independence from Denmark that achieved political success in 1814, but strove for cultural independence throughout the nineteenth century, depended importantly on folklore. Jörgen Moe, in a prospectus of 1840 for the collection of Norwegian folktales he was undertaking with Peter Asbjörnsen, commented that "No cultivated person now doubts the scientific importance of the folk tales . . . they help to determine a people's unique character and outlook" (Falnes 1933:215). And, following Moe's thought, George Webbe Dasent characterized the Norse tales as "bold, outspoken, and humorous, in the true sense of humor. In the midst of every difficulty and danger arises that old Norse feeling of making the best of everything, and keeping a good face to the foe." Moe perceived in the fairy-tale hero Askeladden the spirit of the *landsman* guided by providence, and an Oslo newspaper in 1957 visualized Askeladden as "a crafty, glib Norwegian farmer with the necessary sense and power to win half a kingdom" (Dorson 1964:vi–vii).

In Ireland the drive for cultural nationalism preceded and fed the movement for political independence. The Irish literary renaissance involved such major personalities as William Butler Yeats, Lady Gregory, and John Millington Synge, who actively collected Gaelic folk traditions and incorporated them in poems and plays. Their friend Douglas Hyde published scholarly collections of Irish folk narratives and literary histories of Ireland and became the first president of Ireland. All fought for the revival of the Gaelic tongue and heritage against the stifling cloak of English culture. Hyde mourned that "story, lay, poem, song, aphorism, proverb, and the unique stock-in-trade of an Irish speaker's mind, is gone for ever" (Dorson 1966a:293). Through the Gaelic League, founded in the 1890's, Hyde exhorted the Irish people to recover their inheritance of Gaelic song, dance, music, story, and speech.

In Greece too political and cultural nationalists utilized folklore and enjoyed an advantage over other European scholar-patriots who sought to reconstruct a shadowy Celtic or Norse mythology from fragmentary hints in Märchen and Sagen. Olympus beckoned invitingly across the centuries, and modern Greek folklorists strove to connect their peasant tales with the classic myths. One Greek scholar commented in 1964 that the "science of folklore and the new independent nation of modern Greece were born almost simultaneously; the term folklore was not officially minted until 1846 when Greece already had its new constitution for three years . . . the study of folklore became a nationwide project and a number of studies and collections of folk-literature were published in Greece together with the first modern Greek publication of the ancient authors, for both were deemed equally important" (Oikonomides 1964:vii). In pursuit of their claims, folklorists such as Stilpon Kyriakides beheld vestiges of the Dionysiac revels in the masquerades of the Twelve Days of Christmas, the nymphs of old in the *nereids* of current belief, and myths of the Olympian gods and goddesses in saints' legends and Virgin Mary miracles.

Not only the sentiment of nationalism but also a particular nationalistic ideology may derive support from the content and interpretation of folklore. The course of folkloristics in the Soviet Union provides a ready case in point, well-documented by Felix Oinas (1961, 1966, 1971, 1973). As he recounts the story, government controls over writers, critics, and scholars — including folklorists — tightened from 1929 on with the introduction of Stalin's five-year plans and the organization in 1932 of one inclusive Union of Soviet Writers. In the keynote speech of the first All-Union Congress of Soviet Writers in 1934, Maxim Gorky stressed the values of folklore as an expression of the realities and aspirations of the working classes. From then on government policy strongly supported widespread collecting activities and socialist interpretation of folklore. In November 1936 the staging in Moscow of the comic opera *Bogatyri* (The Epic Heroes), written by Demian Bedny, Soviet poet laureate, evoked the ire of Party officials for disparaging the *byliny* heroes. The opera was withdrawn from the repertoire, and articles in *Pravda* attacked the distortion of Russian history and epic traditions by folklorists. In time folklore scholars shifted their view of the origins of the *byliny* from an aristocratic to peasant sources. In his standard work on Russian folklore Y. M. Sokolov expresses the current ideological attitude of the Communist Party and the Soviet government toward folklore: "what a vastly important artistic force this in the propagandizing of the resplendent ideas of Communism, what a great place folklore occupies in Soviet socialist culture." And: "Never, in all the history of Russia, has the oral poetic word served the social aims so broadly and powerfully as in the Soviet period. Soviet folkloristics has helped to reveal the agitational and propagandist significance of folklore. And thereby, Soviet folkloristics has firmly allied itself with the practical tasks of our social life" (Sokolov 1950:39).

This shift in general attitudes toward the national body of folklore, and indeed the expressed desire for a new and different content of folklore, seems to substantiate my thesis of the contemporaneity of folk traditions. Not only were the older epic songs reinterpreted, but a whole new corpus of revolutionary and industrial-labor lore was collected by trade-school students and workers on collective farms and machine tractor stations. By the 1930's such collectors had recorded a new folklore of Soviet *byliny*, laments, tales, and new songs called *noviny*, often glorifying Lenin, Stalin, Voroshilov, and other political and military figures. So too did folk heroes of the new democracy like Davy Crockett, Mike Fink, and Mose the Bowery b'hoy appear on the American scene half a century after the American Revolution. The same social forces are operating in different countries to produce a folklore, and a folkloristics, reflective of the ideology and ethos of the times. Governments in Finland and Ireland have supported national folklore archives in order to place on record folklore materials that exalt the heritage of their people.

The pressures of government in the United States on the scholar are considerably less than the pressures of the marketplace, and the publication of folklore responds not to official ideology so much as to popular taste, which contains its own latent ideology. In the depression decade of the 1930's leftist folksingers in the United States sought to arouse the working man to a sense of social injustice and a mood of political radicalism through the singing of protest songs. The history of this movement, embracing well-known personalities such as the Almanac Singers, Woody Guthrie, Pete Seeger, Burl Ives, and others, has been ably told by R. Serge Denisoff in *Great day coming: folk music and the American left* and Richard Reuss (1971) in "American folklore and left-wing politics: 1927–1957." In spite of the individual reputations of these singers their strenuous endeavors came to little, since they misunderstood the underlying philosophy of the American working man. One observer pointed out that he had never heard Arkies or Okies singing the Dust Bowl ballads that Woody Guthrie had written expressly to dramatize their distress.

All sorts of questions about ideological, political, and nationalistic uses of folklore invite exploration. The new African nations are a wide open field. In a suggestive article on folklore as an agent of African nationalism, James Fernandez (1962) discusses how folk traditions furnish pan-Africanists and new-state Africans with an oral history and references for statements of negritude and African personality. Folklore can be divisive as well as unifying and contribute to separatist feelings: witness French Canada, Scotland, Wales, Brittany. Political folklore and the relations between politics and folk genres have inspired new courses at the University of Pennsylvania and Western Kentucky State University. Gyula Ortutay, the noted Hungarian folklorist, has related "the way I turned from folklore research to work in politics and how the two came to be united inseparably" (Ortutay 1972:9). As he studied the folk life of peasants and realized their difficulties he perceived, as a folklorist, the need for a political action program. The political philosophies of the modern world, whether following the trail of democracy or socialism, embrace the peoples of the world, and sooner or later will levy on the traditions of the people.

REFERENCES

ABRAHAMS, ROGER D.
  1964–1971   *Deep down in the jungle: Negro narrative folklore from the streets of Philadelphia.* Philadelphia: Hatboro Associates, 1964. Revised edition published by Aldine, 1971.
AFANASYEV
  1865–1869   *The poetic attitudes of the Slavs on nature* [in Russian], three volumes. Moscow: E. Connatehkoba.
BAUSINGER, HERMANN
  1961   *Volkskultur in der technischen welt* [Folk culture in the technical world]. Stuttgart: W. Kohlhammer.
  1968   Folklore research at the university of Tübingen. *Journal of the Folklore Institute* 5:131.
BOATRIGHT, MODY C.
  1945   *Gib Morgan, minstrel of the oil fields.* Texas: Folk-Lore Society Publication 20.
  1963   *Folklore of the oil industry.* Dallas: Southern Methodist University Press.
BOATRIGHT, MODY C., WILLIAM A. OWENS
  1970   *Tales from the derrick floor.* New York: Doubleday.
BOTKIN, BENJAMIN A., ALVIN HARLOW
  1953   *A treasury of railroad folklore.* New York: Crown Publishers.
BRINGÉUS, NILS-ARVID
  1971   "Gunnar Olaf Hylténs-Cavallius," in *Biographica, Nordic folklorists of the past.* Edited by Dag Strömbäck et al., 89–106. Copenhagen: Nordisk Institut for Folkedigtning.
BURNS, TOM
  1969   Folklore in the mass media: television. *Folklore Forum* 2(4): 90–106.
CAMPBELL, JOHN FRANCIS
  1860–1862   *Popular tales of the West Highlands.* Edinburgh: Edmonson and Douglas.
CHAMBERS, ROBERT
  1825   *Traditions of Edinburgh*, two volumes. Edinburgh: printed for W. and C. Tait.

CHILD, FRANCIS JAMES
1882–1894   *The English and Scottish popular ballads*, ten volumes. Boston: Houghton-Mifflin.
CHRISTIANSEN, REIDAR, *editor*
1964   *Folktales of Norway.* Chicago: University of Chicago Press.
CICALA, JOHN
n.d.   Unpublished paper, Folklore Archives, STU–187.
CLODD, EDWARD
1898   *Tom Tit Tot, an essay on savage philosophy in folk-tale.* London: Duckworth.
COFFIN, TRISTRAM P., HENNIG COHEN, *editors*
1973   *Folklore from the working folk of America.* New York: Doubleday.
DÉGH, LINDA
1969   "Two old world narrators in urban setting," in *Kontakte und Grenzen: Festschrift für Gerhard Heilfurth zum 60 Geburtstag*, 71–86. Göttingen: Otto Schwartz.
DENBY, PRISCILLA
1971   Folklore in the mass media. *Folklore Forum* 4(6):113–125.
DENISOFF, R. SERGE
1971   *Great day coming: folk music and the American left.* Urbana: University of Illinois Press.
DORE, R. P.
1958   *City life in Japan.* Berkeley and Los Angeles: University of California Press.
DORSON, RICHARD M.
1962   Folklore and the national defense education act. *Journal of American Folklore*, 75:160–164.
1963   *Studies in Japanese folklore.* Bloomington: Indiana University Press.
1964   "Foreword" in *Folktales of Norway.* Edited by R. T. Christiansen, v–xviii. Chicago: University of Chicago Press.
1965   "Foreword" in *Folktales of Hungary.* Edited by Linda Dégh, v–xx. Chicago: University of Chicago Press.
1966a   The question of folklore in a new nation. *Journal of the Folklore Institute*, 3:277–298.
1966b   "Foreword" in *Folktales of Ireland.* Edited by Sean O'Sullivan, v–xxxi. Chicago: University of Chicago Press.
1966c   "Foreword" in *Folktales of Germany.* Edited by Kurt Ranke, v–xxv. Chicago: University of Chicago Press.
1968a   *The British folklorists, a history.* Chicago: University of Chicago Press.
1968b   *Peasant customs and savage myths*, two volumes. Chicago: University of Chicago Press.
1971   "Is there a folk in the city?" in *The urban experience and folk tradition.* Edited by A. Paredes and E. Stekert, 21–52. Austin and London: University of Texas Press for the American Folklore Society. (Reprinted from *Journal of American Folklore* 83[1970]:185–225).
1973   *America in legend.* New York: Pantheon.
DRAKE, CARLOS
1968   The killer in the back seat. *Indiana Folklore* 1:92–109.
FALNES, OSCAR J.
1933   *National romanticism in Norway.* New York: Columbia University Press.
FERNANDEZ, JAMES W.
1962   Folklore as an agent of nationalism. *African Studies Bulletin* 5(2):3–8.

GARDNER, EMELYN E.
1937   *Folklore from the Schoharie Hills, New York.* Ann Arbor: University of Michigan Press.
GILLIES, A.
1945   *Herder.* Oxford: Basil Blackwell.
GOMME, GEORGE LAURENCE
1883   *Folk-Lore relics of early village life.* London: E. Stock.
1908   *Folklore as an historical science.*
GRIMM, JACOB
1882–1888   *Teutonic mythology,* four volumes. London: George Bell and Sons. (Translated from the fourth edition by James S. Stallybrass, vol. III, xxix.)
GREEN, ARCHIE
1972   *Only a miner.* Urbana: University of Illinois Press.
HAAVIO, MARTI
1971   "Elias Lönnrot," in *Biographica: Nordic folklorists of the past.* Edited by Dag Strömbäck, *et al.,* 1–10. Copenhagen: Nordisk Institut for Folkedigtning.
HARTLAND, EDWIN SIDNEY
1885   *Folk-Lore Journal* 3.
1894–1896   *The legend of Perseus,* three volumes. London: D. Nutt.
HAUTALA, JOUKO
1969   *Finnish folklore research 1828–1918.* Helsinki: Finnish Academy of Sciences.
HAVERNICK, WALTER
1968   The Hamburg school of folklore research. *Journal of the Folklore Institute* 5:113–241.
HEILFURTH, GERHARD
1968   *The Institut für mitteleuropäische volksforschung* [Institute for Middle European folk research at the University of Marburg]. *Journal of the Folklore Institute* 85:221–235.
HOLBEK, BENGT, THORKILD KNUDSEN
1971   Quotation from *Biographica, Nordic folklorists of the past.* Edited by Dag Strömbäck, *et al.,* 249. Copenhagen: Nordisk Institut for Folkedigtning.
HOOGASIAN-VILLA, SUSIE
1966   *One hundred Armenian folktales.* Detroit: Wayne State University Press.
KAMENETSKY, CHRISTA
1972   Folklore as a political tool in Nazi Germany. *Journal of American Folklore* 85:221–235.
KEIL, CHARLES
        Urban blues. Chicago: University of Chicago Press.
KORSON, GEORGE
1938   *Minstrels of the mine patch.* Philadelphia: University of Pennsylvania Press.
1943   *Coal dust on the fiddle.* Philadelphia: University of Pennsylvania Press.
1960   *Black rock.* Baltimore: Johns Hopkins University Press.
McKELVIE, DONALD
1963   Aspects of oral tradition and belief in an industrial region. *Folk Life Studies* 1:77–94.

1965   Proverbial elements in the oral tradition of an English urban industrial region. *Journal of the Folklore Institute* 2:244–261.

MALONE, BILL C.
1968   *Country music, U.S.A.* Austin and London: University of Texas Press.

MAYHEW, HENRY
1968   *London labour and the London poor*, four volumes. New York: Dover Publications. (First published 1861–1862.)

MESSENGER, BETTY
1972   Picking up the linen threads: some folklore of the northern Irish linen industry. *Journal of the Folklore Institute* 9:18–27.

OIKONOMIDES, AL. N.
1964   "Foreword" to *Modern Greek folklore and ancient Greek religion.* Written by John C. Lawson. New York: University Books.

OINAS, FELIX J.
1961   "Folklore activities in Russia" in *Folklore research around the world.* Edited by R. M. Dorson, Bloomington: Indiana University Press.
1966   "Introduction," in *Russian folklore.* Written by Y. M. Sokolov. Translated by Catherine Smith. Hatboro, Pa.: Folklore Associates.
1971   The problem of the aristocratic origin of Russian byliny. *Slavic Review* 3:513–522.
1973   Folklore and politics. *Slavic Review* 32:45–58.

ORTUTAY, GYULA
1972   *Hungarian folklore essays.* Budapest: Akadémiai Kiado.

PATAI, RAPHAEL
1972   *Myth and modern man.* Englewood Cliffs: Prentice-Hall.

PAWLOWSKA, HARRIET M.
1961   *Merrily we sing! 105 Polish folksongs.* Detroit: Wayne State University Press.

PENTIKÄINEN, JUHA
1971   "Julius and Karle Krohn," in *Biographica, Nordic folklorists of the past.* Edited by Dag Strömbäck *et al.*, 10–34. Copenhagen: Nordisk Institut for Folkedigtning.

PIØ, ORN
1971   "Sven Grundtvig," in *Biographica, Nordic folklorists of the past.* Edited by Dag Strömbäck, *et al.*, 189–224. Copenhagen: Nordisk Institut for Folkedigtning.

RANDOLPH, VANCE
1931   *The Ozarks: an American survival of primitive society.* New York: Vanguard.

REUSS, RICHARD
1971   "American folklore and left-wing politics: 1927–57." Unpublished doctoral dissertation, Indiana University, Bloomington.

SANDERSON, STEWART
1969   The folklore of the motor-car. *Folklore* 80:241–252.

SCHLESINGER, ARTHUR M., SR.
1949   *Paths to the present.* New York: Macmillan.

SCHMIDT, OTTO
1943   *Volkstumsarbeit als politische aufgabe.* Hamburg: Hanseatische Verlagsanstalt.

SHARP, CECIL J.
1917/1960   *English folksongs from the southern Appalachians.* Introduction

to the first edition, 1917, xxii–xxiii. New York: Oxford University Press.

SMITH, ALAN
   1969   *Discovering folklore in industry.* Tring: Shire Publications.

SNYDER, LOUIS L.
   1959   Nationalistic aspects of the Grimm brothers' fairy tales. *Journal of* ✓
            Social Psychology 23(1959):219–221.

SOKOLOV, Y. M.
   1950   *Russian folklore.* Translated by Catherine R. Smith. New York: Mac-
            millan.

SOKOLOV, B. M., JU. M. SOKOLOV
   1975   "In search of folktales and songs," in *The study of Russian folklore.* ✓
            Edited and translated by Felix J. Oinas and Stephen Soudakoff, 13–22.
            The Hague: Mouton.

STROBEL, HANS
   1937   *Neue Brauchtumskunde.* Leipzig.

THIGPEN, KENNETH
   1973   "Folklore and the ethnicity factor in the lives of Romanian-
            Americans." Unpublished doctoral dissertation, Indiana University,
            Bloomington, Indiana.

THOMAS, KEITH
   1971   *Religion and the decline of magic.* New York: Scribner's.

THOMPSON, STITH
   1955–1958   *Motif-index of folk literature*, six volumes. Bloomington: Indiana
            University Press.

WILLIAMS, PHYLLIS H.
   1969   *South Italian folkways in Europe and America: a handbook for social*
            workers, visiting nurses, school teachers, and physicians. New York:
            Russell and Russell. (Reprint of 1938 edition).

WILSON, WILLIAM A.
   n.d.   Folklore and nationalism in modern Finland. Quotation from unpub-
            lished paper.
   1976   *Folkore and nationalism in Modern Finland.* Bloomington: Indiana
            University Press.

YANAGITA, KUNIO
   1954   *Studies in fishing village life* (Kaison Seikatsu no Kenkyū) *and Studies*
            in mountain village life (Sanson Seikatsu no Kenkyū). Lexington: Uni-
            versity of Kentucky Press Microcards Series A, Modern Language
            Series 1 and 2.

SECTION ONE

Folklore and the City

Migration and Urbanization of a Traditional Culture: An Italian Experience

CARLA BIANCO

One of Italy's leading folklore scholars, Alberto Cirese, has said that folklorists have no purpose, or just an irrelevant one: ". . . unless the object and the methods of the study are definitely viewed and understood in the living framework of the problems of our times and of the tensions that cross them at all levels" (Cirese 1973:1). This view is now shared by a growing number of scholars, but I think it is useful to reevaluate its theoretical and methodological application.

Since most other disciplines concerned with culture are developing their methods of inquiry in correlation with the political, social, and economic forces that shape cultural phenomena, folklore cannot, or should not, risk earning the label of a "culturally retarded" field of study. This is not to say that folklorists should exactly duplicate what other human scientists are doing or uncritically adopt every linguistic, sociological, or mathematical method and scheme they come across — as is often done. It seems to me that the work of folklorists will be all the more valuable if we keep a reasonable degree of autonomy and identity for our specific field.

Since urbanization, through both internal and external migrations, is more and more becoming a predominant feature of human distribution — and not only in the Western world — the necessity of following the urbanized masses in their new settings has attracted the growing interest of folklorists. I first started working on the folklore of migrants over ten years ago in southern Italy after noting the tremendous impact of American emigration on the folk culture of the village people. An authentic myth of America developed there that not only encouraged an ever-growing disposition to mass emigration but influenced in many other ways the values, the beliefs, and the whole world view of the peasants. Traces of this influence are explicitly contained in the oral traditions — songs, folktales, and proverbs — dealing with America, while probably an even more decisive, though less obvious, part has been assimilated in the culture.

It was during this first contact with emigration themes that I realized the importance of a parallel investigation in the areas of departure and in those of immigration. While the investigation of urban life appears to be most relevant to the study of the relationships and the contrasts between different levels of culture and different ethnic groups, the peasant milieu of the villages and country towns needs also to be viewed in terms of modern life. There is hardly a place in the Western world where the influence of city life and technology has not penetrated to some substantial degree. Today, even a mountain village of southern Italy has a share of refrigerators, television sets, frozen foods, and similar technological products. In spite of the poor economic conditions and the continual exodus of young people, industrial and urban civilization has thousands of channels through which it changes the culture of even the most distant agricultural place. The modern world is now attaching every inch of the countryside, and the result often is emigration and the consequent disruption of the agricultural and demographic balance. The mass media are reaching simultaneously millions of people everywhere, proposing — and imposing — extremely powerful cultural models and values. One example of this is consumer's mentality, which prefers the fashionable, new, and thus nonlasting to the old, enduring, and cherished. The whole traditional concept of thriftiness expressed in such proverbs as *Chi lascia la via vecchia per la nova mal si trova* [Don't leave the old for the new] and *Gallina vecchia fa buon brodo* [What's old yields a lot] is now abruptly reversed by television slogans that stress the value of the new, the young, the rapid. Thus, one sees the shepherd throwing away or exchanging his hand-carved tools for plastic ones and the peasant discarding terra cotta dishes or traditional furniture for mass-manufactured sets bought from a catalog salesperson. The traditional objects, with their exotic simplicity, will later ornament the living rooms of the upper classes, while the peasant is exposed to the incessant hammering of the consumers' society and its symbols. Just as the immigrant peasants in Turin and in Milan are urged — not always indirectly — to forget their Calabrian or Sicilian dialects and folkways and adopt what I heard defined by one migrant as the "more musical" Piedmontese idiom, the peasants in Roseto Valfortore remodel their houses according to the suggestions gleaned from a magazine or received from their American relatives during a summer visit. Thus, the "dirty" fireplaces — symbols of a bitter past of misery and slavery — are dismantled, and cheap, leaking, gas stoves are purchased on credit. Even when the cold season comes and the village is isolated for a month from the nearest town, and the bottled gas is used up, the country people, who now have no way of keeping warm, still feel gratified at resembling the city dwellers.

From my experience, I am convinced that the culture of the urbanized masses of immigrants can be far better understood with a parallel investigation of their original environment. Such an investigation reveals identical social contradictions in different physical settings. Thus, after ten years of research among the Italian immigrants in the United States and Canada, I continued my investigation in peasant Italy, both to examine the Italian side of the migratory phenomenon and to inspect the erosive process of the expanding capitalistic mentality over traditional culture.

A STUDY OF ROSETO, PENNSYLVANIA

Below, I will not attempt to provide a complete description of my field-work or findings. This brief account will, instead, give a cultural profile of Roseto, Pennsylvania for one purpose: to discuss with other folklorists the methods, objects and motives for undertaking the study of urban and immigrant folklore.

My research in the United States consisted of a pilot survey of various regional groups — mainly Sicilian, Calabrian, Sardinian, and Apulian — living in urban centers such as New York City, Newark, New Jersey, and Chicago. Subsequently, I concentrated on a single community in north-eastern Pennsylvania, whose inhabitants all came from the same mountain village in southern Italy. Both the American village and its place of origin are named Roseto, and both share common cultural and social traits. Roseto, Pennsylvania, was founded in 1882 by a small group of Rosetan farmers and 95 percent of its present 1,600 inhabitants are still descendants of Roseto Valfortore, in the province of Foggia, Apulia. The village is situated in the Slate Belt of the Blue Ridge Mountains, and the immigrants were first hired in the local slate quarries, thus forcing a drastic shift from an agricultural to an industrial way of life. Like most immigrant groups elsewhere, the Italian newcomers had to compete with the resistance and suspicion of earlier settlers — Welsh and German — who owned the quarries and despised the new, unskilled laborers. There followed a period of thirty to thirty-five years during which a chain migration from Roseto Valfortore, characterized by continual trips back home, resulted in the official consolidation of the new Italian–American borough of Roseto in 1912. On the other side of the ocean, a whole body of legends, beliefs, fantastic expectations, and hopes developed concomitantly with the departure of the emigrants. The myth of America stood in contrast to hundreds of years of social injustice and fatal resignation. For many decades, and secretly even during the Mussolini fascist period, the dream of America has shaped much of the peasant culture of thousands of similar villages all over Italy. To this day, the myth of

America is well recognizable in the folklore, and the United States would still be the preferred choice as a land of emigration for Italian peasants if restrictive legislation did not force them to flock to northern Italy, central Europe, Australia, and Canada.

By studying the Italian-Americans and the Italian-Canadians, two interrelated communities, I was able to establish connections and to follow a consistent line in tracing, for example, patterns of family relations and of culture change. If the historical criterion of using the past to understand the present is valid for any human action, it is all the more valid for the study of today's folk traditions and, especially, for the study of immigrant folklore. The evident state of decay and disappearance of many such traditions, and the present transformation of traditional values into new and undefined ones, may lead to wrong conclusions, unless one has the opportunity to compare and verify findings with the situation in the area of emigration.[1]

At first glance, the traditional material collected in both Rosetos seems to be equivalent. The same songs, folktales, proverbs, magic practices, legends, games, and diet are to be found in both places, just as the people seem the same — they share the same names, nicknames, dialect, faces, and relations. However, both the traditional material and the whole world view of American Roseto, with its new values and lifestyle, show signs of deep changes of all kinds. Folktales and ballads that are nearly forgotten in Italy or remembered in fragmentary or Italianized forms have been found in America in long and well-preserved versions. New stanzas have sometimes been added to the songs to reflect the new situation, while princes, dukes, castles, and towers have often become the city of Chicago, a motel on a highway, or a casino and its landlady. Storytelling is gradually losing its old prestige and role in both villages, but many hundreds of folktales can still be collected from talented storytellers. While probably a consequence of emigration, men are no longer considered good storytellers in the Italian village. Yet the best narrative material collected by this author came from Italian-American men, both in Roseto and elsewhere in the United States and in Canada. Other differences within the Italian setting are seen in the preference given to realistic, religious, and satirical subjects rather than to tales dealing with animals and supernatural beings, occasions for storytelling, type of audience, and distribution among age and social groups. The best-remembered songs are the long religious ballads — as long as thirty and forty stanzas — dealing with the lives of the saints and the Easter Passion, lullabies, emigration songs, folk prayers, and love songs. It is more difficult to find nursery rhymes, nonreligious ballads, work songs, dancing songs, and songs about local traditional characters. Of the whole

---

[1]   Constance Cronin (1970) did extensive fieldwork in Sicily before undertaking research among urbanized Sicilian immigrants in Australia.

body of oral traditions, proverbs are among the best remembered and most widely quoted. Scarcely a single interview can be conducted without using at least one or two proverbs as a lapidary illustration of a concept. Religion in Roseto, Pennsylvania is still lived in the dramatic and magic, southern Italian way by the first generation and by much of the second, both Catholic and Protestant, though the younger people show a clear tendency to follow the general American pattern of Catholic and Protestant practice. Magic is present in the belief, widespread among all adults, of the evil eye, witches, and ghosts. The most disbelieving informant will state that while witches and ghosts are not found in the United States they do exist in Italy.

Substantially, the sense of the whole ritual complex, once so dramatically essential to human existence, and its rich articulation in dances, songs, and magic encompassed by the unconscious but organic seasonal cycles, has mostly been forgotten in the United States. Some scattered parts have been maintained — such as the ones already mentioned — which often show a fairly organic relationship with the rest of the culture. As in most parts of the Western world, many of the surviving forms have lost their original meaning in the memory of the same culture-bearers. This, however, is not true for those forms of a more realistic and functional character, such as proverbs, religious songs, prayers, and certain forms of magic practice and belief. The evil eye, for example, can be practiced at a distance, over the telephone, and it helps keep contact among relatives as far apart as Toronto and Florida. Prejudice and superstition about sex, birth, pregnancy, and death are still common among the second generation, and both frequent trips to Italy and contact with Pennsylvania Dutch healers help maintain these and other traditional attitudes.

Examining the peasant culture in relationship to that of the dominant classes is still rather simple in many areas of southern Italy, where contact with modern mass culture has not yet caused too many radical changes. The problem is far more complex in the urban areas, especially in the United States. Roseto, Pennsylvania, however, offered several advantages: the opportunity to refer the culture to that of the Italian place of origin; the relative isolation and homogeneity of the group, which gave a fairly controllable situation; and the possibility of collecting folklore in the context of the total Rosetan culture.

Casa sua non mena guerra [home yields no war] is an Italian proverb that stresses the concept that only one's own home and family can offer a safe shelter from outside enemies and perils. An age-old distrust of the "others" (nonrelatives, representatives of law and justice, government, and society at large) is the first warning taught to any Italian child, and most lullabies are based on the recurring theme of the "wolves," i.e., the world outside of the family and the village circle. This theme is still a dominant one among Italian-Americans in general, and Roseto, Pennsylvania, is no exception. In the absence of an understanding and identification with American society, the relatively successful economy of the Rosetan group has helped to overcome insecurity and isolation and has resulted in the strengthening of part of the traditional value system. There is a widespread antagonism among the first and second generations toward the chief values and symbols of American society and a strongly traditional attitude toward family, education of the children, work, law, and authority. The family in particular, has retained much of its traditional importance, at least compared to attitudes toward the family in other ethnic groups in the United States. In spite of the changes that have occurred in the status of women and in the conception of parental control, the fundamental role of the family in relation to society has largely remained. The role of the father, in fact, is even better maintained in the American Roseto than in Roseto Valfortore, where continual emigration may keep fathers away from home for years. Even though, to a lesser degree than in the past, the father is still the person ultimately responsible for the family prestige and reputation in the community.

After so many years of life in America, Rosetans have only slightly modified their attitude toward law and authority. Mainly through the mass media, they have absorbed — rather than matured — a concept of governmental efficiency and learned to expect a certain attention to their rights and needs as citizens. Since most of their personal experience, however, encompasses only the local, Italian reality, the Rosetan notion of state and national laws is almost as alien in their daily life as it was for their fathers when they left Italy more than eighty years earlier. Proverbs are often quoted by Rosetans to express traditional distrust and to warn about the tricks of laws and governmental authority. The way in which most informants constantly refer to themselves ("we") as opposed to the outside world ("they") also reflects the evident dichotomy between the local, familiar, trustworthy environment and the outside, alien, mainstream society. The latter is indicated by the words "the others" and is conceived of as American or just as non-Italian.

Work has always been considered a necessary and mostly physical effort to provide subsistence. From the immigrants, the second generation has learned to accept this daily effort obediently, but they were never taught a fanatical attitude toward work, and no emotional involvement or moral implication was ever transmitted by the immigrants to their children in relation to work. The same observation can be made about the attitude toward money and wealth, but the situation is now rapidly changing with the younger generation; the shift can perhaps be illustrated here by a single example. While peasants in Italy are more and more inclined to accept money for the information they supply to the folklore collector, several American-Rosetans amazed me by asking how much *they* were supposed to pay for being interviewed. While the Italian peasants are discovering that even their culture has some value, the American-Rosetans do not seem to have such an awareness, since they still feel that they must pay if they want their voices heard. This attitude could be viewed as a reflection of acceptance of capitalistic values (both in Italy and in the United States), but the very fact that this attitude coexists with a strong sense of ethnic differentiation adds another meaning to this occurrence. If integration of the immigrant means losing the uneasiness of feeling alone and different, it should also mean the achievement of a new social consciousness, the consciousness of being part of a larger mass of immigrant labor, regardless of the ethnic differences, which is and has been most necessary to the host society. This view would permit the immigrants and their children to understand their own position in the socioeconomic dynamics of that society. On the contrary, there is evidence that the feeling of marginality originally caused by immigration into an alien society tends to crystallize into an ethnic marginality, and all conflicts are viewed in terms of ethnic differences rather than in the broader terms of the contradictions of the whole social system.

An evident sign of shift is noticeable in the food habits that are reversing the traditional thriftiness recommended by proverbial lore to the poor peasant: *Lu poco abbasta e l'assai fa more* [a bit is enough, and a lot makes you die] and *Poche magna, poche dulore* [little food, little pain]. Traditional dishes following the original recipes are still prepared in Italian-American homes, with the important exception that most of them contain a much larger quantity of dressing and additional ingredients. What used to be the traditional pizza (a flat bread with some salt, tomatoes, or onions) now contains an amazing variety of additions: salami, pepperoni, sausages, ham, and even eggs. The same goes for all varieties of the so-called Italian spaghetti with meatballs (meatballs were totally unknown in the original peasant recipe) and sweets, most of which used to be quite plain and not sweet at all with the exception of the Sicilian sweets, which were mostly honey-based. Not infrequently, Rosetan children in America make disgusted faces at the plain *biscotto* [a kind of ritual cookie] made by their old grandmother for Christmas.

The future development of the cultural profile emerging from this study of one Italian-American community is rather uncertain. Second-generation Rosetans who grew up between 1915 and 1940 lived in a totally homogeneous and traditionally oriented society, an atmosphere which permitted the transmission of folklore from one generation to the next. The introduction of the mass media and other technological innovations and the influence of school education have visibly transformed much of the community life and weakened its traditional pillar, the family. The unavoidable dropping of many old ways and the substitution of new patterns caused a widening gap both between generations and between groups of people with different orientations. Besides the Rosetans, who have tended to move away from the Italian culture and seek identification with American society and its middle-class values and positions, there is a whole section of people that keeps intensive contact with Italy — by travel and correspondence — and seems to find more gratification in identifying itself with the ancestral peasant culture. This last group is mostly in its middle age, and shows a conflict attitude toward American society as well as a thorough disapproval of the lifestyle of the younger generation. Its members travel to Italy often, and many of them spend long summer months in Roseto Valfortore with their relatives and friends. In some way, their cultural and social isolation from the mainstream of American society is similar to the isolation of their parents from the dominant Italian culture at the time of their emigration.

As already mentioned, it is not easy to judge now the future outcome of this combination of acceptance and rejection of American life in Roseto. The community is facing a number of conflicts, some of which are common to most small towns in industrial society, and in this picture of old and new — Italian and American — the most conspicuous problem is, again, the exodus of the younger generation. Contrary to what happened in Roseto Valfortore, the American community maintained a stable population balance for a long time; but now, with many children acquiring college education, the town is no longer able to meet the needs of their new skills and professions. Emigration will thus be, once again, the necessary choice for this community of former emigrants. Often heard among Rosetans are these questions: "Will there be a Roseto in Pennsylvania?" and "Who will take over our nice town?"

What is the folklorist's position in this new approach to folklore study? If we are finally to enter the modern world, face the industrial civilization with its rapidly changing culture, then we must assess our present skills. Possibly folklorists need to try to elaborate a new methodology, to reexamine our ideological framework, and, above all, to seek the appropriate ways of cooperating with other disciplines in developing a new perspective. I have often felt an overwhelming sense of inadequacy in doing my study of immigrant culture, mainly because of a lack of an interdisciplinary basis and of at least a general agreement on the conceptual approach to this aspect of folklore study. Collecting folksongs or folktales, indexing them more or less accurately, and drawing observations on maintenance and distribution have often seemed neither sufficient nor justifiable acts. A comparison with the other aspects of the culture seemed essential. Examining the relationships with the dominant society and the relationships between folk views and the choice of a political party or a religious affiliation, between a folk outlook and the degree of personal affluence, between storytelling and fruition of the mass culture, between a traditional conception of work and the present tendency toward waste and consumption — all these aspects, and many more — appear essential to the study of folklore in the modern world.

REFERENCES

CIRESE, ALBERTO M.
   1973   *Cultura egemonica e culture subalterre: rassegna degli study sul mondo tradizionale populare* [Dominant and subordinate cultures: review of the studies on the popular traditional world]. Palermo.
CRONIN, CONSTANCE
   1970   *The sting of change: Sicilians in Sicily and Austria.* Chicago: University of Chicago Press.

An Oil Boom, Women, and Changing Traditions: A Study of Libyan Women in Benghazi

MONA FIKRY

After World War II, Benghazi was a city in ruins, its destruction comparable only to that of Berlin (Bulugma 1968:61). In 1942, when the Italian occupation ended, this flat, coastal area incurred 1,680 air raids, making war correspondents report with horror and sympathy on the worst-hit city of North Africa:

Though independence [December 24, 1951] fulfilled long and long-fought-for aspirations, reconstruction and development required basic resources which unfortunately did not exist. It is true that Benghazi became the first national capital within ten years of the war's end, but it is equally true that the face of the city remained as ruined as it was when the last German vehicle drove off for the last time. Had it not been for the discovery of oil fields in the Syrtic area almost a decade after independence the present condition of Benghazi would no doubt have been little different. Benghazi's location gave it a considerable share in the oil-companies' expenditure during the early years of exploration (Bulugma 1968:13).

Upon this background of desolation, a process of frenetic construction, expansion, urbanism, and rural migration was initiated in the 1960's and is still going on today, bringing about an unsettling swiftness of change over Libya and its population. To what extent, one may ask, have these changes undermined the basis of traditional living?

THE ERRATIC MODERNIZATION OF LIBYA

While the unsettling and disturbing consequences of wars and colonialism indelibly marked Libyan society, these were, nevertheless, known and familiar forces to which expected reactions, actions, and strategies could be applied. But the discovery of oil in 1958 and the resulting economic boom brought about an unfamiliar force — modernization. Its power is difficult to perceive and assess; its effects are more elusive to identify, to repress, and restrain; and yet some of its influences have been willingly and consciously adopted.

In the words of Hermann Hesse, as quoted by Halpern (1963), "Now there are times when a whole generation is caught . . . between two ages, two modes of life, with the consequence that it loses all power to understand itself and has no standard, no security, no simple acquiescence" (1963:30). It would not be an exaggeration to say that this disequilibrium is one of the basic social problems of our times. Its impact on underdeveloped societies, where the tensions between far more distinct dual cultures create imbalance, dissent, and, often, total lack of comprehension, is felt and observed with greater anguish. This situation is particularly striking in Libya, for unlike most colonized countries which acquire a certain amount of modernization through colonial commerce, bureaucracy, and education in Libya under the Italians, Libyans were excluded almost totally from contact with and knowledge of processes that would have helped them acquire modern concepts and skills.[1] During exile to various Arab countries, such as Egypt, Lebanon, Syria, and Turkey, Libyans tasted the bitterness and comfort of modernization, but even this privilege was essentially limited to men. Traditional behavior, education, and attire were largely continued in exile for the women.

In short, Libya did not benefit from the general modernization that is a particular consequence of colonialism. Consequently, not infrequently one hears Libyans, and particularly educated women, speak with envy of the type of colonialism their Algerian counterparts experienced. "At least, that was colonialism that brought with it culture," they say, paying no regard to the deep sense of rootlessness, the loss of identity, and the psychological turmoil that this "culture" brought to the Algerians. No matter. Some Libyans, particularly those from Benghazi, which has always been far more isolated than Tripoli, think they would have preferred the "chance" the Algerians had of making contact with the outside world to their own situation, in which they were prevented from obtaining any sort of an education and from acquiring any modern skills. The only skills imposed upon Libyans throughout colonization involved the menial labor Libyans have traditionally considered, and still consider, undignified, an attitude that has hindered their economic development. The present labor force in Libya is almost entirely constituted of Egyptian and

---

[1]   Following the Italian occupation, which lasted from 1911 to 1942, the Libyans still had no possibility of acquiring any sort of modern skills, for between 1942 and 1945, Libya was under military occupation of the Allied Forces under British command; and between 1945 and 1951, it was administered by the United Nations with Adrian Pelt as the UN Commissioner. In 1951, the year of independence, the ravages of war were still apparent everywhere, and Libya was counted among the poorer nations of the world.

Tunisian skilled and manual laborers (*Economic Development of Libya* 1960:9–10).

While modernization in Europe was a consequence of industrialization, in a country such as Libya it was a consequence of commerce with the West; consumption, not production, is the essential characteristic of a society that takes no part in, and has no knowledge of, the production of its consumer goods. In a society that lacks both a sufficient manual labor force and basic technological skills, the cost of repairing machinery is often exorbitant. Consumption consequently reaches levels of irrationality when money is readily available. Two examples from Libyan experience can illustrate this point. The owner of an apartment house may simply replace defective water heaters in apartments with plumbing problems rather than checking the pipes and elements for defects in the heaters. The next example may appear anecdotal but it is in fact true. A man purchased a refrigerator that he soon discovered did not function. He purchased another, then another, neither of which worked. So he put the machines aside without returning them. A neighbor who heard of the man's plight went to investigate and discovered that the electric wall plugs were defective, not the refrigerators. These examples show that modernization unaccompanied by an understanding of technological skills imposes tragic limitations on countries that have become very wealthy while remaining strongly traditional. The acquisition of useless objects — such as wigs and furs in hot, dusty regions — becomes the sign of ultimate modernity.

This veneer of modernization may be a source of frustration, "a knowledge of attempting to be modern but failing at it" (Apter 1965:47). This awareness is acquired by those who are, to use Daniel Lerner's apt categorizations (1958), the "transitionals," those urbanized individuals whose inner life may still be close to the "traditionals" (1958:71–75). The "moderns," those at the opposite social pole may appreciate traditional living, but are no longer able to identify with it. Consequently, they may reach an even more complex level of frustration, which is expressed in the form of alienation in many aspects of their behavior. This frustration and alienation are more characteristic of the educated and modernized Libyan woman than of the educated man. In no way do these "moderns" regret their level of modernism, but they deeply resent both the traditional society that restrains and criticizes their modernism and simultaneously, their inevitable loss of integration with it. This ambivalence is compounded when, in the face of the growing desire for modernity the traditional society intensifies its assertion of traditional and religious values.

With this background, the painful and erratic process of women's modernization in Libya can be comprehended. Several important elements have fostered a collision between the modern and traditional values of the Libyan women. First, the movement from rural (if not essentially nomadic) to urban settings is often unsettling. For a man this change of environment is accompanied by the acquisition of a new and/or different job. For a woman, on the other hand, it usually means the loss of a job (for in her original setting, she participated in agricultural or handicraft work), or the acquisition of a menial job (such as a hospital lavatory cleaner), which she would never have conceived of doing in her rural setting. Second, in many underdeveloped countries, literacy is and has been the first step toward modernization, even in rural areas. In Libya, this has not been the situation. Although the emphasis of modernization will shift as an increasing number of rural and urban schools are opened for girls, the first most significant step toward modernization occurred in the material aspect: the accumulation of money, cars, houses, land, furs, wigs, and so on. Third, the increased awareness of a world outside that of the extended family has been made possible for Libyan women through contact with the mass media, especially television. In a predominantly illiterate society, seeing is far more impressive than either listening or reading. Unfortunately, television in Libya offers little more than packaged entertainment, greatly diluting the traditional imagination that folklore nourished through the ages. Instead of creating a new sort of imaginativeness, it has often led to an insidious boredom of which both women and youth complain. In the 1950's, Lerner stated a difficulty common in the Middle East that is the very crux of this dangerous consequence of change: boredom. "Needed there," he wrote, "is a massive growth of imaginativeness about alternatives to their present lifeways and a simultaneous growth of institutional means for handling these alternative lifeways" (Lerner 1958:411). This need is left grossly unsatisfied in Libya, as in many Arab countries, because of the very nature of that erratic level of modernization. In Libya, this particularly affects women's growing need to fill their leisure time; for whereas boys and men have the freedom to loiter in the streets after work or during periods of unemployment, or to spend their time in various meeting places, at the movies, soccer games, or the beach, or aimlessly riding in fast cars around town, women are restricted to the *hosh* [home] and their social and intellectual activities are greatly limited. In Libya, two absolutely distinct worlds exist, one of men and another of women, one lived "outside" and the other lived "inside" (Souriau 1969: *passim*).

WOMEN AND CULTURAL OPPRESSION

Even inside the *hosh*, the personalities of women are in constant change. A very small percentage of them fit Lerner's category of the "moderns," that is, educated or even partially educated urban women who can form opinions on general topics and who are no longer self-consciously concerned with being "modern." Most women fit the "transitionals" category. Either they were born in the city and reared in a predominantly traditional setting, or they moved from the village or the desert to the city, greatly desiring to change. One could even make several subdivisions according to the level of education, empathy, and years of urban living of these "transitionals." The last group "traditionals" are greatly diminishing in number, even in the rural areas, for those who fear change and modernization are forcibly abandoning traditional life (Hilal 1967:26–27). In fact, the majority of Libyan men and women could be called "transitionals." Their psychological search is a personal tug-of-war between modern and traditional values.

This ambivalence, so common among modern Libyan women, derives from different psychological and social reasons than those educed by Lerner, who saw ambivalence as a matter of inner uncertainty. To the women of present-day Libya, ambivalence is a consequence of society's religious, if not political, values. The importance of religious belief is drummed into the people through radio and television, newspapers, and magazines. To be born a Muslim and then to doubt one's religion is a very serious matter indeed, as it is in any traditionally religious culture. Thus, any opinion contrary to traditional Islamic concepts cannot be openly voiced. Opposition to polygamy, for example is not tolerated. In contrast to Egyptian, Syrian, and Lebanese women, who officially condemned polygamy in 1972 at the Congress of Arab Women held in Cairo, the educated, modern Libyan women attending the Congress condemned only its abuses. In fact, if the Libyan women had supported a "modernistic argument" against polygamy to its logical end, they would have incurred the double criticism of Libyan political and religious forces, if not that of other Libyan "traditional" or "transitional" women.

The personal drama of change in most underdeveloped countries lies in a consistent imbalance between change in individuals and in their environment, along with an even greater difference in the degree of change between men and women. The physical and psychic mobility of the woman in Libya is determined largely by the male's willingness to view her in a role other than that given her by tradition. Accordingly, the potential progressiveness of Libyan women is greatly curbed, for the nation "provides the channels through which individuals transform their own lives" (Lerner 1958:83).

The psychological spontaneity in the life of women is also greatly suppressed. This spontaneity was taken care of in the traditional setting by the organized repetition of routine, of traditional occasions and festivities accompanied by known and expected participation and performance. Yet many of the educated women, and even those in the process of being educated, feel consciously oppressed. A very strong feeling of empathy, of understanding of one another's problems, characterizes this set of women: "I am really culturally oppressed!" This startling confession by a young, educated woman brought to light the entire problem of alienation, happiness, and traditionality. One first ponders what culture she is referring to. European? Arab? Libyan? Or is it the mixed life she is living, which as yet has no place in the society?

To what extent can these women participate in the traditional life of their culture? They have to participate in various traditional occasions or else be ostracized from their social and family milieu. For the modern, and maybe also for the transitional woman in the last stage, traditional participation is lived piecemeal. She goes to weddings and claps along with the others — but she remains an observer. She goes to funerals and wails and scratches her face like the others — but maybe with less intensity.[2] She rejects what she is not forced to participate in, such as the wearing of a talisman for protection against the evil eye. She is religious to the extent that all those around her are religious, but she can be discriminating in her religiousness by condemning certain abusive social practices tolerated by the religion. She is a secular-religious individual, living her religion in a nonchalant but dutiful fashion, with less inner intensity than outer obedience.

This ambivalent behavior is a determining factor in the level of happiness achieved in the life of the women. Those in the two extreme modes, the traditional and the modern, are the unhappiest. On the one hand, their mobility and self-assertion have been limited; on the other, the continuation of traditions has been threatened. It is also true among the modern or educated Libyan women that, with the disruption of the traditional values in their own daily life, their appreciation of formal education and of "mental" modernization grows. But they are faced with frustrating social and traditional elements that make them even more aware of their inner instability and lack of integration in the society at large. Such awareness made a young educated woman at a wedding observe how much happier the traditional girls (including the "transitionals") were and how much more actively they participated than the few modern girls present. The latter were quiet and expressed little enjoyment.

[2]   One of the most persistent of traditional customs that women help perpetuate in spite of education, purer Islamization, and a lessening of family cohesion is the funerary custom in which women are socially obliged to mourn their dead by weeping, scratching their faces, and pouring ashes on their heads. In fact, even educated girls and women who may not show sufficient earnestness in these manifestations of mourning will be publicly disgraced. The only women exempt from this practice are those who are *hajjas*, that is, those who went to Mecca on a pilgrimage, for this is a custom abhorred in Islam. In fact, a law specifically forbids "the repulsive habits in funerals" (Law 31, 1951, in *Official Journal*, April 4, 1952) and is supported by the prophetic *hadith*, which says: "And they are not one of us who slap their face and tear their clothes."

The concept that happiness is achieved through literacy is expressed in the desire to acquire the minimum sense of independence necessary to city living — the ability to read street signs, dial the telephone, ride the bus without having to ask for assistance. It is also expressed in the desire to fill one's time with "something useful" — such as reading magazines, books, newspapers, and subtitles in foreign movies on television, for example. Moreover, literacy would allow the illiterate woman better to educate her children, who now go to school and ask her questions she cannot answer. Most of all, it would enable her to be independent from her mother-in-law (a significant point to which we will later return) or obtain jobs other than the menial positions open to her now.

All these aspirations toward greater personal happiness and freedom are in no way evaluated by the women as aspects of alienation but, rather, as a means of better integration into the urban society as a whole. The desire to be of use to the country is often expressed; it indicates the extent to which television and radio broadcasts link literacy to greater national usefulness and illiteracy to doom and darkness.

Women realistically evaluate the difference between the happiness generated by life in town and by life in the original rural or Bedouin setting as the difference between the material and the emotional satisfactions that each environment respectively provides. The Bedouin-become-urban-woman realizes that she was happier in her tent surrounded by her family. The unity of the family was far stronger then, if only because crowded living quarters demanded it. Such unity is difficult to find in the city. But she is content with what city living offers her — a house of her own, television, a school for her children, work. In the city, her material needs are satisfied, but her emotional life remains linked with past happiness.

FOLKLORE AND THE MASS MEDIA

Folklore has lost much in its significance since the war years and military campaigns (Rossi 1965:88). In the city of Benghazi, the sudden rural movement to the urban center and the overwhelming use of television, radio, and cassette recorders have served to decrease greatly the folkloric activities in the lives of women and society as a whole.

Traditional handicraft skills have vanished except for the weaving of the traditional *rida'*, perhaps because "Under the Italian occupation, domestic production was unable to compete with cheap machine-made goods" (*Economic Development of Libya* 1960:199). Even though the government has encouraged the formation of folk dance and folk music groups and the University of Libya has opened a center that collects folk poetry, the interest expressed in such activities, especially by the youth, is very limited. Folk poetry, which is recited only by men and traditionally deals essentially with historic epics, today includes current topics such as the ills of traffic, the rudeness of drivers, praise for the 1969 revolution, and, more recently, praise for the Cultural Revolution of Libya of 1973. The radio regularly broadcasts folk poetry and music, as does the television, which also transmits folk dance performances. Attempts to "modernize" the choreography of the dances make the traditional viewer feel that he or she is observing a foreign performance of Libyan dancing. Here young men and women dance together, sometimes holding hands or even each other's waists. Such conscious attempts at change are interesting expressions of the desire to mold the traditional into modern shapes, but the artistic ideas have not as yet matured enough to be satisfactory to either traditional or modern viewers.

Tale-telling, called *khurafat*[3] in Libya, used to be an essential part of family entertainment in towns, villages, and tents, but in the city it has now all but disappeared to be replaced by television. The time that young children spent listening to tales is now spent studying, reading magazines, or watching television. Rare are the occasions when tales are told and few are the young urban women who know any tales to tell. Even the special night devoted to tale-telling during the wedding celebrations is now firmly linked with the past.

Tales used to help fill the leisure time of the women, as did songs, poetry, dancing, and the rhymes that served as lullabies or as childrens' games. Women fifty years old and over remember that, in their youth, they would get together with friends and play traditional instruments and sing and dance for the sole purpose of enjoyment. Such activities are truly nonexistent in the cities and have been largely replaced by television. For women, however, even television does not completely eliminate the boredom that results from their indoor seclusion and diminished contact with husbands and relatives. Television programs in Libya are essentially Egyptian, Lebanese, and American, with the latter having Arabic subtitles; rarely can the majority of the women (that is, the traditional and transitional) identify with the problems and programs aimed at the viewers. Thus, the television is used for entertainment, not educational purposes, even though literacy and counting lessons are presented regularly as are health and cleanliness campaigns. Today, television is increasingly used by the government to project its ideas through specific programs. Also, the speeches of the president of the Revolutionary Command Council are broadcast in their entirety.

[3]   In Libya, tales are called *khurafat*, which literally means "superstitious sayings," or "the meaningless," "the imaginative." It is said that the word *khurafa* originated in the name of a man who claimed he had been captured by a *djinn*, thus explaining the reason for his long disappearance. He used to tell stories about that *djinn* to the people who had neither heard of such things nor could believe them. Such tales were therefore called *khurafat* or *Khurafa* (Al-Kasshat 1968:19).

Undeniably, of course, television has influenced and does still greatly influence women viewers, as well as children. It has given them a wide vision of the world and has exposed them to attitudes beyond the limited traditional family allegiances. It has created new needs, new desires, new aesthetics, and new examples to imitate, even though these have not always been beneficial to them or to the society. A few years ago, an Egyptian series called *The Black Cat* (an imitation of American action movies) was very popular among the youth. It dealt with violence, kidnapping, stealing, and so on. Soon a wave of terrorism appeared in Benghazi: schools were burned down, and notes were left behind signed "The Black Cat"; kidnapping threats signed by "The Black Cat" were sent. The program was discontinued, but it is an indication of how easily the youth may be led toward violence as a means of filling their empty and undirected time.

The traditional aesthetics and signs of beauty have also changed, and television viewing is an important factor in this change. The traditional *washam* or "tattoo" made on the bride before her wedding was considered an embellishment. Each region and town had its particular symbol; Benghazi's was a small palm tree placed on one's chin. This embellishment is now on the wane in the rural areas and has disappeared from the city traditions.

The void created in the lives of the urban Libyan women by the rapidity with which modern mass media entered their lives and deracinated the old traditional customs has not yet been filled. If it has instilled a certain amount of empathy among women, it has also created a certain amount of social and psychological instability. Yet, one of the most important aspects of mass media, and particularly of television in Libya, regardless of its level of excellence, is that to most traditional and transitional women, it is at least a window to the outside world.

RESTRICTIVE LAWS AND MORES

In Libya, it is the husband who shops for food. Yet, he does so not to be helpful to his wife, rather, to prevent her from having unnecessary contact with strangers. Many traditional and religious customs, in particular those pertaining to women, are tenaciously adhered to in spite of, and maybe because of, the surge of modernization and swiftness of urbanization, the apparent breakup of the family system, and the supremacy of money. All these changes erode the basic values of the society. This tenacity is clearly expressed in the laws that do not yet reflect the greater awareness and knowledge that women are acquiring through education, television, and physical mobility. Quite to the contrary, the laws seem to intensify the conservative and religious currents prevalent in Libya.

"Neither laws nor religions are stronger than traditions" is what a young Libyan woman graduate in law once said, implying that social reality is often different from and contrary to legal codifications. In Libya, however, the laws do not fully correct the abuse of women inherent in Islamic law, on which the status of women is based. With the exception of the matter of inheritance — it is illegal to rob a woman of her traditional rights of inheritance (she gets half of what her brother gets) — most other laws dealing with marriage, polygamy, divorce, and repudiation have not embodied a willingness to give the basic rights of self-possession to women.

The continuity of some restrictive traditions is not only the male's doing. Women themselves cannot eradicate deeply rooted traditions in the space of ten or twenty years. The few university graduates — male and female — are not enough to overhaul the traditional concepts severely restricting the urban and modern woman. A case in point is voluntarism, which is, in every way, contrary to traditional behavior, for to do any type of voluntary work outside the family involves a certain amount of contact with strangers, both male and female, and demands a freedom of move-ment that women are neither free nor able to acquire. Not surprisingly, the New Woman's Association of Benghazi is therefore almost at a standstill. With ninety members enrolled in 1973, only six or seven attended meetings, and eleven proposed projects have been left on paper.

The Libyan woman presents a particularly complex and difficult pic-ture. She is living in two acculturated, but starkly different, cultures; her life is divided between indoor and outdoor behavior. Having little contact with the outside world, except through television, she truly has no model as a symbol of progress. Alienation of the woman is seen on all levels of society. The modern woman rejects her traditional counterpart; the traditional is tenaciously holding on to already diluted traditions; the transitional woman is jolted more and more by the inevitable and ines-capable change in the traditional value system.

In the city, the lower-class woman, the one closest to traditional living, has had to shed many of the restrictive traditions by the mere fact of having to leave the house to work among strangers. Outside, even while covered up and observing the world with one eye, she is faced with constant novelties. Once indoors, she continues to live her secluded life. But now she is beginning to overcome a growing feeling of restlessness and solitude by learning how to read and write — to integrate herself and her family in the urban world more successfully.

The educated woman's problem of alienation involves coping with social and religious pressure against identification with the norms and values of the outside world. This conflict makes her feel torn between outdoor contacts and indoor relationships. The tensions from such contrasting lives are not yet resolved, but they find an outlet in a static self-contentment with the status quo and the acceptance of and, more especially, the resignation to a system based on conservative religious values, traditional persistence, and male dominance.

Urbanization, literacy, and mobility have brought about a certain measure of modernization that has directly affected women. It has changed, to a certain degree, their way of life and their role in the changing social system. It has established, in all levels of relationships, an element essential to change — tension — that has helped her to acquire a new consciousness, a new empathy. It has also increased women's self-perception, through physical mobility, literacy, and varied contacts with the mass media.

Television has played an essential part in the life of the Libyan women, especially in the past ten years, for women spend almost all their time indoors at home and center their lives, more than men, on television. Television has widened the woman's perspective and awareness, thereby creating a complex set of feelings: inner instability, a sense of enjoyment, unconscious empathy, and previously unknown modern needs. Television has also effectively diminished the use and significance, on traditional occasions, of folk music, dance, poetry and tale-telling.

There exists and has always existed in the life of the urban Libyan woman a certain amount of contact and interaction, of acceptance and rejection, all of which are essential motor elements to the process of change and acculturation in the society as a whole. Yet, all these new experiences that she has acquired and is acquiring still, all these new attitudes that she is assuming are, in effect, lived behind closed doors.

REFERENCES

AL-KASSHAT, M. S.
   1968   *The folk literature of Libya.* Beirut: Dar Lebman.
APTER, DAVID E.
   1965   *The politics of modernization.* Chicago: University of Chicago Press.
BULUGMA, HADI M.
   1968   *Benghazi through the ages.* Tripoli: Maktabet al-Fikr.
Economic Development of Libya
   1960   *Economic Development of Libya.* Report of a mission organized at the request of the Libyan government. Baltimore: Johns Hopkins University Press.
HALPERN, MANFRED
   1963   *The politics of social change in the Middle East and North Africa.* Princeton N.J.: Princeton University Press.
HILAL, MAJIL M.
   1967   *A sociological study in Libyan social reality.* (Available only in Arabic.) Tripoli: Maktabet al-Fikr.

LERNER, DANIEL
   1958   *The passing of traditional society*. Glencoe, Ill.: Free Press.
ROSSI, P.
   1965   *Libye* [Libya]. Lausanne: Editions Recontre.
SOURIAU, CHRISTIANE
   1969   La société féminine libyenne [The female Libyan society]. *Revue de l'Occident Musulman* 6.

The Impact of Urbanization on
Shukriyya Life and Folk Poetry

SAYYID HURREIZ

The last few years have witnessed a growing interest in the study of urbanization in the Sudan. *African urban notes* (Hale and Hale 1971) devoted a special issue to the Sudan. The Philosophical Society of the Sudan convened and published the proceedings of a conference on urbanization in the Sudan (El Bashra 1972). Besides these works, individual studies have been published in book form or scattered in various journals of African studies.[1] Such literature, however, lacks attempts to relate Sudanese folklore to the processes of urbanization and modernization that are sweeping the country. This paper deals with the impact of urbanization on the Shukriyya as reflected in their folk poetry.

With the coming of the Turks to the Sudan, there commenced a new era, characterized by social and political change and an increasing encroachment of urbanization. New concepts of administration, together with urbanization and processes associated with it such as industrialization, came with the Turkish rule (1820–1881). These cultural changes and modernizing influences were later activated and strengthened by the British occupation (1898–1956).

The beginning of urbanization and industrialization in the Sudan dates back to the time of Meroe (sixth century B.C. to fourth century A.D.). The impact of urbanization on Shukriyya life and folk poetry, however, is more recent. The first part of this paper deals briefly with influences traceable to the Turkish and British eras. The second and major part investigates repercussions of urbanization caused by the resettlement of Nubians and the establishment of the Khashm Al Girba Development Scheme in the Shukriyya homeland.

The Shukriyya are one of the largest nomadic and cattle-owning tribes

[1] For further information on literature pertinent to urbanization see Hale and Hale (1971:150–181).

of the Sudan. According to the first population census of the Sudan, conducted in 1956, the Shukriyya number 121,525 (Department of Statistics 1956:27). Their homeland is the stretch of land between the Nile and the Atbara rivers, traditionally known as the Buṭāna. The Shukriyya live in camps of woven wool tents, which they carry with them as they move from one grazing ground and water source to another. They claim to be descended from the legendary ancestor Shakīr, but the first ancestry with whom oral, historical testimonies are associated is Shā' 'ed-dīn, of the second half of the sixteenth century (Hillelson 1920:33–75). Their tribal history is full of feuds and battles, fought in order to secure their land and maintain supremacy over other tribes such as the Hamaj, the Rikābiyya, and the Baṭāhīn. Oral traditions of the Shukriyya are full of reminiscences of warriors such as Abū 'Alī and 'Awaḍ Al Karīm, who died defending tribal territory. During the Turkish rule some sections of the tribe Shukriyya-t-El. 'Adēk [the Blue Nile Shukriyya] became more inclined toward agriculture and a sedentary life (Hillelson 1920:33–75).

During the Turkish rule, modernization and urbanization were first concentrated in Khartoum, and their impact was gradually diffused to other parts of the country. A police force, government workshops, administrative departments, army barracks, a governor's palace, a hospital, churches, and dockyards appeared in Khartoum in the 1860's (Hale and Hale 1971:12–13). Later, during the British occupation, firearms, trains, trucks, taxis, airplanes and other industrial innovations became part of the urban scene. Such items, or knowledge of their existence, gradually spread to rural and tribal districts and affected the folk mentality in numerous ways. Preoccupation with these technological products was mirrored in the folk poetry of the Shukriyya as well as in oral and literary traditions of other Sudanese tribes.

For instance, the imagery that was traditionally used in the description of camels and women (the two favorite themes in Shukriyya folk poetry) gave way to new concepts and images brought about by the influence of urbanization and modernization. While describing "the beloved," the Shukriyya and other Islamized tribes of the Sudan always stressed how well guarded she was by her family and kinsmen. "A woman's" guard was frequently compared to the he-goat or the stag that protects the flock or keeps it together and to the honey bee that stings those who come to collect honey.

The image of honey that is likely to be tasted by other than the rightful owner refers to "the beloved." Such images throw light on the status of women within that group and on the Shukriyya's social values and attitudes toward women. The he-goat and the stag that protect the flock and keep it intact are reminiscent of nomadic scenes. Also in the poems, the constant fear that girls may be molested and the avowed communal responsibility, especially of male relatives and kin, to safeguard against such an unthinkable event reflect nomadic values.

When the new urban setting, with its novel administrative concepts and vocabulary, began to dominate Shukriyya society at the end of the nineteenth century, some of the old concepts and descriptions (such as the constant reference to "the beloved" as well protected) persisted in the tradition. The role of the protector began to be assumed by a government agent such as a sentinel or *Al Murāsla* [a messenger-porter] rather than by male kinsmen who were symbolized by the stinging bee or the wild he-goat. Traditional poetry compares "the beloved" to a high-ranking official in an administrative setting reminiscent of Turkish administration. The following verses offer some examples of the mixing of old and new images:

I was received by a messenger-porter whom I greeted.
"I am guarding 'the beloved' who is worthy of your love."
"Welcome, friend, who has come from the wilderness
    of the countryside," he replied.
He then rushed back to his squeaking door.

In a second example protection is given by another government agent, a real sentinel this time and not a porter. In the following lines, the poet addresses his camel and urges it to hasten and unite him with his beloved:

Hardoub Mount has appeared before you, can't you see it!
Are you frightened by its huge rugged stones?
Hasten and unite me with "the one" who is always
    advancing towards higher ranks,
Before the sentinel arrives and forbids people
    to hover around "him."

Technical and industrial innovations that were part of the urban scene also found their way into this poetry, especially when it came to the description of speed. For instance, the swiftness of the camel had previously been compared to the wild animal frightened by war drums or the clouds driven by heavy winds. Such stock images were replaced by the train, the truck, and the sewing machine (Hurreiz 1969:7–17).

This set of urban influences, reflected in Shukriyya folk poetry, was an offshoot of the general process of modernization, which affected the country at large and was disseminated from the capital and other urban centers near the Shukriyya homeland. These urban influences did not disrupt the traditional life of the Shukriyya, although they exerted a considerable impact on their life and folk traditions. By and large, modern products could be assimilated into the traditional tribal life experience, since most of them were very peripheral in nature. Tribal bards seem to have been dazzled by the introduction of the new technical devices, which forced them to widen the boundaries of their experience and their world view and, consequently, to extend the diction and imagery of their poetry and the range of their poetic faculties.

The second example of the impact of urbanization on Shukriyya life and folk poetry is more recent, and its effects are more deeply penetrating and far reaching. This urbanization process is associated with the movement of the Nubians and their resettlement on the Buṭāna, the grazing ground and homeland of the Shukriyya tribe.

The causes for this movement go back to the Nile Water Agreement of 1959 and the construction of the High Dam at Egypt. The building of the High Dam led to the flooding of the extreme northern parts of the Sudan, and as a result more than 34,000 people from the Wādī Ḥalfa district had to be evacuated and rehabilitated at the new site in the Buṭāna (Shaw 1967:463). The preparation of the wild grazing ground of the Shukriyya for the resettlement project necessitated the introduction of numerous technical and modern innovations. Among the major changes in this area were the construction of the Khashm Al Girba Dam, a railway system and a sugar refinery, the building of new cities such as New Ḥalfa and Khashm Al Girba, and the introduction of mechanized cultivation.

The movement of the Nubians started in January 1964, and by the middle of 1967, 53,000 Nubians were resettled ('Allām 1971:18). The resettlement also attracted an influx of immigrants from different tribes and language groups, of which the two largest groups were the nomadic Shukriyya and the Nubians, who were sedentary agriculturalists and laborers. The underlying differences, which were aggravated by the bitterness of the Shukriyya, sometimes resulted in tribal feuds, but mostly they were vented in protest poetry (Hurreiz 1974:7–12).

The technical and industrial innovations associated with the new scheme, together with the fact that "the employment structure of émigré population" was urban rather than rural in character, produced an urbanizing and modernizing effect on the Shukriyya (Shaw 1967:487). One consequence was the creation of a new genre of folk poetry called *ghuna Al Buṭāna* [the Buṭāna poetry]. This poetry embodies the responses of the Shukriyya toward urbanization and toward the development scheme with which it was associated.

For various reasons the immediate responses to urbanization reflected in this poetry were negative. First, the nomadic Shukriyya abhor and ridicule agriculture (Hillelson 1920:61–71), and the Khashm Al Girba scheme consisted mainly of mechanized agriculture. Second, new regulations essential for the administration of the changes necessitated the imposition of restrictions on nomadism and grazing rights. Third, the first phase of the plan was designed mainly for the resettlement of Nubians, and not for the Shukriyya, who were allotted land at a later date, some of them as late as 1969. Privileges in services were given to the Nubian immigrants, and the Shukriyya were supplied with inferior services ('Allām 1971:25). Thus, the Nubians had the best of everything, and the indigenous Shukriyya got the leftovers. All these factors reinforced the nostalgia for the old ways of traditional life and denigrated urbanization.

In the following pages, I will survey some examples of this poetry and its reaction to planned development and urbanization. One of the most significant factors in this discussion is that the Shukriyya were mainly nomadic pastoralists and, as such, were reluctant to accept farming and sedentary agriculture. This fact underlies their preliminary rejection of the plan and the subsequent process of urbanization:

Your[2] occupants have moved on camel back.
Sheikh Na' īm's Trees[3] has been inhabited by aliens.
How could those who have tasted milk from the
    udders of light brown camels
Become farmers and accept the life of farming?

The following verse ridicules agriculture in general and specifically the cultivation of certain crops, such as the radish, which seem to the nomad to be of no value:

Al Barāyrob[4] has been utterly destroyed and torn apart.
It is being turned into farms for growing radishes.
At the time of Aḥmed, "The Cutting Sword",[5] everyone who galloped by
    used to avoid it.
Whoever dared to ride by found himself toothless or
    with broken ribs.

There is also an ecological attitude toward the encroaching urbanization embodied in such poetry, which reveals an added sense of bitterness felt by the afflicted nomad:

Al Ḥasan's Acacia Trees have been torn down.
The canal water on the scheme is stored at Al Īdēhim[6]
O! hares bemoan and cry for Aḥmed, "The Cutting Sword."
The cocks of Ḥalfa Nubians are crowing right over
    Al Ma'āgil dune.

The acacia tree, the hares, and the dune are reminiscences of the wild nomadic environment; they contrast with the cock, which is associated with sedentary life.

The Buṭāna was the traditional grazing ground of the Shukriyya, but the establishment of the plan and the cultivation of land made it essential

[2] The pronoun "your" refers to the Buṭāna.
[3] "Sheikh Na'īm's Trees" is a place in the Buṭāna.
[4] A name of a certain valley.
[5] A nickname of Sheikh Ahmed 'Awaḍ Al Karīm, one of the famous Shukriyya chiefs.
[6] "Hasan's Acacia Trees" and Al Idēhim are place names.

to impose restrictions on nomadic habits. In brief, the camels and goats of the Shukriyya could no longer roam about freely. Penalties and fines were levied on the owners of stray animals. During the early phases, the administration of the plan required additional police forces to guard the plantations against the indigenous nomads and their animals ('Allām 1971:21). As a substitute for the lost grazing land, animals had to rely on a limited number of *Shōbāras* for their fodder (a *Shōbāra* is a stretch of land that remains fallow for one year; It is sometimes distributed to farmers on the understanding that it will be used for growing animal fodder):

We have become keen- and hook-eyed on the Shōbāra.
Our milk goats have starved because of the judge's fine.
The Nuer[7] have swaggered proudly regardless of who
   pleases or groans.
May Allah bring back to us the time of our horses which
   were covered by mail.

With the rejection of the new way of life comes the rejection of planned development together with its technology and modernization. In interviews which I conducted a few years ago, some of the informants viewed the digging of canals as devastation of the land:

You have suffered a great misfortune, land of thick, entwined grass.
They dug canals and brought tap water to you.
Many notable warriors have previously roamed on you
   like famous venomous snakes.
Both Ni'ēma and Madame Zhahrab[8] bear witness to that.

After the completion of the scheme, not only did the Halfa Nubians settle at the Butāna, but various other tribes also flocked to the newly developed area. Different cultures and languages came into contact. Such influences together with the new mode of living brought about more complaint. The following lines depict the response of the Shukriyya toward the increasing influx of tribes into the area and the enslavement to agriculture:

Rikēba[9] said to me: look how numerous these people are.
The Dinka[10] and Nuer have spoilt my green color by their
   tough trading feet.
The scarred beautiful girl is embracing cotton.

---

[7]   One of the Nilotic tribes of southern Sudan.
[8]   Names of two famous women who were mistresses of the bard who supposedly has composed this poem.
[9]   Rikēba is the name of the valley in which the city of New Halfa has been built.
[10]   "The Dinka" is a Nilotic tribe.

Is she not afraid that she might be rejected by the
  bridegroom for giving herself up to
  picking cotton?

The poem describes the feeling on the part of the Shukriyya that the homeland, the grazing ground, and the traditional way of life were threatened by modernization and planned development. This feeling of insecurity was counteracted by a reaffirmation of ties with the Buṭāna and a constant recollection of tribal history and traditions. Such oral traditions are governed by a certain tendency to glorify the past:

From the time of Shakīr up to Muḥammad, the present
chief, we have experienced heated battles on this land,
we have controlled our frontiers up to Sarāwīl Māda,
on the Ethiopian border, by the cutting swords on which
  blood is clotting.

Much poetry similar to these examples came into being after the implementation of the Khashm Al Girba Development Scheme and the resettlement of the Nubians. The immigration and resettlement began in 1964, and a year to a year and a half later this Buṭāna poetry started. While some poems are still associated with certain tribal bards, the bulk of this poetry has been adopted, adapted, and folklorized by the masses. Moreover, some of its authors are anonymous.

Analysis of the examples presented shows that the following major themes and subjects occur in this poetry:

1. Usurpation of homeland that forced the Shukriyya to move and acquire a new mode of living.
2. Loss of nomadic life, threatened by urbanization.
3. Reluctance and inability to adjust to agriculture.
4. Positive attitudes of the tribe toward ecology and veneration for land.
5. Ridicule of certain traits associated with agriculture and the life of farming.
6. Nostalgia for the old days when the sword reigned.
7. Limited sources of fodder for animals after the grazing ground had been taken over by the plan.
8. Imposition of restrictions and fines on grazing animals (and consequently on nomadism) by an urbanized, administrative setting with civil courts and police.
9. Resentment by Shukriyya over influx of tribes to the Buṭāna.
10. Ethnically and linguistically different tribes with whom the Shukriyya were forced to share their own land.
11. Digging canals seen as misfortune and destruction of the land.
12. Implicit rejection of technology.

13. Resentment of the new concepts of labor, for example, in cotton picking, that threatened some traditional values.
14. Reaffirmation of ties with land, traditions, and ancestry.
15. Attempt to mobilize tribal forces: plea for action.

Examination of interviews conducted with Shukriyya tribesmen a few years ago showed that their responses to questions related to the Buṭāna and the development scheme emphasize the same themes presented in the poetry.[11] This evidence demonstrates that, though a recent phenomenon, we are dealing with folk, not bardic, poetry[12] that focuses on and verbalizes the responses of the Shukriyya toward the urbanization and modernization represented by the Khashm Al Girba scheme.

One may venture to make the following conclusions and inferences based on the previous discussion of the Khashm Al Girba Development Scheme and its impact on Shukriyya life and folklore. Contrary to the conviction that modernization and technology stifle folklore, the impact of urbanization on the nomadic Shukriyya, especially those living in the Khashm Al Girba area, created a folklore renaissance. This renaissance is centered on the very same things that were threatened by urbanization: namely, land (the ancestral homeland), tradition, and nomadic values.

Folklore also has a positive role to play in developing countries that recently have been exposed to the tremendous influences of urbanization and modernization. It serves as a critique of the changes affecting the community. I propose that folklore, in fact, should be employed to detect potential responses to urbanization before policymakers embark on major development schemes, and it should be examined as well in reassessing such schemes and reconsidering some aspects of their implementation.

The planners and administrators of the Khashm Al Girba Development Scheme did not take into consideration the cultural premises and nomadic values that are clearly and strikingly manifested in the folklore of the groups affected by the scheme. The nomadic Shukriyya, who ridiculed agriculture through the ages, were brought into abrupt contact and confrontation with a system dominated by mechanized agriculture and a sedentary lifestyle. Instead, they should have been transferred smoothly from one stage to another and from one mode of life to a different one. Their folklore would have aided the planner of social and economic development by indicating those actions that would be acceptable or unacceptable. The planners failed to accommodate the traditional nomadic way of life, or at least some of its essential traits, into the newly introduced system.

For example, grazing areas were not secured within the fringes of the

[11]   For recordings of such interviews, see the Institute of African and Asian Studies Archives, University of Khartoum, Subject Index, tapes K(I)10 and K(I)20.
[12]   For a recent examination of folklore and oral literature, see Dorson (1972:10–30).

scheme, nor were enough plots allotted to the nomads for cultivating fodder for their camels. Moreover, a minimum — and almost negligible — number of animals could be kept within the plan. Since the planners and administrators of the scheme failed to accommodate the traditional values and ways of living to modernization, the nomads tried to do that themselves. They tried to keep to nomadism and yet participate in the agricultural development scheme: "The nomads at present live in their original villages which are very remote from the scheme. They come to their *hawashas* [plots] with the intention of spending the shortest time possible at them" (Sorbo 1971:20). Undoubtedly, this was at the expense of the success of the scheme. Though the scheme is already some ten years old, yield is below expectation. According to the Annual Report of the Agricultural Production Corporation (1969/1970), the fact that nomads have not settled is one of the causes for low yields (Sorbo 1971:6).

The response to the process of modernization associated with the Khashm Al Girba Development Scheme, and to the specific manner of implementing it, is incorporated into the poetry discussed earlier. This body of folk poetry offers a useful basis for evaluating the progress of the scheme and for reconsidering some of its aspects.

APPENDIX: INFORMANTS OF FOLK POETRY

The corpus of folk poetry from which the examples discussed in the paper are selected has been recorded from the following informants:

'Abd Allah Al 'Awaḍ is a Shukry presently living at Al Sadda, one of the villages in the Buṭāna. He is a cattleowner and farmer.

Aḥmed 'Awaḍ Al Karīm Abu Sin belongs to the Sinnāb section of the Shukriyya tribe. He is about sixty years of age. He used to live at Rēira, but he moved to 'Arīḍa after the introduction of the scheme. He is a famous bard and presently works as a farmer in the Khashm Al Girba Scheme.

Al 'Āgib 'Abdal-Gādir Mūsa is about fifty years old. He belongs to the 'Aishāb section of the Shukriyya tribe. He lives at Gēili about sixty miles east of Khartoum.

Al 'Awad Abd al-Salām is about fifty years of age. He belongs to the 'Aishāb section of the Shukriyya tribe and lives at Al Ṣufayya. He knows a lot of historical traditions and folk poetry related to tribal feuds and local history.

Al Ṣādig Ḥamad Al Ḥalāl is a famous bard. He was born at Al Ṣufayya in the Buṭāna and spent most of his youth between Rēira and Al Ṣufayya. He belongs to the Khatmiyya Muslim brotherhood and currently works in the Khashm Al Girba Scheme. Much of the poetry related to the scheme is attributed to him.

Khālid Khālid Gilbōs is an elderly man about seventy years of age. He is retired and lives at Al Ṣufayya in the Buṭāna.

REFERENCES

ʿALLĀM, A. H.
    1971   "Khashm Al-Girba agriculture project." Paper presented at the work-
            shop on human settlement in new lands, held in Cairo, Egypt.
DEPARTMENT OF STATISTICS
    1956   *First population census of Sudan: final report*, volume 3. Khartoum:
            Government Press.
DORSON, RICHARD M., *editor*
    1972   *African folklore.* New York: Doubleday.
EL BASHRA, EL-SAYED
    1972   "Urbanization in the Sudan," in *Proceedings of the seventeenth confer-
            ence of the Philosophical Society of Sudan*. Mimeographed. Khartoum,
            Sudan.
HALE, JERRY, SONDRA HALE, *editors*
    1971   *African urban notes*, 6, special issue.
HILLELSON, S.
    1920   Historical poems and traditions of the Shukriyya. *Sudan Notes and
            Records*, 3.
HURREIZ, SAYYID H.
    1969   "An annotated collection of Shukriyya oral poetry." Mimeographed.
            Khartoum: Sudan Research Unit.
    1974   "The use of folk poetry in social and political protest by the Shukriyya,"
            in *Directions in Sudanese lingustics and folklore.* Edited by S. H. Hur-
            reiz and H. W. Bell. Khartoum: Khartoum University Press.
SHAW, D. J.
    1967   Resettlement from the Nile in Sudan. *Middle East Journal* 21.
SORBO, GUNNAR
    1971   *Economic adaptation in Khashm Al-Girba: a study of settlement prob-
            lems in the Sudan.* Khartoum: Sudan Research Unit.

Modern and Traditional Aspects of Somali Drama

B. W. ANDRZEJEWSKI

In the Somali urban environment, one of the main sources of entertainment is the theater. It began, one might conjecture, in response to the stimulus of social change in the mid-1940's (Johnson 1971, 1974; Lewis 1965), a period that also witnessed the rise of the *balwo*, a new poetic genre that developed into the thriving *heello* of today (Johnson 1971, 1974).

My research leads me to feel that Johnson's hypothesis — that the rise of these genres was causally connected with the social changes of the time — can also be validly applied to the Somali theater. Although dialogue and a mimetic element can be found in Somali prose narratives and poetry as far back as oral tradition reaches, drama, conceived as a realistic imitation of life on the stage, was a complete innovation. As far as I was able to ascertain from interviews with people who were involved in the early stages of the Somali theater, the inspiration came from amateur dramatic and operatic productions in English or Italian in schools and military centers. Films brought from abroad played a role as well, but to a lesser extent.

The foreign influence on Somali drama does not, however, go beyond this initial point. The plots and characters of the plays are, with very rare exceptions, drawn from Somali life; Somali is used throughout, and the wit and humor of many of the scenes is due to the mastery of the verbal medium on the part of playwrights and actors. I provided a general account of the Somali drama and its developments in an earlier work (Andrzejewski 1974).[1]

From its inception the Somali theater won the interest of the public

---

[1] Note that so far there is very little published documentation of Somali drama. The excerpts from plays given in this paper are transcripts of tape recordings in the author's possession.

masses, and it soon became a powerful means of influencing public opinion. It has been used throughout the various stages of its brief history to advocate social reforms, to censure abuses through satire, and to promote political views, usually permeated by a deep sense of patriotism.

The audiences who frequent the theater are not limited to any particular social group; the theater attracts huge crowds of people, both men and women, and among them one can find members of the new educated elite just as easily as persons who have had no formal education. Plays are performed not only at the National Theater in Mogadishu, but also in provincial centers, where the spectators include pastoralists and farmers from the surrounding areas. Theater companies often go on tour, both in Somalia and in the Somali-speaking regions of the neighboring countries.

What particularly impresses any outsider who comes into contact with the Somali theater is the strong emotional involvement of the audience. I have met many Somalis who knew by heart whole passages from plays and could recite them with relish and feeling. Some of them attend their favorite plays several times.

The question arises, then, why the theater, a relatively recent innovation in Somali culture, should have such a powerful appeal for the public masses. One of the causes might be the fact that the Somali theater makes extensive use of the traditional culture and folklore of the nation, and in the remaining part of this paper I shall endeavor to substantiate this supposition.

In Somali plays the important parts are usually in poetic form. The use of prose is mainly restricted to humorous scenes or brief snatches of conversation. Initially, some plays were entirely in prose or contained just a few poetic inserts, but authors soon discovered that to succeed in their art they had to satisfy the insatiable craving for poetry among the public. This is not surprising if one considers that poetry composed in alliterative verse is a dominant feature of Somali culture in general.[2] This poetry contains various genres, ancient and modern, diversified in their rhythmic patterns and subject matters, but all sharing the basic alliterative technique and a marked preference for the traditional imagery taken from rural life.

It may seem paradoxical that the Somali theater, which aims at a realistic representation of life and deals mainly with modern life situa-

[2]   For accounts of Somali oral poetry and its social role, see Andrzejewski (1963:22–24, 1967:5–16), Andrzejewski and Lewis (1964), Andrzejewski and Galaal (1963:15–28, 93–100, 190–205), Cerulli (1957, 1959, 1964), Johnson (1971, 1972), Laurence (1970), Legum (1963:503–519), Galaal (1968a:39–55, 1968b, 1969), Nuh (1970, 1972a:41–43, 1972b:19–21), Somali Democratic Republic (1971). For other sources, see Johnson (1969:279–297). Note that some of the most modern developments are covered in a thesis on Somali political poetry prepared by Abdisalan Yassin Mohamed (1973) at the School of Oriental and African Studies, University of London, in conjunction with the Third World Studies program, Goddard College, Plainfield, Vermont.

tions, should make use of such a stylized artistic medium. Yet it is quite likely that this is the most effective means at the playwright's disposal of bridging the gap between the traditional culture and the rapidly changing world of today and of protecting Somali society against a split in its collective personality.

The use of alliterative poetry in the theater is illustrated here by a passage from the play *Kalahaab iyo kalahaad* [Wide apart and flown asunder] written in 1966 by Ali Sugule [Cali Sugulle].[3] The passage is taken from a dialogue between Caateeye and his wife Cutiya; their daughter Marwo is soon to be married, and in a reflective mood they talk about their life together:

CAATEEYE: Wax badan baa harraad iyo gaajo na ina heleen.
Maynu hoodo xumaannin, noloshu waa hagardaamo oo
Waa habeen-ku-dhaxaas. In badan baan haqab soor ah
Iyo hilbo aannu cunayney oo, caano aan hirqanayney.
Habeenno aan la ilaawin iyo maalmo aan la halmaamin
Oo hore sow garan meysid? Haddii Eebee yidhaahdo na
Dar kaloo hibo weyni waa inoo hadhsanyiin.

CUTIYA: Caateeyow, habeennadaan la illaawin iyo maalmahaan
la halmaamini.
Waa heshiiskii dhexdeenna iyo hoy-galkeennii arooska.

CAATEEYE: Runteeda! Ahahaa!

CUTIYA: Hogoshii onkodeysey, hillaacii widhwidhaayey
Hir doog oo ka dhex beermiyo, wixii heeli bislaadee
Higlo ay midho saartay, hohobtaan guranayney iyo
Hoobaantaynu cunayney weligey ma halmaamin oo
Hiyigeygiyo laabtiyo calooshaan ku hayaa.

CAATEEYE: We have suffered a lot from thirst and from hunger,
Yet we did not have bad luck. Life is full of trouble
And as short as a journey needing only one night's
rest. Often we had meager fare
Yet we also ate meat and drank milk in plenty
And there were nights and there were days one does not
forget.
You remember them, don't you? If God allows it
Other wonderful things like that are still in store for us.

CUTIYA: Oh Caateeye, those nights and days one does not forget,
That is what the bond between us, and our first
homecoming together, were all about.

---

[3] The Somali texts in this paper are written in the new national orthography introduced on October 21, 1972, which is identical with that used by Axmed (1966–67). For the explanation of the symbols, see Andrzejewski and Lewis (1964), but note that *ch* used there corresponds to *x* in the new orthography. Somali personal names are written in their conventional anglicized forms, and their equivalents in the Somali orthography are given in brackets, except for Shire Jaamec Axmed, whose name is given in its Somali form only, as in his publications of 1966/1967. In Somalia, family names are seldom used and a person's given name is followed by that of his father and then, sometimes by that of his grandfather. In *References* this order is inverted.

CAATEEYE: [*aside*]   Ah, how right she is!
CUTIYA: The rain clouds that thundered, the lightning that
flashed
And the sight of fresh grass engendered from them
on the horizon, and wild fruit that ripened,
Higlo that put forth berries, and the hohob that we
picked together
And the hoobaan[4] that we ate together — I have never
forgotten these things
I keep them in my mind, my bosom and my heart.[5]

POETIC EXCHANGES

Public verbal exchanges in verse, often involving fierce invective, are very
frequent among Somali poets, who either face each other at a meeting or
send their poems through messenger-reciters. Andrzejewski and Lewis
(1964), Andrzejewski and Galaal (1963), Cerulli (1957, 1959, 1964)
have provided examples with translations. Axmed (1965) has provided
an example in the Somali only.

This mode of poetic debate, which is traditional and thoroughly familiar to all Somalis, is frequently used in plays, and a short passage will be
given here as an illustration. It is taken from *Dhulkeenna dhibaha ka
jooga* [The troubles present in our land] written in 1968 by Ali Ibrahim
Edleh [Cali Ibraahiin Iidle], a play in which Dhiirran, a patriotic young
civil servant, tries to serve his country but is faced with severe pressures
and temptations from his environment. His obscurantist kinsmen, who
include his own father and uncle, try to involve him in illegally procuring
firearms for an interclan war and at the same time some of his young
educated friends show cynical indifference to the nation's struggle for
progress.

In this passage we witness a poetic exchange between Dhiirran and
Dhamac, an irresponsible young man, very much given to the chewing of
khat leaves,[6] the favorite intoxicant of the Horn of Africa, and to the
singing of *heello* poems, which are here referred to poetically as *balwo*,
the original form of this genre:

DHIIRRAD: Dhamacow, ku dhalliilay oo
Dhaddab baad ku jirtaa yoo
Dhoy ba waanad lahayn e!

---

[4]   *Higlo* and *hohob* are bushes that provide edible berries; the term *hoobaan* is sometimes
used for the ripe fruit of the *gob* tree. For botanical identifications, see Glover (1947).
Glover transcribes *higlo* as *higlu*.
[5]   "Heart," literally "abdomen," where the emotions are said to be localized.
[6]   Glover (1947:433–434) provides botanical identification.

<pre>
                Intaad dheelka hablaa iyo
                Qaadkanaad dhilanaysiyo
                Ka hadlayso dhul dhowdhow
                Dhallintii waddankeenniyo
                Dadweynuu ba dhammaan
                Ay ku dhaadanayeen oo
                Dhimaadaad aragtaa ye
                Miyaanay ku dhibeynin?
DHAMAC: Dhiirradow, dhado waa cir
                Dhalanteed biyo weeye
                Dhiman maayo nin nooli
                Haddii aad ku dhawaaqdood
                I dhegeysta tidhaahdo
                In lagaa dhuro mooyee
                Dhab miyaannu u qaadan?
                Adigaa dhaddabay oo
                Ilaahay ku dhaqaajee
                Dhallintaa waddankeenna
                Dhaleecaynta ka daa yoo
                Dhaqaalayso dadkaaga!
DHIIRRAD: Dadyow, dhuuryo lalaysoo
                Garbii dhiico u yeeshay oo
                Dhulka saartay afkiyo
                Raq dhurwaa diley maalin
                Dhiiggeedii u hillaacay
                Haddaad dhuuryo tidhaahdo oo
                Dhagax weyn ka hor geyso
                Adigoon u dhoweyn ba
                Dheg ma kuu jalqisaa?
                Dhallinteennu na maanta
                Runtuun baan ku dhintaa ye
                Waa ba taa, dhalankeeda oo
                In kastood u dhawaaqdo oo
                Barwaaqaynta dhulkoodiyo
                Wixii dheef u dhalaayiyo
                Ugu yeedhdho dhaqaale
                In la dhawrto lahaayood
                U dheereeya tidhaahdo.
                Balwaday dhadhdhansheen baa
                Dhegohooda malaastay oo
                Dhabandaaddo ka yeeshay oo
                Dhaqdhaqaaq laga waa ye.
                Waxba hay dhinac roorin e
                Dhaawac baynu qabnaa yoo
                Dhaleecaynoogu taallee
                Sidii loo dhugan laa yee
                Dhammaan loo tiri laa
                Ku dhaqaaq taladeeda!
DHAMAC: Dhankanaad ka gabyaysiyo
                Hadalkaagan dhanaani
                Dhafoortaabasho weeyee
</pre>

DHIIRRAD: I have contempt for you, oh Dhamac![7]
             You live in a dream
             And practice no reflection.
             Around and about, you just talk
             Of frolicking with the girls
             And tearing off the *khat* leaves for yourself.
             Idle, you look down on
             What the young men of our country
             And the whole nation
             Used to boast of.
             Do not these things fill you with concern?
DHAMAC: If you proclaim,
             Oh Dhiirrad, that dew is rain,
             That a mirage is water
             And that a man who is alive will not die
             And tell people to listen to you,
             Shall we regard it as true
             Unless we get water from you?
             It is you who are dreaming
             And God made you restless.
             Stop censuring
             The youth of our country
             And keep in with your people!
DHIIRRAD: [*To the audience*]:
             Oh people, when a hawk in flight
             Folds his wings
             And turns his beak towards the earth,
             Where the blood flashes to him like lightning
             From a dead beast which a hyena killed one day,
             Will he lend you his ear
             If you call to him, "Oh Hawk!"
             And throw a big stone in his course,
             Unless you are close to him?
             The youth of today
             Are just like that —
             I tell the truth unflinchingly.
             Even though you summon them
             To work for the prosperity of their country
             And for that which profits it,
             And call them to look after
             The economy which it owns,
             And tell them to move fast,
             You can get no movement out of them.
             The *balwo* songs which they relish
             Have silted up their ears
             And turned them into fools.
             [*To Dhamac*]
             Do not deny it hastily;
             We all suffer hurt

---

[7]   Note that to accommodate the substantial divergences between word order in Somali and English, I have transposed in the translation some of the lines of the original, keeping closely, however, to the original version within each line.

And shame is upon us.
Bestir yourself to find the way
In which this could be stopped
And stamped out altogether!
DHAMAC: The topic of your poem
And your bitter words
Provoke one to anger![8]

RIDDLES

In the Somali rural environment, the asking of riddles is a traditional pastime among children. These are called in Somali *googaaleysi* (Nuh 1970:45). They have an introductory formula, and the answers are usually fixed and unique. Adults also have a traditional mode of conversing which is reminiscent of riddles. It consists of asking one's interlocutor a question, usually on some general topic. In the answer, he or she is expected to show wit and wisdom, but neither the question nor the answer is in any way formalized, and there is no set opening formula.

In traditional Somali life such adult riddles have been used as informal intelligence and personality tests in various situations, and especially in the selection of spouses in arranged marriages and in personal courtship. A good example of this is found in the collection assembled by Musa Hajji Ismail Galaal, where some men choose a wife for their cousin from among three girls (Andrzejewski 1956:39–40). They ask them three questions:

1. What is the best way of making boiled millet palatable?
2. What fence offers the best protection for camels?
3. What is the best sleeping mat for men?

While the first two girls go into great technical detail in their answers, the third gives very simple answers, which make the men decide in her favor:

1. To give it to a hungry man.
2. To be born in a powerful clan and to have a wife from a powerful clan.
3. Peace.

This form of questioning also used to be employed in poetic contests integrated into dances. Some one hundred years ago a contest was arranged by one of the chieftains of the Ogaden region between a poet called Dhiidhdhi and a poetess called Geelo, in which the former won. The following four questions were put to Dhiidhdhi by Geelo:

GEELO: Waar, gaarida ma garataa?
Goombaarta na ma garataa?
Geesiga ma garataa?

---

[8] Mumin (1974) provides further examples of poetic exchanges.

Giiryaale na ma garataa?

DHIIDHDHI: Naa, gaarida na waa garan.
Waa guudad weyntay,
Gosha waa xidhxidhataa yoo
Gadhmadoobihii qabay iyo
Gunta ba waa u roontahay oo
Gacantay is marinaysaad
Geelwaaqis mooddaa yoo
Gaaridu bal waa taa.
Goombaar na waa garan oo
Waa ganacyo weyntahay oo
Gosha waanay xidhan karin oo
Gadhmadoobihii qabay iyo
Gunta ba waa u darantahay oo
Aqalkeeda guradiisaad
Geelxeradi mooddaa yoo
Goombaar na waa garan.
Geesiga na waa garan oo
Sarbiciidka ka ma sido oo
Samaydiisu waa xidid
Hubka na furinta goyska ah mooyee
Kiisa kale ka gaada leh
Marka se goobta laysugu tago
Ama guul ka soo qaad
Ama goobta lagu leged yoo
Geesigu na waa kaa.
Giiryaalaha na waa garan oo
Khayli gaasho waaweyniyo
Gaashaan gabiibyo leh mooyee
Hubka kale ka gaada leh
Marka se goobta laysugu yami
Hootadii baan hortii ganay iyo
Mayalkii bayga googgo'ay buu
Geedka shirka na keenaa yoo
Giiryaale waa kaa.

GEELO: Do you know how to tell a good wife?
Do you know how to tell a slut?
Do you know how to tell a brave man?
Do you know how to tell a coward?

DHIIDHDHI: I can tell a good wife:
She has big and neat tresses,
She tidily wraps her waist around;
To the blackbearded man, her husband,
And to the clan leaders she is generous;
The hand with which she washes her body
You might mistake for a *geelwaaqis* flower.
That is what a good wife is like!
I can tell a slut:
She is fat under her ribs,
She cannot wrap her waist tidily;
To the blackbearded man, her husband,

And to the clan leaders she is unkind;
The sleeping recess of her house
You might mistake for a camel pen.
I can tell a slut!
I can tell a brave man:
He does not carry an oryx-hide shield,
The shaft of his spear is made from the root of a tree;
Except for a piece of his attire, wielded as a weapon,
He despises everything that he possesses;
But when people go into the battlefield
For him it is either to win victory
Or to be thrown down in the battlefield.
A brave man is like that!
I can tell a coward:
He wears check-patterned clothes
And a decorated shield;
He despises all other weapons.
But when people come to the battlefield —
"I have already hurled my javelin
But my shield got broken!"
These are the excuses he brings to the assembly tree.
A coward is like that![9]

This kind of adult riddle has great potential on the stage and has been used frequently by playwrights. There is even one play, *Miyi iyo magaalo* [Town and country] written in 1959 by Abdillahi Yusuf Farey [Cabdillaahi Yuusuf Farey], which is entirely constructed around a series of exchanges between a townsman who woos a girl from a village. The humor of the play, which made it a great success with the public, derives from the limitations in their knowledge of each other's background.

This artistic device can also be applied effectively to political themes, as the dialogue that follows illustrates. It comes from *Shabeelnaagood* [Leopard among the women], written in 1968 by Hassan Sheikh Mumin [Xasan Sheekh Muumin], which was composed in the period of political disintegration that preceded the revolution of October 21, 1969. In this dialogue, which was so popular that many spectators immediately learned it by heart, Diiddane, a young patriotic and reformist teacher, puts some burning questions of the day to his friend Diiddan, who is a like-minded woman teacher:

DIIDDANE: Doc kastoo la eego, nolosha dunidu waa dabkee
Markuu dabkii dhaxamoodo, maxaa lagu diiriyaa?
Waa tilmaan la daaho, degdeg ku ma habboonee,
Adoo deggan u fiirso, ujeeddadaa i deeqsii!
DIIDDAN: Ruux haddii la doorto, derejadii la saariyo
Xilkii daryeeli waayo, dab dhaxamooday weeyee
Waa su'aal da' weyn oo, madaxa daalinaysee

[9] The full text of the contest is found in Musa Hajji Ismail Galaal's collection, which is awaiting publication. I am indebted to him for making the text available to me.

Wixii lagu diirinayo, dadweynaha la weydiin!

DIIDDANE: Durdurkaa laga cabbaa, biyihiis lagu dabbaashaa
Hadduu harraad dareemo, darkee laga waraabshaa?
Waa tilmaan la daahoo, degdeg ku ma habboonee
Adoo deggan u fiirso, ujeeddadaa i deeqsii!

DIIDDAN: Ruuxa duunyo haystee, dahabka barkanayee
Wixiisii deeqi waayeen, durdur oomay weeyee
Waa su'aal da' weyn oo, madaxa daalinaysee
Darkii laga waraabin, dadweynahaa la weydiin!

DIIDDANE: Qofkii cudur dilaayo, dawadaa bogsiisee
Hadday dawo bukooto, maxaa lagu dabiibaa?
Waa tilmaan la daahoo, degdeg ku ma habboonee
Adoo deggan u fiirso, ujeeddadaa i deeqsii!

DIIDDAN: Dallaalimada diintiyo, distoorka iyo xeerka
Haddii dabool la saaro, dawo bukootay weeyee
Waa su'aal da' weyn oo, madaxa daalinaysee ·
Wixii lagu dabiibi, dadweynahaa la weydiin!

DIIDDANE: Subagga dufankiisaa, dadku ku dhaashdaan e
Hadduu dufan basaaso, xaggee dux looga doonaa?
Waa tilmaan la daahoo, degdeg ku ma habboonee
Adoo deggan u fiirso, ujeeddadaa i deeqsii!

DIIDDAN: Dhaqanku dugsi weeyaan, dalkiisu uu ku dhaatee
Haddii dadkiisu aaso, dufan basaasay weeyee
Waa su'aal da' weyn oo, madaxa daalinaysee
Halkii dux looga dooni, dadweynahaa la weydiin!

DIIDDANE: Wherever one looks, the life of this world depends on
fire;
But if fire itself feels cold, what can one heat it with?
This is a matter screened off from sight and which does
not profit from haste;
Bestow on me, calmly and at leisure, the gift of your
opinion.

DIIDDAN: When a man is elected and placed in his high office
And yet does nothing to fulfil his trust, he is the fire
which feels cold.
This is a very old question, which makes one's head grow
weary;
It is the people, then, who will be asked how to bring
back the heat to the fire.

DIIDDANE: People drink flowing water, and swim in it, too
But if the water itself feels thirsty, from what trough
can one quench its thirst?
This is a matter screened off from sight and which does
not profit from haste;
Bestow upon me, calmly and at leisure, the gift of your
[opinion]

DIIDDAN: If a man possesses wealth and rests on gold for his pillow
And yet all his riches do not satisfy him, he is the
water stricken with thirst.
This is a very old question, which makes one's head grow
weary;

It is the people, then, who will be asked from what trough
the water can quench its thirst.

DIIDDANE: A medicine brings health to the man whom illness assails,
But if the medicine itself feels ill, what can one cure
it with?
This is a matter screened off from sight and which does
not profit from haste;
Bestow on me, calmly and at leisure, the gift of your
opinion.

DIIDDAN: If the straight path of faith, the constitution and the
laws
Are dimmed and covered up, it is they that are the medicine
which feels ill.
This is a very old question, which makes one's head grow
weary;
It is the people, then, who will be asked what the medicine
can be cured with.

DIIDDANE: It is with an unguent of *ghee* that people oil themselves,
But if the unguent feels dry, where can one look for
oiliness to restore its efficacy?
This is a matter screened off from sight and which does
not profit from haste;
Bestow on me, calmly and at leisure, the gift of your
opinion.

DIIDDAN: Our heritage is a shelter and a refuge, and the country
looks on it with pride
But if its own people bury it, it is an unguent which
feels dry.
This is a very old question, which makes one's head grow
weary;
It is the people, then, who will be asked where one can
look for oiliness to restore its efficacy.

ALLUSIONS TO FOLKTALES

The stories told to Somali children by adults and by older children remain
in their minds to provide them with a repertoire of emotionally colored
images that can be easily revived. Some Somali playwrights make use of
the folktale imagery in a very subtle way, and an example par excellence is
the use of a children's story about the ringed plover in a political play
called *Indhasarcaad* [Clouded vision], written in 1963 by Ali Sugule [Cali
Sugulle]. To understand the emotive power of the playwright's device, it
is necessary for the foreign reader to be told this story which Nuh (1970:9)
has made available. It relates that the ringed plover used to be a bird of
prey and that one day all the birds of prey divided the carcass of a big
animal among themselves. When they had eaten their fill, they decided to
leave the remainder until morning, and they all went to sleep in a tree. In
the middle of the night some birds woke up and called all their friends,

except the plover, together. They ate all the meat, including the plover's share, and flew away. When the plover awakened, it realized that it had been cheated and abandoned, and it made an oath of abstinence from four things in the following song:

Haddaan, Haadow, ku raaco,
Haddaan, Hurdooy, ku seexdo,
Haddaan, Hilibow, ku oonto,
Haddaan, Geedow, ku fuulo,
Aabbahay Xiid baan xarrago dhalin!

Oh Birds of Prey, if I ever go with you,
Oh Sleep, if I ever partake of you,
Oh Meat, if I ever eat you,
Oh Tree, if I ever climb you —
Then I have not been honorably begotten by
    my father Xiid![10]

Ali Sugule's play was composed during the unhappy period of conflict that arose from the desire of Somalis inhabiting northeastern Kenya to join Somalia (Drysdale 1964; Legum 1963:503–519). Many Somali poets and playwrights displayed fierce militancy, calling the nation to arms in support of the Somali guerrilla fighters in Kenya.

The pivotal point in the play is the dialogue that is sung between a character called Diiriye, representing Somalia, and a girl who personifies the former Northern Frontier District of Kenya (NFD). The refrain in the dialogue has a structure similar to the oath of the plover, except that the last line is omitted; the unfinished sentence was to be completed from the listeners' childhood memories. In my translation below I have put the inferred line in square brackets. I give here two stanzas of the poem,[11] which is still remembered by many people, although the fighting itself stopped some years ago and a satisfactory *modus vivendi* has been found between the two countries:

NFD: Inta uu dhulkeennii,
        Qoqobuu dhex yaalliin,
        Ee aan kala dhantaallahay,
        Haddaan, Dhimashooy, ku diido,
        Haddan, Dhalashooy, ku sheegto,
        Haddaan, Dhaqashooy, ku raadsho,
        Haddaan, Dheregow, ku doono . . .

[10]   The Somali name of this bird is *xidinxiito. Xiid* is here the name of the eponymous ancestor of the species.
[11]   Johnson (1971:135–136; 1974) has the full version of this poem. Note that Johnson's version differs slightly from mine, since it appears to have been transcribed from a tape recording of a different performance. Before the introduction of the orthography, performances often diverged, since most actors learned their parts from the playwright by word of mouth and had no scripts of any kind.

DIIRIYE: Intaad dhaxal wareeg tahay,
    Aan dhagar laguu gelin,
    Waa noo dhegxumo weyn e,
    Haddaan, Dhimashooy, ku diido,
    Haddaan, Dhalashooy, ku sheegto,
    Haddaan, Dhaqashooy, ku raadsho,
    Haddaan, Dheregow, ku doono . . .

NFD: As long as within our own land
   There are dividing frontier fences
   And we remain incomplete,
   Oh Death, if I reject you,
   Oh Ancestry, if I claim you,
   Oh Prosperity, if I follow your footprints,
   Oh Satiety, if I seek you,
   [I have not been honorably begotten by our
    common ancestor.]

DIIRIYE: As long as you remain robbed of your inheritance
    And no blood has been shed for you
    It is a great disgrace to us.
    Oh Death, if I reject you,
    Oh Ancestry, if I claim you,
    Oh Prosperity, if I follow your footprints,
    Oh Satiety, if I seek you,
    [I have not been honorably begotten by our
     common ancestor.]

It is, I hope, clear from these examples that there is a close link between the Somali theater and the traditional means of artistic expression of the nation. If research continues in this field, many more facets of this aspect of Somali drama will likely come to light.

It is also likely that the traditional folkloric element in the Somali theater will continue to grow, since the revolutionary government of Somalia is interested in the preservation and development of Somali national heritage, and official support and encouragement are given to various enterprises such as the tape recording and transcribing of oral literature, both old and modern, its extensive use in radio programs, and the organizing of folkdancing displays. In this respect, the Somali Academy of Culture and the Ministry of Information and National Guidance are remarkably active, and their activities could serve as a model for many countries passing through the stage of transition and modernization.

REFERENCES

ANDRZEJEWSKI, B. W.
 1963 Poetry in Somali society. *New Society* 1 (25):22–24.

1967   The art of the miniature in Somali poetry. *African Language Review* 6:5–16.

1974   "Introduction," in *Leopard among the women: Shabeelnaagood. A Somali play.* Written by Sheikh Mumin. Edited and translated by B. W. Andrzejewski. London: Oxford University Press.

1975   The rise of written Somali literature. *African Research and Documentation* 8(9):7–14.

ANDRZEJEWSKI, B. W., *editor*

1956   *Hikmad Soomaali.* London: Oxford University Press.

ANDRZEJEWSKI, B. W., MUSA HAJJI ISMAIL GALAAL

1963   A Somali poetic combat. *Journal of African Languages* 2:15–28, 93–100, 190–205.

ANDRZEJEWSKI, B. W., I. M. LEWIS

1964   *Somali poetry: an introduction.* Oxford: Clarendon Press.

1965   *Gabayo, maahmaah iyo sheekooyin yaryar* [Poems, proverbs and short stories]. Mogadishu: National Printers.

AXMED, SHIRE JAAMAC

1966–1967   *Iftiinka-Aqoonta* [Light of education] (in five sections). Mogadishu.

CERULLI, ENRICO

1957, 1959, 1964   *Somalia: scritti vari editi ed inediti* [Somalia: various edited and unedited writings]. Rome: Instituto Poligrafico Stato.

DRYSDALE, JOHN

1964   *The Somali dispute.* London: Pall Mall Press.

GALAAL, MUSA HAJJI ISMAIL

1968a   "Some observations on Somali culture," in *Perspectives on Somalia.* Somali Institute of Public Administration.

1968b   *The terminology and practice of Somali weather lore, astronomy and astrology.* Mogadishu.

1969   *Seeska hiddadha Soomaalida.* Mogadishu.

GLOVER, P. E.

1947   *A provisional check-list of British and Italian Somaliland trees, shrubs, and herbs.* London: Crown Agents for the Colonies.

JOHNSON, JOHN WILLIAM

1969   A bibliography of the Somali language and literature. *African Language Review* 8:279–297.

1971   "The development of the genre 'heello' in modern Somali poetry." Unpublished M. Phil. thesis, University of London, School of Oriental and African Studies.

1972   The family of miniature genres in Somali oral poetry. *Folklore Forum* 5(3):79–99.

1974   *Heellooy Heelleellooy: the development of the genre 'heello' in modern Somali poetry.* Bloomington: Research Center for Language Sciences, Indiana University.

LAURENCE, MARGARET

1970   A tree for poverty: Somali poetry and prose. Dublin and New York: Irish University Press. (Reprinted from the 1954 edition published in Nairobi by Eagle Press.)

LEGUM, COLIN

1963   Somali liberation songs. *Journal of Modern African Studies* 1(4): 503–519.

LEWIS, I. M.
1965 *The modern history of Somaliland: from nation to state.* London: Weidenfeld and Nicolson.
MOHAMED, ABDISALAN YASSIN
1973 "Political themes and imagery in modern Somali poetry." B.A. thesis, Vermont College, Plainsfield, Vt.
MUMIN, HASSAN SHEIKH
1974 *Leopard among the women: Shabeelnaagood. A Somali play.* Translated with an introduction by B. W. Andrzejewski. London: Oxford University Press.
NUH, OMAR AU
1970 Some general notes on Somali folklore. Mogadishu.
1972a Somali culture and its immense richness. *New Era* 5:41–43.
1972b Songs that derive from folk dances. *New Era* 7:19–21.
SOMALI DEMOCRATIC REPUBLIC
1971 *Adab al-thawra.* Mogadishu: Government Printers.

Aspects of the Folklore of the Jamaican Ethnic Minority in Britain: A Preliminary Consideration

VENETIA NEWALL

Folklore studies in England usually have concentrated on the rural population in the counties or on native peoples throughout the Commonwealth. It is time to consider the new ethnic elements that now comprise an important part of the population of London and other industrial cities.

The folklore of the Jamaican ethnic minority in urban Britain needs to be viewed against the specific socioeconomic background of the West Indian Commonwealth immigrant. In 1968, an estimated one million Commonwealth immigrants were residing in Britain; half of them were West Indian of which 60 percent originated in Jamaica (Abbott 1971:49; Krausz 1971:12). They came under economic pressure, the result of overpopulation and insufficient job potential in the homeland (Huxley 1964:40). Their position as an ethnic minority is somewhat unusual in that they tend, initially, to identify culturally with Britain (Deakin 1970:124, 283). Since, however, there are aspects of social conditions in the receiving country — such as housing, employment, education, overpopulation in urban areas — that are not favorable to immigration, the newcomers experience a feeling of rejection (Peach 1968:52). These opposing sentiments give rise to a dichotomous situation.

Other negative factors include an inauspicious climate, change from an often rural to an intensely urban industrial setting, and the apparent unfriendliness of the host country. To some extent, this last is the outcome of a cultural difference based on traditional English reserve (Calley 1965:137). However, a Gallup opinion poll conducted in November 1961, eight months before the passing of the Commonwealth Immigrants Act on July 1, 1962, showed that 76 percent of the British public favored the proposed measures to control immigration (Peach 1968:52, fn. 2).

The initial reaction on the part of the new arrival is one of withdrawal, which can be observed on physical, cultural, and spiritual levels. For example, recent studies show that large numbers of practicing West Indian Christians adhere to their own Pentecostal and extreme fundamentalist sects, in preference to the more usual British denominations (Hill 1963; Calley 1965). Bearing in mind that the surrounding culture is largely disinterested or even actively hostile to Christianity, this predilection for a form of folk religion has been explained as in part escapist, in part historical accident (the slaves were not evangelized until the mideighteenth century, an exclusion that caused them to form their own sects), and in part compensatory. Those who believe themselves saved, and hence numbered among the elect, receive a feeling of elation and self-esteem that counteracts the persistent belief of white people in supposed black inferiority (Calley 1965:17). Another reason for this spiritual withdrawal may be the tendency to equate the Church of England, the established church, with support for the theory of evolution, which fundamentalists reject. One informant (Gloria Ferguson) vehemently dismissed Darwinism as "rubbish."[1] It is viewed as the thin end of a racist wedge that identifies the black person with evolutionary forms of animal life.

On the physical and cultural levels many West Indian communities in London are well on the way to becoming self-contained units, whose members frequent the same clubs and social gatherings, enjoy their own music, and purchase their own food (Hill 1963:77). The casual visitor in Brixton or Shepherds Bush Market will see a wide variety of goods catering specifically to West Indian needs: local pharmaceutical products, Afro wigs and other hairdressing items, exotic tropical fruits and vegetables, both fresh and canned, and goat meat. These were random examples of the wide range of goods available during the summer of 1972.

Jamaican informants are very conservative in their food patterns. This is a common phenomenon, since traditional cuisine provides tangible physical comfort in an alien environment, as well as an intangible link with the past (Newall 1972:5). Hence, the most popular ethnic dishes remain those that formed the basis of the menu in the homeland: curried goat, chicken with rice and peas, *ackee*, and salt fish. *Ackee*, a tree vegetable, is known as a free food in Jamaica because it is so plentiful (Slater 1970:11).

Food may also serve as a status symbol. An advertisement in the weekly English edition of a Jamaican newspaper described the benefits of Wate On, a patent fattening food (*Gleaner* 1972). It is aimed at both

[1]   In the present article, with the exception of Melda Halliday, this informant and all others cited came from Jamaica to London. Their ages at the time the author received their personal communications were Gloria Ferguson, fifty; Velma Minot, twenty-one; Lorna Aspinal, thirty; Carol Facey, seventeen; Pauline Welsh, eighteen; Ken Luis, thirty; Fay Ferguson, twenty-two; Valerie Bennett, twenty-four; and Melda Halliday, twenty-one. Ms. Halliday came from St. Kitt to Wales at the age of two. She was brought up among Jamaicans and is now a resident of London.

sexes, presumably with intended appeal to the affluent class from a country where many live just above the subsistence level.

Food appears in yet another role, as an aphrodisiac. Coconut milk (called "coconut water") and Irish moss (called "Irish mash"), mixed with overproof rum, are consumed by men. They serve the same purpose as the pills and other concoctions of dubious origin traditionally purchased by British males at London's Charing Cross Road. Love magic practiced by girls is related to the perennial search for a mate and centers on divination by such means as palmistry, cards, and egg white broken in a glass of water (according to Velma Minot).

Sexual frustration often finds expression in the practice of obeah, which appears in a number of the stories recorded from informants (Velma Minot, Lorna Aspinal, Carol Facey, Pauline Welsh). For example, a black Jamaican student teacher wrote in 1896: "The prevalent belief in these days is about the obeah-men and the duppy" (Cundall 1904:94). Eighty years later, this is still a reasonable description. No pressure was exerted on informants to relate stories with a specific theme, but the majority of the tales recorded concern the supernatural. One informant (Carol Facey), who helped to collect the material from her circle of acquaintances, stated that recording the tales herself would have made her nervous in view of their frightening nature.

This indicates a high degree of personal involvement and presents an interesting parallel with the obsessive current British interest in the supernatural. According to a recent survey, one Briton in six believes in ghosts, one in fourteen thinks he or she has actually heard or seen one, and almost one in three has visited a fortune-teller. Another survey, conducted among members of Mensa, an international society requiring a high intelligence quota for membership, showed that 22 percent believed in some form of the occult (Jahoda 1969:25, 27). It is interesting, though perhaps fruitless, to speculate whether this is also a manifestation of the desire to escape from one's current condition. The function of the supernatural in present-day England appears to be escapist, equipping life with a new dimension of interest, and at the same time relaxing tension by providing an outlet and a focal point.

The supernatural can also have a more positive function. Death creates a gap in the community, and a belief in ghosts can help to seal that gap by providing a means of coming to terms with a stressful situation. For Jamaicans, it can also underline the feeling of continuity by providing a link with the past. Much of the recorded material takes the form of *memorates*, which, as Honko has observed, express the living experience of folk belief (1964:10). One informant, a participant-observer (Ken Luis), tells the tale of a Duppy Nun, which by inference serves as a sociohistorical document by looking back from the era of teenage gangs to the period of slavery, the influence of the church, and the traditional ethnobotanical correlation between the duppy and the silk-cotton tree (Leach 1961:210–211, 214; Beckwith 1929:89, 122).

Some tales of Anansi, the spider trickster, were also recorded (Crowley 1966:29; Williams 1934:25; Beckwith 1928:13; Jekyll 1966:xxiii, xxix–x; Sherlock 1966:5). The subject matter varied with the personality of the raconteur. Material provided by Carol Facey, a model and ex-cabaret dancer, was earthy, verging on the obscene. Fay Ferguson, a practicing fundamentalist Christian, disapproved of Anansi's character and the lack of moral guidance that the stories provided for children. She noted that Jamaican children are fascinated at a very early age by a small, spiderlike creature that makes its home in the mud. They dig it out and lay it on the dust to crawl about, chanting: "Nancy! Nancy! Make a map of Jamaica for me." Anansi, despite his low moral caliber, is used as a point of reference. Thus, Valerie Bennett said "Anansi says it's better if troubles come in pairs." Popular collections of Anansi tales are readily available in England, and some of the children of the informants borrow them from the public library.

To date, the material collected contains little that related to calendrical observances. The tendency, in fact, appears to be to adapt those holidays of the host country. One West Indian informant (Melda Halliday) reported with some amusement that a group of black children incongruously collected pennies for Guy Fawkes' Day — a typical English festival with politico-religious connotations. A black dummy was used to represent Guy Fawkes, who had attempted to blow up the Houses of Parliament in 1605. Possibly the calendrical observances of the parent country, in fact, transplant unsatisfactorily. If so, could this be why there is so little interest in festivals in American folklore circles? By contrast, there has emerged a considerable body of material surrounding the sociosexual life cycle of the community, such as love divination, marriage, and practices designed to promote the well-being of a new baby.

When one particularly intelligent informant was very young, she supposed that London was located in the sky, since that was where the airplanes all went. This notion in the mind of a child conveys an attempt to visualize and make concrete a nonvisual situation, an overlapping of the spatial with the metaphysical. It suggests overtones of an earlier colonial era. One may compare this to traditional American attitudes to the Old Country that are still prevalent among many of the tourists who go to England each year (Newall 1972:330). Politically conscious Jamaican immigrants, who appear to be few in number at present, take as their focal point not London, but the United States: the home of black power.

As to the receiving community, it is said that periods of social upheaval and tension are characterized by an increase in superstitious belief (Jahoda 1969:129, 133). Rumors arise in situations where information is inadequate; for example, in notions of the excessive fertility of immigrants (Eversley and Sukdeo 1969:2). These beliefs, related to subconscious fears, have been exploited by racist demagogues (Foot 1969:113–114).

One of the antidotes to demagoguery is laughter. Black humor arrived on Britain's television screens with Charlie Williams, Sammy Thomas, and Jos White, whose declared aim is to assist race relations through comedy. Charlie Williams explained: "These people still have a deep-down fear of the black man. And it's this fear I'm trying to help break down, by telling jokes about it"; Sammy Thomas asserted: "When I tell jokes. . . I'm really hitting at the white man and his ridiculous prejudices" (Irwin 1972:36, 53). Cycles of racist jokes are current among the immigrants, the humor centering on "the ridiculous prejudices of the white man." One informant (Fay Ferguson), referred to a relative who went to Germany and never returned: "Oh, they probably made him into a black lampshade."

The lot of the Jamaican immigrant coming to England's shores is not an easy one, but many are able to respond with patience and good humor to their situation. Gordon Lewis wrote: "He can be seen indeed from this viewpoint as the last of the English gentleman type surviving in a society where the old gentleman class is rapidly on the decline" (Deakin 1970:228). One might add that his corpus of traditional folklore should greatly enrich the indigenous culture of the British Isles.

REFERENCES

ABBOTT, SIMON, *editor*
  1971 *The prevention of racial discrimination in Britain.* London: Oxford University Press.
BECKWITH, MARTHA
  1928 *Jamaica folk-lore.* New York: Stechert.
  1929 *Black roadways.* Chapel Hill: University of North Carolina Press.
CALLEY, MALCOLM
  1965 *God's people: West Indian pentecostal sects in England.* London: Oxford University Press.
CROWLEY, DANIEL
  1966 *I could talk old-story good.* Berkeley and Los Angeles: University of California Press.
CUNDALL, FRANK
  1904 Folklore of the Negroes of Jamaica. *Folk-Lore* 15.
DEAKIN, NICHOLAS
  1970 *Colour citizenship and British society.* London: Panther.
EVERSLEY, DAVID, FRED SUKDEO
  1969 *The dependants of the coloured commonwealth population of England and Wales.* London: Institute of Race Relations.
FOOT, PAUL
  1969 *The rise of Enoch Powell.* Harmondsworth: Penguin.

Gleaner
1972   *Gleaner, The Jamaican Weekly.* July 12.
HILL, CLIFFORD
1963   *West Indian migrants and the London churches.* London: Oxford University Press.
HONKO, LAURI
1964   Memorates and the study of folk beliefs. *Journal of the Folklore Institute* 1.
HUXLEY, ELSPETH
1964   *Back street new worlds.* London: Chatto and Windus.
IRWIN, KEN
1972   *The comedians.* London: Wolfe.
JAHODA, GUSTAV
1969   *The psychology of superstition.* London: Allen Lane.
JEKYLL, WALTER
1966   *Jamaican song and story.* New York: Dover.
KRAUSZ, ERNEST
1971   *Ethnic minorities in Britain.* London: MacGibbon and Kee.
LEACH, MacEDWARD
1961   Jamaican duppy lore. *Journal of American Folklore* 74.
NEWALL, VENETIA
1972   "Race relations in Britain: the role of the folklorist." Paper presented at the American Folklore Society meeting. Austin, Texas.
PEACH, CERI
1968   *West Indian migration to Britain.* London: Oxford University Press.
SHERLOCK, PHILIP
1966   *West Indian folk-tales.* London: Oxford University Press.
SLATER, MARY
1970   *Caribbean cooking for pleasure.* London: Hamlyn.
WILLIAMS, JOSEPH
1934   *Psychic phenomena of Jamaica.* New York: Dial.

Culture Shock and Narrative Creativity

BARBARA KIRSHENBLATT-GIMBLETT

Folklorists have tended to view change negatively, whether it occurs on a small scale in the transmission of particular texts or on a large scale, such as when a community migrates or becomes urbanized.[1] As a result, they have often sought out conservative, tradition-oriented groups and have tended to view isolation from mass media and the modern world gener- ally as a positive force for maintaining the stability and integrity of a community's folklore.[2] Even the conceptualizations of how folklore func- tions have assumed stable social situations as the norm, and folklorists have discussed the role of folklore in maintaining this stability.[3] The more psychologically oriented folklorists, while recognizing that folklore tends to proliferate around points of stress in the life of the individual and the community, have not often taken up social change per se as a source of stress, which it almost invariably is, and, therefore, as a stimulus for the production of folklore. Given this preoccupation with the stability of society and the traditionality of folklore, it is not surprising that so few folklorists have studied change as a positive force, either with regard to the role folklore plays in implementing change or to the stimulus that sociocultural change provides not only for the persistence and revitaliza- tion, but also for the creation of folklore.[4] Consistent with these trends, the immigrant groups in North America are generally studied in terms of

[1] Alan Dundes (1969) provides a discussion of such attitudes to change in terms of the more general devolutionary premise in folklore theory.
[2] For discussions of the controversies regarding the definition and characterization of "folk groups" and the conditions conducive to folklore's vigor, see Bauman (1971:31–41), Ben-Amos (1971:3–15), and Dorson (1970:185–228).
[3] A suggestive exception is Wendy Reich (1971:233–244). Reich adopts a cross-cultural approach in her study of the role of folklore in revitalization movements, an interesting example of culture change in contemporary societies.
[4] Important exceptions are Reich (1971:233–244), Dorson (1948:113–150; 1952; 1960:111–174), Oring (1973:358–366), and Klymasz (1970).

the folklore they lose in the process of settling down in the "golden land" and not in terms of what they gain.[5] Nor is it surprising that the few studies of folkloristic creativity that have been made deal with relatively stable communities, whether it be epic singing in Serbia or narrative in the Bahamas (Lord 1960; Crowley 1966), rather than with communities in the midst of dramatic change.

CHANGE AND CREATIVITY IN THE STUDY OF JEWISH FOLKLORE

The study of Jewish folklore, both in Europe and North America, is no exception. Scholars have focused on the most conservative and tradition-oriented segments of the community — eastern European Jews rather than western European, and the Orthodox and Hasidic Jews rather than the Conservative, Reform or nonobservant (Weinreich and Weinreich 1959; Mintz 1968). Furthermore, even the folkloristic study of Old World Jewish communities, whether from near (Rappoport 1914) or far (Zborowski and Herzog 1962), has overestimated their insularity and stability and has perpetuated the romantic image of an "eternal and pan-East European *shtetl*." With the rare exception,[6] diversity and change in these communities were not properly appreciated or investigated. Multiculturalism, multilingualism, and change were *not* new to the eastern European Jews who emigrated to North America. These were a constant in their homes in Europe, but with a difference. Jewish immigration from eastern Europe to North America entailed radical sociocultural change and considerable trauma when individuals, separated from their families and communities, suddenly found themselves in totally foreign surroundings. In Europe, they grew up and were gradually socialized into their multicultural and multilingual milieu. In North America, they were thrust as full-grown adults into a totally strange situation. Such situations, where change is rapid and traumatic, can and do generate a special culture and, as part of it, a special folklore, even though this culture may be relatively short-lived. An extreme example, and one certainly worthy of investigation, is the rich flowering of Jewish folklore in and about the concentration and displaced-persons camps during World War II (Blumenthal 1963:221–236; *Metodologishe* 1945).

Nonetheless, folkloristically and ethnographically oriented studies of Jewish communities, even in the New World where change is so obvious,

---

[5] Important contributions to the study of immigrant folklore that view change as essentially negative and focus upon the fate of the Old World traditions in the immigrant context are Kaija-Köngäs (1960:117–123; 1963), Georges (1964), and Paulsen (1967). Their studies are among the first full-scale treatments of immigrant folklore.

[6] See the work of Beregovski, Skuditski, and other Soviet-Yiddish folklorists in Weinreich and Weinreich (1959).

have continued to focus on the most conservative segment of the Jewish community, the Hasidim. But even the Hasidim have not survived simply because they have refused to change. On the contrary, their persistence has been facilitated by their creativity in harnessing modern technology to serve their own ends. They use chemical and microscopic tests in a scientific laboratory to help people observe *shatnes* [Jewish law that prohibits the wearing of any garment that has been made of a mixture of wool and linen]. The "Frig-O-Matic Sabbath Zeiger" is an automatic timer attached to the refrigerator which enables the Hasidic Jew to use refrigerators on the Sabbath without violating the law that they must not work or cause others to work. Because the timer regulates the motor and lights, opening the door and letting in warm air does *not* cause the motor to start running as would otherwise be the case (Poll 1962:107).

In contrast with this interest in and respect for the Hasidic communities in North America, American Jewish culture tends to be negatively evaluated and, perhaps for this reason, neither recognized nor studied. In comparison with the "authentic Jewish culture" of Europe and of groups in America who preserve the Old World ways, American Jewish folklore, especially the jokes and songs, is considered to be "in poor taste." Sendrey, in his definitive and comprehensive *Bibliography of Jewish music* (which contains over 10,000 entries) stated that the only category of Jewish music he omitted is Yiddish popular music, much of it a New World creation known as "theater music," because it is "a corruptive element, a deterrent in the development of Jewish musical life" (Sendrey 1951:xxii). Jewish dialect humor has suffered a similar fate:

The so-called dialect Jew-comedian is passé and we need not mourn his demise. With the gradual passing of the immigrant generation, he no longer corresponds to any real living type in American Jewry — if he ever did — and in his day he made no great contribution to an understanding of the American Jewish picture. I also agree that the *Bagels and Lox* type of entertainment has no place on the American public stage or radio, whether seen by Jew or Gentile, not only for reasons of its basic vulgarity but also for its essential spuriousness — it represents no genuine kind of Jewish life existing here other than in the imagination of its script-writers (Kayfetz 1952:285).

Jewish popular culture in North America, which includes the Yiddish theater and its music and professional comedians and their dialect humor, has influenced and has been influenced by Jewish folklore, as we can see clearly in the folksong and folktale repertoires of Jewish immigrants. Dialect humor, which has been so maligned, has been a major expressive form in traditional immigrant narration. The impact of popular culture on Jewish folklore in North America and the higher value accorded the past and faraway have led scholars to undervalue the immigrant folklore contribution.

TRADITIONAL STORYTELLING IN THE TORONTO JEWISH COMMUNITY

In an effort to counteract these emphases in the study of folklore generally and Jewish folklore in particular, change will be examined here as a
stimulus for folkloristic creativity in an immigrant community of Conservative, not Orthodox, Jews. Born for the most part between 1915 and
1930 in eastern Europe (mainly Poland), the informants for the present
study arrived in Canada between the two world wars, primarily between
1925 and 1936. They form a social network of about forty individuals,
male and female, who are friends and relatives of each other. In the
period of 1968–1970, I recorded about 700 of their tales, in addition to a
variety of other folklore materials. The collection as a whole is dominated
by Jewish themes and protagonists and by a secular and humorous cast.
About one-third of the tales were heard in, or associated with, the Old
World. Two-thirds of the corpus, or about 450 tales, were associated
with the New World. Traditional storytelling continues to thrive in this
Jewish community today because of, rather than despite, sociocultural
change.

My focus here will be on one category of New World narrative, what
the narrators call *classics* and what I identify as stories associated with the
"period of initial contact." The following classification of the New World
component of the narrative repertoire of my informants indicates the
place of these tales in the larger scheme:

A. New World Jewish Narratives
  1. Emigration narratives
    a. Motivations for emigration
    b. Preconceptions about America
    c. Departure rituals
    d. The voyage
  2. Period of initial contact
    a. Getting off the boat
    b. First week in Toronto
    c. At home
    d. At school
    e. At work
    f. Buying and selling
    g. Local characters and family sagas
  3. Transitional phase
    a. Intragroup focus
    b. Intergroup focus
  4. Ethnic phase
    a. Not being Jewish enough
    b. What is a Jew?
B. New World Non-Jewish Narratives
  1. Secular legendary narratives
  2. Humorous anecdotes

The data clearly indicate that situations of multilingualism and multicul-turalism, where world views, cultures, and languages clash and undergo massive and rapid change, unleash the creative energies of immigrant raconteurs. These storytellers produce a rich body of special narrative lore that is characterized by distinctive kinds of stylistic elaborations and the preoccupation with being between cultures.

For this special body of narrative lore to emerge, however, it is not enough for one individual to be an immigrant. A whole community needs to share the experience, and in the case of the Toronto Jewish community this experience coincided with the Great Depression, a factor that inten-sified the already formidable difficulties facing the newcomers. Of the four periods — emigration, period of initial contact, transitional phase, and ethnic phase — it is the period of initial contact in the 1920's and 1930's that appears to have generated the longest and most elaborate anecdotes. This was the time when the shock of culture contact was felt most strongly. In these stories, the immigrant protagonists are bunglers who are without culture because they are between cultures, and they suffer the indignities of not being able to find a toilet, of misunderstand-ing what is said to them, and of being in the double bind of not under-standing the new language and culture they confront while not being able to use the old culture they left behind. Personal narratives may take the form of jokes, and jokes may be told as personal narratives. Both tend to be elaborate, long, carefully localized, and prefaced by a detailed, ex-planatory preamble for the benefit of members of the younger generation in the audience who did not live through this period. These stories are called *classics* by the narrators because they are worth retelling and because they do not lose their effectiveness after they have been heard once.

The stories about the transitional phase are concerned with the pro-tagonists' desire to rise socially and to be accepted by both more accul-turated immigrants and by non-Jews. The period of transition is fraught with anxieties. Even when all the symbols of a higher status have been acquired, immigrants fear they will be rejected. They are anxious that they will not be able to maintain their new roles, that they will overplay them, or will reveal that, although the externals have changed, they are immigrants in mentality, after all.

The anecdotes about the ethnic phase are preoccupied with a sense of loss. The price of acceptance was somehow too high. Having "made it," immigrants find themselves in marginal positions, to use Shapiro and Rosenberg's terminology (1958:70–80), and they suffer an identity crisis. They fear total assimilation through conversion, intermarriage, and the secularization of the Jewish religion, and they puzzle over the problem of how they are to define Jewish identity. Are they Jews by religion, by culture, or by nation? Most of the narrators for this study were either in or

just coming out of the transitional phase, and this may explain why very
few ethnic jokes were recorded.

THE CLASSICS OF THE PERIOD OF INITIAL CONTACT

Whereas in connection with the emigration period only two traditional
jokes were found — and both of these were about people who had been in
America and had returned to Poland either on a visit or for good — over
seventy traditional jokes and more than sixty personal narratives about
the immigrant experience of the New World were recorded. As one
informant explained, nothing the emigrants imagined about Canada
when they were still in Poland could ever really approximate what they
found when they got there. And in terms of the selective memory of the
immigrant narrator, the stories about the trauma of culture contact are
not only more recent and more protracted, but also represent the difference between fantasies about what life in Canada would be like and the
innumerable actual experiences in the daily life of an immigrant in
Canada. It appears from the narratives in the Toronto corpus that experience, especially traumatic experience, generates more elaborate tales and
a greater number of them than does fantasy alone. Also, in the case of the
Toronto informants, their arrival was considerably more eventful than
their departure. Judging from the stories they tell, the narrators seem to
find what they came to, of considerably more interest than what they left.
This was not the case for the narrators who arrived after World War II.

In the period between the two world wars, Toronto was the home of a
large immigrant community with a thriving Jewish social and cultural life.
This is the period in which all the narratives about the immigrant experience are set, even though immigrants continued to arrive after World
War II. It appears, therefore, that the necessary prerequisite for this
special body of New World folklore about the immigrant experience is *an
ongoing immigrant community and culture* and that this represents but
one phase of development in the history of the Toronto Jewish community. Immigrants who arrived in Toronto after World War II, when the
Jewish community was making a transition to its ethnic phase, are *not*
good sources of folklore about the immigrant experience, despite the fact
that they are immigrants and recent ones at that. In other words, simply
being an immigrant is not enough. A person needs to have been an
immigrant *at the time when his community was in its immigrant phase* in
order to be a potential bearer of folklore about the immigrant experience.

Furthermore, in the case of Jewish culture in Canada, the larger the
community, the more Yiddish was spoken and the more active was the
Jewish social and cultural life. Therefore, the haven for the development
of folklore about the immigrant experience was *not* the small, isolated,

rural communities but rather the heart of the big cities, where the Jewish population is found in greatest concentration. Immigrants arriving after World War II found the Toronto Jewish community relocated physically and moving into its ethnic phase culturally. This close association between the immigrant era and immigrant folklore suggests that the special body of folklore being considered here emerges only when the immigrant experience is collectivized, when the immigrant experience is shared by a whole community, for only then can an immigrant culture emerge.

Tales about Jewish life in North America fall into three categories that parallel the development of the Jewish community itself through three phases — immigrant, transitional, and ethnic. The first category — stories associated with the period of initial contact — is especially interesting because these stories are among the longest and most elaborate in the Toronto corpus. There is generally a telltale sign that marks a narrative as belonging to this category; namely, a statement in the exposition to the effect that the events in the story occurred the first day or week the immigrant arrived: "He just got off the boat," or "He hadn't been here more than a week." A few years of immigrant life may get telescoped into a week in the world of the narratives. Tales about the immigrant phase are preoccupied with culture shock, name changing, linguistic and cultural unintelligibility both on the part of the immigrant and on the part of the surrounding society, social blunders of all kinds — the ultimate and most popular being the inability to locate a toilet — extreme poverty, and the eccentricities of immigrant characters.

Immigrant stories are often very carefully localized with the names of people and places specified and detailed descriptions provided. In fact, because of the stylistic habit of localizing the tales, there is a tendency for the distinctions between the personal narrative and a traditional joke to become confused. In several instances, the narrator tells the joke in the first person as if it were a true-life experience:

HARRY KATZ: During the depression years, Starkie and I couldn't get jobs in Toronto so we went to Detroit. So we couldn't get any work. So we both looked for work at the same time. So we decided to separate. So we separated. I went one way. He went the other. My money ran out so I, I got hungry. I go up to a big restaurant on Woodward Avenue, big window and there's a beautiful looking girl sitting in there eating. And I pressed my face against the window and and she calls me. She says, "Would you like to eat?"

I says, "I certainly would."

She says, "Well, restaurant food's not the best thing for a young fellow like you." She says, "No."

I says, "No."

She says, "Well, how about you come up to my apartment. I'll make you something nice."

So we go up to her apartment. She makes me a beautiful spread. I eat myself silly. Finally she turns around. She says, "Do you mind if I get comfortable?" So she goes in the other room, comes out with a beautiful negligée. Being a young fellow, I go after her and I chase her here, I chase her there. I grab her here, I grab her there. Finally, I connect. We have a ball and she says, "One?" Once, and one shot deal, and she was really happy and she says, "I appreciate what you did here and I really enjoyed it. Any time you feel like having another session of the same thing, you get hungry again, here's the key to the back door, but just in case I should have the night catch on, you come in through the front door but usually, use the back door."

So I got back and tell Starkie the story. He says he doesn't believe me. I says, "Come on I'll show you." So we go up to the apartment. We go up to the back door. The night catch is on so we can't get in. We go to the front door. Sure enough the door is open. We walk in. It's a big huge vestibule and a big wall in the front with little holes cut out and a bunch of old men are sitting watching looking through these peep holes. So we push a couple of fellows aside, we give a look. I see the same girl with another fellow. They're going at it the same routine as I had. Finally after the half an hour or so, the fellow is through, she's through and she gives him the same treatment as she gave me.

So all the old men turn around and applaud like this [claps] you know except one. One says to the other, he says, "How'd you like the show?"

He says, "Terrific, terrific. But you should have seen the little Jew that was here this afternoon."

On the other hand, personal narratives have been retold many times and have become so similar to traditional tales that it is difficult to tell whether they are jokes or personal narratives:

MARTIN SOKOLOV: A lot of people when they came to this country had very long names. And some of them wanted to shorten their names and they did. And Wasserman became Wasser and Bergmaster became Berg and so forth and so forth. . . . And the names that were shortened from very very long names and cleaned up or brought to where they could be spelled because some of these people couldn't even write let alone spell and they couldn't even sign their names.

But I had a salesman who worked for me. His name was Hyman Lipshitz and he was on the road and came to work for me and I had a watch and the face of my watch was all scratched up so I was getting the face refinished.

So the guy says to me, "What do you want on there, Bulova or Gruen?"

I says, "It's not a Bulova or Gruen. It's a Columbia watch."

He says, "Yeah but it's more prestige. Who knows Columbia here in Canada? Get Bulova or Gruen."

I said, "I'll tell you what, I'll be different. I want to be unique. On my watch put Martin Sokolov." So he put on the front of the watch the name Martin Sokolov and I still have the watch. Candy wants to wear it. It's got my name on the front like when they re-did the face of the watch.

So my salesman Hyman Lipschitz looks at it. He says, "That's nice," he says, "you know, the face on my watch is also scratched up." He says, "I'm going to get it done." So I picked up my watch. . . .

He . . . gives the guy and the guy says, "What is your name?" He says, "Write it out."

He writes out Hyman Lipschitz and it was too long. He couldn't fit it into the space that it had to go into.

So he says, "I'm sorry it's too long."

So he says, "Oh well," he says, "then use the short form of my name because I'm changing my name anyway."

He says, "Oh good, what are you changing it to?"

He says, "Instead of Hyman Lipschitz, call it Hy Lipshitz."

When this personal narrative is compared with Sokolov's immigrant jokes, the "folklorizing process" is evident. Sokolov typically prefaces his immigrant jokes with an explanatory preamble of precisely this kind. Like a joke, this narrative has an exposition followed by dialogue and a punch line. The narration is swift and to the point. Thematically, this personal narrative falls into the genre of name-changing stories, a common immigrant tradition. Furthermore, versions of it appear in published collections of jokes. Despite the fact that Sokolov tells it as a true personal narrative, it is a traditional tale. This does not mean that the event did not actually occur. Rather, this anecdote provides further corroboration for the notion that personal narratives take traditional forms, partly because folktales provide models for reconstructing experience.

Another point worth noting is the extent to which traditional narrative can condition experience. Narrators can incorporate the punch line of a joke into a real-life dialogue and later report on the experience. Technically the report is a personal narrative, but structurally and in terms of motifs and even in terms of style, the story is a traditional folktale. Or traditional narratives will provide the models for reconstructing personal experiences so that the storyteller will cast his report of what happened into a traditional form.

Some narrators such as Jerry Sacks specialize in, and are famous for their personal immigrant narratives, whereas others, such as Martin Sokolov, are famous for their traditional immigrant tales, which they may cast as personal narratives and set in the immigrant period between the two world wars. These two different types of narrators utilize two different processes. One may be called the *immigrantizing* of traditional tales and the other the *folklorizing* of immigrant experiences. Regardless of which process is used, the results bear many features in common. Both the personal narratives and the jokes are often long. They may be full of elaborate detailed descriptions, enriched with code switching and a plentiful use of Yiddish, and set in downtown Toronto during the Depression. It is, therefore, not surprising to find personal narratives that conform to traditional tale types and traditional tale types that bear the stylistic earmarks of personal narratives, such as protestations of truth, first-person narration, and detailed localized descriptions of a specific time and place. Furthermore, the narrators themselves recognize these stories about the early immigrant days as a special category. Sokolov calls them *classics* in contrast to his other stories that he calls *oncers. Classics*, he says, are funny even after you have heard them many times, whereas *oncers* are funny only once. The reason for this, he explains, is that there is more to a *classic* than the punch line; the humor is just as much in the style of narration. When asked to identify his *classics*, Martin pointed to the immigrant stories. Jerry Sacks said of an immigrant joke: "It depends how you tell it and how you build it up. You can make up a whole thing out of it but it's mostly one of these stories that you can just build up. The punch line isn't that much really." The joke he gave as an example was about an immigrant in a drugstore in search of a rectum. From these comments, it appears that characterizations of immigrants and descriptions of their experience are of interest in and of themselves, that a whole category of stories is perceived by the narrators as being the kind that is highly elaborated, and that the resources for this elaboration are drawn from the immigrant culture in Toronto between the two world wars.

IMMIGRANT NARRATIVE CREATIVITY

The creativity of Toronto Jewish narrators is inherent in their ability to cope with culture shock by telling elaborate tales in which they draw from the resources of two conflicting cultures and mediate between them. These narrators and their tales are instrumental in helping them and their audiences to adapt to the changing circumstances (Reich 1971). The narrators accomplish this by serving as a bridge between worlds. They often find themselves performing to audiences in which there are considerable discrepancies in experience, since individuals may have immigrated during different periods. The younger generation may not speak Yiddish, or be familiar with Old World life and the early immigrant days that form the basis for the tales. The narrators, in telling these particular tales and especially in the *way* they tell the tales, create bridges across these gaps in experience, provide the community with a sense of continuity, and define for it the nature of its past.

The mediating role of the immigrant narrator is perhaps most clearly seen in such stylistic features of their storytelling as the (1) extended prologue, (2) glosses (what Dell Hymes has called *metalinguistic interventions* in his discussion of North American Indian myths), (3) code switching, and (4) the ethnographic impulse in the elaboration of the tale's reality. These stylistic features are actually ways of dealing with discrepancies in cultural frames of reference that are extreme in situations of rapid change and intensified by age and generation differences. By such devices, the narrators render cultural experiences intelligible to those who did not live through them.

The prologues to the immigrant tales are sometimes as long as, if not longer than, the body of the tales. The careful description of life in Europe and the period of initial contact in Canada both enlighten the younger generation and appeal to the older listeners who enjoy hearing these descriptions even though they are very familiar. Indeed, narrators who can speak Yiddish as well as English and who can talk knowledge-ably about Jewish culture are highly respected. The *classics* provide an opportunity for immigrant narrators to display these talents, whether in the prologues, the glosses, special Yiddish terminology, or in the detailed localization of the tale action.

The artistry with which the narrators alternate among a wide range of linguistic varieties (distinct languages, dialects, styles, imitations of how immigrants speak) has been analyzed elsewhere (Kirshenblatt-Gimblett 1972). This code switching is an essential feature of immigrant narrative style and is used to create brilliant comic effects. I will consider only one aspect of it here: the gloss and the gloss parody, or mock definition.

Because the immigrant narrators' audiences are usually so mixed, they develop ways to please everyone at the same time. While explaining the basics to the young Canadian-born listeners, they must also captivate the knowledgeable older European listeners. One way they manage this is to gloss special concepts and Yiddish words to help young listeners to follow the story, to "educate" them, and to parody these glosses for the special pleasure this affords their older audience members. The mock definition is perhaps the ultimate in-group joke. In one performance, the narrator glossed *mikve* [ritual bath] as an overheated swimming pool. Another joke is built on the mock gloss for *bal-metsitse* [man who sucks the wound of circumcision] as "cocksucker." In the following excerpt from an extended narrative, the narrator describes an Orthodox Jew who, in his efforts to collect money for charity, finds himself in a whorehouse or "place of reclining refreshments," as one narrator put it. The prostitute proceeds to undress the man, a process that is elaborately and beautifully described by the narrator. When she comes to his "belt," the storyteller says:

Then she took off his *gartl*. The *gartl* was the strap they wore around the waist to separate the *milkhiks* from the *fleyshiks*.

The *gartl* is the belt that Jewish males wear during prayer. According to Jewish dietary law, *milkhiks* [dairy food] must be kept separate from *fleyshiks* [meat foods]. The narrator's mock gloss on the term *gartl* is an in-group joke because to understand it, his audience needs not only to know what a *gartl* is, but also must understand the literal and figurative meanings of *milkhiks* and *fleyshiks* in this context. Figuratively, *milkhiks* refer to breasts and *fleyshiks* to genitals. The humor of this mock gloss thus hinges on the confusion of sacred and profane as well.

CONCLUSIONS

These immigrant narratives provide an opportunity to examine processes that also operate in other sociocultural situations where change is less radical. The processes may be more visible in Toronto because change is more extreme. Only if the study of folklore in situations of radical change and culture shock — in this case, immigrant folklore — is extended beyond the concern with Old World retentions to all the folklore the immigrants know, can one see fully the positive and negative repercussions of culture contact and culture shock on repertoire and performance, both from the point of view of what they lose and of what they gain. Furthermore, the gains need to be seen both in terms of the acquisitions from the surrounding culture and the creativity in generating a special body of New World lore about what it means to live in such an environment. It appears from this author's data that the early immigrant years provide the narrators who had contact with them with the richest resources for developing their narratives. This is the period of vigorous multilingualism and biculturalism, and it appears that such conditions — where world views, cultures, and languages clash — are extremely productive in giving rise to a rich body of special narrative lore. Indeed, change itself becomes a focus of interest and a creative force as gifted narrators draw from the resources of both cultures and mediate between them.

REFERENCES

✓ BEN-AMOS, DAN
 1971   Toward a definition of folklore in context. *Journal of American Folklore* 84:3–15.

✓ BAUMAN, RICHARD
 1971   Differential identity and the social base of folklore. *Journal of American Folklore* 84:31–41.

BLUMENTHAL, NACHMAN
 1963   Magical thinking among the Jews during the Nazi occupation. *Yad Washem Studies on the European Jewish Catastrophe and Resistance* 5:221–236.

CROWLEY, DANIEL J.
 1966   *I could talk old-story good: creativity in Bahamian folklore.* Berkeley and Los Angeles: University of California Press.

DORSON, RICHARD M.
 1948   Dialect stories of the upper peninsula: a new form of American folklore. *Journal of American Folklore* 61:113–150.

 1952   *Bloodstoppers and bearwalkers: folk traditions of the upper peninsula.* Cambridge: Harvard University Press.

 1960   "Jewish-American dialect stories on tape," in *Studies in Biblical and Jewish Folklore.* Edited by Raphael Patai, Francis L. Utley, and Dov Noy. Bloomington: Indiana University Press.

✓ 1970   Is there a folk in the city? *Journal of American Folklore* 83:185–228.

DUNDES, ALAN
 1969   The devolutionary premise in folklore theory. *Journal of the Folklore Institute* 6:5–19.

GEORGES, ROBERT
1964 "Greek-American folk beliefs and narratives: survivals and living tradition." Unpublished Ph.D. dissertation, Indiana University, Bloomington.

KAIJA-KÖNGÄS, ELLI
1960 Immigrant folklore: survival or living tradition? *Midwest Folklore* 10:117–123.
1963 "Finnish-American folklore: quantitative and qualitative analysis." Unpublished Ph.D. dissertation, Indiana University, Bloomington.

KAYFETZ, BEN G.
1952 The vanishing Jewish comedian. *Commentary* 14:285.

KERMISH, YOYSEF, NAKHMAN BLUMENTHAL, NOYAKH GRIS, GENYA SILKES
1945 *Metodologishe onvayzungen tsum oysforshn dem khurbm fun poylishn yidntum. Oysgabes fun der tsentraler yidisher historisher komisye baym tsentral-komitet fun poylishe yidn* [Methodological instructions for investigating the Holocaust of Polish Jewry. Publications of the Central Jewish Commission of the Central Committee of Polish Jewry] no. 5. Lodz.

KIRSHENBLATT-GIMBLETT, BARBARA
1972 "Traditional storytelling in the Toronto Jewish community: a study in performance and creativity in an immigrant culture." Unpublished Ph.D. dissertation, Indiana University, Bloomington.

KLYMASZ, ROBERT B.
1970 "Ukrainian folklore in Canada: an immigrant complex in transition." Unpublished Ph.D. dissertation, Indiana University, Bloomington.

LORD, ALBERT B.
1960 *The singer of tales.* Cambridge: Harvard University Press.

MINTZ, JEROME
1968 *Legends of the Hasidim: an introduction to Hasidic culture and oral tradition in the New World.* Chicago: University of Chicago Press.

ORING, ELLIOTT
1973 "Hey, you've got no character": Chizbat humor and the boundaries of Israeli identity. *Journal of American Folklore* 86:358–366.

PAULSEN, FRANK M.
1967 "Danish-American folk traditions: a study in fading survivals." Unpublished Ph.D. dissertation, Indiana University, Bloomington.

POLL, SOLOMON
1962 *The Hasidic community of Williamsburg: a study in the sociology of religion.* New York: Schocken.

RAPPOPORT, SOLOMON [SH. ANSKI]
1914 *Dos yidishe etnografishe program, ershte teyl, der mentsh.* [The Jewish ethnographical program, first part, the human being.] Petrograd: J. Luria.

REICH, WENDY
1971 The uses of folklore in revitalization movements. *Folklore* 82:233–244.

SENDREY, A.
1951 *Bibliography of Jewish music.* New York: Columbia University Press.

SHAPIRO, GILBERT, BERNARD ROSENBERG
1958 Marginality and Jewish humor. *Midstream* 4:70–80.

WEINREICH, URIEL, BEATRICE WEINREICH
    1959   *Yiddish language and folklore: a selective bibliography for research.* The
            Hague: Mouton.
ZBOROWSKI, MARK, ELIZABETH HERZOG
    1962   *Life is with people: the culture of the* shtetl. New York: Schocken.

SECTION TWO

Folklore and Ideology

Myth and Superstition in Communist China's Drama and Theater

WALTER J. MESERVE and RUTH I. MESERVE

> Angels and ministers of grace defend us!
> Be thou spirit of health or goblin damn'd.
> Bring with thee airs from heaven or blasts
>   from hell,
> Be thy intents wicked or charitable,
> Thou com'st in such a questionable shape
> That I will speak to thee.
>
> HAMLET, Act I, Scene iv

Communism presents rather particular problems for literary artists in China. Although their works may have artistic value and beauty, these must remain secondary in an atmosphere where the political cause determines their art. It is, then, no wonder that China's literary heritage and popular culture — rich with superstition, fate, supernatural beings, and a moving panorama of Taoist and Buddhist gods, goddesses, and demons — should give the Communist Party of China considerable difficulties.

Regardless of its wishes, when the Party came to power in 1949, it assumed a cultural heritage of more than 3,000 years. For this new and struggling government, the need for change was obvious and immediate. The actual reform process, however, would prove to be long and continuing, particularly where "spirits" of the past were not easily dispersed among China's generations, and while time-honored conventions haunted the present and cast shadows toward the future. It was out of this general problem concerning myths and superstitions, interestingly enough, that one of modern China's greatest literary debates grew. The consequences of this debate brought major purges among literary people and, in particular, to those in the theatrical world. Stated simply, the debate questioned whether ghosts and fairies, the myths and superstitions of an ancient heritage, should walk the Chinese Communist stage. Should *Niu-kuei-she-shen*, those "ghosts and monsters" or "ugly beings" who opposed the Chinese Communist Party and the thought of Mao Tse-tung, be recognized in modern China? Were the supernatural and the unreal actually "dregs" of a "feudal" past? Or could they serve the masses in literary creations and help clarify the expression of the "Marxist-Leninist world outlook"?

These questions and the approaching conflict with the Communist Party were a concern of Ts'ao Yü, one of China's greatest modern dramatists, even before the "take-over" in 1949. Always aware of the social ills of old China, he helped define a central problem for the Communist Party in 1946 with this statement:

Under the Imperial Regime, the Chinese were not an articulate people. The plays that could be produced with Imperial approval were bound to be historical ones, supernatural fairy tales, or murder stories. These were the plays that were supposed to cater to the taste of the general public. An examination of the plays from the Yuan Dynasty down to the present time would reveal that, with very few exceptions, there was no seriousness of purpose behind the production of plays nor any attempt to call attention to social or other evils (Wan Chai-pao 1946:35–36).

It was this lack of a "seriousness of purpose," this failure to call "attention to social or other evils," that the Communist Party of China would refer to many times during the early years of the People's Republic. Evils of the past, the Party felt, should be exposed. Because theater had been used by the Communist Party to serve the people since before the war with Japan, it was an accepted propaganda weapon. But could plays with ghosts and fairies, gods and demons, really accomplish Party objectives? This was one question that bothered Party officials. Could the old ideas of "fate" accompany and help explain the new ideas of communism? Or should the dramatist's creatively directed imagination be turned away from myth and superstition and led to a narrower and presumably more reliable path, one reflecting stark reality?

Traditional Chinese drama was not exclusively at fault in this argument. Even communist plays such as the famous *White-haired girl* had been criticized before the "take-over" for their use of "superstition." Here was a popular play that sang the praises of the Communist Eighth Route Army and cursed the evils of a society of landlords who oppressed the peasants. In the early stages of its composition — it was written and revised from 1945 through 1949 — some "comrades" believed that the play was simply a "meaningless fairy tale" to be discarded; others thought that the script should be rewritten to remove elements of superstition; still others stated that the play should be revised to include ideas of "antifeudalism" and "antisuperstition". Clearly, the play presented a difficult problem for the ideologically pure, while those outside the Communist Party fold must have found some interest in a discussion not concerned with a traditional drama. After these arguments came the revisions. And according to Ting I (1952), one of the playwrights, the problems were finally solved by grasping "the positive side of the script, reflecting the antifeudal system and the difference between the two societies." Since then, of course, *The white-haired girl* has passed through other revisions and forms — drama, opera, ballet, film — to be at different times and in different forms one of the most successful communist ventures into the performing arts (Meserve and Meserve, 1977).

Yet, it is basically true that the plays involved in the Party problem of myth and superstition did come from the traditional Chinese theater repertory. And the questioning continued. Possible answers to some of these questions appeared before the new People's Republic of China (PRC) was even officially proclaimed in October 1949. In April of that year, for example, the Cultural Central Committee banned fifty-seven plays from the traditional repertory: twenty-seven for "superstition," fourteen for "licentiousness," four as derogatory to national dignity, four for catering to "slave morality," five for upholding "feudalistic oppression," and seven for "boredom" (Bodde 1957:153). Obviously, this was censorship, but as would soon be clear in the politically careful and astute wording of Communist Party officialdom, the act was masked with a slogan that seemed to proclaim a healthy advance for a new China. One should "Weed through the old to let the new emerge."

In this process, not all plays were either accepted or banned. Many were simply revised to fit Party needs. This was particularly true of plays that were traditional parts of festivals and known by all the people — plays such as *The cowherd and the weaving maid* (also called *Union at the heavenly river*), which is traditionally presented at the Festival of the Cowherd and Weaving Maid on the seventh day of the seventh lunar month. On July 24, 1949, a group of theater people met in Tientsin to discuss ways to bring this play into line with current Party ideology. Although the play emphasized such acceptable Party attitudes as reward for hard work and an implied criticism of arranged marriages, it had its bad points, too — an overemphasis on sex and superstition. Consequently, the theater group decided (1) to add a prologue and an epilogue to explain the weaknesses in the play, (2) to strip the play of all supernatural elements, (3) to delete the heavenly fire which destroys the home of the brother of the cowherd, and (4) to portray the impoverishment of the brother and sister-in-law as the direct result of their own idleness and bad conduct (Bodde 1957:234–235).

Soon this new version of *The cowherd and the weaving maid* was advertised for performances in Peking and Tientsin theaters. When Sinologist Derk Bodde saw the play on August 1, 1949, the major change was the deletion of the final scene, in which the ruler of heaven pronounces the time of rendezvous for the couple (the time traditionally is the seventh day of the seventh lunar month, when magpies form a bridge in heaven on which the couple is to meet). During the afternoon performance, the audience seemingly accepted the deletion. That evening, however, when the curtain fell, the audience shouted "Not finished!" and refused to leave the theater. When a member of the company tried to explain that the cut had been made to "combat superstition," the disgruntled members of the audience showered him with melon seeds and voiced their displeasure for ten minutes before leaving the theater (Bodde 1957:232). During the ten years that followed, this play continued to be revised in order to fit the dictates of the Party, which, through its controlled press, recorded the delight of the audience rather than its dissatisfaction. That first audience's reactions to changes in a traditionally loved play, however, clearly foreshadowed the serious problems the new regime would encounter, not only with revised and banned plays, but also with any manifestation of the traditional myths and superstitions from China's popular culture.

With the revision of *The cowherd and the weaving maid*, the debate on myth and superstition became a serious Party topic, and arguments for and against reform began to materialize. One significant reaction came from the influential Drama and Opera Reform Committee, which included in its membership some of China's foremost literary and theatrical personalities — T'ien Han, Ou-yang Yü-ch'ien, Hung Shen, Lao Shê, Ts'ao Yü, and Chou Hsin-Fang — and had as its chairman the renowned Mei Lan-fang. At a meeting of this committee on July 11, 1950, it was established that censorship should be exercised and would be carried out under three circumstances: (1) if the play "popularized feudal slavism" and "superstition"; (2) if the play "popularized" corruption, viciousness, and murder; and (3) if the play despised and insulted the laboring people. Yet the committee members also found present values in their traditions that made it impossible for them to abandon completely the myths and superstitions of old China. Some fairy tales, they explained, clearly protested against existing society and dramatized a strong desire for a more ideal world (*Wen Hui Pao* 1950).

Perhaps in response to the committee action, classes for sixty-two blind street minstrels were established in December 1950 in an interesting attempt to use the popular past in support of the political present. Proposed by linguist Lo Chang-pei and dramatist Lao Shê, this project was supported by the Bureau of Civil Affairs, the Bureau of Labor, and the Department of Literature and Arts of the Peking Municipal People's Government. After receiving political training, the blind minstrels sang new ballads and told new tales of Mao Tse-tung, the People's Volunteers (CPV's) in Korea, and even old-fashioned mothers-in-law. And this was not all. These minstrels, the reports stated, were sufficiently enlightened to become "discriminating" in their "choice of tales from feudal China. They have set their faces against superstitions [*sic*] of ghosts and evil spirits of such tales as *Lady into fox*" (*People's China* 1951:27).

Censorship, however, as practiced by the Cultural Central Committee and supported by the Drama and Opera Reform Committee, continued in an aggressive fashion. By 1951, the list of acts and actions that were to be abolished from the stage included foot binding, lewdness, torture and killing, beating and kowtowing, men wearing pigtails, unscientific action, blowing one's nose and spitting, horrid masquerades, walking corpses, as well as superstition and horror (Ma Shao-po 1951). Some of these were drastic changes, and all represented strong ties with the past. Obviously, the Chinese people needed encouragement in accepting these reforms. In a psychologically shrewd manner that has been characteristic of the Chinese Communist Party, a government representative tried to help the Chinese people over the hurdle by blandly explaining that they had already achieved that successful acceptance.

Audiences of the New Democracy reject all superstition. The merely weird no longer excites their interest. They love the dramatic character of Pao Cheng, the celebrated judge of the 11th century, who defended the people against the illegal "laws" of the emperor, but they reject the dramatic device whereby he is given supernatural powers and is able to communicate with spirits in Hell who help him make out his briefs (Yu 1951:12).

Events proved that this was a premature declaration, although the reference to an audience of the "New Democracy" was clearly made with care. In the short space of two years, 1949 to 1951, it would seem that the general theater audience would scarcely have appreciated the reforms thrust upon them.

In fact, the complications of an ever-changing theater reform geared to a developing and, therefore, changing Party line must have puzzled many theater-goers. As the drama and theater reforms continued, however, some very noteworthy theater people lent their support. Even Mei Lan-fang (1952), the great Peking opera actor, commented on the need for change. "All plays," he wrote, "that speak against the spirit of nationalism, against the healthy living and thinking of the broad masses, against science and are for superstition must be cancelled." Perhaps he was saying that he preferred to have the scripts completely banned rather than altered beyond reason and relegated to absurdity. Whatever his motives he could never have believed that the Chinese people would accept the changes, for it was as a female impersonator in these plays that Mei Lan-fang had achieved great fame and popular appeal. He himself never acted in the communist propaganda plays. And on the fiftieth anniversary of his stage career in Peking, on April 12, 1955, at a time the Party scorned "spirits" on the stage, he performed scenes from the mythological plays, *Magical lamp* and *Nymph at Lo River* (*Survey of the China Mainland Press* 1954:13).

Argument, support, and opposition to theater reform were acceptable to a certain point — until a unified Party policy was established. On the problem of myth and superstition, it became evident that a genuine and immediate effort to clarify and formulate a concrete Party policy was necessary. At the First National Festival of Classical and Folk Drama, held in Peking in October 1952, the Party spokesman, Chou Yang, carefully defined relevant terminology from the communist point of view, thereby suggesting the direction for literary and theater reform. Recognizing that both myth and superstition are products of the imagination, he pointed out that each had its distinct qualities, making it either "good" or "bad." To Chou (1954) and to the Party, superstition was "always negative and generally serves the interests of the ruling class." Superstition "preaches fatalism and retribution, thus leading people to believe that everything is predetermined and that man must resign himself to fate." (This statement is particularly interesting when related to the concept of fate as expressed in terms of "inevitability" in the communist doctrines from Marx to Mao. Perhaps it shows something of the seriousness that the Party attached to superstition at this time.) Superstition, Chou went on, "claims that men are the playthings of the gods, their slaves and victims," and it "aims at making him [man] a willing slave glorying in his bondage." Mythology and folk legends, on the other hand, were allowed a much more positive treatment from Chou Yang and the Party. Because "a great many folk stories take a positive attitude towards the world and are impregnated with popular character," they were seen as serving the masses. It was, then, the handling of "fate" that determined Party acceptance or rejection. When "folk tales . . . depict man as unyielding before fate and finally triumphing over it in the world of imagination," it was acceptable to the Party. "In mythology, [but not in superstition] men dare to hurl defiance at the gods. . . . Mythology," Chou Yang declared, "always encourages man to break away from his enslavement and seek after the life of the real man" (Chou Yang 1954:115–116). These statements became the main reasons and the basis for the Party's early opposition to superstition and its acceptance of myth and certain folk legends.

Using this distinction, writers began to revise innumerable old plays. It was a slow process and, although Party policy was firm, it needed interpretation. Someone was necessary to hold revision within reason; and this person was, again, Chou Yang, who assumed his role as interpreter at the same time that he defined terminology for the Party. Discouraging those whose answer was simply to ban all the old superstitious plays, Chou also tried to restrain those who wanted to modernize the plays with no sense of historical relevancy. At the 1952 festival, he had initiated the problems in drama revision by criticizing a production of *The cowherd and the weaving maid*. At this performance, the magpies, which traditionally formed the bridge for the lovers' yearly meeting, had been changed to doves, the symbols of peace. The old ox that ploughed the fields had been turned into a modern tractor. And somehow, the playwright-adaptor had also managed to put the President of the United States of America along with airplanes and tanks on the stage. To Chou Yang this was a concrete example of the "anti-historicists" who were "stubbornly determined to turn old legends into reflections of present-day struggles" (Chou Yang 1954:128); and it was distressingly poor, both as drama and as Party reform.

As drama revisions determined by Chou's speech continued, another result of his forthright comments at the 1952 festival appeared. Other writers and critics felt encouraged to comment on and try to expand Party policy. In late October 1952, Chiang Ping-t'ai added fairy tales to the "acceptable" myth category and described the problems of revising fairy tales to eliminate superstitious elements. Chiang's major argument for dramatized fairy tales was that they "often protest against unreasonable social backgrounds and visualize the future, happy, idealistic living. To put it in a proper way, they can stimulate the will for struggle and the desire to pursue truth" (Chiang Ping-t'ai 1952). Quite bluntly, Chiang disagreed with the growing tendency among dramatists to increase the educational value of plays and to introduce reality and science in order to combat superstition: "By trying to intensify the educational meaning of fairy tales, we would have robbed the beautiful vision of simplicity and innocence that are present. This would have erased the activism of the fairy tale role. . . . We must also realize, therefore, that it is impossible to manufacture scientific fairy tales" (Chiang Ping-t'ai 1952). Instead of prohibiting fairy plays from the stage, Chiang suggested that each performance be preceded by an introduction in which the origin and motive of the play would be explained. To him, the preservation of the genre was most important, although he tried to emphasize both the traditional and the revolutionary approaches to art in its defense. "The prohibition of fairy tale plays is an uncivilized attitude we cherish toward our national cultural heritage, and it is an attempt to abandon our ancestors' revolutionary tradition" (Chiang 1952). In later years, such a comment would probably have been rebuffed by Party critics, but at this early point in the development of the People's Republic of China, it was allowed to pass.

Fairies on the stage were one thing; ghosts were quite a different matter. Considered part of superstition, ghosts were not generally acceptable in the new Chinese theater. Consequently, between 1949 and 1956 very few ghost plays were produced, while some old, favorite ghost plays were revised to fit Party demands. One of these was the famous old ghost play, *Visit to the West Lake*, with its ghost, Li Hui-niang. This play tells of Li Hui-niang, the concubine of Chia Shih-tao, who was an influential minister of the Southern Sung Dynasty. Murdered by Chia, Li Hui-niang's spirit becomes a phantom heroine seeking revenge. Rewritten by Ma Chien-ling, who changed Li Hui-niang from a ghost to a human being, the defects of "ghostly and uncanny evil images and the heavy fatalist and superstitious elements" (*Kuang-ming Jih-pao* 1963:2) that existed in the original play were presumably overcome. As with other revised plays, however, the audience's reaction was varied and significant. Some accepted the drastic change without question; others staunchly claimed that the revisions did violence to China's dramatic heritage. In some ways this second reaction was prophetic, but the violence to the past that these people saw as a consequence of the revision was slight compared to the destruction that the ghost of Li Hui-niang would bring to the theater in the future. It is this ghost — Li Hui-niang — who would walk the stage and become the element for purge, of both plays and men, during the Cultural Revolution. At this early time, however, with the problems of myth and superstition now being openly debated, the major task in all instances became the creation of play revisions that would suit the Party, the critic, and the audience — three bodies that had not yet found a common ground for agreement. Unfortunately, revision was particularly difficult at this time, because the Party had not yet categorically decreed that superstition was "bad" and myth and legend were "good."

Coincident with the problems raised by the ghostly appearance of Li Hui-niang was another attempt to revise *The cowherd and the weaving maid*, this time by Ch'in Tz'u, a member of the standing committee of the Kwangsi Literary and Art Association and the "responsible person" of the Drama and Opera Reform Committee. Ch'in's purposes, evidently, were to show the struggle against "feudalism," to abolish superstitions, and to expose the social bondage of the peasant to the landlords. Some critics praised this new version as an accurate expression of "the new democratic literary and art principle." Far too many others found the new script totally unacceptable. It was important to several critics, for example, that the play did not reflect a true picture of the laboring people. One such observer, Fu Sheng (1953), with Party policy clearly in mind, pointed out that Ch'in Tz'u had failed to "express the one truth that the world is created through labor." In addition, because Ch'in did not understand the passion of the laboring people, he had endowed the love affair between the cowherd and the weaving maid "with the passion of the petty bourgeois circle." Having thus described Ch'in as politically uneducated and capable of bourgeois sentiment, Fu Sheng further condemned him for his inept interpretation. Ch'in Tz'u, he maintained, had "not fully understood the basic purpose of this legend which should reveal the inevitable spirit of resistance of the major characters." In this fashion, the

Party tested and questioned attitudes before actually determining policy.

With these two plays — *The cowherd and the weaving maid*, and *Visit to the West Lake* — the progress of the problems that myth and superstition brought to the modern Chinese stage can be clearly traced. When, in 1954, the magazine *Wen-i Pao* called the revising of ghost plays "barbaric," an interesting and pertinent debate immediately followed (*China News Analysis* 1964:1–7). At this time many people still supported ghost plays and even denied that they included superstition. It was perhaps only logical that a *Wen-i Pao* reporter would choose *Visit to the West Lake* to illustrate his positive view of the ghost in Chinese drama. Staunchly opposing the transposition of Li Hui-niang from ghost to human being, the reporter denied the charge levied against the ghost figure and explained the play's contemporary relevance: "The original ghost play basically does not advocate superstition and fatalism as the reviewer maintains, but is a superior creation demonstrating how women continued to resist the feudal power in form of spirits; thus, the typical figures of the feudal rule are not punished in fact; they are punished or . . . overcome [only] in the people's imagination" (*Wen-i Pao* 1954).

Other critics supported this view, among them Chang Chen, who explained his strong convictions concerning the positive value of ghosts:

Such ghosts symbolize the people's curse of the oppressor and the alter-ego of their anger. The ghost images embody their desires and stimulate their ambition to revenge. They have an intimate feeling for such ghosts. . . . The appearance of [Li] Hui-niang's ghost, from the main spirit of the entire work, is not superstition, and it is not proper to delete it. . . . It is the continuation of the struggle in the imagination. Such description is not against realism, but an outcome of the active development of the realistic spirit (Chang Chen 1954).

Clearly, these stated opinions had an effect, and when the two articles quoted from were reprinted in *Chun-chung Jih-pao* and *Shensi Jih-pao*, in June and December 1954, the reason given for the second printing was their "correct" view. Soon Ma Chien-ling reappeared on the scene and, presumably as a consequence of this wave of criticism and its acceptance by the Party, revised *Visit to the West Lake* once more, restoring Li Hui-niang to ghost form.

By 1955 the problems surrounding myth and superstition were becoming much clearer to the Party. Although Chou Yang's 1952 speech condemning superstition and supporting myth and legend had provided an interesting dichotomy, it was a solution whose simplicity could not be maintained once more searching questioners sensed the problems. A refinement appeared with the new development of support for ghosts as well as fairies, and the Party responded by indicating that there could be "good" and "bad" ghosts as well as "good" and "bad" fairies. The result was a beginning for the Party, the critics, and the audiences, and because these years constituted a period of general tolerance in the PRC, myth and superstition in the drama were accordingly granted certain acceptance.

When the Ministry of Culture convened the National Dramatic Works Conference in 1956, one stated objective was to explore the possibility that traditional plays might enrich the contemporary theater repertory. Obviously, the arguments and productions during the previous three-year period had had an effect, and it was quite natural that demands were made and met to redeem ghost plays. For the next five years, press releases and Party commentary showed people enjoying both ghost plays and finding them "harmless." In terms of the political advancement of the PRC, this period of relaxation of previous strictness is understandable, highlighted as it was by the Hundred Flowers Campaign of 1957 and the Big Leap Forward of 1958–1960. For the traditional theater, however, the result was a definite rejuvenation. Plays and operas with ghosts and fairies, phantoms and wizards, and gods and goddesses once again became acceptable theater fare. As one critic explained the new liberal attitude, "We must put all supernatural beings on equal ground and regard them all as creations of artistic imagination and exaggeration" (Li Kang 1957). In one sense, the acceptable critical attitude approached an "art for art's sake" aesthetic encompassing an understanding that, although there might be supernatural beings on the stage, people were sufficiently intelligent to realize that such beings do not exist in everyday life. At any rate, ghosts once again wandered across Chinese stages without fear of retribution from the real political world, and theatrical troupes began performing such works as *Avenging an unusual wrong*, *Visit to the ghost world*, and *Capturing Wang K'uei alive*, all of which feature ghosts. Still it should not be assumed that the political world was far away or that it did not seek to profit from the return of the traditional ghosts and the supernatural elements of the popular culture. In late 1955, for example, a production of *Borrow the east wind* showed the mythological god of war, Kwan Yu, putting Harry S. Truman to death.

Whatever use the Party made of ghosts and the supernatural, audiences seemed to enjoy the return of past pleasures to the theater.

"They like to see operas mirroring present-day struggles and life, but they also like operas on historical themes, fairy tales and romantic fairy tales. There is already a good tradition of this in traditional China. Our audiences see no reason why such themes should not also be seen on the modern operatic stage" (Ma K'o 1957:31).

Both the change in theatrical fare and the switch in Party policy were duly noted by China observers such as C. P. Fitzgerald who explained that the policy that had once branded certain plays as "superstitious" and "feudal" and caused them to be banned, was now "stigmatized as 'incorrect'" (Fitzgerald 1958:141). Within China, however, as the period of tolerance toward art progressed, another attitude appeared. A Party playwright, Ou-yang Yü-ch'ien expressed this most clearly as a new policy of caution and study. "On the whole," he explained, "much that is admirable can be found in the traditional Chinese theater, although some plays have backward features and include certain vulgar elements. To distinguish between good and bad, we must make a thorough study of the theater" (Ou-yang Yü-ch'ien 1959:118).

Part of this thorough study was a concern for the problem of myth and superstition. Once again the Party was preparing the Chinese people for a policy change. Having admitted and built upon the enrichment that myth and superstition brought to a popular culture, and having allowed the people to enjoy those theater elements for a few years, the Party was now ready to persuade the people that slight changes or modifications could be made for the advantage of both the Chinese people and the country. The process of initiating and determining change, however, had to be done, with deception and efficiency. As minor as the theater might seem to some politicians, it had been a cherished part of Chinese culture for many centuries. Any dramatic upheaval dealing with a much loved tradition might produce undesirable events and attitudes toward the new government, and the plays and operas now affected were among the favorites of the people. It was a delicate situation:

These *shen hua chu* [mythological plays] are semi-religious plays, mostly concerned with Buddhism. Their anthropomorphism does not disturb the practical mind of the people, and the interrelation of a supernatural power to provide a happy solution for the play appeals to the taoist and buddhist elements of the Chinese soul. . . . Many have been banned, but since some Russian writers have defended them as folklore, not all have been condemned. . . . The plan now is to change or remake them (*China News Analysis* 1959:4).

Whatever the situation, however, a decision for change had been made and was to be carried out within the next few years.

As usual, the change was to come slowly, at a pace determined by Party diplomacy and popular reaction. For the PRC the objective was a long-range one and momentary setbacks were to be expected. The previous attempt (1952–1955) to change public attitudes toward myth and superstition had been only partially successful. Hence, there would now be a period of tolerance with a few suggestions. From 1955 through the end of 1962, there would be considerable freedom to produce a wide variety of mythological and superstitious plays. These plays were, of course, only a part of a rich and varied Chinese theatrical activity, and they were scattered among numerous productions of plays about communist heroes — plays such as *The white-haired girl, Steeled in battles, A couple learns to read and write, The saleswomen, Comrade, you've taken the wrong path,*

Long live the heroes!, *Loyalty to the Party*, *Red banner community dining hall*, and *Poor little American moon*. A respectable number of Western plays — Ibsen's *A doll's house*, Molière's *The miser*, Schiller's *Cabal and love*, Chekhov's *Three sisters*, and Shakespeare's *Romeo and Juliet* — were performed in the Chinese theaters during these years. It was also during this period that the Chinese celebrated the fiftieth anniversary of their modern drama with a revision of the play that helped introduce Western-style drama to China in 1907 — *Uncle Tom's cabin* (Meserve and Meserve 1974:57–66).

Among the theater pieces employing the supernatural, there was considerable range of style and subject matter — ballets, traditional operas, contemporary plays, adaptations of old tales, as well as dramatizations of contemporary stories and events. One of the most far-fetched uses of a ghost occurred in a play about a statesman of the Three Kingdoms Period (220–589 A.D.) who returned to earth to read the works of Mao Tse-tung and was labeled a "progressive ghost." And it was no surprise that *Li Hui-niang* was revised once more (this time by Meng Ch'ao). The following list of annotated theater productions suggests the varied interest in the supernatural from 1958 through 1962.

Mistress clever (Peking, March 1958): a folktale in which a fairy steps out of a painting to marry a woodcutter.

Magic aster by Jen Teh-yao (Peking, April 1958): a children's play with a fantasy hero, an evil black cat, and animals, birds, flowers, and trees that talk.

The cowherd and the weaving maid (Wuhu, Anhwei Province, December 1958): New Zealand journalist Rewi Alley saw this production and commented, "In this version the irate old queen of the western heavens, denying the weaving lass and the cowherd their yearly privilege of meeting together, is confronted by a group of commune folk who have come right up into the sky to bring down the Milky Way and make it irrigate their land. They build a bridge for the lovers and offer the weaving maid a job in a textile factory in their commune and the cowherd a tractor to drive" (Alley 1961:200).

Precious lotus lantern (Peking, March 1959): a ballet depicting a nymph's love for a mortal.

The ghost seeks revenge (Peking, April 1959): a Szechuan opera-drama in which a scholar, after gaining wealth and position, deserts his wife, causing her to commit suicide. The river god hears of the wife's fate and helps to avenge her.

The feather robe (Peking, November 1959): a Hunan flower drum opera in which a fairy bird is changed into a beautiful woman. When she falls in love with a farmhand, they are protected from a landlord, a magistrate, and the emperor by a magic robe made of feathers.

Snow in midsummer by Kuan Han-ch'ing (Peking, 1958 and 1959): a

Yuan dynasty drama in which the ghost of an unjustly executed girl seeks revenge.

Visit to the West Lake (Peking, February 1960): a Ping-j'u opera in which the ghost of Li Hui-niang seeks revenge.

Spring on earth (Peking, February 1960): a Shaohsing opera in which the God of Plague sends his daughter to poison the people on earth. She disobeys, falls in love with a doctor, and becomes his helpmate.

Swallow of Dragon Lake (Peking, June 1960): a play presented by the Peking Opera Troupe of Kirin Municipality about an evil dragon on Lung Tan [Dragon Lake] Mountain who causes floods and suffering to the neighboring people. A fairy swallow turns into a beautiful girl and, with the aid of the villagers, tames the evil dragon.

The white snake (Peking, December 1961): a Peking opera in which an immortal fairy white snake becomes a beautiful girl and marries a young man. Complications arise when a wicked abbot, Fa Hai, contrives to separate the couple and imprisons the white snake in Leifeng Pagoda. The play has a green snake, angels, the god of longevity, evil deities, water spirits, and cloud spirits.

A cloud seeks her husband (Peking, May 1962): a modern opera drama adapted from a folktale of the Pai minority people in Yunnan Province. A Pai princess falls in love with a brave hunter and defies her stepmother's wish that she marry a haughty official. Fleeing from the palace, she marries the hunter, but the stepmother has a magician turn the hunter to stone. When the princess dies of grief, her spirit takes the form of a cloud and wanders the heavens looking for her husband.

The magic boat by Lao Shê (Peking, June 1962): a children's play in which a woodcutter has a magic boat that he uses to do good deeds for others. A wicked and envious man, Chang, steals the boat and presents it to the lazy emperor, who, in return, makes him prime minister. After a fierce battle, the woodcutter and his friends — a white cat and a stork, among others — regain the boat.

During this period, too, plays of the supernatural were published and/or translated into English and other foreign languages. Under the auspices of Chou Yang, Mao Tun (editor of *Chinese Literature*), and the director of the Foreign Languages Press, such traditional plays as *A slave to money* with strong elements of myth and superstition appeared in print;

LUCK: I am the God of Luck in charge of all ranks
and conditions of men, noble or humble, high
or low. I control both life and death, besides
the eighteen regions of Hell and their seventy-
four divisions. What a pity men are too foolish
to do good! . . . But as the saying goes: Men's
whispered secrets sound loud as thunder in the

ears of the gods, and evil done in the dark cannot
escape the lightning of the god's eyes. This
is very true.

A Slave to Money, Scene 1

FATE: I am the Arbiter of Fate. Kneel and listen to my words!
No mortal born into this world
May flout the will of Heaven and of Earth.
Poverty and Wealth are predestined;
Fools struggle in vain against fate.

A Slave to Money, Scene 4

These speeches would not have escaped the censors prior to 1956, nor would they after 1963.

The year 1963 proved to be a turning point leading to the drastic measures practiced during the Cultural Revolution. From the period starting late in 1955 through 1962, the Party seemed content with performances of the supernatural, as long as audiences liked the political plays equally well and attended them. When in mid-1963 it was reported that audiences in southern China had displayed a strong dislike for a political propaganda play, the government became concerned. What could it do? "It would like to force Chinese opera troupes to perform only plays that 'benefit Socialism,'" wrote one critic, "but cannot do so because audiences would not come, the troupes would go out of business and the government [could] not nowadays afford to support them" (Yang Cheng 1963). Cantonese opera troupes reported that people came for amusement, not education, and that they must, therefore, play to the crowd. Confronted with contradictory demands from the people and the government, theater managers and critics began to categorize their plays as light or serious. The light plays included love stories, murder plays, and ghost plays. The serious plays reflected themes such as modern workers, the peasants' struggles, the history of the revolution, and history plays about ancient heroes. For obvious reasons, the Cantonese opera troupes in 1963 confessed that they tried to avoid the serious plays (Yang Cheng 1963).

In the Party view, this attitude was bad enough, but since it also led to more serious theatrical practices, it had to be stopped no matter how highly approved by both audience and dramatic troupes:

During the Spring Festival, a Canton opera troupe from Fashen was invited to give the opening performance at the inauguration ceremony of a newly built theater of Tungk'ang commune in Tungkuan *hsien*. Before the stage performance was about to begin, this troupe quite unexpectedly started burning incense at the backstage, besides putting on a short act "Offering to the White Tiger" [also known as "Jumping Over the God of Wealth"] on the evening of that day, before the first act of that opera performance was to begin. This short act, symbolizing evil, appeared very frightening to the audience, and was intended according to the established practice of old-fashioned Cantonese opera troupes, to "ward off evil spirits" before the opening performance of any new theater (Yi P'ing 1963).

Obviously the Party could not allow such regressions to past ways. This mixing of gods, myths, and theater activities had to be refuted, and the response came later in 1963, although moderate views continued to be published. "In a class society," one critic observed, "... fairy tales and religions play entirely different roles in society. First, the mythological personalities in fairy tales must not be mixed up with the gods in religions. Gods in religions are tools used by the ruling class to intimidate and benumb the people, while mythological personalities in fairy plays are those created by the laboring people from their imagination on the basis of their lives, struggles, and thoughts" (Shen Yao 1963:2). By this time, however, the Party had started anti-supernatural campaigns in earnest. Articles against the supernatural had already appeared, particularly against the 1961 theory that "ghost plays are harmless." In discussing Meng Ch'ao's 1961 revision of *Li Hui-niang*, which restored the ghost, one critic, Liang Pi-hui (1963), declared that "promoting ghosts is not a progressive and healthy tendency." He felt quite strongly that some ghosts could not be kept and others discarded; they should all be removed from the stage. Liang also revived an earlier distinction between ghosts and myth, using it as his main explanation for the elimination of ghost plays from the stage. "Though both come from the people's superstition about gods and ghosts and the fatalist concept, myths are the products of 'the infancy of mankind,' and they show bravery, diligence, and optimism of mankind, such as the Greek myths and Chinese myths. On the other hand, ghost stories and legends are mostly the products of the feudal society, and harmful" (Liang Pi-hui 1963).

As this new direction in Party policy became clear, more critics supported the idea that ghost plays were definitely harmful, although for different reasons. Ch'ing Ku-hsueh (1963), for example, noted that ghost plays "produced a drugging effect" that was "an escape from reality." Chao Hsun (1963) felt that ghost plays would "hamper the people from accepting the socialist and communist ideologies" as well as cause them to refuse to believe that workers could "use their own two hands to reform society and the world." The concern of these critics for the communist world outlook, which was contrary to the enjoyment the people felt for their traditional popular culture, foreshadowed some of the great turmoil into which China was headed during the purges of the Cultural Revolution.

As the eve of the Cultural Revolution approached, the number of denunciations of ghosts and superstitions increased. In this process, the term "ghosts" was expanded from its strict literary use in stories and plays to include living people who adroitly used the past to criticize the Party. These individuals became known as "ghosts" or "ugly monsters" in Party criticism and were a major object of attack. Ghosts within plays, however, also received special critical attention. At a speech during the opening ceremony of the Festival of Peking Operas on Contemporary Themes, June 5, 1964, Lu Ting-i (1965:79) explained that "ghost operas helped feudal superstitions to raise their ugly heads." Questions about who were these "ugly heads" — those who used the past to criticize the present — would be answered by numerous purges within the ranks of literary people during the Cultural Revolution. Among those purged would be Meng Ch'ao for his ghost character in *Li Hui-niang*. Lao Shê, Chou Hsin-fang, Wu Han, T'ien Han, and Hsia Yen would also be purged, not for creating ghosts in a play or story or essay, but for having "feudal superstitions" in their past or present work. Through transposition, the past itself became a ghost criticizing the present, and the Chinese government could not allow *this* ghost to pass into the future. It was quite like Scrooge's ghosts of Christmas in Charles Dickens' *A Christmas carol:*

"I've told you these were shadows of the things that have been," said the ghost. "That they are what they are, do not blame me!"
    "Remove me!" Scrooge exclaimed, "I cannot bear it!" . . . "Leave me! Take me back! Haunt me no longer"

Charles Dickens, *A Christmas carol*

The past, particularly those events and people from the past that might be used as veiled criticism of the present Chinese government, could not be allowed to haunt the present. Nor could the past be permitted to advance into the future. There was no place for ghosts in a communist utopia. "Armed with Mao Tse-tung's thought, the people are invincible," wrote one believer: "No ogres and monsters, open or hidden, in front of the scenes or behind, can stand a single blow from this mighty force" (Chi Pen-yu 1966:65). Such was the expressed optimism in ridding China of ghosts, past and present. Obviously, the people were supposed to see themselves revealed in the peasant song from An-kang *hsien* in Shensi Province:

In heaven there is no Jade Emperor,
On earth there is no Dragon King.
I am the Jade Emperor,
I am the Dragon King.
I order the Three Mountains and the Five Peaks to give way,
For I am coming (Fan Wen-lan 1958:3).

In the new China there is an urgency to cast away the past, particularly among the young and fervent followers of Mao Tse-tung's thought. It is a casting off not only of the emperors, beauties, and scholars, but also of a vast lore involving the myths and superstitions of the people. In its place is the new communist mythology of superheroes, more real than life itself. And this is a necessary mythology created to change the goals of a traditional China to that of a communist utopia. Yet when the propaganda of the Party has become tiring and monotonous in its frequent refrains, it has been the old plays, the old operas, the old tales of days gone past, filled with exalted emperors, flourishing generals, revenging ghosts, and the mythological rulers of the universe, to which the people have returned — with or without the sanction of the Communist Party of China. This drama is part of the enduring popular cultural heritage of China that will survive the vagaries of current censorship. Essentially, China confronts in it the haunting problem of reality:

When the unreal is taken for the real, then the real becomes unreal;
Where non-existence is taken for existence, then existence becomes non-existence (Ts'ao Hsüeh-ch'in 1958:7).

The problem for the Party is to find an efficient and satisfying means to combine the past with the present to serve the future objectives of the People's Republic of China.

REFERENCES

ALLEY, REWI
1961   *China's hinterland in the big leap forward.* Peking: New World Press.
BODDE, DERK
1957   *Peking diary: a year of revolution.* Greenwich, Conn.: Fawcett.
CHANG CHEN
1954   On the revision of *Visit to the West Lake. Wen-i Pao*, 21. (Translated in November 1963 *Joint Publications Research Service, China*, 21792:18–25.)
CHAO HSUN
1963   Is it harmless to show ghost plays? *Wen-i Pao* 4. (Translated in November 1963 *Joint Publications Research Service, China*, 21792:24–25.)
CHIANG PING-T'AI
1952   On the problems of revising and performing fairy tale plays. *Chun-chung Jih-pao*, October 29. Hong Kong: Union Research Institute, clipping file.
China News Analysis
1959   Literature, quality or quantity? *China News Analysis* 303. November 27.
1964   Ghosts and spirits on the stage. *China News Analysis* 502. January 31.
CH'ING KU-HSUEH
1963   The harm of ghost plays. *Kuang-ming Jih-pao*. May 21–25. (Translated in November 1963 *Joint Publications Research Service, China*, 21792:24.)
CHI PEN-YU
1966   "On the bourgeois stand of *Frontline* and the *Peking Daily*" in *The great socialist cultural revolution in China*, volume 2. Peking: Foreign Languages Press.
CHOU YANG
1954   *China's new literature and art, essays and addresses.* Peking: Foreign Languages Publishing House.

DICKENS, CHARLES
  1967   *A Christmas carol.* New York: James H. Heineman.

FAN WEN-LAN
  1958   P'o-ch'u Mi-hsin [Dispelling superstition]. Peking: *Hung-ch'i.* June 16.
         (Translated in June-August 1958, *Translations from Hung-ch'i* 533.)

FITZGERALD, C. P.
  1958   *Flood tide in China.* London: Cresset.

FU SHENG
  1953   Discussion of the Kwangsi cultural and art circle on *The cowherd and
         the weaving maid.* Wuhan: *Changkiang Daily*, January 7. Hong Kong:
         Union Research Service, clipping file.

Kuang-ming Jih-pao
  1963   The argument on whether "ghost plays" are harmful. *Kuang-ming
         Jih-pao.* September 10.

LI KANG
  1957   *Myths and ghost plays.* Shanghai: Wen-hua Publishing House. (Excerp-
         ted translation in November 1963 *Joint Publications Research Service,
         China* 21792:18–25.)

LIANG PI-HUI
  1963   On the "theory that ghost plays are harmless." *Wen-hue Pao.* May 6 and
         7. (Translated in November 1963 in *Joint Publications Research Ser-
         vice, China,* number 21792:23–24.)

LU TING-I
  1965   "Speech at the opening ceremony of the festival of Peking opera on
         contemporary themes" in *A great revolution on the cultural front.* Pek-
         ing: Foreign Languages Press.

MA K'O
  1957   China's modern opera. *People's China* 14 (17):31.

MA SHAO-PO
  1951   Eliminate the sickly and evil display on stage. *Jen-min Jih-pao.* Sep-
         tember 27. Hong Kong: Union Research Institute, clipping file.

MEI LAN-FANG
  1952   The new orientation of Chinese drama and opera art. *Kuang-ming
         Jih-pao.* September 3. Hong Kong: Union Research Institute, clipping
         file.

MESERVE, WALTER, RUTH MESERVE
  1974   *Uncle Tom's cabin* in China's modern theatre. *Modern Drama*
         17:57–66.
  1977   *The white-haired girl*: a model for continuing revolution. *Theatre Quar-
         terly* 24:26–34.

OU-YANG YÜ-CH'IEN
  1959   The modern Chinese theatre and dramatic tradition. *Chinese Literature*
         11.

People's China
  1951   Blind minstrels of the people. *People's China* 3 (8):27.

Survey of the China Mainland Press
  1954   Mei Lan-fang and Chou Hsin-fang give anniversary performances.
         Survey of the China Mainland Press 1026. April 11–13.

SHEN YAO
  1963   Fairy plays and ghost plays and communist ideology. Peking: *Kuang-
         ming Jih-pao.* November 17. (Translated in January 1964 in *Joint
         Publications Research Service, China,* 22752:43.)

TING I
  1952   The process of making *The white-haired girl. Hsin-hua Jih-pao*. May 20.
         Hong Kong: Union Research Institute, clipping file.
TS'AO HSÜEH-CH'IN
  1958   *Dream of the red chamber*. Garden City, N.Y.: Doubleday.
WAN CHAI-PAO [TS'AO YÜ]
  1946   The modern Chinese theatre. *National Reconstruction*. July.
WEN-I PAO
  1954   A discussion of the revision of *Visit to the West Lake. Wen-i Pao* 5.
         (Translated in November 1963 in *Joint Publications Research Service*,
         21792:18–25.)
Wen Hui Pao
  1950   The Central [People's Government] establishes drama and opera
         reform committee. *Wen Hui Pao*. July 25. Hong Kong: Union Research
         Institute, clipping file.
YANG CHENG
  1963   "Cantonese reject 'political' operas." Canton: *Wan Pao*. June 20. Hong
         Kong: Union Research Institute, clipping file.
YI P'ING
  1963   The undesirable practice of "warding off evil spirits" must be con-
         demned. Canton: *Nan-fang Jih-pao*. June 29. (Translated in August 21,
         1963 *Survey of the China Mainland Press*, 3084: 16–17.)
YU, P. C.
  1951   The reform of the classical Chinese theater. *People's China*. January 1.

SECTION THREE

Folklore and the Mass Media

The Wandering Infant-Noble Theme in Japanese Legends and Mass Media

HIROYUKO ARAKI

The Japanese have a saying, *Hangan-biiki*, which refers to a national sentiment fanatically sympathizing with the tragic fate of a Japanese hero. *Hangan-biiki* has gradually become a common noun meaning sympathy for the mistreated, weaker party. *Hangan* (or *Hogan*) refers both to the rank of an ancient courthouse official and to Yoshitsune (1159–1189), a hero of that rank so popular in Japanese history that *Hangan* has become the synonym for Yoshitsune himself.

When Yoshitsune was seven years old, his father, Yoshitomo, was killed by the army of the Heike clan, and Yoshitsune was put under the care of Kurama Temple. After running away from there, he wandered until he arrived at Fujiwara's. Later, he destroyed the Heike clan at the battle of Dannoura. He was the supreme commander for the army of the Genji (Minamoto) clan, but for all his glorious exploits he was expelled by Shogun Yoritomo, his half brother. After much more wandering, he again returned to Fujiwara's, where he was killed by troops dispatched by Yoritomo.

The saying *Hangan-biiki* has a long history, which appears in *Kefuki-gusa,* a collection of haikus published in 1638 by Shigeyori Matsue. The haiku poem on *Hangan-biiki* goes as follows:

Gentle breeze!
With cherry blossoms and *hangan biiki*
Blooming everywhere.

The origin of the saying has been traced as far back as the Muromachi Era (1392–1573); however, the sentiment must have existed even earlier. This theme has been discussed by Shinobu Origuchi (1966:242–270), a scholar of folklore and literature often classed with Kunio Yanagita, and by Yasaburo Ikeda (1962), a folklorist and professor at Keio University.

They concluded that the source of the sentiment can be traced back to the popularity of the oldest tradition of the "Wandering Infant-Noble." Their discussion maintained that Japan had a tragedy pattern traditionally handed down from generation to generation, which was, so to speak, a psychological attitude or a racial mentality. An infant-noble exiled as punishment from heaven or a place like heaven roams about suffering great hardships. He is usually accompanied by a guardian. After long wandering and privation, he dies and is enshrined at the place where he died. Since remote ages this pattern has found its way repeatedly into the various traditional literatures of Japan.

Thus the *Manyo-shu* [Collection of myriad leaves] informs us that there were many stories about exiled nobles, the most famous of which are about Omi-no-okimi, who was exiled to Iragoga-shima, and Isonokami-no-otomaro, who was banished to Tosa (Takeda 1959:16–17; 353–355). Origuchi asserted that the chapters entitled "Exile at Suma" and "Akashi" in *Genji-monogatari* [The tale of genji] are definitely influenced by the tradition of the Wandering Infant-Noble. Prince Genji who has nothing to do with the Genji clan, was exiled to Suma because of a love affair. Origuchi (1966:261–263) is of the opinion that lamentation on the seaside becomes very important when the tradition of the Wandering Infant-Noble is sublimated into literature. Origuchi quoted a few lines from "Exile at Suma":

At Suma autumn had set in with a vengeance. The little house stood some way back from the sea; but when sudden gusts of wind came "blowing through the gap" [the very wind of Yukihira's poem] it seems as though the waves were at Genji's door. Night after night he lay listening to that melancholy sound and wondering whether in all the world there could be any place where the sadness of autumn was more overwhelming.

The reference of Murasaki-shikibu, author of *Genji-monogatari*, to Yukihira's poem is suggestive, because Yukihira himself is thought to belong to the Wandering Infant-Noble theme. One of Yukihira's poems goes as follows:

Haphazardly asked,
Tell him
That I mingle
With Ama of Suma
Lamenting single.

Here Yukihira mentions that he is mingling with Ama, and Genji's mingling with Ama is also described in the chapter "Exile at Suma."

The highest peak of the literary tradition of the Wandering Infant-Noble is *Gikeiki*, the life of Yoshitsune, first published by an unknown author in the early years of the fourteenth century and profoundly influenced by oral tradition, illustrated in the following tale from *Tango-fudoki-itsubun:*[1]

There was the mountain of Hiji to the northwest of Kori-no-miyake in Tango Province. At the top of the mountain was a pond named Manai and at the foot of it lived an old couple, Wanasa-okina and his wife Wanasa-omuna.[2] The old man found out that eight heavenly Virgins were descending to the pond to bathe. He hid the celestial robe of one of the maidens and finally took her home. After that he gradually became prosperous. The couple turned the maiden away, who subsequently wandered about day and night.[3] When she arrived at the village of Nagu, she said that she felt *nagu* [quiet] and settled there. That is why the village and the temple where she was enshrined were both called Nagu (Akimoto 1958:446–468).

Some other maidens who assert the same origin as the maiden of Nagu are also enshrined in several places in the province of Izumo, where the maidens are called Minuha.[4] Thus we know that many maiden goddesses of the same origin are scattered about in the provinces of Tango and Izumo. To trace the maidens back to their genesis is not so difficult. There is a maiden god enshrined in the hamlet of Wanasa in the province of Awa, one of the most important centers of Ama tribes, to whom the worship of the Infant-god[5] is ascribable.

The tribes of Ama, known as sea tribes, probably came to Japan from the South Seas area by way of the southern islands or southern Korea. One branch is thought to be the tribe of Hayato, appearing in *Kojiki*.[6] They worshiped sea gods such as Watatsumi-no-kami, Munakata, and Sumiyoshi. Engaged in fishery, they wandered about from place to place, settling here and there. The exiled-nobles-mingling-with-Ama motif is very distinct, and it persists in ancient stories and poems related to the Wandering Infant-Noble. The mingling of Prince Genji and Yukihira with Ama has already been noted. Other famous exiled nobles, such as Omi-no-okimi and Isonokami-no-otomaro, are also known by poems to mingle with Ama.

[1]   This refers to *The Fudokis*, the collection of topography and folklore of local provinces compiled in 713 A.D. by order of Emperor Genmyo. Many of the volumes are lost or destroyed, with only five extant. Nevertheless, some lines from the lost *Fudokis* are cited here and there, and they were arranged as an addendum (*Itsuban*) by several scholars. *The Fudokis*, revised and annotated by Akimoto, include these addenda of folklore and topography from Tango province.

[2]   *Okina means "an old man"* and *Omuna*, "an old woman."

[3]   It is clear that this story is a rare combination of the stories of the "Swan-maiden" and the Wandering Infant-Noble. The unkindness of the couple was introduced in the process of combination. Clearly, the man and woman were formerly characterized as the maiden's guardians.

[4]   In the opinion of Origuchi (1966:245–246), Minuha is related to Minuma, a county name at Awa and a central point for the tribes of Ama. He adds that Minuma used to be a maiden-goddess there.

[5]   *Infant* here is used to describe a weak or frail-looking noble, not necessarily a real infant.

[6]   The *Kojiki* is the oldest Japanese chronicle, compiled in 712 A.D., and the main source for the early mythology of Japan.

In the hamlet of Wanasa there is also a shrine consecrated to Wanasa-ohoso (Origuchi 1966:246). *Ohoso* means "grandfather," or simply "old man," and one is quite safe in asserting that Wanasa-okina in Tango province is closely related to Wanasa-ohoso, with the former as a form of the god degenerated into a character of the oral literature and the latter as the original sacred form.

This is but one of many instances of local legends connected with exiled nobles. Some are associated with Emperor Antoku and other court nobles believed to have survived the battle of Dannoura, where Yoshit-sune destroyed the Heike clan. The tale of the Wandering Infant-Noble, describing his suffering and travels, spread over the lands where a group of the worshipers of the Infant-God sojourned or settled. Thus the tradition of the Wandering Infant-Noble was firmly rooted in the Japan-ese mind, and the sympathetic response to the story has been handed down from generation to generation. Japanese never forget the heart-rending thrill they experienced over the tragic story of Sansho-daiyu, and the emotion that stirred in their heart is, I believe, no other sentiment than the ancient sympathy toward the Wandering Infant-Noble. In this story, Anju and her brother Zushio, accompanied by their mother, wife of the lord of Mutsu, went in search of their father, who had been exiled to Tsukushi on a false charge. On the way they were kidnapped and sold as slaves. Their master, Sansho-daiyu, was a cruel man, and Zushio ran away with the help of Anju, who drowned herself to attract the pursuers' attention from her escaping brother. Many years passed and Zushio, risen to an exalted rank, met his mother, who had lost her eyesight in sorrow for her misfortunes. Origuchi (1966:267–268) suggested a relationship be-tween Sansho-daiyu and the Wandering Infant-Noble, using the slave merchant as a clue and comparing him with the gold merchant in *Gikeiki*.

Returning to Yoshitsune, one finds it remarkable and strange in the *Gikeiki* that the best days of Yoshitsune, which were dramatic, brilliant, and gay, are almost entirely omitted. The story concentrates exclusively upon the two tragic wanderings of his early and closing days. Is it probable that the saga of Yoshitsune, one of the most important warriors in Jápanese history, unfolds without describing his flowering period? Why are the author and the audience satisfied with this hiatus? The description of Yoshitsune in his later years as an utterly powerless and dependent person is indeed odd. There is no manly and commanding young Yoshit-sune (he was killed at the age of thirty) as presented in the *Heike-monogatari*. This famous work, which probably came into existence in the early thirteenth century, recounts the vicissitudes of the Heike clan and characterizes Yoshitsune very favorably. Blind minstrels, known as *Heike-zato*, recited the tale of Heike and transmitted many of its episodes orally.

So we return again to the tragic pattern of the Wandering Infant-Noble, where the infantility and weakness of the hero persist. It is not that the real life of Yoshitsune fitted exactly into that pattern, but that the history itself was molded into the pattern of the story. Most suggestive of this conformity to tradition is the fact that the part of Yoshitsune in the Noh play is performed by a *Kokata* [infant actor]. *Kokatas* are supposed to take the roles of real infants, indicated by the suffix *waka* [young] at the end of their names, as in Ume-waka or Matsu-waka. It is no wonder that Ushi-waka, the infant name of Yoshitsune, is played by an infant actor, but even in his manhood Yoshitsune is played by a *Kokata* (Ikeda 1962:306).

Here again the Wandering Infant-Noble theme is reflected in the Noh play of Yoshitsune — a play in which the hero is supposed to be powerless. In *Gikeiki*, especially in the closing part, as we have seen, Yoshitsune is described as weak and helpless. He meets his hardships guarded by his protectors. Among the retainers who attended Yoshitsune during his later wanderings, the most famous was Benkei, at one time a monk at the west temple of Enryaku-ji. He accompanied Yoshitsune as a shadow follows its form. At the end of his wanderings, Yoshitsune has to die without any reward, a perfect counterpart to the Wandering Infant-Noble. The Noh play appropriately tries to express such a characterization of Yoshitsune through the performance of a *Kokata*.

The story of Yoshitsune excited profound public sympathy and caused a considerable stir in the whole country, not because his real life was so tragic and pathetic but because it was adapted to the formula of the Wandering Infant-Noble to which Japanese emotions are always ready to respond. In all probability the sentiment of *Hangan-biiki* existed before the actual history of Yoshitsune began.

Looking to the present day, one sees a pattern that pertinaciously endures, namely that of the "traveling hero." One sees a persistent stereotype in the last scene of each episode of television dramas, movies, and the popular novels called *matatabi-mono* [stories of wandering gamblers] or *kengo-mono* [stories of master fencers or strong samurais]. There is always a departing hero, either with a group of villagers wistfully seeing him off or, in the case of a gambler, aimlessly leaving alone. Either type of hero departs for ceaseless wandering. More than seventy percent of so-called *jidai-geki* [dramas with a samurai or his contemporary as a hero] follow this stereotype, in which one discovers the immortal tradition of the Wandering Infant-Noble.

Needless to say, every samurai or gambler story does not represent this tradition in its entirety. How can we trace the Infant-Noble in the brawny master fencers? How can old Mitsukuni, who is a vice-shogun, represent an infant or the weaker party?

Here consideration should be given to the guardians or sympathizers, who without exception attend the heroes in the stories of wandering master fencers. Mitsukuni is always accompanied by Suke-san and Kaku-san. With Shingo Aoi, Koto-hime [Princess Koto], and Hyogo Tsukikage — the most popular master fencers or women fencers (Koto-hime) on television and in movies — there are always guardians or sympathizers.

The story of traveling Mitsukuni, who is accompanied by Kaku-san, has maintained a nationwide popularity for a long time and been filmed for movies and television over and over again. Vice-Shogun Mitsukuni, in the disguise of a merchant, travels around the country with Suke-san and Kaku-san. He chastises unfair magistrates and punishes the wicked. Shingo Aoi was fostered by Shozaburo, who harbored enmity against Shogun, Singo's real father. A master fencer, Tamon Umei, also shelters Shingo, who wanders about to fight against ten well-known swordsmen. Guardians and protectors are always seen with master fencers. Foster-father Shozaburo and Tamon Umei attend Shingo Aoi; a secret guard accompanies Koto-hime; and Yaizu-no-hanji waits on Hyogo Tsukikage. Some guardians stay close to their hero; others watch over him from a distance; but all are ready to protect him or her in case of emergency. The presence of a guardian is the essential attribute of the pattern of the Wandering Infant-Noble, and the persistence of the element is a most important consideration. Master fencers are supposed to be strong, but those who need guarding or sympathy are the weak. Mitsukuni remains a weak and powerless old man in the disguise of a merchant until Suke-san and Kaku-san hurry to his rescue and reveal his master's exalted rank. Similarly, Shingo Aoi and Koto-hime are both children of a shogun and Hyogo Tsukikage is the nephew of a *daimyo* [feudal lord]. With all the essential elements present in the Wandering Infant-Noble — nobility, weakness, a constant guardian, and a habit of continual wandering — one can properly assert that these traveling noblemen are the direct descendants of the traditional Infant-Noble.

In the personas of traveling gamblers, one discovers no trace of nobility. Is it then farfetched to trace the pattern in these gambler stories? If so, what are those aimless and never-ending wanderings, which seem to be parallel with those of master fencers?

As we have seen, the Wandering Noble is exiled as punishment, and that is the only element that is lacking from the stories of master fencers. In the stories of wandering gamblers, no guardians or sympathizers accompany them; they wander alone. What is discarded in the stories of master fencers, the punishment element, is restored and stressed in the stories of gamblers, and what is stressed in the former is utterly discarded in the latter. Only the wanderings of gamblers seem to be motivated by the commission of crimes.

Gamblers are characterized as outlaws or outsiders. The outsider cannot be strong, since he is deprived of every sympathy and protection. Yoshitsune, bereft of every authoritative protection, is also a pure outsider. Thus we know that there is something in common between the sympathy for gamblers and the sentiment of *Hangan-biiki*. Both share in the sympathy given the mistreated outlaw.

We know that the Infant-Noble is invariably accompanied by a guardian, and the infant himself is supposed to be enshrined. This attention is the only consolation he receives. Where the tradition of the Wandering Infant-Noble is bereft of this consolation and the punishment element comes to the fore, one encounters the pattern of gamblers' stories. The stories of master fencers, which discard the punishment element, are no longer tragic. Conversely, the tragic element predominates in the stories of wandering gamblers, where the punishment is overstressed and the guardian motif is excluded.

A gambler, being severed from every consolation, wanders alone with a birth trauma incised in his heart. One such character who has won overwhelming popularity is named Kogarashi Monjiro. He has really taken the public by storm. Monjiro is exiled to the island of Hachijo on a false charge. He bears the blame for his best friend, who later breaks his promise of silence to proclaim Monjiro's innocence. For Monjiro, nothing is now reliable. He escapes from the island and wanders about aimlessly. He says he is just killing time by wandering because he has no object to live for and no place to go. He does not want to get involved with anything. No one can force him into any action, unless he wants to do so. Justice or sympathy have never served him in any way. For Monjiro, everything in this world is transient and empty. *Kogarashi*, his nickname, means "freezing blast sweeping down from the mountains in winter."

Monjiro is a child born to answer the needs of modern times, when everything humane is hopelessly rejected. Monjiro is no doubt a reflection of today, but at the same time he reflects times of old when the tradition of the Wandering Infant-Noble was well understood. Today as yesterday, Monjiro appears on television and the movie screen. We give enthusiastic applause to the solitary, retreating figure of Monjiro and superimpose on him the never-perishing image of the Wandering Infant-Noble.

REFERENCES

AKIMOTO, K.
  1958 *Tango-fudoki-itsubun* [Lost writings on the physical description of Targo]. Tokyo: Iwanami-shoten.
IKEDA, Y.
  1962 *Nihon geino-densho-ron* [About the transmission of Japanese performing arts]. Tokyo: Chuo-koron-sha.

ORIGUCHI, S.
  1966   *Origuchi Shinobu zenshu* [Origuchi Shinobu's complete works], volume
         7, number 8, Tokyo: Chuo-koron-sha.
TAKEDA, Y.
  1959   *Manyo-shu-zenko* [Complete collection of the *Manyoshu*], volume 1
         (third edition). Tokyo: Meiji-shoin.

Influences of Mass Media on Folklore in Egypt

AHMED RUSHDI SALEH

When Egypt was brought into the orbit of Western culture in the opening years of the nineteenth century, factors of change began to affect traditional life. Folk heritage was exposed to new technical, social, and economic influences that were destined to impart new ideas, ferment new values, implement new customs, and help to change the structure of folk communities. This process began in a slow rhythm and on a limited scale, but it persistently gained strength until it ended in an accelerated, nationwide drive. In the last two decades, technical influences and socially planned changes have reached an unprecedented level.

In the early nineteenth century, printing initiated the contact between the advanced Western technological countries and the traditional culture of Egypt. The first Arabic press, established in the 1930's, was operated by Egyptian printers trained in Italy. One of its early publications was the first edition of *The Arabian nights*. A few years later, new printing presses started publishing magazines in colloquial dialect, collections of jocular tales, pamphlets, jokes, proverbs, and other types of popular literature. As a result, a new era in the life of folklore began.

Before the introduction of printing, folklore was transmitted orally. Only a few manuscripts were available to a small minority of affluent amateurs or educated masters of folk arts. The oral transmission of folklore followed acknowledged traditional patterns. When folk artists sang, narrated, or performed some of the memorized traditions, they did so amid an audience with whom they were psychologically connected. Professional folk artists were the entertainers, the dispensers of wise sayings, the masters of rare skills. All their capacities were at the disposal of their public, for it was this public that patronized the artists and directly responded to the performances.

When a literary text of a folktale is rendered in print, however, the intimate atmosphere between artists and their audiences expires. The reader of a written or printed text reacts to it as an individual, isolated from the rest of the audience of folk literature. Such was the impact of the press on folk literature. The theater also had its effect on folk traditions during the 1870's, as did radio, introduced in the 1930's, and television, in the 1960's. Therefore, for nearly a century the impact of modern mass media on folk culture and folklore has been felt. This impact has had virtues as well as shortcomings. One may admit for example, that it is due to printing that certain types of folk literature, which are no longer in use, were preserved in print. These included the folk epics of *Al cantaria*, *Seif Ibn Zi-Yazin, The Arabian nights*, and other colloquial poetic compositions that were current when printing first began but that now are obsolete.

One can also say that psychological attachment to folk heritage finds an outlet in published folk literary materials. During the closing decades of the nineteenth century, the rise of slogans such as "Egypt for Egyptians" signaled the campaign to stress the authenticity of the Egyptian nation and culture. This stress took the form of an increased interest in ancient Egyptian history as well as in the attempt to arabicize the Egyptian dialects. Some of the earliest collections of folk proverbs and colloquial sayings were printed as the result of a renewed interest in the Arabic language, which aimed at purifying it from non-Arabic influences.

The picture will be incomplete, however, if we fail to mention the efforts of European residents who participated in cultural institutions such as the Royal Geographical Society and the Royal Historical Society. To the Royal Geographical Society, we owe the first ethnological collection, and to the Royal Historical Society, the works of a number of geographers, historians, and antiquarians who published studies of folk practices, beliefs, and sayings.

In the last thirty years, another interesting stage in folklore has come into being. This development was of an academic nature and took the form of M.A. and Ph.D. theses that treated certain subjects of folk literature. These studies began with the examination of *The Arabian nights*, Andalusian colloquial verse, and Egyptian epics. While these studies pioneered in the field of academic research, they suffered through using literary rather than folkloristic criteria. The subjects chosen have their historical value, indeed, but they are not dealt with through the science of folklore, which was then either unknown to academic circles, or ignored by them until quite recently.

In order for folklore to become an accepted academic field, its study had to have a new orientation, its subject matter had to be redefined, and its scope had to be clarified and demarcated.

During the last two decades, folklore studies have usually been based on the discussion of literary types which are examined in their social and cultural contexts. Collecting lore in the field remains an essential task for which fieldwork skills must be developed. In addition, a knowledge of the history, theories, and methods of folklore must be mastered. The social sciences as well as the humanities have contributed to this end.

In 1957, the Center of Folklore was established, and I had the honor of being named its director. Under the auspices of the Center, it was possible to realize some basic work. Nearly 5,000 items of oral folk types were recorded on tape. They were collected from different social levels and from different folk communities. This was the first collection of its kind in Arabic. It was now possible to publish a first annual collection of folklore and to establish the first specialized folklore library. As a result of the Center's activities, some distinguished university graduates were enrolled in European and American universities to study folklore and related social sciences. These activities have produced an unprecedented level of printed material on folklore in the Arabic language. The effort, nevertheless, falls short. In Egypt, folklore research is still virgin land; many tale types and folklore genres remain uncollected.

The new school of folklorists must learn to work with printed sources as well as to record in the field. From the beginning, the introduction of printing led to the publication of collections of folkloric material and observations on folk beliefs, practices, and culture. L. H. Coults's *An annotated bibliography of the Egyptian fellah* (1958), for example, offers outstanding collections of folk literary types and folklore studies. Most of these belong to what may be called the pioneering and scientifically unsystematized stage of modern interest in folklore.

Such works disclose the fact that the writings and collections were issued by persons of different inclinations. There were works by European travelers and Orientalists who were spellbound by the traditional life of the Orient. There were also collections, observations, and studies published by the European residents. Finally, there were folkloric collections by the Egyptian intellectuals, such as Ahmed Taymur's *Popular proverbs* containing 3,000 proverbial sayings.

In the nineteenth century, several editions of *The Arabian nights* were printed. The first appeared in Cairo, the second, known as the "expurgated" version, was published in Beirut. Names of nineteenth century authors, such as Edward William Lane (1839–1941, 1902) and Bayle St. John (1852) are to be added to those of the twentieth century, such as Gaston Maspero (1882) and Fernand Leprette (1939). The printing of folklore was carried on in Egypt as well as abroad. Consequently a remarkable amount of printed matter became available to highbrow readers.

In the 1870's, printed works were made available to the ordinary reader — low- and middle-brow — in the form of cheap pamphlets, dailies, and weeklies written in colloquial Arabic. The impact of such publications on folklore and the folk imagination was significant. The reasons are many. The birth of the humorous colloquial press coincided with an upsurge of nationalism. The first influential magazines of this type were imbued with Arabic political thought.[1] The magazine *Abu Naddara Zarga*[2] [The man with blue glasses] reached an impressive circulation of 5,000 copies in a culture marked by prevailing illiteracy. *Al Tankeet wal Tabkeet* [Joking and blaming] was published by the famous political agitator of the Arabic cause, Abdullah al Nadeem. The pages of such periodicals included various forms of folklore. Among these were the *nukta*, a pun, joke, or humorous series of phrases connected into a whole called a *Kafia*. The *Mawal* was a kind of folk lyric poem, said to have migrated eastward from its birthplace in Iraq under the Abbassides. It is now one of the most popular forms of folk poetry in the Arabic dialects. The *Zagal*, another kind of folk poetry, originated in Muslim Spain. Other kinds of folk materials, such as jocular tales, also appeared in the periodicals.

Humorous folk characters were created expressly for these publications. For instance, Goha the fool was a satiric figure featured in thousands of humorous tales, jokes and proverbs in Arabic and Turkish dialects. He was portrayed variously as a simpleton, a rascal, a shrewd person, a wise man, an oppressed layman, a clever cheat, a liar, a social critic. Abu Nawas, an outstanding classical poet of the Abbasside period, was transformed, by the folk imagination, into a humorous character. He became a drunkard, a sexual pervert, a satirist, a charlatan, who usually appeared with the Caliph Harun al-Rashid and his prime minister, Ga'far.

Hence, traditional literary forms were used as vehicles for the expression of modern social demands, i.e., no taxation without legislation or parliamentary representation, social and economic reformations based on the principle of universal suffrage, emancipation of women, introduction of compulsory education, and so on. It is clear that such ideas were influenced by the Western principles of democracy, liberty, and equality. They were disseminated through magazines, as well as through theater and songs. Hence, printing incorporated folk types of literature traditionally connected with entertainment. As a result, numerous magazines and publications confined themselves to jokes, humorous tales, and cartoons that made use solely of traditional forms of literary compositions to "propagate" urban concepts.

---

[1]   In the 1870's, the Arabic movement appeared as an expression of Egyptian nationalism. Its tendencies were clearly republican and reformist. The intelligentsia was attracted by it and brought to it slogans of a social and politically modern spirit. The magazines referred to here echo these views.
[2]   The publisher of this magazine was Ya'coub ibn Sanōa, a well-known poet, actor, and political agitator.

Since the press was concentrated in the capital, Cairo, its printed material diffused from the summit of the cultural pyramid to the lower levels of society. The more advanced strata of society used certain kinds of folk literary forms to express themselves to the illiterate majority. This process had its virtues for folklore, but it resulted in distortions as well. Some printed works came to be known by heart by peasants, for example, the sharply satirical criticism of the peasants' customs and beliefs that was written by an anonymous educated author and published under the title, *Hazz El Kuhuf fi Sharh Kasidat Abu Shad uf*. In fact, one may trace a considerable number of popular songs, comic tales, and jokes to these fabricated works that were printed in the vernacular.

In the field of modern theatrical plays and shows, folk material such as tales, songs, dances exchanged influence with these works.

The impact of printing and the theater however, is surpassed by the influence on folkways and culture of radio and television. The limited public for printed material and the limited audience for theater has been superseded by the unlimited masses who listen to radio programs or view television.

With the advent of radio the listening peasants fall prey to the wide network of urban values. They are entertained by songs, music, and plays that are alien to their artistic traditions. Other programs, such as discussion, news, and commentary influence their inner conceptions and orient them toward prevailing lines of thought.

The attitude of those who listen to mass media differs from that of those who listen to folk songs or folk narrations. With radio and television, the listeners are subjects acted upon. With oral folk songs or narratives, they are participants in the action. They listen, but they may influence the recitation; they receive what is given of folk arts, but they can choose what they want. Performing artists are at the disposal of their audiences, whereas radio listeners are under the control of the program producers.

These ubiquitous and highly influential media are concentrated in the metropolis. The values they diffuse reflect more modern, urban ways of life, as seen and practiced by the city intelligentsia (thinkers, artists, men of letters, and social, political, and cultural leaders).

When folkloric material is produced on radio or television, it is submitted to a series of influencing conditions. Usually the material chosen is presented for its value as entertainment, not for its folkloric value or its function in the owners' daily life. For example, if a ceremonial dance is presented on television, it has to be interesting to the audience; and if a folksong is broadcast on radio, it has to be understandable to the listeners. These are the first marketing criteria applied to the "raw" folk material. in addition, folksongs, dances, and music are usually shortened and taken out of their original cultural and social context. When folksingers, musicians, or dancers are transferred from their original setting to the studio, they are planted in a totally new atmosphere. They feel strange in front of cameras, microphones, and technical equipment. Electric lights, stage sets, and even the language of announcers, producers, and other radio or television workers are apt to make folk artists feel self-conscious and detached. When folk artists perform under such conditions, they are no longer themselves. The "artist" in them becomes an "artisan." The flavor of performing before a public they know or to whom they feel attached is replaced with the awe of a public they do not know. My personal experience in presenting folk items on television convinces me that the very transfer of folk artists to the studio subtracts what is genuine from their performance. One must not expect folksongs, music, and dances to appear on television as they do in real folk life, for radio and television have their special techniques, criteria, and functions that are not similar, parallel, or even connected with the tradition of performing folk arts.

When modern mass media arose in advanced industrial cultures, they completed a process of change already begun in the relationship between the audience of modern Western culture and its advanced technology. But when the same media were brought into the life of developing agrarian cultures, they brought about a far reaching and pervasive change on the structure of the traditional culture.

The presentation of songs, music, and dances through the mass media can subject these traditions to misunderstanding, distortion, and misrepresentation. There are other causes that deform these arts. One of them is the attempt to "reconstruct" dances or choreograph them to fit into the television show format. What is known as popular theatrical dance or popular television dance is not folk dance but a fabrication of folk dance molded to fit the techniques of these modern media.

Folksongs are subdued in a similar manner. Texts are rewritten, purged of harsh or immoral expressions or idioms that do not become refined tastes. Musical arrangement is also exposed to changes; the instruments used in media performances are not always folk musical instruments.

To summarize, radio and television inflict deplorable changes on the folk arts. Songs, music, and dances performed on modern mass media can sometimes draw from the old folk types, but usually not without considerable change.

Mass media exercise their persistent influence on folklore (1) as a means of diffusing modern urban values and concepts; (2) as a means of propagating new forms and fabrications; and (3) as a means of orienting the non-participating public to such values and concepts. Finally, they have the power to plant conforming judgments into folk tastes.

My intention here is not to underscore the drawbacks of television and radio as technical factors of change on folklore. The media may be viewed instead as part of a problematic series of phenomena that were brought into the life of the Egyptians as the logical outcome of social change. The mass media are not an evil in themselves. The fashion in which they are used determines their relative virtues or shortcomings.

The disintegration of traditional cultures under the stress of technical, economic, and social factors of change is a fact that controls the destiny of these cultures in the contemporary world, but efforts to protect these cultures from disintegration can succeed if modern technology is adapted to the needs and nature of traditional cultures. One must be aware that these cultures have an innate power to resist change, even though the power to resist is not the decisive factor in the preservation of the cultural heritage. Social planners are expected to deal with problems such as social change and cultural disintegration. Folklorists are to collect as many traditional types as they can, observe customs, record beliefs and practices, and acknowledge the importance of folk heritage. However, they cannot stand in the way of this objective reality, the constant change taking place in the structure of traditional culture.

Egyptian folklore, one of the richest and oldest of Arab folk cultures, was not as fortunate as European folklore from the historical point of view. We do not have very many written texts. Moreover, collections printed in the nineteenth and twentieth centuries include but a small part of our total folkloric treasure. The bulk of it is still transmitted orally. Social and cultural contexts of the traditional culture do not disappear, however, for in spite of the accelerating factors of change, folk life retains the essence of its heritage. But within the foreseeable future, this situation will change drastically. What people still retain of folk life will no longer be a vigorous reality; all too soon it will become only the remnant of a bygone way of life.

Modernization began as a slow, scattered, and superficial trend as Egypt was brought into the orbit of Western culture. But one hundred and fifty years of active dialogue with the West introduced powerful factors of social, economic, and cultural change. In the last two decades, these factors have been consciously accelerated by social planning, and the scope of folk life is now far more limited and far more exposed to technical changes. Folk life in Egypt is now confronted by the same fate as other traditional cultures in developing countries in this changing world. Scientific efforts can help in preserving or protecting folk heritage from disintegration, and folklore as a science must serve such an end in communities exposed to the tremendous influences of modern technology.

REFERENCES

COULTS, L. H.
  1958   *An annotated bibliography of the Egyptian fellah*. Miami: University of Miami Press.
LANE, EDWARD WILLIAMS
  1839–1841   *The thousand and one nights*, three volumes. London: Charles Knights.
  1902   *An account of the manners and customs of the modern Egyptians*. London and New York: Ward, Lock.
LEPRETTE, FERNAND
  1939   *Egypte, terre du Nil* [Egypt, land of the Nile]. Paris: Plon.
MASPERO, GASTON
  1882   *Les contes populaires de l'Egypte ancienne* [The popular stories of ancient Egypt]. Paris. J. Maison-neuve.
ST. JOHN, BAYLE
  1852   *Village life in Egypt*. London: Chapman and Hall. (Reprinted 1973. New York: Arno Press.)

Traditional Culture, Folklore, and Mass Culture in Contemporary Yugoslavia

DUNJA RIHTMAN-AUGUŠTIN

In the years preceding World War II, four-fifths of Yugoslavia's population lived in rural areas; by the 1971 census, only about one-third of Yugoslav citizens lived in villages. This demographic framework cannot be left out of consideration when discussing the relationship of traditional culture, folklore, and mass culture in Yugoslavia today. Yugoslavia's cultural pluralism is a commonplace: it is in this country that, through the ages, three world religions and several European or Mediterranean cultural patterns have met to build a cultural and ethnic mosaic. The recent rural-urban migrations have only added to this complexity. It should be mentioned here that the rural exodus in European countries usually lasted a century or even more and that it was completed (for example, in Germany) at the beginning of this century. The point is that in those countries industrial and urban development proceeded at different rates and in different historical periods. In Yugoslavia, on the other hand, rural-urban migrations have come about during the last twenty-five or thirty years, along with the industrialization and modernization of the country.

This is, of course, the setting of cultural dynamics which is implied in our hypothesis of traditional culture persisting in some way in the contemporary complex culture in Yugoslavia and in Yugoslav society.

We conceive of a culture as a product of historical events, but we also wish to underline the process of adaptation of yesterday's cultural patterns to those of today and tomorrow, as well as the adaptation of present culture to historical patterns. The research of culture change carried out by the author in recent years has brought to the surface certain relevant facts concerning the presence of traditional culture in contemporary sociocultural development in Yugoslavia. It is obvious that traditional culture determines behavior, sometimes on unexpected levels. We shall briefly examine only three examples to illustrate this.

Interesting differences can be observed, for instance, in the pattern of savings behavior in different regions in Yugoslavia. Private savings in Slovenia and Macedonia are proportionally higher than in other regions or constituent republics. Although this behavior in Slovenia may be explained by the advanced level of economic development, this is not the case in Macedonia, which is one of the less well-developed republics. However, there exists ethnographic evidence of a greater propensity to save money in traditional Macedonian culture, even during the times of Turkish occupation (Rihtman-Auguštin 1971a:274–284).

Another example: an analysis of Yugoslav folk poetry devoted to the sea points to a differentiation of two value orientations — a continental one and a maritime one (Bošković-Stulli 1962:523–524). The former, characterized by a failure to understand the sea intimately, had a strong impact on the maritime policies of the country between the two world wars and after World War II.

Finally, the presence of traditional culture can be observed in conflicts over pasture land between a certain number of still-nomadic herdsmen and local peasants. Such conflicts were a regular feature of earlier periods, but even now they still occur every autumn and involve some modern institutions.[1]

It seems that evidence of this kind supports the hypothesis of a continual but implicit impact of traditional culture on everyday life in this country.

From the standpoint of explicit culture and its institutions, the problem appears somewhat different, but it can be perceived through the relationship between explicit and traditional culture. Various changes have occurred in the last thirty years and four different periods can be discerned. Since the relationship between explicit culture and traditional culture is of relevance in this discussion, brief sketches of those four periods are necessary.

1.   Although the impulse to oppose the enemy originated in the cities and in the Communist party, the stage of the drama of the National War of Liberation was rural. It can therefore be argued that the war was conducted within the framework of peasant culture patterns. One of the most important factors of partisan war is a more or less autarchically organized peasant economy. It so happened that peasant culture provided a most effective environment for the war of liberation.[2] To this, we should add the fact that the ideological program of the National War and of the national and social revolution was reinforced by traditional values

[1]   The problem was debated in the Croatian parliament in 1968 (Rihtman-Auguštin 1971b:4–6).
[2]   The same observation has been made by other anthropologists in cases of Algeria, China, and Vietnam, where partisan war was, or has been, conducted within the peasant sociocultural systems. Compare Marcin Zbigniew Kowalewsky's comment on the review article by G. Dalton, (1969:85, 86).

such as heroism, fighting spirit, and equality. Even the institutions organized in those days did not lack authenticity in the sense used by Lévi-Strauss (1958:400–401).

The period is documented in folk art with a considerable amount of oral prose and poetry conceived in the style, meter, and general form of traditional oral literature.

2.   Immediately after World War II, the first waves of rural migrations brought to the cities not only the revolutionary mentality but also this new cultural amalgamation. The direction of those migrations was not the usual one, from the village to the suburb and into industry. A specific kind of postwar urbanization brought rural immigrants to the centers of cities as representatives of new political and social power. A penetration of peasant culture patterns into the cities is again documented in folk art.

Kolo and other folk dances were performed in city streets and squares in those days by groups of young people and by professional groups. Folklore was highly valued as part of the national value-orientation.

3.   In the years 1950–1960, two groups of phenomena had a strong impact on the relationship between society and tradition. First, industrialization was in full swing, with the fastest rate of growth in the world at that time. Many predominantly young people from the rural parts of the country moved to cities for work and study. They shared one dominant value, which could be described as an urgent desire to get rid of the village spirit, to wipe out all traces of peasant origin, to become urbanized as soon as possible. The desire was reinforced by the ideology and the program of development, which did not, at that time, rely on agriculture. The second phenomenon was that of political centralism, which favored a unification of national and regional specific traits.

The devaluation of tradition was evident: everybody was ashamed of "traditional primitivism." Folklore and other expressions of folk life were labeled as reactionary; they were banned from cultural programs as incompatible with, or even detrimental to, economic development. Scientific institutions in the field of ethnology and folklore struggled simply to survive.

4.   The period beginning in the late 1960's is characterized by a democratization of social life. The self-management system, with its decentralization of political and social power, had revitalized tradition on national and local levels. On the other hand, market economy had made a strong impact on mass culture. Folklore tended to be treated as a particular kind of consumable good in the tourism and entertainment industries. *Folklorismus* became *ante portas*.[3] To this condition was added the general problem of value change. Thousands and thousands of rural migrants, lost in the lonely crowd of newly industrialized cities, were in search

---

[3]   *Folklorismus*, as defined by Hans Moser (1962:180) and Herman Bausinger (1969: *passim*, is a "second existence of folklore."

of values. They had abandoned the old ones as inadequate in their new lives, but they had no new values available for a new life. To many people tradition suddenly seemed to offer something that was firm and safe, a kind of familiar refuge. It is no wonder that the revitalization of tradition results sometimes in romantic glorification and sometimes in vulgar commercial forms.

The above delimitation of the four periods is not elaborate; a pedantic socioanthropological analysis would probably uncover more relevant details. Our purpose in this discussion, however, is simply to demonstrate the changing attitudes toward tradition: from very positive to the very negative and back again to the positive. The pendulum swings all the time: at its explicit levels, the sociocultural system cannot afford to be neutral regarding its own tradition. On its implicit levels, on the other hand, the flight from villages, conflicts with the old environment, mimicry in the cities, and, finally, identification with the new environment and its culture, as well as the search for one's roots in tradition, have resulted in a noteworthy social process, which will be discussed presently.

To digress first, however, it should be noted that although the aforementioned swing of the pendulum is commonplace, Yugoslav ethnology and folkloristics, not to mention the sociology of culture, have failed systematically to approach the problem. Caught in the vicious circle of their own changing position, these disciplines have lacked the strength to explicate, in an adequate manner, the latency of traditional culture as well as the imminence of *Folklorismus*.

The two exceptions, and in our opinion, turning points, are marked by an article on *Folklorismus* published in a journal devoted to workers' cultural action (Bošković-Stulli 1970) and a sociological paper on the links between traditional and mass culture in Slovenia (Kermauner 1970). The destiny of both papers is very illustrative. The article on *Folklorismus* was judged as something that had strayed by mistake into that cultural action journal. The paper on traditional and mass culture enjoyed a somewhat better fate: sociologists regarded it as a valuable piece of literature, though not as a scientifically sound contribution. Thus the relationship between tradition and contemporary life, between folk and mass culture, continues to be left to subjective individual evaluations and is not submitted to serious, scientific study.

In the meantime, in Yugoslavia we are witnessing a process known in other countries and analyzed by some ethnologists interested in present-day ethnology; wherein one meets the structure of folktales in films, comics, and other products in the entertainment industry. In television quiz programs, the atmosphere of popular riddles and games is renewed. Children and adults repeat advertising jingles.

A process of merging of the traditional and the mass culture into one has clearly begun. Various examples could be given to demonstrate that in mass culture, in a very selective and efficient way, some symbols and inner meanings now operate that were developed within the framework of traditional culture.[4] This can easily be explained by the function of mass culture in contemporary complex societies. We agree with the statement by Denzin:

> The legitimation of an art object (or artist) at any point in time gives individuals a point around which social relationships and images of self can be built. One's identity is, in part, established by his location on the shifting modalities of popular culture. One is "in" or "out" of fashion according to the actions he takes toward the legitimated features of his culture. Thus members of mass society must be constantly adding to their acquisitions of popular culture — an act which may go no further than the purchasing of every new record produced by a popular artist (1970:1037–1038).

A new identity is built on the basis of a combination of old folklore patterns and a pattern of European popular culture.

The national television network used to run a long-time quiz series, *Malo ja, malo ti*, in which married couples were invited to participate. Structurally, it was a combination of various riddles and games of traditional, more or less folkloristic provenance and a modern quiz, constructed according to a western European or United States model. A deep knowledge of any topic was not required; the audience was quite satisfied when the participants proved to be at all skilled or clever. Critics sometimes worried about the low level of knowledge displayed by the participants, but this did not disturb the audience at all. The audience believed that it was not knowledge but good luck that was decisive. It was evident that the audience did not like some of the more successful participants, people who, in their opinion, had earned too much money in the quiz. A young man of exceptional intelligence, who seemed to be interested in money, found no sympathy in the audience when he was finally defeated. Charity donations from the participants were welcomed. Both these facts seem to point to a dominant national value — that of egalitarianism, which some sociologists argue is the dominant value orientation of contemporary Yugoslav society (Županov 1970).

One other kind of television program that attracts massive audiences is a show written and performed in dialect. It makes no difference whether the dialect originates from a small community or from a broad region: such serials or programs are welcomed in all parts of the country. It seems that the new heterogeneity resulting from the great rural-urban migrations makes for a better understanding of various culture patterns. Moreover, there are folkloristic characters with whom one easily iden-

---

[4] Most critics, on the contrary, are of the opinion that mass culture in Yugoslavia is a pure import from the East or the West. This conclusion is true only in part.

tifies. *Long, Hot Summer*, a United States serial broadcast in Yugoslavia a few years ago, also deserves to be mentioned here, along with its hero, Ben Quick. The success of the serial in Yugoslavia was unique. Nowhere else in the world did the program or its hero, played by an actor of quite average capabilities, achieve such popularity.

Ben Quick, a poor boy, lived through a series of black-and-white situations: he was honest and courageous, and he fought against the rich and evil. This is the structure of a folktale, of course. What won the hero nationwide popularity in Yugoslavia was his origin and his behavior. A farm boy, not unlike thousands of Yugoslav peasant boys he behaved as if he were a rebel: he fought against the local authorities, against those who were rich and in positions of power. The rebellious features of his temperament and his peasant origin fit well into the traditional cultural pattern, and therein we find the secret of his exceptional success.

In analyzing one more phenomenon in mass culture, one finds that the most popular figure in Slovene comics is not the clever and resourceful fox called Zvitorepec but, rather, the wolf Lakotnik, "who is interested above all in good food. All other personalities regard him as an ignorant and naive person. But, ignorant as he is, the wolf succeeds in everthing!" (Zupan 1970:28). Simpleminded and brave, he manages to defeat some strong, authoritarian personalities, feats that bring him great popularity. That type of personality is not unknown in folkloristic tradition and therein may lie the roots of his contemporary popularity.

All the above examples show the everyday presence of traditional culture, which operates as a selector in various situations of contemporary mass culture. They prove also the existence of an interaction of various cultural factors on an implicit level.

In much the same way, the relationship between traditional folklore and contemporary mass culture could be discussed on an explicit level. The process of the transformation of traditional folklore is emerging as an explicit fact and different levels of transformation could be presented as a continuum. A tentative classification of transformation levels might be:

1. Folklore living in its original expressions.
2. Folklore living its second existence — *Folklorismus* — and changing in several ways until finally transformed into and adopted by mass culture on several levels.
   a. Traditional forms adapting themselves to modern media without losing their original artistic integrity.
   b. Traditional folkloristic expressions losing many, if not all, of their original traits, and then, as "new folk," appearing on the market of modern mass culture.
3. Folklore as an inspiration in all kinds of cultural activity offering to modern art its motives, rhythms, content, and ideas.

Folklore living in its original expression (point 1) is demonstrated in those regions of Yugoslavia where folk art still lives in its original forms. Many modern publications, as well as unpublished research material with contemporary oral prose, poetry, music, and dance, testify to the contemporary existence of authentic peasant folk art created according to the rules and structures of older folk production. In small and rather closed communities where such production is going on, mass culture has not yet penetrated. Although the number of those communities is rapidly diminishing, and although ethnologists and folklorists are worried about the danger of their disappearance, the fact remains that at the moment they still exist and produce.

Folklore in its second existence (point 2) poses a problem of its own that is not unique to Yugoslavia. This problem was well known in other European countries, and it will be known in all developing countries in Asia, Africa, and in the Americas. Although it is a problem of modern times, it is not a new problem, having been registered in Austria and in Switzerland since the eighteenth century.

The point is that small peasant communities where folklore was created, with their primitive technology, including the technology of musical instruments and the technology of communication, are disappearing in the modern world. Radio, television, films, and records are used to distribute messages. As those small communities disappear, folklore is changing to mass culture and has to satisfy new requirements of technology and the rules of a specific market. The moment of direct transformation is achieved in various ways and with different methods. Many of these methods are not approved by experts; an educated ear or eye can hardly accept them: critics are unanimous in their condemnation of new forms, if they find them worthy of discussion at all.

Some illustrations are needed of the two levels of the transformation of folklore mentioned above. Traditional forms adapt themselves without losing integrity (point 2a) when forms of traditional folklore are transmitted by the modern mass media without adaptation or with a minimum of adaptation. Such is the case of Dalmatian singing groups called *klape*. Informally organized peer groups of young men traditionally used to meet in small towns on the coast. For several springs, summers, or autumns, they sang in the squares, in the streets, under the window of a local beauty, or in the local inn. It often happened during World War II that such groups, together with their guitars, disappeared during the night to appear again as partisans. The songs that these groups sang were peculiar combinations of peasant folk tunes from the continent and the Mediterranean area.

After the war, the groups virtually disappeared; changes affecting the country affected small towns, too. Only rarely would one hear a tune and catch a glimpse of a group of singing Dalmatian students. In recent years, however, *klape* have been revived and brought to television, bringing "old" nostalgia and introducing some newer tunes and habits. Critics who express resentment over the "new look" and the new tunes of the old *klape* forget that had it not been for television, the people would have only memories of such Dalmatian singing groups. The atmosphere and mentality of small communities have changed; the local beauty is interested in becoming a student or in taking part in a beauty contest, and all the music she needs she can get from the radio or television. In the local inn, of course, a jukebox offers a more interesting choice of songs. Even the boys have changed their attitude toward how they spend their time; they have jobs to do.

In this case television has played an important role in reviving a particular form of folk art. Traditional forms are not neglected. Only some minor adaptation to a new medium has occurred.

That traditional folkloristic expressions lose many, if not all, of their original traits (point 2b) is demonstrated by "new folk" music which consists of a series of newly composed songs. The composers are more or less skilled and qualified people. Some are urban, others — the more successful ones — are urban with a folk background. Texts are banal: they describe the happiness of someone getting a new apartment or the misery of someone leaving for work in a foreign country. A more or less vivid connection with the tradition can be traced in the melodies of "new folk," in its texts, or in a combination of both.

New folksongs are extremely popular. Records are sold in hundreds of thousands of copies, always more copies by far than other popular and commercial music. The performers of new folk are leading personalities in commercial entertainment and mass culture. They have clubs and fans. Even skilled and professional jazz and other popular musicians are unable to compete with new folk performers. When new folk is performed in Germany and other European countries for Yugoslav migrant workers, it provokes tears, sighs, and nostalgia of a more intense kind than any other type of art or genuine folklore.

Even with the most benevolent attitude and a desire to be as objective as possible, it is very difficult to say anything good regarding the quality of new folk music. Critics and experts, as a rule, blame producers and distributors of new folk music for lack of honesty and professional conscience, accusing them of unfairness in business and of only seeking profits.

What is the secret of success of new folk? A parallel analysis of original folk texts and those of new folk, as well as a comparison of tradition and new folk music, may give an answer to this question. A tentative comparison of texts brings out the following points:

First, in the case of original folk texts, the real world is transposed into artistic expression through the experience of many generations and the use of condensed artistic sensation. Second, in the case of new folk, the emphasis is laid on a blueprint for an affluent society. In the struggle to achieve success in the society of consumption, some old tunes are given a new shape, some traditional words, phrases, and figures are seen as perhaps the only source of badly needed security, a reminiscence of something true and firm that existed in the past. These important features are sometimes hidden in a clumsy rhythm, in a combination of old and new elements in the melody, in the rhyme. No one can be certain precisely where these features are located, but they do exist, and they evoke a sense of tradition without actually being traditional. Moreover, it is the much debated modern form of new folk that provides the warranty of "being in fashion," which, as has been pointed out, in a path toward new personal integrity.

As far as folklore is an inspiration (point 3), not only in mass culture but also in contemporary national art, it is difficult to say now whether this aspect of folk art has been pursued in the appropriate way. Since the beginning of the twentieth century, the atmosphere among intellectuals and artists has varied from the romantic adoration of folklore to its total rejection as a possible source of art. This attitude has some links to the "swing of the pendulum" in the evaluation of traditional culture, but it also has its own motives, such as the impact of Western art in the education of artists. It is only in recent years that a generation of artists who approach folklore critically and with greater objectivity seems to be emerging. Some film and theater performances built on an atmosphere of folk culture and folklore seem, after all, to bring the public and critics closer together.

This discussion of the relationship between traditional culture, folklore, and mass culture in Yugoslavia has pointed to the complexity of forms and structures. Many of those forms, structures, and relationships have not been studied yet. Structures of new folk are unknown and remain a challenge for the modern folklorist. The cultural and folkloristic laboratory in Yugoslavia is very rich, containing specimens at each level of the continuum and many changing forms and phenomena in between.

REFERENCES

BAUSINGER, HERMANN
  1969   Kritik der tradition [Critique of tradition]. *Zeitschrift für Volkskunde*
          65/II:232–250.
BOŠKOVIĆ-STULLI, MAJA
  1962   Pormorska tematika u našoj narodnoj književnosti [Nautical themes in
          our national literature]. *Pomorski zbornik* 1:505–536.
  1970   O suvremenom folklorizmu [On contemporary folklorism]. *Kulturni
          Radnik* 5:45–66.

DALTON, G.
1969   Issues in economic anthropology, *Current Anthropology* 10:85, 86.

DENZIN, K. NORMAN
1970   Problems in analyzing elements of mass culture: notes on the popular song and other artistic productions. *American Journal of Sociology* 75:1035–1038.

KERMAUNER, TARAS
1970   Masovna kultura kao rodeno mada nepriznato čedo tradicionalne kulture [Mass culture as an unrecognized result of traditional culture]. *Kultura i razvoj jugoslovenskog društva*, passim.

LÉVI-STRAUSS, CLAUDE
1958   *Anthropologie structurale* [Structural anthropology]. Paris: Plon.

MOSER, HANS
1962   Vom *Folklorismus* in unserer Zeit [From *Folklorismus* in our time]. *Zeitschrift für Volkskunde* 58:177–209.

RIHTMAN-AUGUŠTIN, DUNJA
1971a Stednja-jedan uvid u motivacije i globalne orijentacije [Saving-one type of motivation and global orientation]. *Ekonomiski pregled* 5–6: 270–298.

1971b Položaj tradicionalne kulture u suvremenom društvu [Status of traditional culture in contemporary society]. *Narodna umjetnost* 8:3–17.

ZUPAN, FRANCE
1970   Masovna Kultura-strip [Mass culture-strip]. *Kultura* 2:23–56.

ŽUPANOV, JOSIP
1970   Egalitarizam i industrijalizam [Egalitarianism and industrialism]. *Naše teme* 2:237–295.

Folklore and Industrialism

Tourist Archeofolklore in Greece

DEMETRIOS LOUKATOS

In Greece there has always been a tendency to recall the life of the nation's ancestors, be it in architecture and performances of mythological subjects, in symbols and proper names of societies and schools, or in artistic creations. This tendency has become especially pronounced since Grecian independence in 1830. It has been most evident among the upper classes and the intelligentsia, but it nonetheless has attracted the attention of the lower classes, who like mythology and plays with legendary themes.

One could add that the idea of the 1821 uprising was itself promoted by a recollection of the glorious events and characters of ancient Greece. Already in 1796, in the first imaginary map of a free Greece, printed in Vienna by the learned martyr Rigas Feraeos, many names and figures of gods, mythological scenes, and ancient sites were printed and then popularized (Ubicini 1881; Branoussis 1954; Laios 1960). During this period, the ambitious practice of engraving characters of antiquity on weapons and ornaments, especially such heroes and warrior gods and goddesses as Athene, Heracles, and Alexander the Great, also prevailed.

The movement that promoted a neoclassical architecture in the country (at the time of the reconstruction of Athens, from 1834 onward) influenced the people of the towns and villages, who liked to decorate their humble dwellings with elements drawn in the old style, such as the pediments and the columns much loved by the Greeks (Biris 1938). Furthermore, after independence, the streets of the Greek capital and of other cities were given names recalling the Hellenic past, a fact that is still true today in every new town and settlement.

Throughout the nineteenth century, the ancient legends continued to nourish the nation's hope for a total liberation of every region, and in consequence of this emotion, the figure of Alexander the Great, conqueror and avenger, was elevated to an imposing position in legends and in the presentations of the popular theater (Loukatos 1958; Zora 1960).

With the advent of archeological excavations (begun in 1831–1833), the opening of museums, and the publication of illustrated history books, Greek knowledge of its ancient civilization broadened, and a rich, artistic creativity from sculpture to weaving developed. Young girls learned to embroider mythological themes or motifs, and a painter of the primitive school, Theophilos (1866–1934), decorated the walls of cafes and inns with ancient characters and scenes (Tsarouhis 1966; Makris 1939). The imitation of classical architecture and sculpture even reached the neo-Hellenic cemeteries, many of which offer great possibilities for study (particularly at Athens, Syros, Andros, Argostoli, and others).

The public's psychology concerning the ancient life and the use of its representational elements has changed greatly, especially since 1927, when the first Festival of Ancient Greek Theater, combined with an exhibition of neo-Hellenic art, was organized in Delphi (on the initiative of the Greek poet Anghelos Sikelocnos and his American wife, the scholar Eva Palmer-Sikelianou).[1] Contact with these elements of costumes, jewels, names, scenes, words, as well as the opportunity to wear similar clothes oneself, or to use archeological motifs in a new art form, has promoted an enhanced familiarity with the life of the ancient Greeks. This Greek awareness was followed by the international tourist boom. The Delphi Festivals have been expanded into huge summer festivals in Athens, Epidaurus, Philippi, Dodona, and elsewhere, and the first exhibition of Greek popular art gave birth to the tourist-trade shops of today.

It is for today's tourist clientele, so numerous and insatiable, that the skilled Greek craftworkers have searched through reviews and books or examined actual objects for classical motifs that can be used in salable reproductions. The National Organization of Hellenic Handicrafts (EOEX) came to their assistance and still provides them with directions and designs inspired by authentic ancient art forms.[2]

Thus today, in the tourist stores and in the shops and stalls near archeological sites, one finds, besides the usual souvenirs, all sorts of archaic objects and ornaments that one would have thought were made for the people of an ancient time. Today, all the branches of the Greek tourist trade offer, in addition to their specimens from the ethnographic life of the country, a variety of archeologically inspired objects, a real

[1]   In 1967, nos. 103–107 of *EOS* (Illustrated Monthly Review) were dedicated to Eva Palmer-Sikelianou. These issues appeared in Greek and English.

[2]   *EOEX* has issued, at this writing, the following publications pertinent to the artisans' work: *Greek Decorative Motifs*, vol. 1 (Athens, 1961); *Greek Decorative Motifs*, vol. 2 (Athens, 1965); *Greek Ornament*, 2nd ed. (Athens, 1972); *Quality*, nos. 1–17 (1968–1972).

"archeofolklore", inspired by the mythology, art, and ethnography of the ancient Greeks. All the branches of Greek craftsmanship — pottery, metallurgy, jewelry, plastic arts, sculpture, woodworking, painting, weaving, embroidery, tapestry, ornamentation, posters — are represented. Indeed, one might also think that the ancient divine patrons of these crafts, Athene-Ergane and Hephaestus, were once again watching over the work.

One may speak here of a self-perpetuating circle: as the tourists' demand for souvenirs increases, the more inspired and productive the craftsworkers become; the more they produce, the more the tourists buy. Of course, one must be aware of the abuses that commercialization provokes and also of the bad taste so often evident in some arbitrary sales articles. All too frequently, the ancient symbols lose their original significance and become mere decorations. One sees, for example, motifs of ancient vases woven into a peasant bag, the head of Athena sculpted onto a paperweight, Achilles's chariot engraved on a snuffbox, and Poseidon's trident embroidered on a bathing suit.

This phenomenon of commercialization is international and is seen in every country that can display an ancient civilization (Marinus 1958:43–63; Dorson 1972:43; Roberts 1972:238). Visitors like to relive the atmosphere of ancient cultures, and the indigenous populations take advantage of this. In this situation, the tourist movement has multiplied relations not only among peoples but among epochs. Everything becomes a mixture of cultural elements, from clothing and fashions to commercial insignia and hotels, all of which refer to names and sites from the "national" past.

In Greece, where the ancient culture seems to belong to every native as well as to every tourist who visits the Acropolis, the imitation of the past is especially evident. At first, there were a few intellectuals, Greeks and foreigners (particularly women), who enjoyed dressing like the ancients and walking the streets of Athens as if they were fellow-citizens of Pericles. Now everyone wants to wear something from the ancient dress — sandals, a draped skirt, a belt with a chiseled buckle, a pendant with the head of Apollo or Artemis, a shirt bordered in the Athenian fashion, bracelets in the form of snakes, Mycenaean spiral rings, or earrings *à la* Cleopatra. One is no longer surprised to meet in the streets of Athens or on the highways and boats of Greece travelers who wear this type of costume and jewelry quite simply and negligently, as if they had just emerged from an ancient fairground. It is, therefore, on the basis of the "biological" behavior, so to speak, of Greeks and foreigners alike that one can consider all this a living archeofolklore. I include in this grouping the people who manufacture the articles, those who buy them, the people who wear them, and even the articles themselves because of their function in the life of the people and their new status as modern necessities.

So, several factors have influenced this psychology of folklorization of ancient objects and designs. These include:

1.   Direct knowledge of the objects and culture of ancient Greece has been promoted through group visits to museums and archeological sites. Particularly when one stands before the showcases of the museums, which display these objects in a very attractive manner (for example, the Mycenaean room of the Athens Archeological Museum), the desire to dress in the same way or wear jewelry of the same type becomes an archeofolkloric temptation.

2.   The fashion houses and the important jewelers of Athens strengthen this desire by copying clothing and jewelry from the museums and by creating a demand for them. The EOEX does the same thing by presenting archeofolkloric adaptions in exhibitions and periodicals.

3.   Tourists are always looking for souvenirs to take home from the countries they visit as proof of their trip abroad. These souvenirs must be as representative as possible of the historical and cultural atmosphere of the country visited; and, since authentic specimens are unobtainable, the tourists must make do with copies and imitations, the value of which depends on their price.

4.   Visitors to archeological sites and ruins are, in a sense, pilgrimages; one glance at what happens everyday beneath the entrance to the Acropolis of Athens is adequate confirmation. The people climb toward it in silence; they look up reverently at the lofty height of the columns; then they stop, quite moved, before the sight of the Parthenon. When they reach it, they touch the marble with pious gentleness; they lean against the "sacred" columns (a good chance for a photo); they meditate; then they descend its stairs, again in silence, to the adjacent museum, where another pilgrimage, to the statues of the well-dressed *Kores* [maidens] and the scenes from the frieze of the Parthenon, detains them. The whole visit is made in a magical and archaic atmosphere. Even people who know nothing of the history or the importance of the Acropolis let themselves be "sanctified" by the simple fact that they have seen it.

Near the exit of any archeological site, small markets offer all sorts of articles and photographs reproducing the monuments and objects just seen. Thus, as visitors to the Acropolis leave, they buy some "religious" souvenirs, irrespective of their quality, or else they take a pebble, if they are allowed to do so or a flower from the ground, much as they would have bought a little cross or a little flower from the grotto at Lourdes.

5.   Nowadays young people like to dress freely and arbitrarily. Negligence in dress is nothing other than a movement for freedom.[3] Young tourists in Greece find an excellent opportunity to combine freedom of dress with the charm of ancient Greek clothing. Girls, in particular, satisfy

---

[3]   Earlier generations found the same opportunity during Carnival, when they could dress as they pleased, but today one can do this year-round without embarrassment.

their love of elegance with attractive imitations of the clothing, hairstyles, and jewelry of the ancient Greeks, and they are proud to stroll through the archeological sites with the gait of a Spartan. It should be observed that the notions of young foreigners concerning the ancient Greeks, their mythology, and their way of life are much more poetic and inspiring than those of Greek youth.

6.   In Greek public and commercial life there had always been a tendency to use names and titles taken from antiquity for streets, industrial enterprises, scientific societies, bookstores, and high schools, as well as for the motifs on postage stamps and coins. But with the tourist boom, businesses and trades have tried even more to adapt themselves to the enthusiasm for antiquity, and they choose their names and symbols (their insignia and titles) from among the ancient gods, sages, and artists, and from mythological places. Hence most of the hotels, agencies, cafes, movie theaters, and fashion or antique shops bear names recalling antiquity that are designed to attract customers and allow their imagination to journey into the glorious and romantic past of the country. It could be added that almost every boat that makes summer trips across the Aegean Sea has a name borrowed from Greek mythology: Adonis, Aeolus, Alkyone, Aphrodite, Apollo, Atalanta, Helle, Hermes, Jason, Kydon, Minos, Mycenae, Naiad, Odysseus, Orpheus, Pegasus, Poseidon, Zeus.

7.   With the aid of magazines and posters, the official tourist board (The National Department of Greek Tourism) does all it can to draw attention to every aspect of archeology potentially attractive to both foreigners and Greeks (note also its initiative since 1959 to present in front of the Acropolis a *son et lumiere* show that is both educational and impressive). At the same time, the great festivals of Epidaurus, Athens, and other cities — dating from 1955 — revitalize the archeofolklore movement in the country so that the names, actions, and songs from the plays performed are sometimes repeated in a "folkloric" way by the people.

All this is very pleasant. In our modern society, so anxious and so confined within its material preoccupations, it is comforting to see people, especially the young, coming out into the fresh air of Greek antiquity and looking for sources of pleasure in its culture and lifestyle.

A few words must also be written on the work of contemporary Greek craftworkers and its adaptation to the archeofolklore movement. The origins, locations, and development of Greek craftsmanship receive an interesting treatment in the work of folklorist Angélique Hajimihali (1895–1965). In *L'art populaire grec*, the author speaks of a "*mouvement en faveur de l'art populaire, commencé en 1921*" [movement towards popular art, begun in 1921] (1937:45–46). On the subject of archeofolklore, one reads that already in 1900, a native ceramist, Nicolas Rodios, had set up his own workshop on the Isle of Skopolos to produce earthenware articles resembling the pottery of ancient Greece *"tant par la forme que par la finesse du travail"*[as much in its form as in the excellence of the work] (1937:38). Similarly, one reads that the society of potters, Keramikos, founded in 1920, decorated its vases with motifs *"pris à la Grèce antique* [taken from Greek antiquity]" (1937:37). And as for weaving, *"Un centre professionnel d'art textile a été créé (vers 1925, en Crète) sous la firme 'Diplous Pélekys'* [Double Hache] [a professional center for textile arts was created (*circa* 1925, in Crete) by the firm named 'Double Hache']" (1937:22) — whose title and designs were inspired by the Minoan epoch.

To a large extent, all branches of Greek popular art today take their inspiration from antique subjects, and, in the spirit of this movement, all craftworkers create with an enthusiasm that matches their profits. All over Athens and in the other towns of Greece, one has only to look at the windows of shops and stores, operated not only for the tourists but also for local customers, from the jeweler's shop to the bakery, to find the "ancient Greek" element, on cloth and metal, on plaster and clay, on boxes and wrapping paper. At the wharves of the large ports — Piraeus, Phaleron, and elsewhere — each time the sailors of a foreign fleet disembark, one sees the picturesque exhibition of statuettes of gods, goddesses, heroes, and mythological scenes set out on the ground or on benches. White in color, made of alum or plaster, and sold very cheaply, these statuettes educate the sailors in the mythology of the country and provide a form of local color just as popular as the *evzones*. These same "archeological" objects are also sold in shops, along with objects of popular art. The sale of the statuettes, which began after the exhibition-festival at Delphi in 1927, again stresses the folkloric nature of all these examples of antiquity.

In Athens I paid a visit to the workshop of an engraver of insignia and molds for goldsmiths. There I found a number of albums and illustrated books — museum catalogs, archeological reviews, prospectuses, prints, and newspapers — containing drawings and pictures of every object and figure from Greek antiquity, from vases to coins. I was told that an interested client looks for the motif he or she prefers or else asks the engravers for advice. In Delphi, I have also watched a vase being decorated with mythological designs. In one of the numerous Greek arts shops, an artist who painted ceramics would first show the customers several books with illustrations of ancient Greek vases, as well as a choice of unpainted vases; and as soon as he had received an order, he would reproduce with remarkable skill the requested design.

All the branches of contemporary popular art find their motifs for archaic ornamentation in books (published in Greece or abroad), in posters, or from photographs and archeological postcards. The craftsmen examine each example very carefully, and constantly enrich their imagination. But at the same time the considered advice of the National Organization of Hellenic Handicrafts has since 1958 guided the artisans' work by furnishing them with motifs and designs, of both past and present tradition. I should mention here its series of publications, *Greek Ornament*, which displays decorative motifs from Minoan and Cycladic art as well as the later classical, Byzantine and neo-Hellenic styles. Also the review *Quality* (1968–present) has presented every possible application of archaic designs to modern art and life.

The mixture of antique and neo-Hellenic motifs especially appeals to the general public, a fact evidenced in the furnishings of the ordinary people's houses; the public accepts, with its traditional openness, everything that the designers, publicists, and humorists present.

One characteristic example of the "folklorization" of ancient life is the parody made of it in modern songs ("The gods descend to drink resin-wine at Plaka"), in the mural paintings of the taverns and also on current postcards. Jupiter can be seen watching television, Neptune being cosseted by beautiful Sirens, Bacchus drinking *ouzo*, and Mercury selling "Greek art" to Americans. I might add that the carnival celebrations in Greece and, more recently, Greek films often feature burlesque performances, whose subjects are taken from ancient mythology and literature.

All this — and all else that could be mentioned or shown in photography — in my opinion, constitutes archeofolklore, a segment of contemporary urban folklore that ought to be studied further. In general, although everything we borrow from another culture in order to complement or replace our own folk customs becomes an aspect of folklore, this phenomenon of retrospective borrowing, stimulated by tourism, is motivated by elements that are as much historical and cultural as they are social. In our comfortable lives, saturated with every element of contemporary culture (including recent tradition), we are gratified to look for "new" ideas in the lives of our ancestors. This attention to ancient life also seems to lead to a more natural and a freer vision of life, as reflected in the past, and probably occurs in other countries with important ancient civilizations. The attention paid to the life and culture of the ancient Greeks offers, at the same time, a return to a world of artistic and spiritual equilibrium, well suited to alleviating the anxieties of modern society.

REFERENCES

BIRIS, COSTAS
1938   *Athenian studies*. Athens.
BRANOUSSIS, LEANDER
1954   *Rigas*, number 10. Athens: Bassiki Library.

DORSON, RICHARD M.
   1972   "Concepts of folklore and folklife studies" in *Folklore and folklife: an introduction*. Edited by Richard M. Dorson. Chicago: University of Chicago Press.
HAJIMIHALI, ANGÉLIQUE
   1937   *L'art populaire grec* [Popular Greek art]. Athens: Pyrsos.
LAIOS, GEORGE
   1960   "The Maps of Rigas." *Deltion of the Historical and Ethnological Society of Greece* 14:231–312.
LOUKATOS, DEMETRIOS
   1958   "La tradition et la vie populaire grecques dans les représentations de Karaghiozis" [Greek tradition and popular life in the representations of Karaghiozis] in *Quand les mariennettes du monde se donnent la main* [When the marionnettes of the world shake hands], 232–244. Belgium: Musée de Liège.
MAKRIS, KITSOS
   1939   *The painter Theophilos at Pelion*. Volos.
MARINUS, ALBERT
   1958   *Essais sur la tradition* [Essays on tradition]. Brussels: Moens.
ROBERTS, WARREN E.
   1972   "Folk crafts" in *Folklore and folklife: an introduction*. Edited by Richard M. Dorson. Chicago: University of Chicago Press.
TSAROUHIS, G.
   1966   *Theophilos*. Athens: Commercial Bank of Greece.
UBICINI, A.
   1881   La grande carte de la Grèce par Rhigas [The great map of Greece by Rhigas]. *Revue de Géographie* 8:241–259; 9:9–25.
ZORA, POPI
   1960   The Siren (*gorgona*) in Greek popular art. *Parnassos* 2:331–365.

Syllogisms of Association: Some Modern Extensions of Asturian Deepsong

JAMES W. FERNANDEZ

This paper will examine some aspects of a variety of folksong, the *Asturianada*, which is still very much alive in Asturian mountain municipalities. In particular, we will account for the unexpected persistence of this genre among the miners. The municipality of Aller, in which most of these songs can be heard, extends from the divide fronting with Castilla (Puerto de San Isidro at 1,530 meters in altitude) to the mining town of Moreda (at 298 meters), 46 kilometers to the northwest. This valley is one of those in the south central Asturias that have come to be known as the "Cuencas Mineras." The northern half of the municipality from the county seat, Cabanaquinta, to the line with the *concejo* of Mieres, has been devoted to deep mining of bituminous coal since the late nineteenth century; but, as is characteristic of Asturian miners, most men who work the mines still hold on to land. What cows they are able to keep graze in abundance in green meadows in the heart of the mining zone.

Cattle keeping is an ancient cultural pattern in Asturias, and the burden of hay making in the summer months falls in varying degrees on all valley dwellers. During the hay making months, the mines go into reduced production — the inescapable acquiesence of coal to grass. In the upper reaches of the valley, cattle keeping is still dominant, though miners may be found in all seventeen villages and towns that make up the *concejo*. In the upper valley villages, a transhumant life is still prevalent. The cattle are moved in May (and stay through October) to graze in the

The deepsong discussed in this paper was heard either by my wife or me in the municipality of Aller. However, it is surely not exclusive to this locale. Songs recorded at the provincial championships of 1971 are also discussed, as are those in the collection of E. M. Torner (1920). We are indebted to the National Science Foundation for their support of the research on comparative culture change in the Asturian mountains. I have also benefited from the comments made on this paper by Richard Detwiler, Sidney Kasfir, and Juan Noriega.

high public pastures and divide-plateaus (*paramos*) so typical of the Cantabrian range. In former days, one or two family members accompanied the cattle until the end of the hay season, when they were joined in the rough stone *caserias* by the entire family. In recent years, however, the time spent by families in the *caserias* has been much reduced because so many family members are miners who can devote themselves only to the haying but not the herding. There is more commuting back and forth from the village than before. Children have to be sent down in mid-September for schooling. There is still nostalgia for life under the peaks, but as more and more conveniences come into village life, extended sojourns in the uplands carry with them a sense of deprivation by comparison with village life.

One has to speak of a tension between two lifestyles that is present in every village, in many families and, often enough, in individuals. It is one thing to drive cattle to upland meadows to fatten them for a fall market; it is another thing to descend for daily wages into the depths of the earth. The former is a family-centered way of life, and though arrangements for herding may be made with other families, responsibility for one's cattle always rests finally within various generations of the family. In the miner's life, the male working bond is more important. Although it is rare for that bond to extend beyond four or five work companions in any truly effective way, there is a general sense of solidarity among Asturian miners. This, in part, accounts for the chronic strike situation that has long prevailed in the Asturian mines — even though, since the Spanish Civil War, the miners view themselves as having no labor organization that truly represents their interests. It is relatively easy to prevail upon Asturian miners to strike in their own interests, but it would be difficult, if not impossible, to prevail upon any cattle keeper (*ganadero*) to strike. This family-centeredness and unwillingness to cooperate in the interests of improvement of breed, prices, or conditions of marketing has been the despair of many a forward-looking veterinarian.

Many reasons account for the difference in solidarity between the two lifestyles. The family-centeredness of the cattle keeper's life carries with it the age-old enmity among families who are, in a sense, competing for scarce goods in a situation of relatively high human and cattle density. It carries with it all the enmities of generations of family interaction. The miner's life is no doubt subject to class-structure analysis. The miners are not really competing with each other in the exploitation of scarce resources, rather, they are thrown into a subterranean cooperation against what, in their view, is a superfluous class of well-off managers and owners who rarely descend into the mines. When the miner returns to the surface after his arduous and dangerous labor, his resentment is inevitably aroused by his contact with the clean-faced men who organize, manage, and, in some ways, own him, and who yet have had no part in his dark feats of production. By contrast, when the cattle keeper returns to the village from the high pastures, the warmth of his homecoming is mottled by his having to pass people to whom, for many reasons, he and his own family do not even nod their heads. Up in the mountain pastures during the day, the very strict stone demarcations of the *minifundia* landscape keep families apart more than they bring them together. Good stone fences keep neighbors in their place; they do not necessarily make good and helpful neighbors. These fences constantly remind one of family property, but they do not suggest interfamily solidarities. Farther up in the mountains, where herds graze in common on public lands, there is some collective herding and interfamily solidarity, yet the familism of the valley reasserts itself in quarrels over the size of herds and limited grazing resources. There is a solidarity in life in the mountain heights for the cattle keeper, yet the familism of the valley is the predominant mood. The solidarity of the mines is at odds with the familialism of the valleys, but it is not overcome by it. Miners are easily inspired to collective sentiments beyond the family; cattle keepers are not. Asturian deepsong plays an important role in that inspiration.

There are many kinds of social science analyses — economic, socio-structural, and political — that must be brought to bear upon the differences between miner and cattle keeper. Wage and class-structure differences alone may be sufficient explanations for many of the frictions. Yet these analytical categories are all epiphenomenal insofar as the Asturian villagers are concerned, and I believe that no explanations can be made that fail to allow for what is real experience for the miners and the cattle keepers: a tradition of song and verse that is still very much alive as a primary activity despite the overlay of newspaper, television, and dance hall culture now present in even the most isolated hamlet. In the solidarity and divisiveness of this song and verse, one may no doubt see other structures reflected. Songs and verses may not be final causes of interpersonal relations, but they are surely efficient causes for the way cattle keepers and miners represent their situation to themselves.

What I specifically propose to examine is the way the men and women of these Asturian mining valleys extend themselves into the lyrics of their deepsongs — lyrics that are, on the whole, quite short and simple. By using the term *extension*, I refer to that fundamental mechanism in the problem-solving process by which persons take experience from one domain, where it is more concretely apprehended and more easily conceptualized, and use it as a model for a domain of greater abstraction and much fuzzier and more ambiguous perception. In the expressive life, this extension takes the form of metaphoric and metonymic predications upon the various inchoate pronouns of social life (Fernandez 1970; 1972; 1974). Such predications instill qualities in pronouns when they, as subjects, are brought into association with the objects of predication.

What are the qualities predicated upon or associated with the various Asturian pronouns as a consequence of the singing of these songs? There is an important problem of modernization involved, for deepsong has remained very contemporary — very modern! How has it managed to do so when other folklore has failed? How has a song largely rooted in an agricultural and pastoral world become also the favored song of miners?

THE SURVIVAL OF DEEPSONG

As is everywhere the case, the Austurian mountain countryfolk have suffered the inroads of mass communications and mass amusements. Men and women used to memorize long historical romances in verse. In any village, people can be found who can still recite these poems for hours on end. The poems largely had a nineteenth-century locus, such as the wars in Morocco or the Carlist Rebellion. But the didactic and entertaining functions of these recitations have been appropriated — for those many whose reading still does not enable them to take to the paperback novel — by the serial *novelas* and the dramatized twentieth-century newsreels (*Espana Siglo XX*) on television.

There was also a rich lyrical tradition in courtship songs and the lyrics accompanying the variety of folk dances; the characteristic Asturian *Giraldillas*, the *bailes de pandero* of the *vaqueiros de Alzada*, the *bailes de los pollos* were typical.

In E. M. Torner's classic collection *Cancionero musical de la lirica popular Asturiana* (1920), more than half of the lyrics collected — 261 of 500 — are associated with dances. The greatest proportion of these, 182, are lyrics for the Asturian *Giraldilla*. These songs and dances are no longer popularly maintained — they are defunct in the villages — though the Spanish National Movement is making valiant efforts through its feminine section to keep them alive. They have been replaced by the pop music of the village dance halls (*las pistas*), which, though an old institution in the cities of Asturias, do not date beyond the 1930's in the *pueblos* and *aldeas*, and are really a development of the postwar period.

The rich repertoire of courtships songs (*canciones de Ronda*)[1] is also much depleted and scarcely heard today because young men no longer form singing groups and spend their evenings courting in other villages. Village girls now attend school for four or five years and, with their new reading skills, have turned from the folklore of such itinerant courtship to the *fotonovelas* — jejune accounts in many pictures and few words of pubescent intrigue. These days young men and young women congregate

---

[1]   Forty-nine of the songs in the Torner collection were specifically labeled *de ronda* by his informants. One hundred and eighty-four songs in the collection were not labeled, but of this number ninety-two would also seem to be of this usage.

weekly in the steamy hubbub of the overcrowded dance halls — hardly a lyrical arena, whatever other fancies may be titillated.

As the villages have experienced decentering — the failure to maintain themselves as the focus of life for their inhabitants — so also have those songs of communal labor vanished, whether in the interest of village improvement (*sextiferia*), or in group labor in the fields (*andecha*). Like the folk dances, they once celebrated a community spirit beyond the family.

Nevertheless, deepsong maintains its strength in these mountain communities. By Asturian deepsong[2] I mean that highly personalized song, also called *Asturianada* or *canción Asturiana*,[3] in which rhythm is of the least importance and in which the singers, male or female, seem to search deep within for those resources of endurance and timbre that they can bring to bear, with high emotional expressivity, upon relatively simple lyrics. The intense concentration upon melismatic vocalization of each syllable means that very often the lyric seems lost in the song production. But the lyric is always there, and its meaning can be of equal interest to listeners, however caught up they might be in the quality of vocalization.

Our inquiry here will be directed primarily at the songs sung by men. However, this genre formerly belonged to both men and women. In the provincial championships this is still the case, as there are equal numbers of participants from both sexes, and male and female champions are chosen. In an overview, no striking difference in the content of the songs chosen by men and women emerges. There is no differing commitment to lyric or narrative deepsong, for example. In fact, in the provincial championships, women sing mining songs about as frequently as men.

Asturian deepsong, when well done, presents profound challenges to

---

[2]   To call these Asturian melismatic airs *deepsong* brings to mind the Andalusian deepsong *cante hondo*, which, in my view and in the view of others who have heard the Asturian song, is similar. A first response of many listeners to the *Asturianada* — as to *cante hondo* — is that it sounds very Arabic. No doubt this comparison rises to mind because of the arhythmic quality and the melismatic quavering in the voice. I know of no extant study of deepsong in Asturias — one of the few parts of Spain that effectively resisted Moorish domination. This Arabic quality may arise from the Mozarabic influx into the kingdom of Asturias in the first several centuries after the Moorish conquest of the rest of Spain. In any case, I employ the term *deepsong* not for musical reasons but because, in the *Asturianada* as in *cante hondo*, the singer seems to be reaching within himself to give voice to very deep sentiments.

[3]   The question of nomenclature for the *Asturianada* is a difficult one. At the present time and in the biannual championships, it is known as *Canción Asturiana*. But I agree with Gonzalez Garcia that the term *canción* should be applied to nonmelismatic song in which rhythm is important. The *Asturianada* should fall under the category of *cantar*. As she points out: "el cantar sería de indole más subjetiva, propia para la entonación a solo, mientras que la canción sería menos susceptible de posibles variantes y podría ser cantado por un coro . . . al cantar corresponde en Asturias la melodía arritmica . . . la canción propiamente dicha, esta comuesta por melodias acompasadas" ("Asturias folklorica y ethnografica," in *El libro de Asturias* (1970:180). Striking a distinction between *cantar* and *canción* is much more difficult in respect to our interest here: the content of the lyrics. They may both treat the same subject matter with rather more light-hearted lyrics characteristic of *canción* and somber declaration of *cantar*.

the human voice. If there is any cultural preparation on the listener's part to receive it, and if the singer's voice can rise triumphantly beyond the obvious physical effort, then these *Asturianadas* can be moving indeed. Annual championships in this song genre pack provincial opera houses; the unruly crowds from the countryside, quick to catcall inadequate singers, are as quick to manifest admiration at some powerful voice especially fertile in the intricacy of its melismatic embellishments.

There are many reasons why this genre persists. Its intensely personal quality is one vital factor. Traditionally, the *Asturianada* was the song of the lone countryman or woman, sung late in the evening, while climbing with the cows up to the pastures after milking them or winding down a long trail after cutting hay. This song *in situ* should properly be heard in early morning or late evening, across a valley. The singer cannot be made out, but the intricate song drifts clearly across the void. Though it bursts out regularly in bars or public gatherings, it is not, and never was, a song for active group participation. Either the group may go on in its hubbub ignoring the singer, or the singer's voice and song commands their attention, and people fall silent in appreciation of the singer's efforts. A fine voice may sometimes be exploited by a group of men in *juerga*, moving on a Saturday or Sunday afternoon from bar to bar. The voice may not even belong to a man who has previous comradeship with the group or who by class belongs in the group. He is invited along to intone *Asturianadas* in bar after bar in order to impose the group's presence — through its association with his voice — upon the bar. Such abuse of deepsong, which should more naturally arise as an end product of intense communication either with the self or with others, is quite naturally resented by many if the voice is not of sufficient quality.

As the communal spirit has gone out of Asturian villages under the impact of wage labor and the individually oriented attractions and amusements of the modern city culture (magazines, books, movie theaters, television), so the folklore that was a part of that communalism — the dance lyrics, the lyrics of courtship — has also died. In an epoch of increasing family autonomy and economic individualism, the old group songs have appeared less appropriate to the age. But the genre that is individualistic *par excellence* appears even more appropriate to the age that more and more celebrates the individual — or the individual celebrity. In this age the *Asturianada* is fully at home. The singer in any gathering is always a celebrity. He does not demand the appreciation of the crowd, only silent, and not necessarily positive, spectatorship. There is certainly intense communication involved in the *Asturianadas*, but it arises from personal display and not from group participation. If collective sentiments are finally provoked by the *Asturianada*, this occurs because the singer has managed to raise the song to the status of a symbol with which all listeners may merge their identity, and not because all participants are merged collectively into the act of singing the song.

The *Asturianada* has also survived — indeed it flourishes — because it is a song style that has proved congenial to the Asturian miners who, for courtship, prefer the hurly-burly of the dance hall to the straggling about in *ronda* and who, for group amusement, prefer the camaraderie of the bars to street dances and celebrations. *Rondas* and street-dance songs are not their style — *Asturianadas* are. Thus, this song can be heard in solitary rendition in distant galleries of the mines. And after several glasses of wine, it almost inevitably rises to the surface in the bars as an alternate and deeper mode of communication among drinking comrades who in ordinary discourse are limited to a public language (Bernstein 1959) with all the tough-minded restrictions on subtle communication of any kind.

As men in the bars, in their increasingly flushed intercommunication, arrive at the speechless level, they turn to Asturian deepsong for deeper sentiments and deeper meanings. Deepsong thus becomes a form of profound communication among three or four drinking companions as first one and then another tries his voice on a *tonada*. It is not only among miners that drinking produces this musical effect. Cattle keepers with a wineskin who are gathered around a pot of stew (*cazuela*) in the *caserias* soon turn to *Asturianadas* to communicate more deeply among themselves. Countrymen of the old culture seem to have had a wider and more subtle range of verbal art at their disposition (*refranes*, for example) and were not as committed to a shallow public language. Indeed, Asturian villagers love stories of the simple-minded sagacity of the countrypeople who, having no sophisticated language at their disposal, make observations of an outrageous obviousness that, on second thought, show a deeper understanding.

In village bars, where there may be no miners present, unmarried countrymen not long in their cups soon are caught up in deepsong. These musical exchanges almost always occur between bachelors celebrating a camaraderie that will be lost when they are married and begin to take up the burden of family quarrels — begin, that is, to fit into that network of social resentments that will make it increasingly difficult to break out in deepsong in the bars of their own village. On trips to other villages, old comrades of the summer's high pastures or of cattle- or horse-trading ventures may be encountered in bars, and their camaraderie, unfettered by family antagonisms, soon leads to deepsong.

BREAKING INTO DEEPSONG

What are the profound emotions communicated by deepsong? What does the song mean and what do the lyrics mean? In many cases, it is the breaking into song that is meaningful, and little attention is paid to the lyrics. Still, how is one to say what breaking into song means? It is an event that surpasses understanding and about which it is difficult to elicit comment. The situation seems ripe; a companion has confidence in his voice, so he launches into song for any number of reasons. His song may be an attempt to express the ineffable, equivalent to saying: "Our comradeship has qualities that cannot be expressed in words, and I propose now to sing you a song." Such a move must both flatter and slightly embarrass a comrade, for it is a shift to a level of feeling higher than is normal in the public relationship of men. As in most communications between comrades, there is also an element of challenge — a kind of throat wrestling. As one launches into song, there is also, therefore, the statement: "Match this if you can, my friend." Indeed, this may be the dominant statement in many songs.

THE ATTACHMENT TO PLACE

If the voice is a very good one and the song well done, then the event becomes symbolic, that is, it comes to stand for much more than itself and the immediate participants. Such a song, regardless of the meaning of its lyrics, raises in the Asturian listeners pride in their province and its lore; at the very least, it arouses local pride. Approval of the song may be murmured or shouted: "¡*Vaya guaje ésto es de cantar!*", said in the sense and spirit of "That's what it is to be an Asturian!" or "That's what Asturias is all about!" or "That's what it is to be from Bimenes (or Langreo)!" or "What a splendid thing it is to be an Asturian (or a Langreano)!" or "What fine songs and what fine singers we Asturians have!" Thus it is that the lyrics of many of these songs do little more than celebrate a provincial or local origin. They mainly add color to locality with words conveying hardly any meaning. The title of one of these songs, "Viva el lugar," is exactly what they are all about. They celebrate province (*concejo*, *pueblo*, or *lugar*). The song "Soy de Langreo" ("I Am from Langreo") has various endings, all difficult to decipher, so overshadowed are they by the fourfold repetition of the *pueblo* identification. Because of melismatic elaboration, the song takes much longer to sing than might be suspected; the elaboration is primarily expended upon the four-line claims to local identity:

1. Soy de Langreo | I am of Langreo
    Soy de Langreo, mira | I am of Langreo, look you
    Soy Langreano | I am of Langreo
    Soy Langreano, mira | I am of Langreo, look you
    Soy Langreano y minero | I am of Langreo and a miner
    Y de eso muy fiero. | And of this fiercely proud.

Or the song, still concentrating on the same first four lines, may conclude:

1a. Por darte un beso suave	For giving you a soft kiss
Lloraba tu madre un dia.	Your mother cried one day.
Para darme, tu, un a mi	For you to give one to me
A ver si lloraba la mia.	Let's see if mine will cry.

The provincial champion of 1971 (a male) sang as one of his championship songs his own composition, which follows:

2. Soy del pueblin de Bimenes	I am of the little town of Bimenes
Baxe de una montana.	I came down from a mountain.
Que me mandan a cantar	They sent me to sing
Una cancion Asturiana.	An Asturian song.

It is clear that the *campanilismo* is the important motive in the song, the fact that he and his song represent, are *naturales de*, Bimenes.[4] Though it is difficult to be equally proud of more than one place at a time, men can and do develop loyalties to several villages, and there is also a slight tendency toward uxorilocality in Asturias. Here, in its entirety, is a deepsong that handles the problem with a touch of humor[5] and with what faithfulness is possible to four locales:

3. Naci en la Pola de Lena,	I was born in Pola de Lena,
Cortexe en Pola de Sierro,	I courted in Pola de Sierro,
Caseme en Pola de Tsaciana,	I married in Pola de Tsaciana,
Y vivo en Pola de Somiedo.	I live in Pola de Somiedo.

Even though the singer may not associate himself with a place in the song, place names figure boldly in most songs. Here is an example:

4. Entre La Pola y el Pino	Between La Pola and El Pino
Hay una piedra redonda	There is a round stone
Donde se sienten los mozos	Where the young men sit
Cuando vienen de la ronda.	When they come from the *ronda*.

[4] We are dealing with a folk tradition in which there is both stability and change in the elements. There are, for example, a series of well-known songs celebrating places — "*Soy de Langreo*" or "*Soy de Pravia*," both collected by Torner (1920:41, 185) — but the elaboration of their lyrics may change according to the singer. In the case of the Bimenes song, we have virtually a new composition, in the view of the singer. But countless other very similar place-celebrating songs have been heard in Asturias. Also to be noted in these songs are elements of the Asturian dialect, *bable*, and, in particular, that of *bable central* (Castellano 1964:210–232).

[5] Part of the humor in this song develops from the allegiance declared to four different *Polas* — the Asturian form of *Puebla*. These municipal entities created in the Middle Ages (the twelfth or thirteenth century) by Royal Letters of Privilege are readily recognizable as Asturian town names, but are quite exceptional names in the total provincial nomenclature.

In support of the theory that these songs are primarily a celebration of place with little additional meaning is the fact that neither the inhabitants of El Pino or La Pola (Aller), pleased as they were to hear their towns mentioned in the song, knew of any such rendezvous stone as the *piedra redonda*. Some people pointed to a kilometer stone between the two towns, but it was, in fact, put up well after the song had obtained currency. The song was originally collected as a dance song from a town neighboring the two towns mentioned (Torner 1920:113). For the same locale, this song, like example 1a, deals with unifying of separate personalities through a common action:

5. La primera vez de mia vida   The first time in my life
    Fuiste al Carmin de la Pola   You went to Carmin de La Pola
    La primera vez de mia vida   The first time in my life
    Que fui al Carmin de la Pola   That I went to Carmin de La Pola

There may be romantic references in these songs, as in the woman's version of the Langreo song, but they still are subordinate to the place element and are mainly vehicles for deepening the tenor of the song. This is well seen in the following song:

6. Asturiana, Asturianina,   Asturian woman, Asturian girl,
    Como quieres tu   Why do you wish
    Que yo non te quiero?   I should not love you?
    Asturias, Asturias!   Asturias, Asturias!

After addressing itself to an Asturian girl, the song transforms her into Asturias itself; the attachment to person transforms itself into attachment to place.

In Asturian folklore, there is a very powerful association of women with the province. The province has a feminine quality assigned to it — *Las Asturias*. And the matriarchal quality of family life is readily recognized by Asturian men: *"nuestro matriarcado,"* men say ruefully! Women (*Asturianinas*), it is often said, are strongly attached to the province and will not leave it: "Marry an Asturiana, marry Asturias." There is an historical basis to this attachment. Men have been leaving women behind to maintain the home and village in Asturias since the time of the reconquest. They went off to battle across the mountains in Castile and stayed to settle. They also have been going to the New World since its discovery, but particularly emigrated in the nineteenth century. And Asturian men coming from the rich grass country of the Cantabrian slope have long been in demand as mowers and reapers in northern Castile and León; and in the late summer and early fall, they leave the province, scythe over shoulder, to spend several months in the grass and grain fields of León, Zamora, and Valladolid. At the present time, many more men than women migrate to jobs in the rest of Europe, though the rate of labor migration is below that for other Spanish provinces. Considering all these masculine vagaries, there is ample reason for the association between Asturias and its womenfolk and for the large number of *Asturianadas* that play upon the deep emotions aroused in men by the accustomed farewells both to the province and to its womenfolk:

7. Cuando yo sali de Asturias When I left Asturias
    De la mas alto montana From the highest mountain
    Me dexaron prisionero They left me prisoner
    Los gueyos de una Asturiana! The eyes of an Asturian woman!

Or the same emotion and identification in a well-known song called "Adios Asturias":

8. Pase el puerto de Payares. I passed through the port of Payares.
    Pase el puerto de Payares. I passed through the port of Payares.
    Paselu con una grande pena. I passed it with great pain.
    Paselu con una grande pena. I passed it with great pain.
    Porque dexaba la moza, Because I was leaving the girl,
    Paselu con una grande pena. I passed it with great pain.

A final testimony to the evocation of place in Asturian deepsong is one of the longest — and least spontaneous — songs composed in this mode:

9. Soy Asturianiana. I am a true Asturian girl.
    Soy lo de verdad. I was born in La Corridoria.
    Nacida en la Corridoria. He who was born here in Asturias
    Todo el que en Asturia nace Can say he was born in glory.
    Puede decir que nacio en la Blessed land where I was born
      gloria. I cannot live without you Asturias.
    Bendita tierra donde naci I adore her so much
    No puedo Asturias vivir sin ti. That I cry for her and would die for
    Es tanto lo que la adoro her.
    Que por ella lloro y por ella I cannot live without you Asturias,
      morira. Blessed Asturias.
    No puedo Asturias vivir sin ti,
    Bendita Asturias.

A fundamental meaning of Asturian deepsong, then, is some locality or set of localities within Asturias and, in the larger context, Asturias itself. Since Asturias is strongly associated with its womenfolk, a relationship to a woman celebrated in a deepsong may easily transform into the celebration of a relationship to Asturias. The opposite transformation may also occur. Examples 6 and 7 typify these transformations. Although the collective sentiment aroused by a singer is the sentiment of belonging to a locality, a fine singer will arouse in many of his hearers who are not of his locality — a sentiment of belonging to Asturias itself. Any of the following forms of the statement is possible:

Ordinary singing provoking exclusive feelings:

I am [we are] to Langreo
As you [singular or plural] are to Pravia.

Fine singing provoking inclusive feelings:

I am [we are] to Langreo
As we all are to Asturias.

Various forms expressing the sentiment of attachment to the opposite sex and hence to Asturias are possible:

I [male] am to you [female] as we are to Asturias [example 6].
I [male] am to Asturias as I am to you [female] [example 7].
I [female] am to you [male] as Asturias is to you [us] [no example given].
I [female] am to you [without gender] as Asturias is to us [example 9].

The evocations of collective sentiments of locality continue to be a main characteristic of deepsong even though, relative to emigration in former years, the development of mining and heavy industry in Asturias has made possible more local employment and, as a result, there has been much less movement of men to the outside world. Industrialization also accounts for the rural exodus, a decentering of the villages and a lessening of allegiance to them. Asturians still think of themselves as mountain-locked on the Cantabrian Sea with poor communications with Castile, although there is much more coming and going than there was formerly. Although men and women may live in the industrial center, they still identify with, return to, and frequently hold land in, their native villages. Regionalism — in this case, provincialism because Asturias, the region, is coterminous with the province of Oviedo — is still pronounced, and so is a kind of nostalgic localism. There is, therefore, plenty of sentiment — both attachment to place, and an associated attachment to women in their various manifestations as sweethearts, mothers, or wives — that can be played upon by deepsong, employing the predominant traditional idiom. Deepsong in this sense retains its modernity by remaining the same. The association of womenfolk with locality no doubt reinforces the persistence of deepsong.

MORE SUBTLE SENTIMENTS AND ASSOCIATIONS

While the simple celebration of place is present in many *Asturianadas* and may be a part of the meaning of any deepsong, more subtle meanings may be discovered in the lyrics of many of these songs. I give below an example from an *espicha* I attended in a village in Alto Aller. An *espicha* is a celebration at which the first barrel of relatively green cider from the last harvest is tapped. There is much food, dancing, and general hilarity.

In this particular case, there were about equal numbers of miners and cattle keepers. Characteristically, the miners gathered more boisterously in the center of the room and around the barrel while the cattle keepers sat quietly at the tables around the side of the room. I was with a group of young miners and one older, retired miner (the father of one of them), when we were accosted by a small, powerfully built, dark-haired man from a neighboring village. Formerly a miner, but now retired with mild silicosis,[6] and an owner of a small bar, he began immediately, with arms around one of the young men, to tax him about the easy conditions of present-day work in the mine. He described how hard conditions used to be. "But now, with all this injection of water into the seams to hold down the dust, and all the machinery, mining is soft work," he said. The young man responded with a lively defense of present-day work conditions, the higher wages, and the greater productiveness — better mining in every way. "How could the older miners ever have worked for such slave wages?" he asked. He seemed to be getting the better of the debate when the older man suddenly stepped back a bit from him — still remaining quite close — and broke into song:

10. San Xuan creó les cerezes.   Saint John created cherries.
    San Bartolomé la escanda.   Saint Bartholmy the spelt wheat.
    ¡ Viva San Bartolomé!   Long live Saint Bartholmy!
    Que les cerezes son piedra y agua.   Cherries are stone and water.

The reaction to this song was impressive. It brought tears to the eyes of the other older, retired miner in our company. "*Cuanto me emocionó*," he said later. And it brought a smile to the face of the young man who had been in argument with the singer. At the end of the song, the young man intoned, "Whey ohh!" and encouraged the bar owner to repeat his deepsong.

Beyond the music and the quality of voice were the associations brought to mind by the lyrics, moving in themselves. In the first place, the patron saint of the village in which the *espicha* was taking place was San Bartolomy — also patron saint of spelt wheat (*escanda*)! A small chapel dedicated to him was directly across from the bar where the tapping was taking place. A reference to, and a *viva* for the local patron saint were

---

[6] Silicosis, or black lung, is a grave problem in the Asturian mines, for the coal is very dirty and the conditions of extraction very difficult. Until recently, the expected working life before onset of silicosis for *picadors* and *barrenists* was between twelve and eighteen years. The reduced lung capacity brought on by this condition greatly hampers the ability to sing deepsong and is one of the consequences of black lung most regretted by miners.

bound to provoke emotion and promote feelings of solidarity. But beyond that, the reference to cherries and spelt wheat was very apt in this context. The discussion had been mainly concerned with the injection of the water into the coal seams as protection against silicosis. And the reference to water in the mines and water in the cherry may have, more than with the patron saint, associated the song with the situation in the singer's mind. The aptness lies in the singer's association of the young miners with the cherry; although fat and "sweetened" by high wages, they were still just water and stone (the old miner had suggested that there was no more good coal left in the mines).

At the same time, the singer was linking himself to spelt wheat: the ancient cereal crop (*Triticum spelta*) cultivated until very recently in the poorer soil regions of the Cantabrian and particularly in the mountains. Spelt wheat is smaller and tougher-bodied than bread wheat (*Triticum vulgare*). It possesses a double hull, which is difficult to thresh free from the grain and which protects it much better from cold and the year-round rains, mists, and sleets of the Cantabrian Mountains, where common wheat would hardly grow. Spelt wheat has a very tough and spiny body, exactly the characteristics the singer had been lauding in the miners of old and which were evident in himself. Quite beside his own linkage to spelt wheat, a reference to it in the song was bound to be evocative, for as flour has become more readily available, more and more attention has been paid to the planting of potatoes and corn. The growing of spelt wheat has been largely abandoned, though, as with seasonal pastoralism, not without nostalgia. For example, to everyone's regret, common wheat flour has replaced *escanda* in the making of the bread offerings (*Ramu*) baked for patronal festivals and auctioned after the Mass. The dark flour of *escanda* is felt by many to be the only proper ingredient for the bread on this occasion.

I would suggest a further level of meaning very likely touched by this song: the distinction between the mountain people of Asturias and the maritime peoples of the same province, that is, between *maraniegos* [the maritime people] and *maraguellos* [the mountain and upper valley people]. Although cherry trees appear occasionally in the mountains, the fruit zone is the Asturian littoral, and cherries are primarily associated with seaside valleys.

The mountain people have always felt they were different from the people who lived near the sea. This feeling is complex and is, in part, admiration for the greater fertility and productivity of the lands by the seaside, the greater size of the seaside cattle, and the greater worldliness of the maritime people. But there is also a feeling of greater toughness in the mountaineers, who are the products of a much harsher climate. The difference is aptly represented in spelt wheat and the cherry. In the social interaction preceding the song, no reference was made to the mountain maritime distinction, but enough such references are made in the bars and in village life to justify the view that the "spelt wheat-cherry" contrast brought to mind differences between the mountains and the maritime, and worked on the young miners' sense of solidarity with their heritage in the following way:

I [the singer] am of San Bartolomy and spelt wheat
[Which is tough durable and of us mountaineers]
As you [young miners] are of San Xuan and cherries
[Which are soft, ephemeral and of the other
Asturians].

The celebration of place — in this case, the mountains — still is important in this song, but it is under- and overlaid with these more subtle sentiments of association.

The old miner went on to sing one more song that, though less emotive for his listeners, was instructive as well. He sang:

11.	Tengo que comprarte un areu	I must buy you a plow
	Que revuelve bien la tierra;	That turns well the earth;
	Que tu pa' mayar terrones,	For you to break the earth,
	Tienes muy mala ma'era.	You have very bad wood.

This song is generally understood as a courtship song and was so described by participants. In it, the man figuratively offers his services as plowman to the woman because she has very bad wood for turning and breaking up the earth. Men and women participate together in the plowing, but it is the men's job to sink and force the plow, and the women's job to pull and guide the cow team. Women, physically speaking, do not have the "wood," or the physique, to handle the plow, which, in any case, is a male-associated instrument (no doubt sexual associations are present in this song as well). In this noncourtship context, the song was aptly chosen by the singer. It is apt, first, because the exchange of deepsong among men in these small-group situations has something of the air of courtship about it: high affective evaluation of one another and a desire to win that other over to one's own viewpoint.

Second, the song was apt because the old miner had been attacking the young miners for having lost the real skills of mining with pick and shovel. Everything has been appropriated, he said, by machinery and the mere leading about of machines. The young men did not really know how to bust up the earth, and so their constitutions, their "wood," were the worse for it. The equation is as follows:

Mining with machinery is to old-hand mining
As the women's dragging about of cows is to the
Hard work of forcing the plow to break up the earth.

Here again we see the singer play upon nostalgia for a former way of life to which all the miners to whom he sang were still in some way committed, if only to such tasks as mowing, in the summer. And we see in this song how a traditional agricultural subject, on the face of it inappropriate to a friendly argument between mining men, can still subtly serve as apt commentary upon that argument.

One could provide countless examples from contemporary bar life in which deepsong is used to communicate more deeply than public language. In many of these "spontaneous" songs, there is a subtle aptness as traditional topics are reworked for modern application — agriculture to mining — and as topics more appropriate to one domain, such as courtship, are applied to another, such as jocular rivalry between male working companions. This adaptability of deepsong is certainly another explanation for its vigorous survival in the modern Asturian world.

The extension of experience from one domain into another for purposes of more concrete comprehension is present throughout the more traditional deepsong. Such metaphorical and metonymic linkages to the subjects of these songs should hardly surprise us, for such topic extensions are fundamental to folklore. What may be more surprising is the ease with which the lore of the agricultural life can be aptly employed for communication between miners. In part, this power to speak about the affairs of miners in agricultural terms arises because practically all Asturian miners are *mixtos*, which means they preserve, by choice or necessity, some tie with the agricultural life through possession of cattle and responsibilities to haying. Metaphoric references to the agricultural life are not dead metaphors to them.

The principal metaphoric and metonymic linkages made to the pronominal subjects of Asturian deepsong (the *I* of the singer, the *he* or *she* of the courtship songs, the *they* of other towns, other parts of the province, or other provinces, and the *we* of the same town, valley, region, or province) are a study in themselves. It has already been shown that some of these linkages are locality related. Others have just emerged:

We [mountain Asturians] are spelt wheat;
They [maritime Asturians] are cherries;
We [men, or old miners] are tough wood of the plow breaking the earth;
They [women or new miners] are the soft hand tugging at cows.

Asturians themselves are well attuned to the metaphoric mode (Aramayor 1962). A reading of the 500 songs collected by E. M. Torner (1920) shows young courting men (*mozos, galanes*) being represented or representing themselves metaphorically as mules, fishes fished from the river or the sea, lost sheep, the sun, a bull bellowing to enter a meadow, mail carriers wandering around the town with intimate letters for every girl, trees, the wood of various trees (oak, ash, or, at a later date, softer woods), and metonymically, as handkerchiefs (part of the courtship attire). Women in courtship (*mozas* and *mozaquinas*) are represented as flowers, doves invited to perch in trees or locked in the cages of their fathers' homes, the moon, a magical snake (*cuelebre*) singing its enchantments, the mountain stone hut into which the pastor desires to drive his cattle, a meadow lush with grass into which the bellowing bull or the herd of cattle desires to enter, a Moorish castle difficult to besiege, a white flag announcing a war in which a young man would feign to enlist, a thorny rosebush, a willow wand, a gardenia bush, and, metonymically, a white underskirt. Married women are represented as old leather bags, unpredictable jumping goats, bundled corn stalks, muddy roads. Married men hardly ever appear in Torner's collection, except indirectly as fathers opposed in some way to a prospective marriage. They appear generally in pronominal reference unqualified by metaphoric or metonymic predications.

Not only personal pronouns but also impersonal ones — particularly the *it*[7] of courtship and lovemaking — obtain metaphoric elaboration. One of the prevalent metaphoric modes for this activity is sating one's thirst or bathing with water. The invitation to come drink from a crystal mountain spring represents an invitation to make love. Lovers' trysts are made at favorite springs. A lover invites his loved one, figuratively, to go swimming with him though neither can swim a stroke. A member of one sex gazing down at water flowing under a bridge is reminded of his or her loved one or of their love together. It is not surprising that this association, when taken together with the association of threshing, mowing, haying (the separation of the seed or the fruit from the plant) with love making, should make the miller and the miller's life highly suggestive. He or she grinds seed by the power of falling water. The milling gear is itself suggestive. The miller, his wife, or his daughter appear in these songs as evocative representations of the *it* to which the singer by indirection is concentrating his attention.

THE EMERGENCE OF MINER'S SONGS

If millers, their situation, and their trade seem so evocative of the sensual life in the Asturian mountains (and not only there, as Chaucer's "Miller's Tale" teaches us), then surely miners in their trade and situation, delving in the bowels of the earth, would be evocative as well. In fact, in a

---

[7]   Readers who feel that this pronoun does not have the referent implied may wish to recall Clara Bow, the "It girl." She had "it" — sex appeal — to employ the barbarous abstraction. But the Asturian mountaineers have more resource of metaphoric and metonymic image than to content themselves with such a barbarism — one that leaves the pronoun in this manner exposed.

well-known, late nineteenth-century Spanish novel of life in these mountains, *La aldea perdida* (1903), written by the Asturian Palacio Valdes,
the dark and debauched life of the miner is set against the ruddy pastoral
virtues of the countryfolk. The villain in this book is a dark-featured,
violent-tempered miner who attempts to waylay sexually the heroine in
an abandoned mine shaft. The association between mining and sexuality
has long been present in Asturias, but miners hardly appear in Torner's
collection. Only two songs out of the 500 make any reference to miners,
and these, only indirectly. In example 12, collected by Torner (1920:45),
the miner, referred to diminutively as *un pobre carbonerillo*, is the victim
of his sweetheart's whims. As in so many songs written of the miners, his
most attractive quality is found in the money he earns:

12.	Una nina bordadora	A seamstress girl
	Cuando sale de bordar	When she leaves her seams
	Mande razon a su amante, el minero	Directs her lover, the miner
	Que la venga a pasear	That he should come and walk
	Y que la lleve al cafe.	And take her for coffee.
	Y el pobre carbonerillo, el minero	And the poor little coalman, the miner
	Triste, afligido, se ve.	Appears sad and afflicted
	No lo puede remediar;	And cannot respond;
	Una peseta que gana el minero	The peseta that the miner earns
	No tiene para gastar.	He does not have to spend.

Regarding the only other song referring to miners in Torner's collection (1920:76), example 13, the compiler has to explain in the footnotes
that it is a song of mockery. The people of the *concejo* of Aller are sung of
by miners from a neighboring *concejo*, Quiros. The association of the
miner with sensuality is present. The men from Quiros have been living in
Aller close to the mines and now, returning home with their savings, they
call out to the Alleranos to take good care of the children they have sired
and are leaving behind. Mining is still a temporary thing in the song.
Countryfolk come down to the mines, but they soon return to the land:

13.	Adios concejo de Aller	Good bye valley of Aller
	Adios nobles Alleranos	Good bye noble Allerians
	Teneis que criar los fijos	You must care for the children
	De los mozos Quirosanos.	Of the men of Quiros.

The lack of miners' songs in Torner's collection has a number of
explanations. He does not seem to have purposefully ignored these songs,
although he may have phrased his interest in collection in a way so as to
encourage songs of the nostalgic past — exclusively agricultural-pastoral

rather than industrial. The lack of such songs is first explained by the fact that the great majority of songs available to Torner, the most popular songs of the period, were either courtship songs — *rondas* — or dance songs in which both men and women were involved. The content of these songs would more naturally refer to the agricultural-pastoral life in which men and women participate together virtually even-handedly, rather than to the mining life, which is exclusive to men. Second, given the *ruralismo* that Asturians ascribe to themselves (Cabezas 1964:138–164), there has been resistance to thinking of mining songs as being in any way typically Asturian. There has been, and this was surely the case in Torner's time, a tendency to think of mining as a way of life that was curious, amusing, sometimes threatening, and surely dangerous. Still, as in example 13 above, it was regarded only as a temporary occupation and not truly an Asturian one. Third, since the more traditional songs of field, meadow, and high pasture could by extension be made relevant to the concerns of miners, who as *mixtos* kept one foot in the agricultural and pastoral life, there was less pressure from them to change the content of deepsong. They could revitalize the old songs by extension. Since a great many Asturian miners, moreover, continued to live in the villages along with agriculturalists mixing with them in the bars, they have hesitated, in my experience, to impose mining songs. Finally, there was a satisfaction for the miners in singing the old songs.

Nevertheless, Asturian song has always valued spontaneity and contemporaneity; the ability to compose rapidly and sing topical verse (*andar cantares*) has always been much admired. Jovellanos gives us an example from the late eighteenth century of a group of youth in *romería* improvising a song of jocular defiance to a local prelate who thought to prohibit their festivities (Jovellanos 1884:591). Experience today in practically any Asturian village would reveal two or three villagers well known for their abilities to *andar a cantares* [walk-forth songs] of a mocking or laudatory character. Even at the time of Torner, there were, no doubt, a great many songs being sung about miners and the mining life — active mining had then been in existence more than fifty years — but probably they had not achieved the status of "traditional deepsong repertoire." They were not regarded as Asturian.

But events occurring since Torner published his collection — the Asturian miners' union movement of the first three decades of the twentieth century, the miners' 1934 revolution in Asturias, and the central role played by the miners in the Spanish Civil War — have permanently linked Asturias with its miners both in the minds of Asturians and in the eyes of all Spaniards. Deepsong directed to miners (and mining as subject matter) is now everywhere recognized as Asturian deepsong and not simply as a curious and ephemeral hybrid. Moreover, while most Asturian miners preserve strong ties with country and cattle, an increasing number of miners — most from outside the province — live in urban housing projects and devote themselves solely to mining. Deepsong is heard in these projects, but it is a deepsong tied less to the agricultural-pastoral tradition. There is still no adequate collection of the folklore of these mining communities.

In the provincial championships of deepsong in the spring of 1971, mining songs had a more realistic representation; still, only five of the forty songs presented in the competition could be so categorized. This was the case even though at least half of the twenty competitors had worked in the mines. Since the Civil War, there have been, no doubt, constraints upon the miners' self-celebration in public performance, particularly at times when illegal walkouts were in progress.

The five songs below, recorded during an actual performance, give a representative range of deepsong devoted to mining. The two shortest songs (with respect to the lyrics) celebrate in a simple way the miner's role. Example 14 is a simple *vivar*; example 15 is a pious hope for the salvation of the miner, a role easily associated with the infernal depths of earth and the devil's work:

14. Viva la xente minera   Long live the mining people
     De Laviana, Carbayin,   From Laviana, Carbayin,
     La xente minera!   The mining people!

15. Dios quiere que   God desires that
     Al cielo vaya   To heaven should go
     El alma de los mineros.   The soul of the miners.

The longest song in the competition, unusually long with respect to lyrics, concentrates its attention, as do so many miners' songs, upon the tragic accidents to which the miner's life is exposed. This song also celebrates a family solidarity between brothers and their mother, which is unusual. Generally, miners' songs celebrate the solidarity of *we*, that is, all the miners, as in songs 14 and 15 above:

16. Dexame pasar que voy.   Let me pass I am going.
     Quiero baxar a la mina.   I want to go down in the mine.
     Tengo el mio hermano   I have my brother
     Encerrado y quiero sacarlu,   Trapped and I wish to free him,
     Salvar la vida.   Save his life.
     Aquel hermanin, madre.   That little brother, mother,
     Que siempre fue un gran minero. He was always a great miner.
     Voy a sacarlu con vida.   I will free him alive.
     Y si non de pena muero!   If not I will die of pain!

The final two songs celebrated two talents for which the Asturian miner is famous: his skill with dynamite and his skill in organizing demonstrations and strikes. In the first of these songs, sung by a woman, the miner is slightly mocked,[8] for with all his powers of dynamite, he is not able to buy her a coral necklace. This readiness to mock a pretentious male role and particularly that of the miner is a recurrent expression of the matriarchal orientation in deepsong. There is an association in this song between opening the mine with dynamite and opening a way to the girl's heart with a red coral necklace. The same kind of association is present in example 11: opening the earth with a good plow and opening a way to the girl's heart with a present:

17. Si yo fuera picador   If I were a picador
     A mi amor le compraría   I would buy my love
     Un collar de rojos corales   A necklace of red coral
     Como quince cartuchos de   Like fifteen sticks of dynamite.
        dynamita.
     Y no me pudiste comprar collar   And you couldn't buy for me a
        de rojos corales.   necklace of red coral.

In the second song, sung by men, the solidarity of the *we* is suggested by a metonymic reference to a common item of clothing — the countryman's beret. There is something of a boast in this, for it is the custom to wear hard hats in the mine and not berets. It serves also as a reference to their status as countryfolk first, rather than miners — an identity that brings them readily out of the mine in protest, as the song goes on to say:

18. Los mineros del Fondon   The miners of Fondon
     Todos gastamos boina.   All of us sport a beret.
     Con un letreru   With a placard
     Todos salimos de la mina.   We march out of the mine.

There have been at least three moods to the deepsong of miners and mining: (1) the mood of mild mockery of miners by countryfolk and, particularly, by the Asturian matriarchate (examples 12 and 18) or the reverse, a mockery by the miners of the countryfolk (example 13); (2) the vaunting mood of miners lauding their powers and solidarity (examples 14 and 15); and (3) the mood of pathos most often thought of as the essence of the miner's deepsong, in which the tragic nature of the mining way of life is explored in its various aspects (example 16). There has been, over the years, a tendency for the deepsong of the mines to move away from the first mood to the second and, finally, to the third. There is much that is politic about this development. There has also been a tendency toward greater narration than is characteristic of the more traditional deepsong.

---

[8] In other versions of this song quite a different mood is established shifting this "matriarchal mockery of the male" to the tragic view of the miner and his life. Killed by dynamite, the miner is unable to bring a present, reminiscent of that very dynamite, to his loved one.

CONCLUSION: DEEP MOODS AND DEEP ARGUMENTS

This paper has explored some of the moods and associations evoked by Asturian deepsong in an attempt to account for its continuing vitality. Deepsong is first of all a genre that is in accord with the personalism and celebrity orientation of modern western Europe. It is, second, in its celebration of place, evocative of provincial and local sentiments still very much alive in Spain and Asturias despite increasing decentering of the rural villages. It is, third, a kind of folksong that continues to appeal to miners, whereas this is not the case for other kinds of song. It appeals in part because it takes reservoirs of strength and endurance to sing deepsong well, and this requirement conforms to the miners' image of themselves. It appeals also because most of the Asturian miners are *mixtos*, who keep some interest in the land and in cattle and have to work at these concerns some part of the year. The *mixtos* preserve a nostalgic interest in the subject matter of the more traditional deepsong. Even if there is no interest in the song itself, the subject matter can be reinterpreted and figuratively extended to cover quite contemporary situations.

Despite the presence of mining in the central mountain valleys of Asturias for almost a hundred years, the development of deepsong with a strictly mining content — its modernization in this sense — has been slow. This is explained in part by the reasons already given for its persistence, and in part by the "ruralism" of the Asturian and his resistance to thinking of the miner's deepsong as typically Asturian. Recent history, however, has firmly linked the miners to Asturias, and there has been some development of mining deepsong. The tendency in this song has been to move from a mood of mild mockery between miners and countryfolk to a mood of pathos. Such an observation as this, however, and indeed all the explanations for the modernization of deepsong, can be treated only as propositions that must be used to confront a fuller compilation of the materials. Present collections of deepsong are not adequate for conclusive explanation.

Underlying our exposition has been a more theoretical interest in what might be called *syllogisms of association*. We have also delved into the connections between extensions in figures of speech and extensions of human experience in time, which is *modernization*. While *Asturianadas* are often simple songs that seek only to establish certain moods about people and places, some of them make an argument that lies beneath the mood they establish. In this sense, they are syllogistic: if one admits their premises, one is led to necessary conclusions. Of course, the logical necessities are those not of identity but of analogy and association by similarity and contiguity. They look like this in a courtship song such as example 6:

I [male] am to You [female]
As You [female] are to It [Asturias].
Therefore I [male] am to It [Asturias].

Or consider example 10:

We [old miners] are to spelt wheat
As You [young miners] are to cherries.
Spelt wheat is to Us [mountain Asturians]
As cherries are to Them [lowland Asturians].
Therefore You [young miners] are of We and not of Them.

Such deep arguments are still persuasive because the metaphors upon
which they are based exploit domains of experience that remain vital to
the great majority of Asturians. They are a people who, amid extensive
mining operations and a large steel industry, continue to retain a strong
allegiance to the rural character of their province and their localities. It
remains to be seen whether this allegiance will continue to survive the
superficial excitements of dance hall culture and mass communications;
these purvey a metropolitan popular culture with very little of the flavor
or substance of rural locality. The evidence from miners is heartening.
Not only do they subtly extend the rural to their contemporary situation,
but, insofar as their experience has shifted away from the rural, they have
yet stayed with deepsong, inventing new content, and continuing to find
in it one of the very best methods for passing beyond a superficial public
language and a canned popular culture to real depths of feeling and
association.

REFERENCES

ARAMAYOR, OLIVIA
    1962   La metafora y la fauna de caso [Metaphor and fauna in Caso]. *Boletin
            del Instituto de Estudios Asturianos* 47:5–22.
BERNSTEIN, BASIL A.
    1959   A public language: some sociological implications of a linguistic form.
            British Journal of Sociology 10:311–326.
CABEZAS, JUAN ANTONIO
    1964   "Asturias," in *La España de Cada Provincia* [The Spain of each pro-
            vince]. Madrid: Publicaciones Espanolas.
CASTELLANO, LORENZO RODRIQUES
    1970   "El dialect Asturiano" [The Asturian dialect], in *El libro de Austurias*,
            210–232. Oviedo: Prensa del Norte.
FERNANDEZ, JAMES W.
    1970   "What it means to be moved; the operation of metaphor in religious
            behavior." Unpublished manuscript.
    1972   Persuasions and performances: of the beast in everybody and the
            metaphors in everyman. *Daedalus* 101 (Winter):39–60.

1974   The mission of metaphor in expressive culture. *Current Anthropology* 15:119–145.

GONZALEZ, GARCIA
1970   "Asturias folklorica y ethnografica," in *El libro de Austurias*, 170–207. Oviedo: Prensa del Norte.

JOVELLANOS, GASPAR M.
1884   "Romerias de Asturias" [Asturian romerias] in *Cartas a varias personas*. Reprinted 1925 in *Costumbristas españoles*, volume 1. Madrid.

TORNER, E. M.
1920   *Cancionero musical de la lirica popular asturiana* [The songbook of Asturian lyrics]. Madrid: Akal.

VALDES, PALACIO
1903   *La aldea perdida* [The lost village]. Madrid: Espasa Calpe.

Folklore and Culture Change: Lau Riddles of Modernization

ELLI KÖNGÄS MARANDA

This paper delves into "contact riddles" among the Lau of Malaita, British Solomon Islands. The Lau are a Melanesian society, speaking a Melanesian language and possessing a rich and viable indigenous culture based on fishing and horticulture supplemented by trade with neighboring inland populations. Lau religion is of the common Melanesian type; ancestor worship expressed in complex ceremonialism and mythology.

The point of this paper is not to describe traditional Lau life; rather, it is to show how Lau cope with external cultural pressures. The outsiders — Chinese tradespeople, Christian missionaries, British colonial government officials — offer goods and procedures that are new to the Lau. These novelties have to be faced; they have to be understood; and they have to be accepted or rejected. The thesis in this paper is that the riddle, a genre of traditional Lau literature, has come to serve as a tool in this coping because it functions as a cognitive device to analyze and evaluate alien cultural introductions.

The function just described is not the only function of Lau riddles. There are several kinds of riddles among the Lau. One group, which strikes the outsider as "classical," describes features of the human body in terms of formations of the landscape. This subgenre is so extensive and so clear that it can be seen as a specific metaphor system. There is no Lau name for it, but when such riddles were extracted from the total corpus and presented to a group of Canadian students, the students were quickly able to give correct answers to most of the riddles. This serves to make the

Fieldwork among the Lau comprised nearly two years, 1966–68. Pierre Maranda and I worked together, although each of us had independent projects in the field. We have published together (Maranda and Maranda 1970:829–861) and separately (Maranda 1971:11–15; 1972:51–61; 1973:3–13). Further aspects of Lau ethnology have been discussed in Maranda (1970a:155–162). Riddle and myth among the Lau are contrasted in detail in Maranda (1970b).

point that although one of the main tasks of the fieldworker is, indeed, to cover and discover the native generic classifications and any native theory of the genres and of performance that may exist, the outsider's analysis still has its contribution to make, if for no other end than to make the indigenous culture intelligible to outsiders.

When riddling began in Lau is unknown. There is no other Melanesian culture for which riddles and riddling have been recorded,[1] but one has to apply the principle of *ex nihilo nihil* and resist thinking that the lack of evidence proves that riddles are not there. The eldest Lau alive, estimated to be over eighty years of age, maintains that riddling (*faleiirilaa*) was a popular pastime in his childhood. Also, it is hard to envisage the first missionaries teaching riddles (the current missionaries would not, at any rate). However, despite Lau reluctance to give up traditional culture, Western forms have slowly crept in — for example, in songs, in what is called *Tahitian style* by ethnomusicologists — that, with their Western rhythms and scales, correspond to modern European popular music. Such music is propagated by radio and records; riddles are not. Thus, one cannot rule out the genre as a possibly Western introduction, but documentation that such really is the case is hard to establish. The point is moot, and the fact remains that Lau have riddles and use them a great deal.

Riddles contrast with the great genre of Lau oral literature, myth (*'ai-ni-mae*). Lau mythology is concerned with the origins of social and cultural phenomena and with early tribal history. Nature is mostly perceived as given, culture as developed by people in interaction with supernaturals (*agalo*) [spirits]. Myths support the social and religious hierarchy and also serve as charters of land tenure. Additionally, they serve important cognitive, symbolic, and aesthetic functions. Myths are presented in grandiose memorial feasts to honor ancestors; specialists sing them in all-night sessions. In several ways, Lau myths can be seen as agents of conservatism. According to Bascom (1954), they are "an important mechanism for maintaining the stability of culture." They instruct members of the society in why things are as they are. And, of course they are *abu* [sacred].

Riddles are *mola* [neutral]. They neither belong to any specialist nor to special formal occasions. In contrast to myths, riddles question the order of society. They may, indeed, be quite close to something Bascom did not believe to exist, "instances of folklore . . . which suggest that the individual destroy or even disregard the institutions and conventions of his society." Where myths validate existing institutions (Malinowski 1955:93–148), riddles seem to reach for the new.

---

[1] For Micronesia, fourteen Marshallese riddles reported by Davenport (1962:265–266) attest to the genre's existence. Davenport says that "pieces of land . . . are known to have been won in ancient riddling contests."

The process of cultural change due to contact with white people is going on, albeit slowly and selectively. The Lau seem to be relatively cautious in accepting white innovations. Observe, for example, that the Melanesian mission and other missions have worked among the Lau from the beginning of this century; and yet the society, despite the presence of Christian converts, is dominated by pagans. White culture is not always applicable. For traveling, motorboats are faster than dugouts, but what can be done with the minutes or even hours saved? Where does one get the fuel necessary for running the boat?

When innovations are proposed, either internally or externally, an informal, but quite clear process is set into motion. People get together to discuss the new thing, to express opinions, to offer explanations, and to work it through together. Such discussion is continually going on in the evenings and at slack times of the day; it is the content of informal gatherings called *rebolaa* [chatting]. *Rebolaa* is a recognized form of behavior but not a recognized literary genre, so that, for example, people would never say that *rebolaa* was done well or badly, although *falegemolaa* [riddling], could be so evaluated. Here we have a general hint to establish a difference between expressive (artistic) behavior and everyday social behavior.

Every new thing that happens will, of course, not cause an immediate gathering of people to analyze it, although some dramatic events will lead to such analysis. When a seaplane was seen in the lagoon for the first time in Lau history, many people dropped whatever they were doing to observe and discuss the novelty. Normally, an evening gathering would "cover" recent events. Just as new introductions can be discussed in *rebolaa*, they can also become subjects in riddling. And just as anyone can participate in informal chats, anyone can express a view, insight, or observation in riddling, because everyone, even a child, is permitted to present riddles.

Since traditional Lau culture is quite rigid and past oriented, men, especially prestigious men such as priests and chiefs, are reluctant to embrace change. Women never were held sacred in the traditional religion and thus more women than men become converts to Christian faiths. Also, women, together with children and unmarried men (*daraa*), seem to introduce linguistic, including phonetic, change.

"WESTERN TECHNOLOGY IS EFFECTIVE"

The following riddles of modernization seem to give unconditional support to Western technology, which is seen as effective and superior to traditional Lau technology. [Solutions are in italics.]

1. Riddle a riddle.
    A thing, even if a tree is hard, it eats it all up today. *Ax*.

2. A leaf, when the wind blows, and even when it rains and you are cold, if you cover your body with it, you won't be cold. *Blanket*.

3. Riddle.
    A thing waits for the time when you are cold. *Blanket*.

4. Riddle.
    A thing, if it just stays there, it does not spoil. It must be broken to spoil. *A big bottle*.

5. Riddle.
    A thing, when it is angry, it is very strong. *Ball*.

6. A small child carries a big man. *Chair*.

7. Riddle.
    A thing that if they fix a house with it, it is very strong. *Cement*.

8. A ship flies like a bird. *Airplane*.

9. Riddle.
    One thing, at a landing place, one man dives and gets there. *Anchor*.

10. A man looks after your canoe. Even when there is a storm, he holds on to it. *Anchor*.

11. A man stands on one leg. When he comes from a village and arrives, he stands on his one leg. *A ship with its anchor*.

12. Two fellow riddle.
    Even if a thing goes into the surf, into the wind, it does not sink. *A big ship*.

13. Even when it goes into the surf, it is not threatened. *A big ship*.

14. Riddle.
    A big man, when he comes and arrives, he stands only on one leg. *Ship*.

15. Riddle.
    A thing, even when he comes angry, when he comes and arrives, he stands only on one leg. Even when the storm is big, he stands only on one leg. *Ship*.

16. Riddle.
    A thing goes with a tree that stands in the sea. *Ship*.

17. A big ship, many men are inside, and one man paddles it. *Steamer. Propeller moves the ship.*

18. Riddle.
    Four men, they paddle a big thing. *Propeller.*

19. Three men carry a big island. *Propeller.*

20. Riddle.
    A thing that people desire very much. *Cooking pot.*

21. A small child comes and sometimes gives us to eat from his mouth. *Spoon.*

22. A man, you cook some food for him, but he will not burn his hand. *Spoon.*

23. Riddle.
    A man speaks in a distant place. You hear his speech in another place. *Radio.*

24. A man, when he speaks, all villages here hear. *Radio.*

25. A man, even if he comes from America, when he arrives in our village, his cry is just the same. *Rifle.*

26. A riddle a thing.
    A thing eats with one tooth. *Sewing machine.*

27. A man this man is a little man, well, sometimes he still beats a big man. *Record.*

28. A man, if you say a word to him and he hears, even after a year, he says it. *Tape recorder.*

29. A big man and a little child. When the little child arrives, the big man flees. *Darkness and a lantern.*

30. Riddle.
    A man, his teeth are very many and very long. *Saw.*

31. Riddle.
    A thing, its mouth is very rough, then its face takes very much. *Saw.*

32. A fruit, if you place it even in bitter water, it will be sweet. *Sugar.*

33. Riddle a riddle.
    A thing has only one mast, but it takes twelve sails. *White man's rainmat.*

34. Riddle.
    A boat has only one mast, but it has eight covers. *White man's rainmat*.

35. A ship arrives, if we step into it, our feet won't be dirty. *Boots*.

36. Riddle.
    A thing is there for making a ship go straight towards the island where it is going. *Compass*.

37. Riddle a riddle.
    A man is master of a door, only when he arrives, the door opens. *Key*.

38. A man, however many tens of us stay with him, when he says we must go to work, it is impossible for us to refuse. *The bell that tolls for work*.

39. A man, when we send him on an errand, he walks on one leg. *Dice*.

40. A thing, even when it is far away, when it is sent, it arrives, it does not speak, and we understand it. *Letter*.

41. A thing counts days and nights. *Handwatch*.

42. A small box, sometimes even a thousand people stay inside it. *Picture*.

43. Eight men who speak with four different accents. *Mandolin*.

44. Riddle.
    A thing, when it opens its mouth, it is very big. *Box*.

45. Two fellow riddle.
    These two things are not with us, and it is bad. *A knife and an ax*.

46. Riddle.
    A thing very good to drink. *A cup of tea*.

47. Small men only, but even when we are very sick, they heal us. *Medicine*.

48. Twelve days.   All the world knows them. *Christmas*.

49. Riddle.
    A rope for tying, when a man has it, he cannot return, that rope holds him. *A thief and the law holds him*.

First, each of the objects and phenomena referred to in the riddles are alien introductions to the Lau, a point attested to by the fact that their names are borrowed words or, in a few cases, translation loans. For example:

ENGLISH	LAU	RIDDLE NUMBER
anchor	*aga*	9, 10, 11
ax	*hakisi*	1
ball	*bolo*	5
bell	*belo*	38
blanket	*bulanikete*	2, 3
boots	*butu*	35
bottle	*botele*	4
box	*bokisi*	44
cement	*semede*	7
chair	*sea*	6
Christmas	*keresimasi*	48
compass	*kabasi*	36
cooking pot	*kuki ni/*	
	kukilaa	20
dice	*daisi*	39
handwatch	*hanowasi*	41
key (lock)	*loko*	37
knife	*neife*	45
lantern (light)	*laeta*	29
law	*loo*	49
letter	*leta*	40
machine	*misini*	26
mandolin	*madeleni*	43
medicine	*meresina*	47
picture	*bikisa*	42
propeller	*borobela*	18, 19
propeller	*belabela*	17
radio (wireless)	*waelesi*	23, 24
record	*rikoti*	27
saw	*soo*	30, 31
spoon	*subuni*	21, 22
steamer	*sitima*	17
sugar	*suka*	32
tape recorder	*teberekodi*	28
tea	*tii*	46

Other translation loans or analogical formations include *kwanga*, which originally meant "thunder," for rifle fire (25); *kaufa*, which originally was "rainmat" for umbrella (33, 34); *faka lolofo*, literally meaning "flying ship," for airplane (8); *maetii*, literally meaning "a container full of tea," for a cup of tea (46); and *faka* [ship] which is a Polynesian loanword in Lau (14, 15, 16).

These riddles, which recommend Western objects, take one function of the object and point out its effectiveness. A little thing does big things: a propeller pushes a ship, a spoon feeds a man, the one tooth of a sewing machine "eats" cloth, a picture holds the images of a thousand men, a wooden box is effective as a container, a key keeps the box locked. Glass bottles do not deteriorate, if not broken. Cement is found superior to the native building materials because it lasts longer. A tape recording preserves the spoken word. To my knowledge, our tape recorders were the first ever seen in Lau Lagoon; the riddle concerning the tape recorder has thus a definite *terminus post quem*. The effectiveness of an ax is praised because it cuts the hardest wood; a blanket has warmth; a football flies fast and so does an airplane. A message sent by Western means — by letter or by radio — reaches even a distant destination unchanged. Finally, the churchbell of the Seventh Day Adventist church must be obeyed by the believers, and the government-induced law, like an unbreakable rope, holds a thief.

That Western cultural traits are subject of Lau riddling does not mean that the Lau possess these traits. In some cases, they have only a hint of knowledge of them and the riddle's work is aimed toward expanding and cultivating such knowledge. No Lau has ever seen a camel, but there are riddles about a camel:

50. Riddle a riddle.
     A man eats for a year and drinks for a year. *Camel.*

51. A man if he drinks today, he will wait six months; when the sixth month comes, he will drink again. *Camel.*

Encountering such riddles, I inquired where the information about camels came. This is the answer I received: *"Nununa faafia sigarete ba gera ngalia la firua ba"* ["its picture was on the cigarettes they had in that war"]. "That war" was the war of Guadalcanal, where some Lau men assisted the Americans and learned a few things from them (for example, how to bake bread).

"Western Technology Demands More Western Technology"

Innovations have their difficult points, too, in Lau perception. Consider the following:

52. Riddle a riddle.
     A thing, only when his food arrives, he cries. If it does not arrive, he never cries. *Engine.*

53. A man, if he stays without eating for a month, he still sits and waits it out. *Engine.*

54. Riddle.
     A thing has to drink before he can speak. *Engine.*

55. Riddle.
    A thing, if there is water, he walks; if not, he just stays put.
    Engine.

56. Riddle.
    A thing runs with the water made for it earlier. *Engine*.

57. Riddle.
    A man, when they hit him, he goes; if they do not hit him, he
    cannot go. *Engine*.

58. Riddle.
    A man, if his food does not arrive, it is impossible for him to speak
    with us. *Radio*.

59. Riddle.
    A thing, if it does not have any rope for sewing, it does not come;
    it only stays put, it does not work. *Sewing machine*.

60. Riddle.
    A thing lives in houses, then a person must reach for it before it
    eats. *Sewing machine*.

61. Riddle a riddle.
    A thing, only when its food comes is it hot; if not, it is not hot.
    Lantern.

62. Riddle.
    A thing drinks but does not get full. *Lantern*.

63. A man must stand in the sea to live; if his foot is dry, he dies.
    Lantern.

64. Riddle.
    A white man drinks up an ocean. *Lantern*.

65. Riddle.
    A thing drinks up a river. *Lantern*.

66. A man that they feed with wind; if not, he dies. *Ball*.

67. Riddle a riddle.
    A thing, only when they hit it, it cries; if not, it stays as is. *Guitar*.

"WESTERN THINGS ARE PERISHABLE"

68. Riddle a riddle.
    A big men's house, very many men live in it. If they come out,
    they die. *Matches*.

69. Riddle a riddle.
    Thirty men, one noise kills them all. *Matches*.

70. Riddle.
    Things that die in one place. *Matches*.

71. A thing is big, big; then when a thousand persons come, it perishes. *Ants and sugar*.

72. Riddle.
    A thing, when they put it in water, it perishes. *Sugar*.

"WESTERN THINGS ARE HARD TO ACQUIRE; LOSE THEIR ATTRACTIVENESS OR ARE DANGEROUS"

73. Riddle a riddle.
    A thing, when a man stays put, he cannot see it. He must look for it to see it. *Shilling*.

74. Riddle a riddle.
    A thing, when we start doing it, it is good; when we do it long, it is bad. *Schooling* (that is, going into a mission, joining a mission).

75. Riddle.
    A thing, when it hits a man, he dies. *Truck*.

Western machinery and tools — motorboat engines, kerosene lanterns, sewing machines, and radios — need more Western goods if they are to work. Gasoline, kerosene, batteries for a radio, even cotton thread are costly for a Lau, for, as another riddle says, you must look for a shilling. Sugar ants make the keeping of sugar difficult. Missions and mission schools may hold initial attraction, but in the long run their attraction fades. Trucks (or cars) have not been seen in the area where the Lau live, but people who visited the government post in Auki had seen them and could report on their speed, its advantages and dangers.

The important consideration is not whether Lau riddles recommend change or point out its disadvantages, but, rather, that riddles serve as a form that discusses new phenomena and makes people familiar with their different properties. The function of such riddles is, then, mainly cognitive.

Bascom (1954) wrote in his classic article "Four functions of folklore":

Although I have spoken loosely of the "functions of folklore," it is important to remember that the functions of the myth, legend, folktale, proverb, riddle, song, and each of the other forms of folklore are to some extent distinctive and must be analyzed separately . . . To fully understand folklore and its role in man's life, we must have more knowledge of the specific functions of each of these forms in various societies, literate and nonliterate, and more of the tedious but extremely rewarding comparisons of the details of folklore texts with those of culture and actual behavior (1954:347–348).

This paper is an attempt to discern functions of folklore in a small society that is subjected to some external pressure from religious, technological, and other influences. Riddles are not the only mechanism of coping with such influences for the Lau, and coping with modernization is not the only function Lau riddles have. However, if my observations and analyses are true, there are functions that Bascom did not discover. Bascom spoke of the "inability of folklore to adapt itself to cultural change." The materials presented in this paper seem to contradict this assumption. Perhaps folklore does not only "insure conformity." Indeed, the modest group of riddles presented here would seem to function to insure the viability of the culture, rather than "stability" in a static sense. Since there is no defense against change — and one can indeed assume that change has always been going on in all cultures — then cohesion can be maintained by working new things into the system. And if one views folklore as a living phenomenon, not as a survival, one can afford to admit that stability does not mean standing put but being in control.

REFERENCES

BASCOM, WILLIAM R.
1954   Four functions of folklore. *Journal of American Folklore* 67:333–349. (Reprinted in 1965 in *The study of folklore*. Edited by Alan Dundes. Englewood Cliffs, N.J.: Prentice-Hall.)
DAVENPORT, WILLIAM H.
1962   Fourteen Marshallese riddles. *Journal of American Folklore.* 65:265–266.
MALINOWSKI, BRONISLAW
1955   "Myth in primitive psychology," in *Magic, science, and religion and other essays*. Garden City, N.Y.: Doubleday Anchor Books. (Originally printed in 1926 in one volume.)
MARANDA, E. K.
1970a   Les femmes Lau — Malaita, îles Solomon — dans l'espace socialisé. *Journal de la Société des Océanistes* 26:155–162.
1970b   "Structures and genres of Melanesian narratives," in *Proceedings of the symposium on the structures and genres of ethnic literature, Palermo.*
1971   "Toward the investigation of narrative combinations: introduction," in *Structural models in folklore and transformational essays*. Edited by E. K. Maranda and Pierre Maranda. The Hague: Mouton.
1972   "Theory and practice of riddle analysis," in *Toward new perspectives in folklore*. Edited by Americo Paredes and Richard Bauman, 51–61. Austin: University of Texas Press for the American Folklore Society.

1973   Five interpretations of a Melanesian myth. *Journal of American Folklore* 86:3–13.

MARANDA, PIERRE, ELLI KÖNGÄS MARANDA
1970   "Le Crane et l'utérus: deux théorèmes nord-malaitains," in *Échanges et communications: mélanges offerts à Claude Lévi-Strauss.* Edited by Jean Pouillon and Pierre Maranda. The Hague: Mouton.

PART TWO

Introduction: Part Two

RICHARD M. DORSON

The papers in Part Two do not fall directly within the four main rubrics of the conference at Indiana University, but they impinge to some extent on the same themes, and they all deal with folklore and its processes in today's world rather than in a past era. Thus Roger D. Abrahams and Susan Kalčik deal to some extent with urban folklore in their essay on folklore and cultural pluralism; Linda Dégh and Andrew Vázsonyi include a section on folklore in the mass media in their treatise on dialectics of the legend; Robert B. Klymasz, in an eyebrow-raising paper, suggests industrial applications to the scientific breeding of plants through the playing of folk music. In other contributions, one sees adaptations of traditional forms — oral history in Nigeria, folk theater in Afghanistan, folk lyrics in villages of Spain — to modern influences. Robert A. Georges writes about life attitudes communicated to Greeks living today from tales of long ago, and Juha Pentikäinen drafts a model of the channels through which folk wisdom flows in contemporary society.

All the papers in this volume address the conference theme, namely that folklorists no longer view their subject as a matter of antiquities and survivals but approach it as a record and reflection of current concerns. √

Folklore and Cultural Pluralism

ROGER D. ABRAHAMS and SUSAN KALČIK

Folklorists have been concerned with traditions, with expressions of cultural persistence, since the beginnings of the discipline. Yet now that ethnic persistence is a focal area of social concern, there is no rush on the part of folklorists to bring their accumulated knowledge and insights to bear on the basic questions that are raised when culturally different populations begin dramatizing their differences. This paper explores how the folklorist might bring special knowledge and perspectives to the study of ethnicity in the United States.

From a simplistic sociological perspective, it might be asked how an individual can be both American and Italian-American, Jewish-American, or Irish-American. This concept is a problem only for those who wish to be regarded both as American and as some kind of ethnic. In such a case, a person is apt to handle the problem by a selective manipulation of symbols of ethnic identification, setting aside certain times and places where the ethnic role may be played out. It is often, for instance, the green beer drunk ceremonially and festively on St. Patty's Day each year that has become one of the means by which some Irish-Americans have dramatized their vision and valuation of the continuity of culture. Such drinking is their little piece of obligatory behavior, shared joyously with the rest of America, which they regard as immutably Irish. It is a historically interesting act because of the stereotype of the Irish as sentimental drunkards, a stereotype that has operated greatly to the detriment of the Irish. This capitalization on an exoteric view of an ethnic group is not unusual in the development of group pride.

This paper was written while one of us (Abrahams) was on a grant from the Center for Urban Ethnography. Our thanks are due to its director, John F. Szwed, for his counsel on questions of ethnicity, and to our colleagues Américo Paredes and Richard Bauman, as well.

Certainly the drinking of beer dyed with food coloring is an ersatz and cheap way of playing the cultural game and says nothing about how any folk perform to and with each other. If anything, we would have to call it *fakelore* and dismiss it from our folkloristic consideration. But folklorists today are interested in a wider range of problems than when such a hard-and-fast distinction between the real thing and its imitation was made. Furthermore, public interest demands that folklorists look not only at what folklore is but at how it is used, both within a folk community and when it becomes an expression of popular culture for the ethnic group that "goes public" by getting involved in the more complex, culturally heterogeneous situation of contemporary America.

Paradoxically, various ethnic groups today are dramatizing their cultural apartness by making a more and more public display of traditional practices. These developments in going public often bring about severe departures from — and, many would argue, disruptions of — these traditional practices. Yet if such public displays are the means by which ethnic identity is maintained or recaptured, who is the folklorist to damn the proceedings by invoking the claims of legitimacy and branding the phenomenon as *fakelore*?

When Richard M. Dorson (1950) originally argued for a hard-and-fast distinction between folklore and fakelore, the choice was a clearer and easier one to make. Mass culture was taking over and threatening everyone, particularly those who cling to the ideal of the small, homogeneous community with its local and regional colorations preserved in their full strength. One had to agree with Dorson — and many other intellectuals of that day — that mass culture was indeed "highly commercial, blatant, loud, aggressive" and that fakelore as a product of mass culture was a debasement, and therefore, malodorous. Fakelore took on the coloration of the "quaint, cute, whimsical, syrupy" and was observably beset by "gooey fabrications" in which traditional performance was sentimentalized and prettified (Dorson 1971:5–8). Folklore, on the other hand, was "virile, coarse-grained."

That these traditional performance pieces were primarily to be recovered in backwater and generally poverty-stricken areas was ignored. What mattered was that folk traditions endured and that they could be used as a measure of what was happening to culture, on the national level, especially as it was being fabricated on Madison Avenue.

It has become evident that this distinction between real and ersatz traditions is losing much of its ideological usefulness. The image of the enemy has changed somewhat, and the need to maintain one's ethnic identity wherever one happens to find it — in city or country — has become self-evident and more persistent.

One dimension of the national self-criticism of the 1960's was to point out that traditionalism of the sort idealized by folklorists also meant an inability of those traditional populations either to negotiate effectively with agencies of national power or to move to where the work was. The fierce independence of the mountain and hill people all too easily became intransigence, leading, in part, to abject poverty, as well as an inability to adapt successfully to new and more populous environments.

The more one looked around in the 1960's, the more one saw other such groups who had been "left behind." The Black presence had been there all along, but now Chicanos and Indians were rediscovered. Their self-publicization has led not only to a rediscovery of some vestige of cultural continuity and integrity, but to what seems to be a parallel investigation on the part of many Euro-Americans. Looking at one's sense of community and tradition has been especially characteristic of central, eastern, and southern European Catholic working-class groups, which are now being called the "white ethnics."

It is not just the self-publicization of racial groups that has affected ethnics and mainstream Americans but the success of that activity. To some degree, this success has led to the achievement of political integration and the gaining of power and organizational strength. Perhaps more important is the notion that such movements did not destroy America; it survived the Black Panther and Black Power movements; it survived and continues to survive nonconformity. What these movements say then is that the melting pot theory and other 100-percent-American theories are not imperative for the United States to survive, and that the kind of conformity demanded in the "Americanization" movement that led to the Immigration Act of 1924 and culminated in the dullness of the 1950's and the rebellion of the 1960's is not the only way to go. There seems to have been a change in the definition of the nation and its people, as well as a change in the confidence in America's ability to survive as a cultural plurality.

This growing sense of ethnic difference challenges the image of what is American, and more than that, forces us to recognize that the tradition-bound characteristics that have made Appalachia and the Ozarks into a version of Arcadia do not provide a very useful model of community and tradition now that we recognize the poverty and isolation of these areas. Thus, we cannot rely just on such WASP rural communities as our guarantee that our cultural diversity will be recognized and maintained. We must look as well to the ethnic communities that have maintained their ethnicity, even while becoming a part of American society, to find out how such cultural pluralism operates. And the more we observe such communities, the more we are forced to recognize in their development elements of their folklore that move toward popularization for mass approval, that move indeed close to the domain of fakelore. We witness a dramatization of selected ethnic traditions into public performance (or products) intended for an audience that goes far beyond the ethnic community itself. Yet this development may permit the community to maintain other culturally distinctive traits — indeed, it may serve as the organizing phenomenon around which the community comes to celebrate itself — although it does so often in the company of outsiders.

With ethnic "minorities" such as Blacks and Chicanos, the recognition of cultural differences is not such a problem. They have been segregated geographically and socially for so long that an entire complex of linguistic and cultural differences has been maintained. Thus, in developing their ethnic pride, these minority communities have a great fund of culturally different practices and behaviors to draw upon as means of announcing integrity and presence. (Ironically, their consciousness of these traits is often introduced by outsiders, through stereotyping or through anthropological study, or both.) With white ethnics, the situation is different because they have convinced themselves and been convinced that they have been acculturated into some supposed American mainstream culture.

Admittedly we bias the argument a bit by looking at the establishment of ethnicity from the perspective of such peripheral social practices as drinking green beer or any such annual phenomenon. We certainly need to distinguish between those Irish-Americans who assert their Irishness only on St. Patrick's Day (and at other convenient times) but who live by essentially American middle-class styles, manners, and values, on the one hand, and those, on the other, who live in enclaves, marry within a community, and carry on certain traditions as regular features of their lives. These latter Irish-Americans may regularly attend *ceilidhs* where they perform Irish music and dance, and they may practice modified Irish courtship and family behaviors. This they do just as self-consciously as the man who drinks the green beer; it is just as earnest an attempt to identify oneself publicly as an Irish-American, but the public audience is different, as is the intensity, duration and periodicity of the performance.

The St. Patrick's Day Irish are drawing upon their supposed heritage as part of their general approach to life. Being Irish is just one of many roles they play; they cling to their ancestry as a means of maximizing the number of roles available to them. Their Irishness is one way to manipulate their own sense of identity, thus preserving their intuitions of freedom — for freedom is, in its middle-American variant, the recognition of a range of behavioral alternatives and the ability to make choices that play out the opportunities fully and successfully. This is quite different from the everyday Irish-American, who has little ability or interest in recognizing lifestyle alternatives, much less in operating in terms of such choice. This person generally lives in a working-class, post-agrarian world — post-agrarian in that his lifestyle is still tied to agrarian or at least *auld sod* behaviors and familistic ideals.

Ethnicity involves a range of behavior or performance, involving the conscious and the unconscious, as well as the public and private. There may be two continua operating from private to public and from unconscious to conscious performance. The study of one extreme may shed light on the other, and the study of the continua can help us see at what point and in what situation ethnic performance was and is permitted or encouraged by the larger culture. Some investigators have talked about a kind of code-switching between "American" and ethnic styles. Part of the white ethnic movement may thus involve the decision to code-switch less often and to display greater freedom in performing publicly what was once reserved for family or other in-group situations, although this behavior may still have its dangers arising from a lack of cultural understanding. White ethnic representatives claim, for example, that the American public's reaction to Spiro Agnew involved his ethnic style, which some could relate to and which others found offensive. It has been suggested, too, that Edmund Muskie's tears over the attack of his wife in New Hampshire during the 1972 primaries represented an emotional response distasteful to those not familiar with this ethnic style and that it led to his downfall.

Strangely enough, it was the immigrant Catholic groups — the Polish-, Slovak-, Italian-, or Irish-Americans — who were once considered the very models of assimilated populations, for they were the ones who "made it" in America. But with the various power movements of the 1960's, there occurred a sudden recognition in such groups that in many crucial ways the question of assimilation was quite beside the point and that in their most important, if private and familial, dimensions of life, they had remained Old World in their living patterns. It was a matter of providing outside legitimization for what was still there, and this came by way of the cultural-difference model of American society, dramatized by Blacks, Chicanos, and Native Americans — thus the coming-out party for white ethnics.

Grouping these various communities together may be somewhat misleading. It is important to bear in mind — especially from a folkloristic point of view — that there is a major difference between white ethnics and others. Although the Irish, for instance, provided the first slave labor in the New World, and they, along with Italians, Jews, Slavs, and other late nineteenth-century immigrant groups, were socially excluded from entrance into society's mainstream, they nevertheless found access to political, economic, and social power sources and, therefore, had some choices of lifestyles. On the other hand, browns, reds, blacks, and, to some extent, yellows were restricted to reservations or ghettoes. There is a high correlation between the level of cultural distinctiveness and the degree to which a community has been excluded. Thus, to include the white ethnics as ethnics at all, one must establish a sliding scale of ethnicity.

Fredrick Barth's discussion (1969:10–11) of ethnic communities and the establishment of boundaries helps in setting up such a scale. An ethnic group, he postulates, is a population that (1) is largely biologically self-perpetuating; (2) shares fundamental cultural values, realized in overt unity in cultural forms; (3) makes up a field of communication and interaction; and (4) has a membership that identifies itself and is identified by others, as constituting a category distinguishable from other categories of the same order. In-group criteria of community membership such as these are not totally unexplored in folklore scholarship. William Hugh Jansen's ground-breaking article (1959) on the esoteric-exoteric factor in folklore argues forcibly not only that groups have stereotypical concepts of themselves, of others, and of what others think of them, but that such notions are most forcibly and memorably embodied in jokes, anecdotes, legends, slurs, and other traditional expressive genres. Furthermore, a number of folklorists have studied how such factors operate in the folklore of specific communities. (One thinks immediately of Dorson's multiethnic study, *Bloodstoppers and bearwalkers* (1952), Neil Rosenberg's dissertation on southern white "Rastus and Mandy" stories (1970), and the study of stereotype inversion in Afro-American folklore in Abrahams' *Positively black* (1970).

But what folklorists have not been sufficiently cognizant of is how devices of folklore are used by community members as a means of establishing the major parameters of a community's concept of itself. This has been left to our colleagues in anthropology, who until recently have dealt with aboriginal or non-European peasant groups. Folklorists have not concerned themselves with the symbolic load of performances because they really have not been much concerned with performance. Rather, ours has been an antiquarian, or historically oriented, discipline, devoting its efforts to the preservation of items of performance so that we may study the way in which they were constructed and the paths by which they have been disseminated. Essentially, this has meant that folklorists have assumed an ideal "folk" group, uncontaminated by the incursions of mass culture and its accompanying media of record (such as print and phonograph records). Dorson's distinction between folklore and fakelore gave a name to the fear that the existence of folk culture was threatened, that nothing was so inimical to folk culture as blatant and sweetened-up imitations of folk performance. Yet this put folklorists in the strange position of acting as guardians of the purity of the folk. We were really guarding our own purity, however; we weren't concerned with the folk at all — only with their items of performance. All of this changed in the post-World War II era as folklorists became more and more involved with informants and their problems and it became evident that these problems did not arise just because of incursions of mass culture into their lives.

That the distinction between folk and mass culture was on our folkloristic minds in the 1940's and 1950's is easily discovered in the studies of the time. Francis Lee Utley (1961) made a survey of the accumulated wisdom of the profession with regard to the definition of folklore in the *Funk and Wagnall's standard dictionary of folklore, mythology and legend*. Utley found that the single common element in the twenty-one definitions related to the "traditional" nature of the items of lore under study, traditionality being ascertained by evidence of the oral transmission of items of performance. Evidence of oral transmission comes not, in this view, from actual elicitation of the lore as it is performed but, rather, from evidence adduced from the texts themselves with regard to their style and the amount and range of variation among texts of the same or related items. As Dan Ben-Amos (1972) argues, this view of folklore implicitly argues for a definition of folk performance as well as for the lore itself. Folklore, in this view, exists only in groups in which the performers come from the community, are known personally to some or all members of the audience, and perform on a face-to-face basis to these friends and neighbors.

All this reveals the intellectual underpinnings of the concept of folklore. *Folklore* is folklore-type performances uncontaminated by the presentational techniques appropriate to the mass media. No wonder that D. K. Wilgus (1971), Archie Green (1972), and many others have had such a hard time convincing fellow folklorists of the usefulness of phonograph recordings in the study of traditional song. The very existence of such a media was considered *prima facie* evidence of the incursion of devices of mass culture. Anything that would question the definition of folklore as items of performances carried solely by such word-of-mouth transmission would undermine the belief in the purity and persistence of the homogeneous folk community. The coining of the concept of fakelore was a valiant attempt to put a stop to such contaminating forces.

This is not to argue that there is no meaningful distinction between folklore and popular culture. To the contrary, there is, although it is not a firm one, or does it carry the implicit valuation given good folklore and bad popular culture. Rather, folklore and popular culture are simply different because they call for a different relationship between performer and audience and a different, if often related, set of materials.

What seems ironic, in retrospect, is that merely asking folklorists to define folklore became a force in a rethinking of the entire discipline. Until the late 1940's, folklore was thought of as the product of folk performance; one knew intuitively which specific items were traditional and which were not because one had worked with the materials long enough to feel the difference immediately — even when performers gave voice to a popular song or story on the same occasion that they performed an archaic, traditional item. When folklore was defined with an emphasis on the centrality of oral transmission, however, the relationship of the performers and audience was then introduced into the discussion, and this necessitated an acknowledgment of the place of the actual performers in the transmission process. The result was a call to add a discussion of performers and the context of performance to the publication of the texts (it should be noted here that folksong scholars such as Gerould, Pound, Gummere, and, in a different tradition of scholarship, the Lomaxes, were the first to pursue these interests).

It is significant that this change was going on at both centers of folklore study at the same time — the University of Pennsylvania and Indiana University. Just as Dorson was publishing important studies incorporating nontextual materials from his recording sessions in the field and giving strong, if impressionistic, descriptions of his informants and their style of delivery, so MacEdward Leach (1961; 1963), who headed the program at the University of Pennsylvania, was making his memorably stirring calls for the addition of such "contextual" material as "The Singer *and* the Song" and "What shall we do with 'little Mattie Groves'" in his speeches.

As so often happens, when the students from these institutions heeded this call and directed their gazes away from texts to the larger cultural matrices in which the performances persist, there was some consternation among the old masters. Among other things, it has led Dorson in self-defense to coin a new title, "the contextual school" of folkloristics, thereby putting us in our place. But to give credit where due, this is a movement which he has not only done much to father but to publicize as well.

When the study of folklore is concerned primarily with reconstructing the past, it must of necessity be tied to what are assumed to be the records of the past. Thus, folklorists studied texts as the external recording of performances made possible with the development of writing and print. In the 1940's and 1950's, when the discontent began within the folklore ranks in the United States, it was the limitations of these media of record that were fastened onto, especially the publication of song texts without melodies. Yet a tune is only one of many elements of song performance that is lost when the song is committed to print, and it was just these dimensions that were missed most by the folklore students of that era. With the development of phonograph recordings and films, some misgivings have been taken care of, even though such media simply abstract the performance items without situating them very effectively. Still lacking was the human behavioral dimension of performance. The new generation of folklorists began searching for ways to redefine the central terms of the discipline so that they might refocus away from these surface renderings toward what the performer and the audience carried into the performance-interaction.

There ensued a search for models of analysis, a process that continues today. Rather than looking to literary and historical techniques of study, folklorists tried ethnographic, linguistic, and communications models. Significantly, all of these are synchronic and ahistorical models that fly in the face of the diachronic antiquarians. Among other things, their use means that the central term of folklore — tradition — has to be eschewed or redefined.

Many of us delighted in Ben-Amos' solution (1971) to the problem; he was able to define folklore without recourse to the word *tradition* by choosing to emphasize instead patterned communication within a group meeting together regularly on a face-to-face basis for the purpose of self-entertainment and instruction (Ben-Amos 1971:3–15). The rejection of the concept of tradition, or at least the retreat from its centrality in folkloristics, is crucial if folklorists are to consider such phenomena as St. Patrick's Day in any useful way. And it seems important for folklorists to concern themselves with the "rise of ethnicity," for it is in the area of performance (and with performances developed out of what are regarded by the ethnic communities as traditional) that this ethnicity is being dramatized. Because folklore has turned its attention to performance, and because of a growing inclination to see folklore as embracing a wide range of performance, the informal and everyday as well as the formal, it seems particularly well suited for the study of ethnicity. The folklorist cannot only record and study the range of ethnic behavior, from its everyday elements such as gesture and conversational genres to the more elaborate festivals such as weddings and the occasions of group celebration such as a yearly "Czech fest" but also can trace the connection between the formal and informal, the public and the private. Such investigations of ethnic performance will likely lead both to a greater understanding of cognitive differences among ethnic groups, as well as a definition of ethnicity and how it operates.

But in making such a study of folklore and ethnicity, we would be wise to eschew the kinds of value judgments involved in distinguishing between the real and the fake and rather become concerned with a description of the change in performer-audience relationship and in setting and how these changes affect the form and content of the performance. By doing this, we will in effect describe the changeover from the folk to the popular, but this change does not need carry with it any feeling of debasement, for the popular dramatization of ethnic diversity carries with it the reestablishment of the sense of legitimacy of being ethnically different. The concern, then, is the increasingly public use of esoteric performances, for the survival of certain aspects of folk-level ethnic identity in both urban and suburban settings suggests certain major questions and areas of study for the folklorist with regard to how, what, and why ethnicity survives.

From this point, our remarks take the form of suggestions rather than folkloric reporting because the data to support any conclusions is not yet available.

It is clear that all minority groups, especially the white ethnics, have been acculturated to some degree into the mainstream. It would seem that the white ethnics' apparent success in assimilation has had to do with their ability to relegate their ethnic traits to areas that have been acceptable and nonthreatening to the mainstream culture. They have, in effect, been able to render to Caesar while maintaining a kind of underground ethnicity. Many ethnic and immigrant novels and publicly given personal narratives, such as that by Spiro Agnew before his fall, present a picture of successful assimilation, but there are others that describe a compromise, the establishment of an equilibrium between things American and things ethnic.

It is just such a distinction to which the folklorist can usefully address himself, for it is primarily in the personal anecdote — the illustrative "story" — that this kind of counterassimilationist message can be discovered. These involve incidents that are recounted or people that are talked about within a personal, face-to-face encounter in which some reprehensible rejection from one's ethnic past is dramatized. Frequent stories concern how so-and-so, who had rejected the old ways of the parents, after their death, in guilt, takes a trip to the homeland and recaptures a sense of identity, and how someone else who is Slovak but claims to be Irish changes his name and begins to manufacture stories of his spurious heritage. Eventually he goes to Ireland and returns, bringing more stories and the inevitable souvenirs, including a *shillelagh*. The Slovaks who work with him have the last laugh, of course, when they discover the *shillelagh* was made in Japan.

Such stories illustrate how important it is to study ethnicity and self-image in all of its manifestations. Assimilation may occur in individuals, families, even whole communities, in certain dimensions, while other aspects of behavior and identity remain unchanged. In fact, the national forces imposing the assimilationist model are selective in the areas of life in which they want to — or can — effect changes. Such forces seem to have more direct access to public than to private institutions. For instance, culturally or linguistically different behaviors are discouraged in governmental service agencies, especially the schools, as the Amish, the supporters of parochial schools, and minority groups in the public school systems can attest. But certain more private institutional areas tolerate differences, such as food consumption, the celebration of festivals and rites of passage, and some aspects of religious behavior. These are family-connected for the most part. Mikulski (Clancy 1970:562) claims that "the ethnic quality comes through especially in two kinds of celebrations. First of all there are the weddings, funerals and baptisms. Then there are the big feasts."

One way of investigating these areas of permitted ethnicity would be to identify those aspects of ethnicity that groups are willing to make public and even profitable. Public approval and acceptance can be a key or bridge to those areas of private life in which ethnic expression is given license. And the white ethnic movement can be studied for insights into the aspects of ethnicity that have served as rallying points for the ethnic minority in America.

The study of performance, public and private, among white ethnics can also lead to an understanding of the more intangible aspects of ethnicity such as world view. Some impressionistic discussion of this has appeared in the ethnic power literature, such as Novak's (1972) statement that the American experience melted the surfaces or appearances of the ethnics but not their "inner feelings, aspirations, symbolic patterns" or their reactions "to pain, to authority, to dissent or rebellion, to fatherhood or family life, to mobility or home ownership," and his claim that the Anglo model is very different from the ethnic's model of life, which revolves around community and family (Novak 1972:48). Where in people's daily lives should the folklorist look for signs of ethnicity, and how have these been regulated by the larger American culture? Has there been a change recently in regulating or accepting ethnic behavior of this sort? The answers to these questions would shed light on the questions of where ethnicity went when it was banished from the public scene (except for special occasions) and how it was maintained and transmitted in family and in-group situations.

Also, by studying the aspects of ethnicity that the movement has chosen to reveal and emphasize, we can approach another important area of inquiry. The parallels between the growth of ethnic awareness and the black movement are clear, and the connection is reinforced by the fact that many of its leaders were trained in the civil rights movement before "whitey" was thrown out. The ethnics, like the blacks, have seemingly chosen to emphasize the things about themselves that are different from Anglo or mainstream American culture; in effect, they have chosen to reverse, in part, their own assimilation process. The white ethnics' choice is significant because, as was not the case for Blacks or Chicanos or indians, the differences could be and have been disguised. By looking into such matters, folklorists may find themselves pursuing a different range of problems with familiar data. In the past we have been inadvertently studying the process of acculturation; now we may find ourselves observing its very opposite.

The adoption or bringing into the open of ethnic traits is a kind of self-pollution. For example, the term *PIGS*, adopted by the ethnic movement to refer to Poles, Italians, Germans, Greeks, Slovaks, is an insulting, self-polluting label, and the claim to belong to the margins of society rather than to be a part of the center or establishment also reverses the assimilation process and brings down on ethnics' heads the charge of being different, non-Anglo. Consciously or unconsciously, white ethnics have seen that power can exist at the margins of society. As Novak (1972:440) says, "Many an Irish telephone operator, watching her Afro-American colleagues protest and demand, has felt confused emotions, both of respect and of horror. 'And all these years, we were docile and obedient. Why didn't we speak up like they're doing?'" Unsuccessful as the Blacks in working through the system, the white ethnics may have found marginality a source of power or energy from which this segment of the working class could organize.

There are numerous other questions that the white ethnic movement raises. Can this movement be linked to a wider, national or even international revitalization movement? Can it be seen as an aspect of what Cora Bell (1972) calls the "re-tribalization" of parts of the world in a post-imperial age? It may be that the movement points to an important need of modern society. Novak speaks of "the need for concrete, historical identity in a machine-like world" (1972:440), and Mikulski describes "an ethnic collectivity" as a way to "resist homogenization," to work against alienation and toward "personalism" (Clancy 1970:558). The counter-culture movement in the United States and elsewhere seems to be a middle- and upper-class form of neotribalism, while the racial and ethnic movements provide a lower-class parallel.

Recent work (*Daedalus* 1972) on "post-traditional" societies offers some insights on the segregation and interplay of tradition and modernity that could prove useful to a study of ethnicity in the United States. One reason that modern societies differ greatly from the traditional and transitional ones is that earlier identities expressed in differing traditions have not been lost. In the United States, where modern institutions have been integrated with many and various traditions, cultural pluralism is not a choice but an unavoidable reality. Some investigators have found that traditional elements are reactivated in times of crisis and by those most threatened, which may help explain the impetus for the white ethnic movement among a group of people who argue that they have been forgotten politically and socially in this nation. It also has been suggested that the social scientists' concept of tradition and of traditional societies inherited from Tönnies (1972) and Redfield (1967) is not flexible enough, that traditional practices, since they involve the way a society deals with the most fundamental questions, offer no final formulations and should not be studied as if they did. Hence, earlier arguments, that older models of what tradition is and where it resides in the culture need to be reexamined.

Another question that needs to be resolved regards whether white ethnics have been accepted by mainstream American culture. Social scientists seem, in the main, to have ignored this question. A comparison of the literature on Blacks, Chicanos, and Native Americans with that on white ethnics — considerable mainly in the areas of historical studies of immigration and assimilation and in sociology — leads to queries concerning the existence of a bias against white ethnics. All of these questions are ones to which folklorists as well as sociologists might usefully address themselves. It would be reassuring to think that folklorists might thus use our techniques of studying traditions and performances on new and more self-conscious expressions of tradition and on new self-publicizing modes of performance. The line between folk and popular culture in this area is a hard one to draw; but need folklorists fear contamination any longer?

REFERENCES

ABRAHAMS, ROGER D.
   1970   *Positively black*. Englewood Cliffs, N.J.: Prentice-Hall.
BARTH, FREDERICK
   1969   *Ethnic groups and boundaries: the social organization of culture difference*. Boston: Little, Brown.
BELL, CORA
   1972   The new tribalism. *Nation* 214 (January 10).
BEN-AMOS, DANIEL
   1971   Toward a definition of folklore in context. *Journal of American Folklore* 84.
CLANCY, THOMAS H., editor
   1970   The ethnic American: an interview with Barbara Mikulski. *America* 123 (December 26).
Daedalus
   1972   102 (Winter).
DORSON, RICHARD M.
   1950   Folklore and fakelore. *American Mercury* 70.
   1952   *Bloodstoppers and bearwalkers*. Cambridge: Harvard University Press.
   1971   *American folklore and the historian*. Chicago: University of Chicago Press.
GREEN, ARCHIE
   1972   *Only a miner*. Urbana: University of Illinois Press.
JANSEN, WILLIAM HUGH
   1959   "The esoteric-exoteric factor in folklore. *Fabula* 2. (Reprinted in *The study of folklore*. Edited by Alan Dundes. Englewood Cliffs, N.J.: Prentice-Hall, 1965.)
LEACH, MacEDWARD
   1961   "The singer and the song," in *Singers and storytellers*. Dallas: Southern Methodist University Press.
   1963   What shall we do with "little Mattie Groves?" *Journal of American Folklore* 76.
NOVAK, MICHAEL
   1972   What the melting pot didn't melt. *Christian Century* 89 (April 19).
REDFIELD, ROBERT
   1967   *The primitive world and its transformations*. Ithaca: Cornell University Press.

ROSENBERG, NEIL V.
1970   "Stereotype and tradition: white folklore about blacks." Unpublished doctoral dissertation, Indiana University, Bloomington.
TÖNNIES, FERDINAND
1972   *Community and society*. New York: Harper.
UTLEY, FRANCIS L.
1961   Folk literature: an operational definition. *Journal of American Folklore* 74.
WILGUS, D. K.
1971   "Country-western music and the urban hillbilly," in *The urban experience and folk tradition*. Edited by Américo Paredes and Ellen J. Stekert. Austin and London: Published for the American Folklore Society by the University of Texas Press.

Oral Transmission of Knowledge

JUHA PENTIKÄINEN

A HOLISTIC VIEW OF THE ORAL TRANSMISSION PROCESS

Folkloristics is most emphatically a discipline in which, to a large extent, progress follows trends within neighboring disciplines. Stimuli have been taken from fields such as history, comparative literature, psychology, sociology, cultural anthropology, comparative religion, and linguistics. It would seem, however, that many of the stimulating impulses available at present will be ignored and not applied to folkloristic problems if folklorists do not recognize that not only should traditional texts be the object of their study but also that the events that accompany the transmission of the tradition should be so treated. Today this means that both oral communication and the channels by which mass lore is conveyed need to be studied and explained together with the interaction that takes place between written and oral means of communication. In fact, this is but one basic model of human intercourse. The transmission of tradition from one generation to another is the process on which the teaching of the knowledge of culture, "social transfer," is based (Hulkrantz 1960:69–76).

The informing process within a society is usually divided into (1) the transmission of information on tradition and (2) the contribution to the formation of information, which can be divided into teaching and upbringing.

In a modern civilization, teaching is carried out primarily by the schools, from preschool institutions to universities. Upbringing, which consists of making individuals acquainted with or oriented to rules of behavior or norms that are demanded for the security of an individual, is carried out predominantly by the primary groups surrounding an individual, such as the family. The formation of information includes, besides the actual creative sciences and humanities, the free action of information, which is taken care of in modern society by literature, the press, radio, and television.

In an oral society, the channels of information are less complicated than in a modern society, and the formation of new information occurs less rapidly. Illiterate societies are more homogeneous in their social structure and hierarchy, and then, too, the institutions for the transmission and formation of information are in many cases the same as in a literate society. In cultural anthropology, information transmitted from one generation to another is described generally by the concept "culture." The formation of new information is tied up with the culture's spawning inventions. One can say that individuals who come by birth to a community do not develop and create culture of their own but, rather, that the culture develops them. The hegemony of people in the world is secured not primarily by their ability constantly to invent new things, but by their capability to adopt, transfer, and apply tradition. In studying the transmission of tradition, one can distinguish between enculturation — the internalization of culture — and socialization — the integration into society and its norms. In an illiterate society, these processes are oral; in a literate society, they are both written and oral.

The concept of *oral tradition* is the counterpart to literary tradition. Albert B. Lord (1964:5–7) points out that oral tradition — he refers especially to verse tradition — is learned and transmitted orally. The minimal definition of tradition includes "culture (elements) handed down from one generation to another" (Hulkrantz 1960:229–231). The Latin verb *tradere* carries the connotation of continuity. Another criterion of tradition is its social character. "Tradition" and "individual knowledge" are concepts that are not to be confused with one another. Individual knowledge, in general, is unwritten information retained by persons in their memory; information is tied up with the human mechanism of memory, and for that reason, it is prone to different transformations. The changes may result from the memory failure and from contamination by the rest of the material collected in the memory. With tradition, the case is similar, but all memory information is not tradition, nor does all individual knowledge become tradition. (In the process of adapting into tradition the choices made by the society, social control also is crucial.) Besides collective tradition, one finds group tradition and craft tradition in a community. The preservation by individuals, from one generation to another, of information not generally known by the community, characterizes individual tradition. Idiosyncrasies, pieces of behavior typical of just one individual, are generally excluded from individual traditions. These will only seldom become tradition. If the information carried by an individual has no continuity, if it is not handed down, if the whole society or one of its groups, does not accept it, one is not dealing with the tradition (Pentikäinen 1968:109–112).

Historically, the problems of oral tradition have belonged to folklorists; however, not many folklorists actually study oral tradition. Instead they study folklore, which is given different meanings by scholars.

It is surprising that many international terminologies of folklore do not even mention oral tradition. The *Dictionary of folklore, mythology and legend* (Leach 1949–1950:308–403) gives a list of views of twenty-one scholars concerning folklore and does not define the concept normatively. Even the title of the book is curious, for it places the terms *folklore*, *mythology*, and *legend* side by side, as if the latter two could not be included in the first. Content analysis of the ideas of the twenty-one writers reveals the heterogeneity of their views. In their characterizations of folklore, the most frequently repeated words are *tradition* (which appears 13 times), *oral* (13), *transmission* (6), *survival* (6), and *social* (6). Most of these writers (13) agree that folklore is found in both primitive and civilized societies. Eighteen writers include literature in folklore; 12 include religion; 5 include crafts, and 3 include folk speech. The view of the majority is that the definitive criterion of folklore is simply oral transmission (Utley 1961:193–206). Alan Dundes (1965:1–3) points out that this cannot be the only criterion, and he is undoubtedly right. On the other hand, one cannot approve of Dundes's pessimistic attitude toward operational definitions. In his *The study of folklore* (1965), Dundes does not define the concept "folklore" at all; he is content merely to list some of its forms.

The differences between such views may be explained in terms of the difference between literature (aesthetics), on one hand, and anthropology, on the other. In the former case, folklore is considered a species of literature; in the latter, it is considered a central element of culture of an entity. When the approach is aesthetic, the folklorist uses critical analysis of texts, but an anthropologically oriented folklorist pays principal attention to the context of the tradition and aims at explaining the use, meaning, and function of a tradition. The position of folklore within anthropology has been considered by William R. Bascom in his numerous articles. He writes:

Folklore, to the anthropologist, is a part of culture but not the whole of culture. It includes myths, legends, tales, proverbs, riddles, the texts of ballads and other songs, and other forms of lesser importance, but not folk art, folk dance, folk music, folk costume, folk medicine, folk custom, or folk belief . . . All folklore is orally transmitted, but not all that is orally transmitted is folklore (Bascom in Dundes 1965:28).

Bascom's definition is regarded as too narrow by many folklorists because many categories, for example, belief tradition and the musicological subjects of ballads and other folksongs, are left outside the concept "folklore." For Bascom, folklore is verbal art (Bascom 1955:245–252). The idea of differentiating the two terms is good. If folklore and oral tradition were classified as one entity, all information in nonliterate cultures would be included under the term *folklore*. Differentiation between the terms is advantageous, also, because it is not necessary to attach the criterion *oral* to folklore. In practice, a folklorist confronts literary tradition (booklore) as well as either wholly or partly nonverbal material. The meaning of oral tradition depends crucially on what is understood by the words *oral* and *tradition*, whereas the meaning of folklore consists of the meanings of the words *folk* and *lore*. The task of a student of folklore is both wider and narrower than that of one who deals with oral tradition. Students of oral tradition study all orally transmitted tradition information, the former study only a part of it, but the folklore student may, in addition to verbal tradition, also consider nonverbal material and written material as well. The central problem of the study of oral tradition is the process by which tradition is transmitted in speech from speaker to hearer.

In their quest for text materials, folklorists have all too often been content to approach their research as if it were a question of merely locating and examining written documents. The care taken in trying to locate every single item of information on a subject from archives and literary sources for comparative research has been commendable. On the other hand, how the texts came to be in the archives, how they came to be recorded and in what context they existed as living tradition have often been ignored. What Malinowski said as early as 1926 has been forgotten: "The text, of course, is extremely important, but without the context it remains lifeless" (1926:24). The significance of written variants has also been overestimated when attempts have been made by diffusionists to arrive at the original function of a folktale by, for example, interpreting texts. It is true that a skillful text critic can reach certain conclusions on the basis of the text alone, but a reliable taxonomy of tradition necessitates careful analysis of both source and context at the fieldwork stage. Dundes (1966:505–516) writes, "One cannot always guess the meaning from context. For this reason, folklorists must actively seek to elicit the meaning of folklore from the folk."

A holistic view of the transmission process is an attempt to arrive at a synthesis by analyzing systematically the variables of oral communication. In this way, scholars must direct their attention to all the factors that can influence the transmission of tradition, those factors that concern the culture, the community, the individual, or the deep structure of the tradition itself, and they must further examine the interaction among all these factors.

TRANSMISSION OF TRADITION AS A SOCIAL, COMMUNICATIVE EVENT

Communication theory provides a specialized approach to problems encountered in the study of the transmission (communication) of a message (information) from one source to another. This study is essentially based on the systematics of probability, working with information-theoretic models. The basic formula of the system of communication has five elements: (1) the information source, (2) the transmitter, (3) the channel of transmission, (4) the receiver, and (5) the destination (cf. Shannon, Weaver 1959:4–6, 98–99; Cherry 1959:3–29). The information source produces messages to be communicated and chooses the desired message from possible alternatives. The transmitter turns the message into a signal and sends it through different channels of transmission to the receiver. The function of the receiver is to transform the information into a message again and to deliver it to the destination. From this point of view, oral transmission can be characterized as a process by which the source of information is the brain of the speaker; the transmitter is the speech organs; the channel is the air; the receiver is the ears of the hearer; and the destination is the brain of the hearer. Like any information, oral tradition is liable to distortion from different transformations caused by disturbances that are labeled *noise* in communication theory. The concept includes all the factors influencing the transmission and causing the received message to be anything other than identical with sent message.

The transmission process of oral tradition can be illustrated diagrammatically (cf. Jakobson 1960:353):

$$\text{Context}$$
$$\text{Message}$$

Storyteller ————————————————————————————Listener(s)

$$\text{Contact}$$
$$\text{Code}$$

Oral transmission presupposes the existence of interaction between at least two persons. Both a storyteller and a listener (or group of listeners) are required. In case A, when the story is told to one listener, the pattern is a chain. In case B, with a group of listeners there is an active social institution: the circle. It has no organization; it is relatively free in its form; and there is no chosen leader (cf. Bavelas 1953:493–494):

A. Chain __ __ __ __   B. Circle

For a community to exist at least two individuals are required. Storytelling is consequently a social event (Georges 1969:317–318), in which the participants do not function simply as individuals but, rather, control each other and adopt certain role behavior, which is determined by their social status and relationships. The storytelling situation is also a communicative process; the verbal message is transferred directly from the transmitter to the receiver by means of personal contact.

Interaction at the verbal level is not possible if the storyteller and the listener do not understand each other; that is, if they do not share a common linguistic and paralinguistic code (Hymes 1964:2–13). A fund of common knowledge and common expectations — a common culture — is also needed. Context gives the message meaning in a given situation. One mistake made by folklorists in the past has been to regard storytelling as a stereotyped process that could not be changed in its details and that always followed a fixed pattern. Yet studies have shown that each storytelling situation is unique by nature; it is an event that occurs only once in the same temporal, spatial, and social circumstances (cf. Georges 1969:316–319).

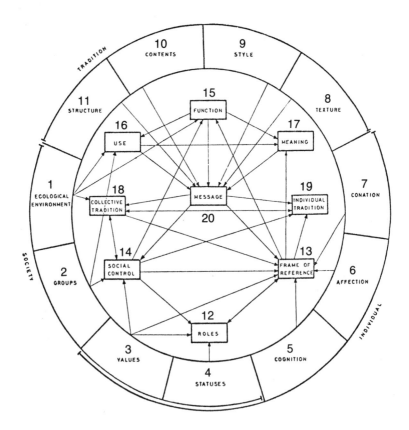

Figure 1. The dimensions of oral tradition

Figure 1 illustrates the author's view of the dimensions that should be considered when studying holistically the transmission of oral tradition. The segmental dimensions have been divided into three levels. Level A includes: (1) ecological environment and (2) groups. Level B is individually psychological[1] and includes: (3) values, (4) statuses, (5) cognition, (6) affection, and (7) conation. Level C, the depth structure of tradition, includes: (8) texture, (9) style, (10) contents, and (11) structure. The variables inside the circle have been grouped into three levels. The lowest level, D, concerns the individual and social psychological factors that influence the formation of a tradition: (12) social roles, (13) frame of reference, and (14) social control. The highest level, E, concerns the context of a tradition message and is divided into (15) function, (16) use, and (17) meaning. The central level inside the circle, F, illustrates the phases of social transmission: (18) collective tradition, (19) individual tradition, and (20) transmission of the tradition message.

The ecological environment (1) includes the cultural-ecological approach required for the observation of oral tradition. Tradition has a temporal and local dependence on the cultural environment of its transmission. An ecological study of tradition tends, among other things, to take into account the dependence of a tradition on the local residents, to eliminate the variables due to contacts with other cultures (acculturation), and to shed light on other related questions, such as if membership in a group with a particular source of livelihood bears any consequent influence upon tradition, its context, functions, and contents.

Groups (2) form the social environment of people and maintain the culture that is taught to an individual. Groups are responsible for social control and determine the values, norms, and sanctions that are desired in an individual's behavior. Characteristics of a group are continuity; reciprocity; an organized nature; solidarity among the members; common norms, aims, and values; and the presence of many members.

Values (3) are the goals toward which people aim in their social behavior; the behavior of an individual is a choice between different social values. Values have many sources — economic, religious, and others — but whatever their origin, they affect the uniformity of behavior within the community. A value is a goal; a social norm is a rule regulating behavior that is supported by sanctions. Tradition depends on values in many respects: values influence the role behavior of an individual, his or her frame of reference, social control by the community, the personal norms adopted, the social norms maintained by the society, and the context and functions of a tradition.

Statuses (4) are social positions of a system of people with common aims. A status is a collection of certain rights, duties, privileges, and

---

[1] The divisions of conscious experience formulated by perception psychologists are the foundation for the level of individual psychology.

norms that, theoretically, at least, are possessed and followed by an individual of a certain social standing. Statuses concern both the society and the individual. A society is a system of individuals who occupy statuses and who, in their behavior, show a dependence upon their statuses. The dynamic aspect of status is role.

Cognition (5) refers to conscious realization in perception.

Affection (6) describes the emotional side of an individual.

Conation (7) denotes desire and mental effort.

The above three divisions of conscious experience can be illustrated as follows: In the case of religious tradition, cognition includes the process of various attitudes and ideas becoming conscious (for example, the view of the world and the system of values that influence frame of reference, dogmas, and ideas an individual has about the cosmos and supranormal beings); affection includes religious emotion and experience; and conation concerns the behavior of an individual directed toward achieving some end. Conation frequently involves a rite, for example, a means by which an individual or a community tries to find contact with the supranormal being (Strunk 1962:39–105).

Texture (8) includes the linguistic aspect of oral tradition, the system of phonemes and morphemes that is manifested in every tradition message. This level also comprises the phonetic features typical of each language, for example, the durational characteristics, the stress, the variations in the fundamental frequency of vocal folds, intonation, and other phonetic coloring of the text. The more marked the textural features of each genre, the more difficult it is to translate it into another language.

Style (9) includes the use of various formulas, alliteration, rhyme, and so on.

Content (10) differs from texture in that it usually can be translated, whereas texture generally is not easy to transfer from one language to another. The text is any version of a folktale, proverb, riddle, or rune that can be analyzed on the levels of translatable contents and the untranslatable texture. The content comprises, among other things, the plot elements of a story, which may be transferred in tradition messages from one culture to another without obstacles to diffusion caused by language boundaries.

Structural analysis (11) is a method that is useful for the study of language and content, since it involves the process of distinguishing structural elements in narrative entities.

Social roles (12) are abstractions that cannot be observed in practice. It is possible, however, to observe a behavior or presentation that belongs to a certain role. There is an interdependence between the status and the role; the occupant of a status is expected to behave in a certain way, or, in other words, to fulfill the role expectations directed to him or her by society. A great number of "own-roles" and alternatively "counter-

THE UNWRITTEN RULES OF ORAL NARRATION

One of the characteristics of tradition is its great stability with respect to form. Content may vary, but form is relatively unchanged and stereotyped. However, despite the stability of form and the opportunities for its study, the formal composition of a folklore item has proved much less challenging to folklorists than has the task of searching for that item's origin (Dundes 1965:127). The view that has long limited folkloristic research, namely, that tradition texts are indivisible units, must, therefore, be rejected. It would be more useful to analyze the same text from several different angles and at different levels, for example, with a focus on content, form, style, structure, texture, function, use, and meaning. The question of the interdependence of the different factors must not, however, be ignored. Folkloristic structuralism would find itself faced with a crisis if it were not able to relate its observations to other aspects of folklore research.

The question of the laws of narrative tradition has been given special attention by Axel Olrik, who, as early as 1908, put forward his theory of "epic laws" (Olrik 1908), which apply to all European folklore:

> Against the background of the overwhelming uniformity of these laws, national characteristics seem to be only dialectic peculiarities. Even the traditional categories of folk narrative are all governed by these principles of *Sage* construction. We call these principles 'laws' because they limited the freedom of composition of oral literature in a much different and more rigid way than in our literature (Olrik in Dundes 1965:131).

According to Olrik's theory, the concept of *"Sagenwelt"* and the world of *Sage* plays a central role. In his view, *Sage* is a comprehensive concept governing all narrative genres such as myth, folktale, memorate, legend, or epic song. By definition, then, epic laws apply to all other narrative genres and, in principle, to all other branches of folklore as well as to folktales. As Dundes (1965:129–130) notes in his introduction to Olrik's article, epic laws are similar to the superorganic concept, which has been written about widely in cultural anthropology. According to this concept, there is not only an organic level that is controlled by people but also a superorganic level above people. Because Olrik's laws are superorganic, they control individual storytellers. He supposes that the narrators must obey the rules blindly. In an extreme form, the concept of epic laws may lead to an underestimation of the individual and the social contribution made when a tradition is disseminated. Examples of this can be found in the concepts and hypotheses put forward by followers of the geographical-historical method; for example, Kaarle Krohn's automigration (1922:21) or Walter Anderson's law of self-correction (1923:397–403). Such concepts, however, mean that the practical problem concerning epic laws as part of the actual transmission process is disregarded. At what levels can these laws be studied? Are the epic laws known to the bearer of the tradition? Do they function overtly or covertly? Is transformation of tradition a cognitive or an intuitive process?

A STUDY OF THE EPIC LAWS IN MARINA TAKALO'S STORYTELLING

One can answer the questions surrounding epic laws by analyzing the narrative repertoire of one tradition bearer, Marina Takalo (born in Russian Karelia, 1890: died in Finland, 1970). Takalo was illiterate, so for her oral communication was the sole process by which information was formed and transmitted. Her repertoire — the amount of the taped material is about 100 hours — included all the genres of Karelian and Finnish tradition. Takalo seemed aware of the different meanings and use of various narrative genres. She categorized the stories using her own natural terminology (Honko 1962:48–64) and seemed to be well aware of the differences. When she related a folktale, she referred to narratives as "*tales*: stories that have no truth in them, amusing anecdotes." A *saint's legend* was a "story of holy men"; a *legend*, "story, hearsay, event" and *memorate*, "experienced event, close event." She also had a feeling for the meaning, the function, and the use of different stories, and in the course of telling them she selected the code appropriate for the genre from the possible alternatives. In each case, this meant a choice between different norms governing content, form, style, texture, and structure. In distinct contrast to what Olrik supposes, most epic laws did not seem — at least, on the basis of Takalo's material — to apply to all narrative genres. On the other hand, many folktales do seem to follow them.

All the folktales told by Takalo contain a formal beginning and a formal end, according to the "law of opening" and the "law of closing." An existential phrase was used to introduce briefly the main characters of the story, and by means of the once-upon-a-time formula, both the narrator and the audience were transported from everyday reality to the world of fiction. The action of the story took place between the formal opening and closing sequences. Repetition (the "law of repetition") occurs at many levels; for example, events, dialogues, phrases, or single words are often repeated three times (the "law of three"). Repetition is also, of course, a kind of rhythmic emphasis at different levels. There were usually only two persons occupying the stage at any one time (the "law of two to a scene"). Opposing character types (rich and poor) came into confrontation (the "law of contrast"). The weakest or youngest is proved to be the strongest or cleverest and triumphs over the others (the "law of the importance of final position"). There can be no doubt that Takalo, guided as she was by tradition, was aware of these stylistic patterns. She knew what the style of each folktale should be, and she used this knowledge quite consciously in creating autobiographical poems from narrative material or in reproducing complete stories from remembered fragments (cf. Pentikäinen 1971:90–96).

The epic laws operating at the stylistic level correspond to the rhythm of the story and to its language. The most distinctive characteristic of the language used in folk stories is its simplicity and archaic quality; for example, the language used by Takalo in her folktales contained considerably more Karelian words and expressions than the ordinary language she used, which had been greatly influenced by Finnish. Language is related to content; the vocabulary is bound to the motif and is consequently foreign to ordinary speech. The form of language is also determined by the epic "law of action"; the story is made more interesting by actions rather than by the attributes of its characters, and the story progresses from event to event in accordance with the plot ("unity of plot," "epic unity"), with the emphasis given to events involving the main character. In its structure, therefore, the story language is much more fixed than ordinary language and permits jumps from one association to another. The storyteller must capture the audience's interest and sustain it, taking his listeners with him and fulfilling their role expectations at the same time. The presentation of a tradition is socially controlled behavior, meaning that in storytelling the story becomes stereotyped, fixed, and has rhythmic tension. Because the action is central to the story, verbs play a stronger role in the narrative than in ordinary language. Takalo followed the Karelian style of narration in her abundant use of the historic present.

Linda Dégh has written:

Many have pointed out that the text is nothing but the skeleton of the performed folktale, and that it is necessary to fill out this skeleton by recording the inflection, cadence, and tempo — the rhythm — of the narrator. Gestures, facial expressions, and dramatic interplay must be retained (Dégh 1969:53).

An examination of the rhythm of Takalo's folktales (Pentikäinen 1973) has shown that rhythm is no random factor in narration but something that is in many ways related to other levels of the transmission of tradition; for example, the content, style, form, structure, language, meaning, function, and use. Rhythm is without doubt partly social, formalized style. The individual's idiosyncratic differences, however, are reflected in the rhythm of his or her narrative. This was shown in Takalo's stories by the fact that, as the family mentor, she emphasized the didactic sections of the story.

Marina Takalo belongs to a group of emigrant bearers of tradition. Her stories, like most of her other traditions, stem from the part of Karelia bordering on the White Sea where she spent the first thirty-two years of her life (1890–1922). Her folktales remained latent for about two decades until she was stimulated into recalling them in 1944 by spending two years in her home area. Thereafter she related the stories to great-grandchildren in the family, to other Karelians, and to collectors of tradition. It was principally the direct-interview approach of collectors that inspired her to an intensive period of folktale reproduction in the 1960's. This led to a considerable increase in the numbers of folktales on record. In 1960, Takalo was encouraged to relate quite freely the folk-tales she remembered and personally preferred. The collection of folk-tales gathered in this way was relatively small compared to the final results achieved (only 17.6 percent of the whole material). Systematic interviews carried out in the course of 1962 led to a doubling of her repertoire; furthermore, Takalo was able to recall at this stage a number of sporadic extracts from other folktales without, however, being able to put them together into a single, logical whole. By 1966, several folktales of which she had been able to remember only fragments earlier had been polished enough to be included in her repertoire. (*Repertoire* refers to the fund of traditions that the informant can actively recall and that he or she can relate without halting, spontaneously and in a stereotyped manner, when the topic of the story is mentioned. It is possible to speak of a repertoire threshold, which a tradition overcomes once it has been related and ceases, through this activation, to be latent.) In the case of Takalo's folktales, the development was as follows:

Total number of tales	Active repertoire
1960 6	6
1962 25	12
1966 34	18

In general, Takalo was able to relate a folktale simply by relying on her own memory; only on a few occasions did she receive help from other Karelians. In spite of the absence of any social control, the stories she was able to recreate in their entirety are reminiscent of the collections of folktales gathered in the White Sea area of Karelia. Sometimes bearers of a tradition change the folktale to conform to their own individual per-sonalities and *Weltanschauung*. When a tradition is reproduced, it is a question not only of the preservation of a tradition learned by the infor-mants but also of transformation. It would seem to be possible, in prin-ciple, to study the way in which a tradition is formed in the same way that transformational-generative grammar studies utterances (performances) in order to determine how language is created. The key to creating language is competence. Skillful bearers of tradition are not only able to reproduce what they have learned but also to change (transform) the material with which they are already acquainted and to give it different forms. This they do partly by following certain rules that were learned and partly by following their own personalities and views of the world. Interesting questions involve what degree these rules vary for different genres and what degree of individual variation is permitted in different genres. In the case of folktales, Takalo's example suggests the posing of the hypothesis that bearers of tradition who are fully acquainted with the style, structure, rhythm, content, and language norms of storytelling may themselves compose folktales or reproduce suitable narratives from memorized material.

REFERENCES

ANDERSON, W.
   1923   *Kaiser und abt*. Helsinki: Folklore Fellows Communications 42.
BASCOM, WILLIAM R.
   1955   Verbal art. *Journal of American Folklore* 68:245–252.
BAVELAS, A.
   1953   "Communication patterns in task-oriented groups," in *Group dynamics*. Edited by Dorwin Cartwright and Alvin Zander. Evanston, Ill.: Row, Peterson.
CHERRY, C.
   1957   *On human communication: a review, a survey, and a criticism*. Cambridge, Mass.: Technology Press, MIT.
COHEN, A. R.
   1964   *Attitude change and social change*. New York: Basic.
DÉGH, LINDA
   1969   *Folktales and society: storytelling in a Hungarian peasant community*. Bloomington: Indiana University Press.
DUNDES, ALAN
   1966   Metafolklore and oral literary criticism. *The Monist* 4:505–516.
DUNDES, ALAN, *editor*
   1965   *The study of folklore*. Englewood Cliffs, N.J.: Prentice-Hall.
GEORGES, ROBERT A.
   1969   Toward an understanding of storytelling events. *Journal of American Folklore* 82:317–318.
HONKO, LAURI
   1962   *Geisterglaube in Ingermanland I*. Helsinki: Folklore Communications 185.
HULKRANTZ, A.
   1960   *General ethnological concepts*. Copenhagen: International Dictionary of Regional European Ethnology and Folklore I.
HYMES, DELL
   1964   Toward ethnographies of communication. *American Anthropologist* 66:2–13.

JAKOBSON, ROMAN
1960   "Closing statement: linguistics and poetics," in *Style in language*. Edited by Thomas A. Sebeok. Cambridge: Technology Press of Massachusetts Institute of Technology.

KROHN, KAARLE
1922   *Skandinavisk Mytologi*. Helsinki: H. Schidts förlagsaktietolag.

LEACH, MARIA, *editor*
1949–1950   *Dictionary of folklore, mythology, and legend*, two volumes. New York: Funk and Wagnalls.

LORD, ALBERT B.
1964   *The singer of tales*. Cambridge: Harvard Studies in Comparative Literature 24.

MALINOWSKI, BRONISLAW
1926   *Myth in primitive psychology*. Westport, Conn.: Negro Universities Press.

MERTON, R. K.
1949   *Social theory and social structure*. Glencoe, Ill.: Free Press.

OLRIK, A.
1908   *Nogle grundsaetninger for sagnforskning*. Copenhagen: Det Schønbergske Forlag.

PENTIKÄINEN, JUHA
1968   *The nordic dead-child tradition*. Helsinki: Folklore Fellows Communication 202.
1971   *Marina Takalon uskonto*. Forssa.
1973   "Individual, tradition repertoire and world view." Unpublished manuscript in possession of author.

SHANNON, C. E., W. WEAVER
1959   *The mathematical theory of communication*. Urbana: University of Illinois Press.

STRUNK, O.
1962   *Religion: a psychological interpretation*. New York: Abingdon Press.

UTLEY, FRANCIS L.
1961   Folk literature: an operational definition. *Journal of American Folklore* 74:193–206.

The Crack on the Red Goblet or Truth and Modern Legend

LINDA DÉGH and ANDREW VÁZSONYI

Friedrich Ranke's 1925 definition of the folk legend has generally been accepted for many years. According to Ranke: "the folk legend is a popular narrative with an objectively untrue imaginary content" (Ranke 1969:4) and "by its nature claims to be given credit on the part of the teller as well as the listener" (Ranke 1969:3). Since Ranke's time, field-workers have assembled a more representative, scientifically recorded corpus of legends which indicates that both of his statements need revision. Nevertheless, Ranke's definition lingers on, and questions concerning its validity have been raised only recently (Georges 1971:1–19). The authors of this essay in particular tried to demonstrate that "although objective truth and the presence, quality and quantity of subjective belief are irrelevant, it is all the more relevant that any legend . . . makes its case. It takes a stand and calls for the expression of opinions in the question of truth and belief" (Dégh and Vázsonyi 1971:301).

Speaking of the currently observable modern legend, this essential feature becomes more conspicuous because legends now focus more on paranormal, horrible, bizarre, and thus controversial encounters which demand, by their nature, statements of opinion from the members of legend-telling events. The legend is more conversational than other genres, and a true legend-telling event is not therefore the solo performance of one accredited person to whom the others passively listen. It is a dispute — a dialectic duel of ideas, principles, beliefs, and passions. It resembles strongly the theological polemics of the Age of Reformation and Counterreformation in its topics, methods, and atmosphere. Peuckert wrote of it as the conflict of two world views, two belief worlds (Peuckert 1965:35).

Belief, however, is a matter of gradation. "You believe more in one idea than the other" wrote Hultkrantz (1968:80). Wesselski

(1931:24–53), too, noted the ambivalent nature of legend belief, saying that the legend is "half believed." On a scale running from total belief to total nonbelief there are numerous grades. But the real opposite of a belief is not an indifferent, impartial, more imaginary nonbelief but rather another active belief which disproves the first. We will identify such belief as "negative belief" and the legend based on it as "negative legend." If, for example, someone were to relate the legend, reduced here to its minimum, for the sake of simplicity, that: "Monday morning the house on N. Street was haunted," or, in a fuller form, "I believe that on Monday morning the house on N. Street was haunted," the proponent would qualify as a believer. If, on the other hand, someone were to state: "I do not believe that on Monday morning the house was haunted," he would be looked upon as an unbeliever. In most cases, the sentence could be reformulated, without the modification of its essential meaning, as follows: "I believe that on Monday morning the house on N. Street was not haunted." In this form the proponent shows himself to be a believer even if the belief is preceded by a negative sign. He is the counterpart of the previously mentioned individual, and thus a participant in the dialectics of the legend process. In his disclaimer he does not use rational counterproof, and accordingly, his disapproval does not divert the legend from the legend conduit[1] that progresses frequently from the believer to the negative believer and vice versa. Therefore, in such cases we will use the label "negative legend" instead of "antilegend," which has been proposed by folklorists[2] to denote narratives that discredit an account expressive of another kind of belief on the basis of a negative belief.

The following are the basic variables of the legend considered in relationship to belief:

Positive legend

I believe that on Monday morning the house on N. Street was haunted.

Negative legend

I do not believe that on Monday morning the house on N. Street was haunted.

[1]   "We have termed the lines of transmission of legends which were created by affinities between certain people *legend conduit*. By this term we understand the contact that becomes established between individuals who qualify as legend receivers or transmitters" (Dégh and Vázsonyi 1975:211).
[2]   For a summary statement see John M. Vlach (1971:124–125).

Or, in a more candid phrasing:

I believe that   on Monday morning the house on
                                            N. Street was not haunted.

The situation is entirely different if the opponents derive their statements not from belief but draw evidence conceived as objective and correct according to the norms of society. In this case the statement might be called an antilegend.

Antilegend

I know that it is not true that   on Monday morning the house on
                                           N. Street was haunted.

   Or:

I know that it is true that   on Monday morning the house on
                                           N. Street was not haunted.

The real difference between the antilegend and the negative legend is not that the teller of the former refers to knowledge, cognition, observation, or facts. This kind of reference is often made by the mediator of both positive and negative legends, although not necessarily with the use of the same nomenclature. What matters is that the denial in the antilegend was not conceived in the "legend climate," as Peuckert (1965:34) expresses it, but in a "rational climate." With its rational emphasis, the antilegend does not substitute one belief for another but intends to attack and destroy the legend as a whole. Legends are, according to Peuckert, documents of wrestling of a magic or mythic *Weltanschauung* with that of the rational, the sensible."[3]

In the case of the spook of the house on N. Street, as well as many other common legends, the representative of rationalism will obviously seldom find objective proof because of the nature of legend situations. But this example can be abandoned for another that shows more aptly this analysis.

There is a legend transmitted to college freshmen by sophomore girls mainly in September and October as a part of the newcomers' initiation into group membership. It is about a young college girl who goes on a blind date with a fraternity boy to a party at his fraternity house. The boy slips Spanish fly (cantharides) into her drink, and she is seduced

---

[3] Peuckert also asserts here that the legend is an important device for expressing both mythical and rational world views.

(Greenberg 1973). *Consumer Reports* in 1972 informed its readers that, according to scientific tests, "cantharides is not an aphrodisiac, despite its popular reputation." This communication could be the basis of an anti-legend:

Positive legend

I believe that   cantharides is an aphrodisiac and a boy seduced a girl by mixing it into her drink.

Negative legend

I do not believe that   cantharides is an aphrodisiac and a boy seduced a girl by mixing it into her drink.

Or:

I believe that   cantharides is not an aphrodisiac and a boy did not seduce a girl by mixing it into her drink.

Antilegend

I know that it is not true that   cantharides is an aphrodisiac and a boy seduced a girl by mixing it into her drink.

The antilegend, based on socially accepted objective knowledge, cannot be classified with the regular legends. The antilegend did not originate in the atmosphere in which legend-creating forces can act. On the contrary, its tendency is destructive to the legend; under normal conditions, it does not venture forth on the legend conduit of either positive or negative believers. It does not belong to folklore, just as incidental, contrary opinion of another expert that cantharides is indeed an aphrodisiac would also not belong. However, it does make a difference if, for example, in the course of a discussion between believers and nonbelievers, the antilegend becomes refuted in a way other than by an argument on the basis of a contrary belief. The new formation thus created perhaps does not have to be named — either seriously or humorously — "anti-antilegend." The double denial would convert the much traveled story into a secondary positive legend:

Secondary positive legend

I do not believe that it is not true that   cantharides is an aphrodisiac and a boy seduced a girl by mixing it into her drink.

That is:

I believe that it is true that   cantharides is an aphrodisiac, and a boy seduced a girl by mixing it into her drink.

One hopes that the given nomenclature with the appertaining schemes is not too reminiscent of scholasticism. The intention is to make a clear distinction between, on one hand, positive and negative belief, and, on the other, nonbelief based on positive or negative cognizance. Although nonbelief might also be a vehicle of legends — legend accounts might be appended to a nonbelieving statement — and occasionally might help a legend to pass from the sender to the receiver, nonbelief is seldom an active part of the legend formation process.

In the foregoing, we mentioned knowledge, cognition, observation, and facts as being contrary to the objectively unestablished legend belief. Our reader may wonder if we are thereby giving free play to the principle of Friedrich Ranke and others with whom we have already taken issue (Dégh and Vázsonyi 1971:282). By no means do we suggest that the legend statement is definitely untrue and that, consequently, the counter-statement is definitely true. It might happen that the legend belief coincides with the truth and the contrary knowledge turns out to be untrue. It is possible, we propose, to believe the truth and to know the untruth. Moreover, it is possible to doubt both. The legend belief has not much to do with plain reason and common sense; indeed, in most cases, it can defy them successfully. One person's belief might be the conviction of another, and vice versa. People, for example, earlier believed, without any scientific evidence, in many curative methods that medicine verified later. Following the verification of such practice, the cure belongs equally to rational medical science and to irrational folk belief. Dundes (1961:37) wrote: "The homeopathic magic of many cures has, . . . been found to be the scientific basis of immunization through inoculations. . . . There are true as well as false superstitions." If, let us suppose, research can verify, or has already verified, certain paranormal phenomena, folk narratives about such phenomena will invariably remain legends. It is not the scientific cognition of experts that will verify them for the legend-producing folk but the sustaining folk faith, the dialectics of positive and negative belief. The legend is able not only to defy reason but also to extricate itself from its unwanted support. In general, it remains unaffected by friendly or hostile encounters with reality.

The most organized, guileful attempt of the antilegend to invade the legend belief system in the modern world has come from the occult sciences, parapsychology in particular. This realm of knowledge/belief attained academic status when, yielding to Margaret Mead's proposal, the American Association for the Advancement of Science admitted the Parapsychological Association to its membership in 1969. Currently, about 100 colleges in the United States offer courses in parapsychology and related fields. Parapsychologists or paranormalists, as Professor Joseph Rhine, the path-breaking pioneer of Duke University calls himself and his followers, are mostly concerned with clairvoyance, out-of-body experience, psychokinesis, and precognition. They contend that such phenomena are caused by natural forces and dissociate themselves from researchers dealing with the supernatural. Nevertheless, the growing prestige of parapsychology inevitably spreads over a great many occult explorations, movements, and business enterprises. Hence, in consideration of the relationship between legend belief and truth, the current position of parapsychology has to be taken into account.

With reference to factual observations, precision instruments, and elaborate theories, researchers state that what had been considered before as the concomitant of semiconsciousness (*Dämmerzustand*), illusion, gullibility, accidental circumstances, or the product of creative fantasy is, in many cases, true. That is to say, this area of knowledge does not try to disprove the belief contained in legends and does not only reach conclusions independent from, but identical with, belief, as some other disciplines occasionally do. Instead, it enters an alliance with belief and proves it. The memorates — the apparent evidences of fabulates — not only theoretically but also practically figure as testimonies in the system of parapsychology. Parapsychology rates paranormal phenomena, the subject of most contemporary legends, as truth; hence, it accepts pertinent personal narratives as objective reality reports. Folkloristically speaking, it attempts to liquidate the legend itself as a genre or at least to transfer it from the category "legend" into the category "true story." However, is parapsychology successful in this attempt?

There is a red goblet on the mantlepiece of our living room. It is shaped like a graceful tulip; two deer in rich gold dust were painted on it by a skilled craftsman some time in the late Biedermeier era. A small crack on its upper rim is hardly noticeable. The crack probably lowers the goblet's value somewhat, but for us, this minute flaw makes the goblet special. It is the source and the bearer of a legend. The antique glass is a gift from Mrs. D., the wife of an affluent retired Hungarian farmer of W., in Canada. She gave it to us as a souvenir, a token of friendship, and also because she "does not like broken things in her home." Broken glass might cause bad luck. Besides, she had wanted to get rid of it for a long time anyway because of the ominous story of its crack. Mrs. D. received the goblet from a favorite aunt in the Old Country and brought it along when she emigrated; for decades, it stood with other knicknacks on a shelf in her china cabinet. One day, not so long ago, she thought she heard a soft clink from inside the glass case. When she looked to see what was the matter, she was horrified to see the sudden fracture on the goblet. Of course, she sensed what it portended, and a letter came a week later with the sad message confirming her fear that her aunt had died the same minute the glass cracked. "I do not believe in such things," she told us, finishing her account, "but in this case . . . there must be something to it . . . maybe. She died right in *that* moment. What do you say?"

The life token motif — death of a person indicated through the mysterious self-destruction of a related object — is as universal (Motif E760–67) as the multifarious notions about death portents that signal the death of a faraway person to a beloved kin (Bächtold-Stäubli and Geiger 1927–1942:1000–1003). Mrs. D. was probably aware of the fact that her experience was not unique. This is why she said, standing in front of the china cabinet with the goblet in her hand, that she does not believe in *such* things. She did not say that she does not believe in *this* concrete phenomenon that she herself observed; nor did she say that she fully believes it, without having any second thought. She was hesitant, undecided about what to think. Her conclusion was that there *might* be something to it. She expected us, outsiders representing the judgment of society, to advise her. "Who knows?" was our response. We still think it was the best answer under current circumstances of scientific knowledge. It deserved a nod of assent from Mrs. D.

Taking all things into consideration, the problem of the cracked goblet might be of interest to quite a few people besides the parapsychologists — for example, the husband who wants to learn more about the personality of his wife to increase his understanding of her views. It might also be of interest to the family doctor in his treatment of Mrs. D.'s eventual nervous complaints; to the antique dealer concerned with the preservation of perishable old glasses; to the glass manufacturer who wants to know why glass objects sometimes crack without direct impact; to the woman herself in view of her own sensory and extrasensory perceptions; to the minister because of the possible conflict between official religion and folk belief; to the friends and relatives of the dead and the living woman; and, in general, to all who desire to believe, to hesitate, or to disbelieve. There is only one category of people uninterested in the mystery of the cracked glass, provided they choose to remain within the limits of their profession — the folklorists.

Strictly speaking, however, Heilfurth (1967:31) has already gone beyond this limit. In one of his books, he commented: "The [paranormal] phenomena became recently the object of research in parapsychology." This sounds like a factual remark, yet one can deduce something from it.

By putting this sentence into a folklore study, he declared that parapsychological research is relevant to folkloristics. Others are even more explicit: Harkort (1968:103) cites his own precognitive dreams; Virtanen (1976:345) claims to rely on an unknown power in acquiring information. It seems that some folklorists believe that parapsychological or any other of the occult researches can be instrumental in the future formulation of standpoints of the discipline. Can this really be true?

For the sake of simplicity, let us assume that the numinous[4] quality so much emphasized by many contemporary legend scholars will be totally clarified in the near future. Let us assume that researchers will be able to measure the presence of paranormal energies with the help of a brilliant new invention, the numinometer, which will perform with *deca-numen* precision. In this way, they will find out that a part of the perception attributed to hallucination, daydreams, error, fantasy, or overstatement are real facts. They will verify that paranormal experiences are concerned not with delusions but with functions of formerly unrecognized senses. But they will find this for only a segment of the range of paranormal experiences, and not for all of them. The visions of psychotics, the sensory errors of normal people under great emotional strain, or the innocent exaggerations of raconteurs will nonetheless, again and again be manifested. But if these phenomena do not cease to exist, and psychology does not lose its validity beside parapsychology, then neurotics, dreamers, ravers, and narrators will continue to tell ego stories that parallel the accounts of people who command extrasensory perception. There will be no apparent difference between them. Both kinds of tellers will allude, as before, to testimony of their own eyes. And of those who pass the accounts on, some will state under scientific warranty that a paranormal phenomenon actually had occurred at a particular place at a particular hour, whereas others will continue to refer to trustworthy old Uncle Steve who experienced it himself.

It is questionable whether a truthful report of real experience is more persuasive than the product of robust hallucination or vigorous fantasy. André Gide (1949:5) noted an unpublished story by Oscar Wilde about the man who used to entertain his fellow villagers with his enticing lies at nightly get-togethers. Once he told about a faun he saw playing the flute in the forest and a troop of woodland creatures dancing around. Then he told about three mermaids he saw on the seashore, combing their green hair with a golden comb. But once the man actually saw the faun and the woodland creatures in the forest and the mermaids on the seashore! When, as usual, the villagers asked him: "What did you see?" he ans-

---

[4] This term, adopted from Rudolf Otto (1958), is widely used in the works of Heilfurth, Lüthi, Peuckert, K. Ranke, Röhrich, and many others. Honko linked this concept to the *supranormal* experience (1962:88–93), retaining *numen* for a basic underdeveloped stage of supernatural cognition (1965:16–17).

wered: "I saw nothing." Evidently, Wilde's narrator belonged to that brand of people whom truth does not inspire but embarrass. We do not think such people are very rare.

Ultimately, legends will survive the attacks of the occult sciences. A legend will arise whether the paranormal phenomenon actually took place or not; the result of the event will be a legend with, without, or in spite of the assistance of parapsychology or any other scholarly assertion of truth. It will move on through the legend conduit whether or not it is true. It seems possible, however, that the number of legends that will antagonize the modern discipline will multiply in the future. These negative legends will probably claim that the cases described by scientists were not real. Accordingly, there already are floating legends that suggest that people have not been on the moon at all; we could read in the newspaper about a Southern farmer who took his son out of a school in which such ridiculous, nonsensical tales are taught as truths. We also were informed that the axis of the Earth was altered by the underground nuclear tests, thus the predictions of astrology are no longer valid. In this vein, Uncle Steve is still the most trustworthy witness for the legend recipients who live in the "mythical climate"[5] and will continue to stay in it for a while, if not forever. The Southern farmer is more prepared to hear the fiddle tune of David accompanied by St. Cecilia from the moon than the televised reports from the astronauts.

So far, parapsychology has had only one significant effect on folkloristics. It seems to infuse new authority into the concept of the "objectively untrue" postulated by Friedrich Ranke and his followers. From the viewpoint of legend theory, there is only one reason to investigate whether the paranormal phenomenon featured in a story has or has not really taken place, and that is when some kind of inference can be drawn from the result of the investigation. There can be only one inference; namely, that if the event really happened, the narrative that tells about it should be treated differently than the way it would be treated if it had not happened. Here we have the old, often refuted definition element in a new shape (Dégh and Vázsonyi 1971:282–286).

Obviously, Ranke's "objectively untrue" and von Sydow's statement (1934:75) that legends "cannot have happened" were not rejected by all authors. Moreover, some see the legend as "solidified rumor." Allport and Postman (1947:162) conventionalized versions of accounts that were originally rumors. According to Shibutani (1966:155) this is a misconception that is derived from the presumed falsity of orally transmitted phenomena. Littleton (1965:21) states that in the definitions "from Max Müller to Malinowski, from Hartland to Bidney," the first, basic criterion is almost always "the extent to which a narrative is or is not

---

[5] This term, introduced by Will-Erich Peuckert (1938:111), has been in general use since its first application.

based upon objectively determinable facts or scientifically acceptable hypotheses." Burkhardt (Isler 1971:3) says that it is not reliable to assert that, by definition, legend contents are in any case objectively untrue, because they would disclaim *a priori* the existence of spirits. That is to say, the legend does not cease to exist as a legend just because it deals with "objectively true," or occult, phenomena.

This is, however, acceptable as a principle that concerns not only paranormal phenomena but also any legend subject. It need not be proven that legend tellers, unless they are persons of unique encyclopedic knowledge, cannot have ample information of all possible legend topics. The legend is frequently identified, after von Sydow, as *Glaubenfabulate* [belief fabulate]; this view actually narrows the concept of the legend. Even if we believed that legend tellers can obtain proof through laborious search whether a certain event has objectively taken place, what kind of attitude do we expect from them? If they found that the account was untrue, should they pass the story on, offering as true what they know is untrue? If, on the other hand, they found that the account is true, should they be exercising a senseless restraint, be silent about it? This is the behavior not of *Homo narrans* (Ranke 1967:4–12) but, indeed, of the pathological liar. An even more demanding criterion is the one that requires a "scientifically acceptable hypothesis" (Littleton 1965:21). The word *acceptable* implies the capability of independent and correct judgment. Such skill cannot be expected from the legend recipient, who later assumes the teller's role. Since objective facts cannot govern the recipient's attitudes, the concept of truth or its elevated form, the scientific hypothesis, is irrelevant to the determination of the legend.

The rapid accumulation of successive events, the modification of ideas, the discovery of new facts, the repudiation of old ones and their rehabilitation are processes that can hardly be followed by the average educated person, or even the scientist. The common awareness of the folk develops and changes in continuation with, and often parallel to, scientific accomplishment, sometimes in opposition to and even independently from it, under the impact of diverse factors. This, however, does not imply the "knowledge of objective truth" and the acceptance of "scientific hypotheses." On the contrary, common knowledge incorporates these very slowly, almost reluctantly. Humanity hardly ever stepped over the confines of geocentrism.

The mutable judgments on objective truth, therefore, have neither theoretical bearing on legend definition nor do they have any practical effect on the world view of the legend. What was born as a legend, within the "legend climate," what was transmitted as legend and received as legend, or, in other words, what traveled through the legend conduit in society, stays a legend even if its content turns out to be true. Shibutani (1966:156) cites the example of a historic personality's legendary accounts, which do not differ significantly from documentary records. Likewise, a story spread as incontestably true cannot be classified as a legend only because its content turns out to be untrue — unless, of course, it remains alive after it is generally disproved. It will be enough to call to mind the usually inscrutable objective truth of historic legends, but a couple of examples of contemporary legends also should illuminate this point.

An acquaintance, who is an enthusiastic rumormonger and legend teller, related the following story: Once a bachelor prepared to take a bath in his apartment in a highrise building. He had undressed, the bath water was running, and he was prepared to step into the tub when he heard the newsboy throwing the paper against the front door. The man opened the door slightly and looked out to see if there was anyone around. Seeing no one on the stairway, he stepped out and stooped down to pick up the paper. In the same moment, a draft slammed the door behind him, and the bachelor stood stark naked on the stairway. Not knowing what to do, he pressed the doorbell of the nearest neighbor, who was shocked to see this lunatic and would not let him in. So he tried something else, running amuck between the floors while the bath water flowed in a small stream from under his door. After several adventures, the janitor came to his rescue. As is usual, our informant gave details concerning the accident location and also named the credible source. Shortly afterward, and for weeks thereafter, we kept hearing the same story with slight variations. After a while, it started to fade. No doubt, this was a typical urban legend that spread and evaporated quickly. A year later, we encountered the story again printed in the Russian novel *Twelve chairs* (1961), by Ilf and Petrov. The legend, believed to be local, appeared in almost the same form. Evidently, this was the source of the versions we had heard. The credible modern urban stories were most probably siblings of the several decades old Russian story and therefore objectively untrue.

Soon after this experience, our accomplished legend narrator surprised us with another credible story. This time it was about a young hothead who took part in a political conspiracy during the late 1950's. When he was about to be apprehended, he tried to save his skin by illegal flight across the Hungarian border. He did not make it, so he secretly returned to Budapest, where his widowed mother hid him in her two-room apartment, all the while spreading rumors that he was dead. There the young man lived for years. When someone rang the bell, he crawled under the bed or stepped into the closet. He never dared to talk aloud, cough, or even breathe or sneeze vigorously for fear that the neighbors or an occasional visitor might notice something. One day, after five years had elapsed, he could not stand it any longer. He ripped open the window and started to yell, scream, and cry so that people on the street gathered beneath him; the young man had a fit. An ambulance was summoned and he was taken to the psychiatric ward of a hospital. He is still there. As a tragicomic epilogue and conclusion to this well-dramatized story, it turned out that he had no reason for his seclusion, for he had been granted amnesty years earlier. When our informant waited for our reaction, we just smiled knowingly, because we recognized the original, the *Urform*. It seemed obvious that this was a simplified, actualized oral retelling of Sartre's drama, *The condemned of Altona*. Our informant vehemently protested. He insisted that he knew the mother and had met the son. Actually, they had been neighbors when they were children. He could also name the hospital where the man was treated for his nervous breakdown. Our informant acted just like any ambitious legend teller attempting to make his story sound truthful. After having heard the same story repeated by others with the same claim for credence, we followed up the leads. It was true. Two witnesses, the mother of the legend hero and the doctor who treated him in the hospital, said so. This legend — what else could we call it — was actually true. After almost a decade, we again came across the legend in a news report in the *Indianapolis Star* of May 6, 1972.

Moscow (*UPI*) — A Russian who collaborated with Nazi invaders during World War II has emerged after hiding for 20 years behind his mother's stove, it was reported yesterday. The newspaper, *Soviet Byelorussia*, said P. L. Lavnik, now 48 years old, went into hiding after the war while his mother spread rumors he was dead. He came out of hiding, the newspaper said, in response to a government offer to pardon collaborators and army deserters.

The Louisville Courier-Journal of March 17, 1968 (p. 2) reported a similar and even a longer-lasting hiding story:

San Fernando, Spain (*AP*) — Juan Rodriguez Aragon, 67, who locked himself up in his house when the Spanish civil war started July 18, 1936, has surrendered to the authorities, the Spanish news agency, Cifra, reported. Aragon, a carpenter when hostilities began, told officials he was afraid that political articles he used to write in a local magazine might bring reprisals. Cifra said his family used to tell friends Juan had disappeared. Authorities indicated he would be questioned and then released since there were no charges against him.

Are these all corrupted versions of the Sartre drama? Or did the Budapest folk legend reach the Soviet Union and Spain in ten years? Or are they factual occurrences? No matter what the truth is, the legend did and will recur. Hiding, after all, is an even older, more elementary concept than stories about hiding.

Here is a third story in which truth and untruth intermingle within even greater complexity. The original story is a model of the classical historic legend. All children in Budapest know this story, although none can tell where they learned it. Perhaps parents communicate it to their children as part of their enculturation. It might once have also been printed in an elementary school reader. In other words, the legend is common knowledge to everyone who was born and reared or who lived for a while in the Hungarian capital. It is about the Chain Bridge, the first to connect the two parts of the city, which is divided by the Danube. This bridge, decorated with two lion statues on both ends, was built in 1842 by Adam Clark, a British engineer. At the opening ceremonies, Clark proudly stated that he had completed his work to perfection — not even a nail was missing. A cobbler's apprentice delivering boots to costumers happened to pass by and heard what the engineer said. "The lions have no tongues!" yelled the boy in front of the audience of eminent townspeople, whereupon the embarrassed builder jumped into the river and drowned. It is commonly known that the story of Adam Clark's suicide is objectively untrue. He did not jump into the Danube but lived for a number of years after returning to England; he even built several other bridges.

At a recent international folklore conference, one of the coauthors related this example during an informal talk with friends, who agreed that legends might not even need a special occasion for their communication. They can be part of a group's common knowledge, a group whose members cannot remember when and how they learned them. M. M. related that the same story had a similar currency in his native Ljubljana [Yugoslavia], which proves that the story is not a local legend, but a migratory one. "The punchline of the account is that the lions actually *have* their tongues in their mouths," commented T. D., of the University of Budapest, robbing the narrative of its epic credibility. In discussing the case further with Hungarians, we decided on a second punchline: "The lions have no tongues." We definitely remembered this as the truth. The debate would have been easy to resolve, since the lions are still at the abutments of the bridge, but we did not expect folklore theory to benefit significantly were the dispute settled. But our friend in Budapest did not leave it at that. She climbed up the platform, photographed one of the lions at close range, and sent the picture to us. There was a tongue in the lion's mouth. This came as a surprise, so we continued our inquiry whereupon we unearthed a new legend: the city council recently ordered the originally missing tongues to be made. We do not pursue the matter any further. This is enough to demonstrate the many facets of truth in legend. Even this plain story could be transformed from legend to negative legend, to secondary positive legend, to antilegend and again, to legend.

Thinking of less tangible topics, such as the paranormal that so many hold as the main subject of modern legend, we still insist that, in terms of legend process and social functions, it makes no difference what was or will be proven by factual knowledge. Likewise, it is irrelevant whether the legend narrator acquired the ingredients of his account through *ESP* or by telephone.

What happens if, instead of on weak reality, one legend belief impinges upon another equally powerful legend belief? In such a case, a peculiar phenomenon can be witnessed. There is an unwritten code of procedure that offers the proponent of the positive legend, mostly the believer, a technical advantage over the teller of the negative legend, representative of a more rational world view. The positive legend teller can use formally unobjectionable arguments, such as "I have seen it myself," "It happened to my father," or "I heard it from a trustworthy friend." On the other hand, the teller of the negative legend can bring up only vague generalities, such as "I have not seen it," "There are no such things," "This is just a superstition," or, "Such things do not exist anymore," or "Such things cannot happen here."

Such statements, which pay no heed to the truth, cannot be accepted as proofs by themselves. In rare instances, the negative legend is able to offer proof *vis-à-vis* the positive legend by confronting one belief with another. Mrs. H. of Gary, Indiana, an outstanding raconteur, told about one of her extraordinary experiences. As a young girl, she used to enjoy the cool breeze with her girlfriends on hot summer nights along a brook outside her home town. The place was quite close to the graveyard; the white tombstones seemed to gleam through the hedges, and the girls always shuddered when they walked by, remembering oft-heard ghost stories. One night, terror-stricken, they spotted a white apparition as it swayed in the moonlight on the plank across the rivulet. Peuckert (1965:58), who asserted that "the bridge, as well as, or even more so the brook, is a place surrounded by the feeling of dread from the Beyond," would not have been surprised to hear that the site was a recognized locus for supernatural encounters in Mrs. H.'s birthplace. The girls, shaken by fear, ran toward the main street. Much later, they found out that one of the local youths had played a nasty trick on them. "So, you mean, there are no ghosts?" we queried. She answered the same way as we did to the owner of the goblet with the telekinetic crack on its rim: "Who knows?"

What does this negative story prove? Nothing more than that there was no ghost in a certain situation at a certain place. Peuckert (1965:88) cited similar accounts, what he calls *Gegensage* [counterlegend or antilegend]. One is about a country sexton who chases away a black sheep, while yelling to the great glee of others: "Get thee behind me, Satan!" Another widespread legend mentioned by the same author (Peuckert 1965:91), is about the village drunk who lays a wager for a dare with his cronies. He visits a cemetery at midnight, accidentally nails his coat to a grave marker, and loses his mind from fright. Departing from these and similar negative legends, only arbitrary and unjustified analogues could lead to the assumption that, since there were no occult forces or supernatural beings involved in these cases, there could not have been occult forces or supernatural beings involved in other cases elsewhere. That is, Satan did not join another man on another occasion in the guise of a black sheep, and the dead man disturbed in his grave did not grab the coat of another nightly prowler in the cemetery. This kind of negative legend can prove only that there are delusions and that there might be deliberate deceit as well. Nevertheless, this is too weak an argument to upset, at least formally, the magico-mythic belief supported by "evidence."

In the peculiar atmosphere of the legend, the affirmative statement would be the winner over the negative if it were to capitalize only on the advantage of the fallacy of *argumentum ad ignorantiam*: the fact that statements the opposite of which are unprovable seem to be true. However, the superiority of the positive legend over the negative is built on a "legal" basis. "The burden of proving the existence or nonexistence of a given fact lies upon [he] who alleges it (Kling 1966:419). Hence, the reason for the "legal" mastery of the positive legend can be attributed not only to the negative legend's inability to provide proof, but also to the fact that the positive legend shows the ability to do so. The legend belief defies rational motive, common sense, contrary knowledge — all the things of which the antilegend is made. In most cases it is successful in defying contrary belief offered by the negative legend. It even survives the competition of occult sciences and also refuses their help. The legend cannot use any truth but its own. Once in a while a legend dies. But if it does so, it dies of natural causes and because the time of its demise has come.

As we have seen, the negative legend limits its own validity to a few cases (mostly only to one) and the inferences offered by them are limited as well. The shrunken negative legend example: "On Monday morning the house on N. Street was not haunted" has no further logical consequences. On the other hand an immense number of consecutive deductions can be derived from a positive legend, such as "On Monday the house on N. Street was haunted." We must infer that ghosts most probably do exist. If there was one somewhere at a given time, we can count on another somewhere else at some other time. Yet if ghosts exist, they must act according to the unknown rules of their existence. They can appear whimsically. The worst they can do is cry, wail, moan, knock, rattle chains, throw objects, and hover incorporeally in sheets thus undermining people's faith in the calculable order of things and their confidence in rationality and causality, upon which the average person's feeling of the continuity of earthly existence is based. Some of the occult sciences — parapsychology in particular — disclaim dealings with the supernatural and declare that the object of their investigation belongs not in the paranormal but in the strictly normal world. The followers of these trends, however, do not seem to honor the distinction. What the investigators consider as knowledge is turned to belief by the masses, and what is meant as a theory appears as a new vocabulary for old legends. Hence, the social effect of the occult sciences, whether they concern themselves with the natural or the supernatural, does not show notable differences. It would seem that the question of whether that particular ghost did or did not haunt the house on N. Street at that particular time or whether that crack on the red goblet is or is not a psychic phenomenon, has a greater significance than one would have assumed.

This is, fortunately, more theory than practice. People seldom thoroughly examine their own thoughts, let alone those of others. Believers usually do not draw a lesson from the consequences of their beliefs. The plebes occupying room 4714 at the West Point Military Academy who saw the life-sized apparition of a nineteenth-century officer emerge from a wall (*Time*, December 4, 1972:6), did not unconditionally agree with each other. Some suspected a hoax or looked for another common-sense explanation. Others, such as the cadet captain who investigated the event and was "still a firm unbeliever, admitted that the designated point of evaporation, which is normally quite warm, felt icy to the touch." Presumably, the vision was a reinforcement of supernatural belief for some; and there were several cadets who, like so many legend tellers, began their account like this: "I certainly do not believe in such things, but this one I have seen with my own two eyes."

In general, people eclectically select from the treasure trove of folk belief. Some believe in witches but do not believe in werewolves; others believe in werewolves but do not believe in the evil eye. Some believe in the evil eye but do not believe in vampires, or they believe in vampires but do not believe in the return of the mummy. Some do not believe in transcendental inspiration but do believe in precognition. A high school senior in a Canadian rural town, an enthusiast of scientific occultism, explained to us: "There are no ghosts. This is a superstition. But there *are* astral bodies and it is easy to confuse them with ghosts." In addition, many people believe in their own official religion, which prohibits the belief in witches, werewolves, the evil eye, vampires, living mummy, transcendental inspiration and precognition, ghosts, and astral bodies. Even if believers do not generalize their beliefs, the question to be raised is of great importance. Indeed, the *question*, not the *answer*, is essential. The world view of people is extremely complex and durable. In general, it does not change significantly under the influence of some persuasive argument or counterargument. Few people of magico-mythical disposition could be turned into rationalist thinkers through the thoughtful advice of a friend, and few rationalist thinkers have given up their reservations about what is commonly known as superstition under the influence of a legend. Persons who have once had a taste of a belief, no matter how and where, will hardly reconsider it throughout their lives.

The attitude toward the legend develops in time into a well-constructed and well-set role and even into a dialogue or a repeated group rite. The cast is remarkably stable; not even the text of the roles is modified considerably over time.

In Indiana Harbor, we met an elderly couple who were eager to tell us all the stories they knew. The man specialized in jokes, and his wife was an accomplished legend teller (Dégh 1976). We visited them repeatedly for several years. In addition to the always interesting new stories from their inexhaustible supply, the woman recited each time her favorite supernatural experience. Once, she heard loud sobbing while she was cooking in the kitchen. She opened the door to see who was crying but could not find anyone outside. Only much later did she learn that her sister's daughter had died at the same time, far away, at the other end of the town. They loved each other dearly, and this is why the old woman heard her dying niece crying. The text of the narrative was almost exactly the same each time. The husband always listened patiently as she unfolded the story — who knows for how many hundreds of times in front of varied audiences of occasional visitors! — and like an actor on cue, he interjected at regular intervals: "Oh, baloney! There are no such things! I don't believe one word of it!" Whereupon his wife responded in due course with such retorts: "Oh, come on! It wasn't just me who heard it. There were two other people here visiting me, and they heard it, too!" At this point, the man became irritated: "They haven't heard a thing. They were just imagining things like yourself!" This ritual wordy warfare took at least five minutes every time. The woman became more and more excited, and the man, more and more stubborn. Then suddenly, without any noticeable reason, the debate would end. Naturally, it had no outcome. How could there have been a resolution if the couple had not been able for decades to come to terms on this matter? The question that apparently played a rather important role in the life of the otherwise peaceful, relaxed, tolerant, and emphatically rational old couple continued to remain a question.

Similarly, no agreement could be reached by a mother and daughter concerning the existence of supernatural beings in Crown Point (Dégh and Vázsonyi 1971:294). The recorded dialogue of the two women could be conceived as a legend-telling session in which the aged mother related her witch stories with remarkable verbosity and eloquence and her daughter, a middle-aged woman, responded with a counterstory to each. The stories and counterstories, the arguments and counterarguments, the legends and negative legends fitted smoothly, so that, if nothing else, the heated and persistent ideological debate seemed to be not an improvised, but rather a well-rehearsed dramatic act.

It has been found that accidental pairs or groups of people who have no opportunity to learn and rehearse their parts act very much the same way.

People gathered at a party, customers standing by chance next to each other at a bar, new residents of a student dormitory, participants of a slumber party, or travelers on a long train trip sharing the same compartment know the essentials of their roles. Each of these actors will faithfully present his or her accepted image assumed for one or more occasions, or sometimes for a lifetime, like the players in a *commedia dell'arte*. Pantalone, the captain, the doctor, Arlecchino, Brighella, and the others all knew what behavior was allotted to them by tradition. Similarly, in the legend-telling groups, stereotypical characters are necessary for the believer, the objective observer, the undecided, the skeptic, the negative-believer, the rationalist, and the others. The stereotypes appear not only as individuals but also as representatives of segments of society, as spokesmen of diverse beliefs and convictions.[6] Nowadays the parapsychologist and his congeners also appear on the stage. They stand for the antilegend, but involuntarily serve the cause of the legend.

The roles of all actors in the performance also become ambiguous. It is not clear any more who represents whom. Earlier there were backward, unschooled, superstitious, often older people whose firm belief stood opposed to the disbelief of the enlightened, schooled, progressive younger generation. Contrarily, nowadays it is more the young generation who seem to be inclined toward mysticism and belief in the occult. The young promulgate both old-fashioned ghost stories and modern legends related to growing cults and occult practices and sciences. Their identification with legend is not modest and defensive like that of superstitious people of yesterday: it is aggressive and self-conscious. Their arguments are not incoherent and naive but sophisticated, sometimes philosophical. The legend event is no longer limited to the narrow confines of small groups isolated from larger society. Through the intervention of the media, legends reach out to the masses and make participants of almost everyone in society.

What brought about the change? What technical means were essential to make it happen? How was the dissemination of legend furthered by them? These questions require further investigation. It should be noted that the study of the social avenues and functions of the legend, not only as the most popular but also as the most characteristic folklore genre of modern industrial society, may lead to new learning about the world in which we live.

---

[6]   "Actually tradition is maintained not by certain individuals, but by social roles" (Honko 1965:14).

REFERENCES

ALLPORT, GORDON, LEO POSTMAN
1947   *The psychology of rumor*. New York: Henry Holt.
BÄCHTOLD-STÄUBLI, HANNS, PAUL GEIGER, *editors*
1927–1942 *Handwörterbuch des deutschen Aberglaubens* [Dictionary of German superstition], ten volumes. Berlin: Walter de Gruyter.
DÉGH, LINDA
1976   "Symbiosis of joke and legend: a case of conversational folklore," in *Folklore today: a Festschrift for Richard M. Dorson*. Edited by L. Dégh, H. Glassie, and F. J. Oinas, 101–122. Bloomington: Indiana University.
DÉGH, LINDA, ANDREW VÁZSONYI
1971   Legend and belief. *Genre* 4:281–304.
1975   "Hypothesis of multi-conduit transmission in folklore," in *Folklore, performance and communication*. Edited by Dan Ben-Amos and Kenneth S. Goldstein, 207–252. The Hague: Mouton.
DUNDES, ALAN
1961   Brown County superstitions. *Midwest Folklore* 9:25–33.
GEORGES, ROBERT A.
1971   "The general concept of legend: some assumptions to be re-examined and reassessed," in *American folk legend: a symposium*. Edited by Wayland D. Hand. Berkeley: University of California.
GIDE, ANDRÉ
1949   *Oscar Wilde in memorium (reminiscences)* de profundis. Translated from the French by Bernard Frechtman. New York: Philosophical Library.
GREENBERG, ANDREA
1973   Drugged and seduced: a contemporary legend. *New York Folklore Quarterly* 29:131–158.
HARKORT, FRITZ
1968   "Volkserzählungsforschung und Parapsychologie," in *Volksüberlieferung*. Edited by F. Harkort, K. C. Peeters, and R. Wildhaber, 89–105. Göttingen: Otto Schwartz.
HEILFURTH, GERHARD
1967   *Bergbau und Bergmann in der deutschsprachigen Sagenüberlieferung Mitteleuropas* [Mining and mines in German speaking legend tradition]. Marburg: N. G. Elwert.
HONKO, LAURI
1962   *Geisterglaube in Ingermanland*. Folklore Fellows Communications 185. Helsinki: Suomalainen Tiedeakatemia.
1965   Memorates and the study of folk-beliefs. *Journal of the Folklore Institute* 1:5–19.
HULTKRANTZ, ÅKE
1968   Miscellaneous beliefs. Some points of view concerning the informal religious sayings. *Temenos* 3:76–82.
ILF, JLIA ARNOLD, JEVGENII PETROV
1961   *The twelve chairs*. New York: Vintage Books.
ISLER, GOTTHILF
1971   Die Sennenpuppe. Eine Untersuchung über die religiöse Funktion einiger Alpensagen [The Alpine doll. Study of religious function of

some Alpine legends]. *Schriften der Schweizerischen Gesellschaft für Volkskunde* Band 52. Basel: Verlag G. Krebs.

LITTLETON, SCOTT C.
1965   A two-dimensional scheme for the classification of narratives. *Journal of American Folklore* 78:21–27.

KLING, SAMUAL G., *editor*
1966   *Legal encyclopedia for home and business*. New York: Benco editions.

OTTO, RUDOLF
1958   The idea of the holy: an inquiry into the non-rational factor in the idea of the divine and its relation to the rational. Oxford: Oxford University Press.

PEUCKERT, WILL-ERICH
1938   *Deutsche Volkstum in Märchen and Sage, Schwank und Rätsel*. Berlin: Walter de Gruyter.
1965   *Sagen, Geburt, und Antwort des mythischen Welt*. Berlin: Erich Schmidt.

RANKE, FRIEDRICH
1969   "Grundfragen der Volkssagenforschung" [Basic problems of folk-legend research], in *Probleme der Sagenforschung*. Edited by Leander Petzoldt, 1–20. Darmstadt: Wissenschaftliche Buchgesellschaft.

RANKE, KURT
1967   Kategorienprobleme der Volksprosa [Category-problems of Folk-prose]. *Fabula* 9:4–12.

SHIBUTANI, TAMOTSOU
1966   *Improvised news: A sociological study of rumor*. Indianapolis: Bobbs-Merill Co.

Time
1972   Ghost at the point. *Time*, December 4, p. 6.

VIRTANEN, LEEA
1976   "Paranormale Spontanerlebnisse," in *Folk Narrative Research: Studia Fennica*, No. 20. Edited by J. Pentikäinen and Tuula Juurikka. Helsinki: Suomalainen Tiedeakatemia.

VLACH, JOHN M.
1971   One black eye and other horrors: a case for the humorous anti-legend. *Indiana Folklore* 4:95–125.

VON SYDOW, CARL WILHELM
1934   "Kategorien der Prosa-Volksdichtung [Categories of prose folk literature]" in *Volkskundliche Gaben: John Meier zum siebzichsten Geburtstage dargebracht*. Berlin: Walter de Gruyter.

WESSELSKI, ALBERT
1931   *Versuch einer Theorie des Märchens* [Attempt at a theory of the Märchen]. Reichenberg i Böhmen: Sudetendeutscher Verlag Franz Kraus.

The Science in Folklore: The Case of Motif D1275 — "Magic Song"

ROBERT B. KLYMASZ

Like the estimable Sir James George Frazer (1961:372), who anticipated that "the dreams of magic may one day be the waking realities of science," subsequent researchers have from time to time engaged in sporadic efforts to explore and, wherever possible, validate, the historicity, efficacy, and veracity of various folkloric phenomena associated with magic, myth, and belief (Eliade 1963; Grabner 1968:152–157; Jackson 1971:341–342; Vansina 1965; Vogt and Hyman 1959). Frequently, generally inconclusive evidence, along with the lack of suitable testing procedures, has compelled most folklorists and their colleagues to expend their energies in a manner that has transformed the realm of magic, myth, and belief into one of the most speculative areas in all of folklore. Especially sensitive to those phenomena that appear to contravene the physical laws of nature, the research has largely concentrated on collation and descriptive reportage (Bächtold-Stäubli 1927–1942), and included discussions on psychological reality (Bidney 1965), "adventitious reinforcement" (Henslin 1967), functional logic (Tambiah 1968), distinctions between science and magic (Malinowski 1948) and even the negation of any need whatsoever to consider the degree of veracity (Dégh and Vázsonyi 1971). In some of these works, one can detect a certain awkward vacillation in approach to the subject of magic — "the one and only specific power, a force unique of its kind, residing exclusively in man" (Malinowski 1948:76) — where "rituals produce what they predict" (Tambiah 1968:200) and "the mere thought that such a thing is possible makes the magic work" (Bowra 1963:256). Recent trends indicate, however, the growing impact of the so-called "exact" sciences (Marinus 1961–1962), whose representatives from such diverse fields as medicine and geology (Krippner and Davidson 1972; Vitaliano 1968, 1971; Kiev 1964) have not only narrowed the gap between fact and fiction but also helped to place the world of modern folkloristics at the threshold of rediscovery and a new awareness.

THE MAGIC SONG

An abundance of scholarly data and anecdotal observations indicate the incorporation of folklore as a sort of magical or semimagical feature in the agrarian and hunting catechisms of societies in almost every part of the globe. In some cultures, the telling of fairy tales is believed to exercise a magical influence on new crops (Malinowski 1935:156); in others, singing is considered efficacious as a spell on birds and other animals so that they can be controlled, approached, or hunted down without difficulty (Bowra 1963:83, 115, 118–149). The main focus of attention here, however, is on the belief that song has a positive effect on plant growth. In this regard, one can readily assume that all agrarian folksong cycles incorporate the notion of abundant plant growth. Many song items serve as incantations and appear to command the plants to grow well and tall, the roots deep, herbs and grains to be fruitful, and trees to be decked with flowers and fruit. Reports on such ostensible manifestations of song magic are usually couched in descriptions of agrarian rites and practices, as found, for example, in Frazer's outline (1961:351) of the *Grannasmias* ceremony in France, Bowra's account (1963:113) of "nature-songs" among the Semang on the Malay Peninsula, Malinowski's analysis (1935:134–310) of planting chants in the Trobriand Islands, Kolpakova's textual survey (1962:32–46) of Russian agrarian incantatory songs, and Thiselton-Dyer's classic volume, *The folk-lore of plants* (1889; Jain 1964). Inextricably related to the notion of song magic and its impact on plant growth is the importance of sound in ritual, as noted, for instance, by Gimbutas (1958:117–122), Anthony Jackson (1968:293–299), and Kaharov (1928:21–56). Finally, it is important to note Stith Thompson's tabulation of the entire song-magic complex in his monumental *Motif-index of folk literature* (1955–1958) under section "D. Magic."[1]

Typical of the kind of work is Ruth Underhill's fanciful description (1938:43–44) of song magic among the Papago Indians of southern Arizona in the United States. Included, for example, is the following account of "singing up the corn":

Night after night, the planter walks around his field "singing up the corn." There is a song for corn as high as his knee, for corn waist high, and for corn with the tassel forming. Sometimes, all the men of the village meet together and sing all

---

[1]   See D1275, "Magic song"; D1275.1, "Magic music"; and D1275.2, "Magic melody." See also D523, "Transformation through song"; D1335.12, "Magic song gives strength" and D1210, "Magic musical instruments" (Thompson 1955–1958).

night, not only for the corn but also for the beans, the squash, and the wild things. . . .

Song texts themselves are a primary source of reference, as reflected in the following English translation of a Lithuanian folksong recorded by Kenneth Peacock in 1967 for the Canadian Centre for Folk Culture Studies at the National Museum of Man in Ottawa, Canada (CCFCS archival finding no. PEA 368–2552):

This singing of men,
This beautifully green rye of theirs,
They sang and they sang,
And their rye grew green.

This singing of women,
This green cabbage of theirs,
They sang and they sang,
And their cabbage grew green.

This singing of the young sisters,
This beautiful green rue of theirs,
They sang and sang
And their rue grew green.

Quite independently of any of the folkloristic accounts of song magic exemplified by the materials just cited, the popular press in recent years has been especially productive in reporting relevant phenomena such as *The power of prayer on plants* (Loehr 1969; Gordon 1966:146–158), "Growing corn to music" (Hicks 1963; Swedlow 1961), and "Evidence of a primary perception in plant life" (Backster 1968). Concomitantly, botanists in various parts of the world have undertaken experiments to correlate increases in plant growth with certain musical selections (Singh, Gnanam 1965:78–99; Measures, Weinberger 1970:659–662). There is proof that some sound frequencies at specific amplitudes do in fact stimulate plant growth, but the implications of this experimentation with sound-treated seeds, sound-treated water on seeds, and sound-treated plants have largely gone unnoticed by folklorists.

When, in the early part of 1968, Dr. Carmen Roy, chief of the Folklore Division[2] at Canada's National Museum of Man, learned of sound-plant experiments being conducted at Ottawa University under the supervision of Dr. Pearl Weinberger (Weinberger, Measures 1968), it was decided to engage the services of Dr. Weinberger to "conduct scientifically controlled experiments on the effects of vocal and instrumental sounds on the germination and growth of plants, using selected material from the Folklore Division's sound archives, which, in popular belief and traditional folklore scholarship, suggested a connection between acoustic

[2]   In 1970 the name of the Folklore Division was changed to the Canadian Centre for Folk Culture Studies (CCFCS).

phenomena and plant growth in agrarian cultures."[3] As outlined in Weinberger's report to the museum of February 27, 1969, the work was concerned (1) with the effect of special musical selections on the germination of selected seed species and (2) with the subsequent growth and development of seedlings and plants (up to eight weeks old) (Weinberger 1969). Of the six musical items provided by the museum for the experiments, four were vocal numbers with texts having incantatory references to cucumber, oats, flax, and hay. Two of these, along with the two solo instrumental numbers, were submitted to a power spectral density analysis.

Germination Studies

This preliminary aspect of the experimentation used the seeds of eight plant species (alfalfa, bean, corn, cucumber, flax, lettuce, oats, and pea). These were allowed to germinate under a constant temperature in dark cabinets, and were all exposed to sound treatment (except for a control group). The experiments were carried out in triplicate. For each plant species, a minimum of 300 seeds was used for each of the six musical items as well as for the control group (no sound). Different batches of each species were allowed to germinate for forty-eight hours, and all but the control group were exposed for twelve-hour periods to the tunes. Music and control cabinets were rotated with each repetition of the experiment in order to eliminate any possible cabinet effects. Each hour the percentage germination of the sound-treated and control seeds was noted.

As reported by Weinberger, the results of the germination experiments indicated that in no case was a statistically significant stimulation of germination obtained, although three of the six musical items appeared consistently to effect the rate of germination.

Growth Studies

For the controlled-growth studies, two of the three productive musical items that seemed to have a slight influence on the rate of germination (tunes II and VI in the experiment) were played to seeds of cucumber, corn, and oats. During the germination of these seeds and the subsequent eight-week plant growth period, each species was exposed for eight hours a day, five days a week to the same tune in parallel experiments using the two selected musical items. The growth experiments were replicated five times, thus requiring a total of fifty plants of each species.

[3] From the terms of the Weinberger contract with the National Museum of Man for 1968–1969.

The results of the 1968–1969 growth studies indicated that one musical item in particular, a Ukrainian flute melody played on the *sopilka*, evoked a striking increase in the overall growth of cucumber plants. This flute melody was also beneficial for oats and in some cases stimulated the leafy growth of corn plants to an unusual degree. Three times the number of buds were produced when the plants were exposed to this tune, and a significant increase in the number of leaves was also observed. This rather unexpected development disappointed those observers who had hoped that the experiments would throw some light on the impact of *vocal* folk music on plant growth. On the other hand, the productivity of the Ukrainian flute melody seemed to match the findings of Singh and his colleagues in India (Singh, Gnanam 1965:78–99), who had exposed paddy grown in fields to daily half-hour periods of music played on the *nadeshwaram*, a pipe musical instrument of South India.[4]

Concerning musical analysis in terms of power density and frequency, Weinberger's final report (1969:12–13) speculated:

Since the germination studies showed that the effect of the tunes was slight, correlation with tune structure will not be attempted. One may, however, try to link the highly stimulated growth of cucumber plants exposed to tune VI to the structure of the latter. However, the pattern of tune VI is very similar to that of II and the latter only stimulated bud development. One may speculate that the presence of very low frequency components in II had a dampening effect on the other growth parameters. Further analysis to show the time variation of the power at various frequencies, and the use of randomized frequency distributions within the range noted in tunes II and VI, may reveal other differences between the tunes and give insights into the relative importance of rhythm and tune structure in relation to stimulated plant growth.

The report concluded that

. . . there is thus some indication that certain of the melodies connected in folklore with agrarian practices might indeed enhance the growth of some plants. More work is required to define what musical elements in the tunes actually stimulated growth. Further growth studies should also be carried out using plants named in the tune titles to determine whether the tunes affect later plant development and thus supplement the earlier investigation relating solely to germination (Weinberger 1969:13).

A series of follow-up experiments (Weinberger, Ste-Marie 1970) conducted during 1969–1970 used pertinent musical items recorded in Africa for comparative purposes. This second batch of tests, however, only reconfirmed the efficacy of the *sopilka*-flute tune, which, though randomized with regard to melodic sequence, was again found to be a most productive influence on the growth of the test plants.

[4]   In this same connection, it is interesting to note the corresponding motifs in the Thompson *Motif index of folk literature*: D1210, "Magic musical instruments"; D1223.1, "Magic flute"; and D1224, "Magic pipe [musical]" (Thompson 1955–1958).

CONCLUSION

Although the Ottawa experiments of 1968–1970 were inadequate to support the working hypothesis regarding the "magic song" belief corpus, they did not, at the same time, contradict them. The lack of a clear, statistically significant correlation between the song material and the test plants was especially disappointing. Still, this could have been influenced by a host of variables that can easily operate within the context of any live, music-making situation and that hardly obtain, given the artificiality of testing under contrived ("controlled") laboratory conditions, as well as the narrow focus on recorded sound alone. On the other hand, the surprising productivity of the Ukrainian flute melody does indicate that it would be premature to abandon the hypothesis *in toto*; rather, it signals a need to develop field methods that would be more sensitive to the investigative techniques employed by the natural sciences — especially in the event that the latter are adopted for the testing of the credibility of belief phenomena.

Above all, the experiments of 1968–1970 are especially important for having brought together the working forces of two disciplines on a problem central to the interests of both. The suggestion of a new and powerful linkup with the natural sciences has much to offer as a supplementary adjunct to the more established avenues of approach to the investigation of folklore. The range of possibilities for such interdisciplinary, science-in-folklore studies has yet to be surveyed, and their implications for folkloristics remain largely unexplored. Nonetheless, there can be no doubt that the kind of research envisioned by the Ottawa experiments of 1968–1970 will stimulate a renewed and profound appreciation for folklore old and new and make its own special contribution to the basic issues that surround our current perception of folklore in the modern world.

REFERENCES

BACKSTER, CLEVE
   1968   Evidence of a primary perception in plant life. *International Journal of Parapsychology* 10:329–348.
BÄCHTOLD-STÄUBLI, HANNS
   1927–1942   *Handwörterbuch des deutschen Aberglaubens*. Berlin and Leipzig: Walter de Gruyter.
BIDNEY, DAVID
   1965   "Myth, symbolism, and truth," in *Myth: a symposium*. Edited by Thomas Sebeok. Bloomington: Indiana University Press (Midland paperback edition).
BOWRA, C. M.
   1963   *Primitive song*. Toronto: New American Library (Mentor paperback edition).

DÉGH, LINDA, ANDREW VÁZSONYI
1971 Legend and belief. *Genre* 4:281–304.
ÉLIADE, MIRCEA
1963 *Myth and reality*. Translated by Willard R. Trask. New York: Harper & Row.
FRAZER, JAMES GEORGE
1961 *The new golden bough: a new abridgement of the classic work*. Edited by Theodor H. Gaster. Garden City, N.Y.: Doubleday (Anchor paperback edition).
GIMBUTAS, MARIJA
1958 *Ancient symbolism in Lithuanian folk art*. Philadelphia: American Folklore Society.
GORDON, THEODORE J.
1966 *Ideas in conflict*. New York: St. Martin's Press.
GRABNER, EIFRIEDE
1968 The history of research in folk medicine in German-speaking countries. *Journal of the Folklore Institute* 5:152–157.
HENSLIN, JAMES M.
1967 Crops and magic. *American Journal of Sociology* 73:316–330.
HICKS, CLIFFORD B.
1963 Growing corn to music. *Popular Mechanics* 119:118–121, 183.
JACKSON, BRUCE
1971 Vagina dentata and cystic teratoni. *Journal of American Folklore* 84:341–342.
JACKSON, ANTHONY
1968 "Sound and ritual," in *Man*, n.s. 3:293–299.
JAIN, S. K.
1964 The role of the botanist in folklore research. *Folklore, India's Only Monthly Journal on Folk Culture* 5:145–150.
KAHAROV, JEVHEN
1928 "Formy to elementy narodn'oji obrjadovosty" [The forms and elements of folk ritual]. *Pervisne Hromadjanstvo* 1:21–56.
KIEV, ARI, *editor*
1964 *Magic, faith and healing: studies in primitive psychiatry today*. New York: Free Press.
KOLPAKOVA, N. P.
1962 Russkaja narodnaja bytovaja [The Russian folk everyday song]. Moscow-Leningrad: Akademija nauk SSSR.
KRIPPNER, STANLEY, RICHARD DAVIDSON
1972 Parapsychology in the USSR. *Saturday Review* 55 (March 18):56–60.
LOEHR, FRANKLIN
1969 *The power of prayer on plants*. New York: American Library (Signet paperback edition).
MALINOWSKI, BRONISLAW
1935 *Coral gardens and their magic*. New York: American Book Company.
1948 *Magic, science and religion and other essays*. Garden City, N.Y.: Doubleday (Anchor paperback edition).
MARINUS, ALBERT
1961–1962 Folklore vivant. *Annuaire de la Commission Royale Belge de Folklore*.

MEASURES, MARY, PEARL WEINBERGER
  1970   The effect of four audible sound frequencies on the growth of Marquis spring wheat. *Canadian Journal of Botany* 48:659–662.

SINGH, T. C. N., A. GNANAM
  1965   Studies of the effect of sound waves of *Nadeshwaram* on the growth and yield of paddy. *Journal of Annamalai University* 26:78–79.

SWEDLOW, EVELYN
  1961   Grow your plants to music. *Science Digest* 49:53–56.

TAMBIAH, S. J.
  1968   The magical power of words. *Man*, n.s. 3:175–208.

THISELTON-DYER, T. F.
  1899   *The folk-lore of plants*. London: Chatto and Windus. (Reprinted in 1968 by Singing Tree Press, Detroit.)

THOMPSON, STITH
  1955–1958 *Motif-index of folk literature*, six volumes, Bloomington: Indiana University Press.

UNDERHILL, RUTH MURRAY
  1938   *Singing for power*. Berkeley and Los Angeles: University of California Press.

VANSINA, JAN
  1965   *Oral tradition: a study in historical methodology*. Translated by H. M. Wright. Chicago: Aldine.

VITALIANO, DOROTHY B.
  1968   Geomythology: the impact of geologic events on history and legend with specific reference to Atlantis. *Journal of the Folklore Institute* 5:5–30.
  1971   Atlantis: a review essay. *Journal of the Folklore Institute* 8:66–76.

VOGT, EVON Z., RAY HYMAN
  1959   *Water witching, U.S.A.* Chicago: University of Chicago Press.

WEINBERGER, PEARL
  1969   "The effect of some vocal and instrumental music on the growth of selected plant species. Unpublished report submitted under contract and deposited with the Archives of the Canadian Centre for Folk Culture Studies, National Museum of Man, Ottawa.

WEINBERGER, PEARL, MARY MEASURES
  1968   The effect of two audible sound frequencies on the termination and growth of spring and winter wheat. *Canadian Journal of Botany* 46:1151–1158.

WEINBERGER, PEARL, GENEVIÈVE STE-MARIE
  1970   "The effect of noise and two seed planting tunes on the growth of three plant species." Unpublished report submitted under contract and deposited with the Archives of the Canadian Centre for Folk Culture Studies, National Museum of Man, Ottawa.

Verbal Art in Modern Rural Galicia

CARMELO LISON TOLOSANA

One winter morning, while perusing notes gathered the night before in the hamlets of Cebrego,[1] I began to hear in the distance the song (*canto*, in the local expression) or noise of the rural one-horse cart. The impression left was that a column of horse carts, rather than one cart, was approaching and, noticing that many of the doors that faced the street were opening, I too went out. Slowly, with the peaceful gait of a cow, eight carts filed along the main street and disappeared around a bend. The dignified, solemn appearance of the tumbrel drivers, who looked straight ahead, not acknowledging any greeting, and the irony displayed by the local people in their comments on the affectation and severity of these strangers, stimulated my curiosity. Watching them withdraw resembled witnessing what the Germans call *das Eintreten des Ernstfalles*, "the appearance of obscurely significant behavior." Some neighbors commented: "It is the *carreto*." With a ballpoint pen and a sheaf of papers, I walked toward the drivers' hamlet.

CARRETO

The term *carreto* refers to the free assistance offered by neighbors to someone building a house — to the contribution of personal labor, the

The author's field research in Galicia from 1964 to 1965 was supported by the Gulbenkian Foundation. Everything reported, if not otherwise indicated, refers to those dates.

[1] In the province of Lugo, Galicia. The Galician region occupies the northwestern corner of Spain. It has four provinces — Coruna, Lugo, Orense, and Pontevedra — with an area of 29,434 square kilometers, and a population of about two million persons living in towns of up to 2,000 inhabitants. The main rural occupation is livestock breeding and farming. Many people in towns on the coast make their livings from the sea. Industrialization is beginning to take on a certain importance, but only in very limited areas. Galacia is predominantly rural.

cart, and the animals that pull it, as well as to cart slate, stone, or other building materials.[2] At night, the person who has benefited from the community's assistance entertains all who have contributed at a splendid supper. Around midnight, after much eating and drinking, and between cups of coffee and glasses of cognac, someone begins to sing what they call toasts (*brindis*) or *loias* (quatrains in which the second and fourth verses are in assonance). *Loias* are improvised as they are intoned and addressed to one person, who has to answer, also in song, with another improvised quatrain, of which the first word must be the same as the last word of the quatrain addressed to him. The second person may start his eight syllables with a word that rhymes with the last word. The second person may reply to the first, a common procedure, or direct his quatrain to a third person. The latter, in turn, must answer in the required form. The singer's glance, the gestures, and the content of the song reveal quite early who is the target of the verses. The completion of the melody is followed by applause, laughter or guffaws, rubbing of hands, and comments, all of which provide a few moments for the person alluded to to prepare his reply. If, in the opinion of those assembled, the latter delays too long, or rhymes badly, or does not respect the literary rules, he is the object of laughter and shouts, such as "Sack him," or "It was badly put together." In some places, everyone sings to someone who does not know how to reply:

Teno un albardina feita,	I have a saddle ready,
feita o meu parecer	Ready as I like it
Pra lle poner a ese burro	To put on that ass
Que non sabe responder.	Who does not know how to reply.

In such cases, the first singer can renew his poetic attack against the victim or choose another of those present as his target.

Direct and keen verbal assault gives rise to great excitement among the listeners; allusive looks are flashed around the room before being fixed on the injured party. All wait for a strong counterattack. It is clear to the outside observer that these dramatic moments not only are awaited, but that they constitute the critical points that provide most of the enjoyment for the listening audience. As soon as possible, the victim launches even sharper and subtler darts against his neighbor, but he still has to adapt their final expression to the verbal form of the attack directed against

---

[2]   According to my notes, this custom is practiced today in Villarin do Monte, Teixoeiras, Coterces, Busnullan, Barxa Maior, Hospital, Fonteferreira, Zanfoga, Riocereixa, Santalla, and Pacios, all villages under the municipal government of Piedrafita, and in Silvela (Nogales), Noceda (Caurel), and Corneantes (Cervantes). As a simple means of neighborly help, it also is found in Sobrado (Pinor), in some villages in Sarria, Cedeira, and Noya, in Rodeiro and Baredo (Bayona), Mens (Malpica de Bergantinos), Carnes (Vimianzo), etc. These last are centers that, like Noya, call the practice *carretada*.

him. Those moments of silence and expectation; the satirical, ironic, acid, and biting responses; the endless cups of coffee and cognac (produced by the women); the strong desire for personal assertion in the face of one's neighbor; and the pleasure provided by the numerous verbal duels — all prolong the versifying until well after dawn. Usually what started in the morning as a manifestation of neighborly solidarity becomes a ceremonial gathering of neighbors in the evening and ends at dawn with deep resentment among several of them; even personal physical aggression between some of the participants is not unlikely.[3] How can such antithetical forces be put into play at the same time between the same persons? Does not the succession of episodes reveal a structural contradiction? What relation does this activity have to that *fine fleur* that is poetry?[4]

BRINDIS

Brindis or *loias*[5] are not associated only with the *carreto* or *carretada*. *Brindis* also occur during the slaughter of pigs, on carnival nights or around carnival days, at weddings and at celebrations of some local holiday, or any other time there is a gathering of a group of neighbors invited by someone wishing to reply to favors received, the sharing of a table, and camaraderie.

The *loia* also occurs at weddings and is started by those not invited to the nuptial banquet. When *loia* participants believe that the wedding meal is about to end, they go to the house, place themselves in front of one of its windows, and intone a quatrain asking for tobacco. One *loia* from Zanfoga is as follows:

Me valgo Dios de los cielos,	May God in heaven be my witness,
yo no me llamo Navarro,	My name is not Navarron.
que le digo senor novio	I request the bridegroom
que me de el cigarro.	To give me a cigar.

The bridegroom or groomsman, and any guest who wishes to take up the challenge, come to the window to accept the poetic challenge and refuse to give the tobacco. The singers accuse him of being stingy; the guests

---

[3] In Lugo province, the people told me of a death that occurred as a result of poetic aggression. If the allegation is true, one would assume that the verses must have precipitated into action a preexisting state of intense enmity.

[4] There is no need to underline the fact that the eye of the ethnologist and that of the historian of literature and the linguist do not necessarily focus on the same phenomenon. Furthermore, the dimensions of poetry are also abundant for the ethnologist; and in this essay, for lack of sufficient time to do otherwise, I am limiting myself to only a few.

[5] Even in an area as small as Cebrero mountain, one finds other name variants: *berindes*, *brindos*, and *berindos*.

reply that the singers are being inopportune and intrusive. The polemical versifying continues to the enjoyment of virtually the whole village. And when the bridegroom or groomsman judges that the form or content of the verbal challenge coming from below has attained a certain quality, he throws down cigarettes or packets of tobacco. The *loia* singers praise that magnanimity in rhyme, as long as their demands are satisfied. Similarly, on the night of the *carreta*, the poetic duel opens by praising the culinary skill of the women who prepared the supper. In these cases, once gratitude has been expressed, the group breaks up.

REGUEIFA

Verbal artistic forms appear in other contexts using specific local names or expressions and properties; nevertheless, the features of drama, struggle, offensive, and counteroffensive are prominent in all of them. Such is the case of the improvised ceremonial poetic melody known as the *regueifa*. *Regueifa* refers to the large loaf of flour, eggs, and sugar received as a prize by the winner or winners of a literary duel. Thus, the latter is given the same name, perhaps by semantic extension. The *regueifa* as a literary contest accompanies the *carretada*, weddings, carnivals, and parish feasts. Vimienzo and Muxia are the towns with the greatest *regueifa* tradition.[6]

The wedding *regueifa* is similar to the Lugo *loia*. Outsiders or the not invited hurl verses rhymed with irony and sarcasm to the newlyweds and groomsmen. According to a villager in a hamlet of Santa Comba: "They insult each other in improvised verses. Now the *regueifa* is sung, but the *regueifa* is not made because they are quarreling, because it gave rise to scrapes; they even insulted the bride . . . They take advantage of these occasions to insult each other."

Regueifas differ from *brindis* in that the reply verse does not have to begin with the last word of the challenger's quatrain; the new verse is unrestricted.

At times, the people also celebrate the completion of a house with a *regueifa*. "Some singers were above, on the scaffolding, and others below.

---

[6]   Both belong to Cornua province. But they are not the only ones; Camarinas (Puente del Puerto), Cee (Lires, Tedin), Corcubion, Cerceda (Adro), Mazaricos (Picota), Cabana (Cesullas), Arnes (Bertamirans), Teo (Mouromorto and Luou), Muros (Louro), Puente-Ceso (Campara), Malpica (Linero, Mens, Razo, Rabuceiros), and Carballo (Ornados) are other towns and villages that enjoy the *regueifa*. In Laxe, I have notes on *regueifas* in the villages of Traba and Serantes; Carantona, Berdoyas, Pedra do Fraire, Brano, Bainas, Ogas, Calo, Salto, Carmpolongo, Moreira, Devesa, Montecelos, Cures, and Tufiones in Vimianzo. Finally, according to my notes, they are also celebrated in the following villages of Muxia: Molinos, Villarmide, Frige, Senande, Gatarante, Leis, Sujo, Quintans, Castelo, San Martino de Ozon, Moraime, Castro de Frige, Morquintion, and Tourinan.

One attacked another very strongly. Things became bad and to avoid a fight, I sang" said a well-known *regueifa* singer.

The *regueifa* is often a parochial poetic contest.[7] It is organized by a parochial commission made up of four or five residents of the parish. In the towns, most *regueifa* singers celebrate two or even three *regueifas* in each parish in a year. Those commissioned to perform one visit the houses of the parish asking for money to organize the contest. About two weeks before it is to take place, they begin to spread the word through the district, indicating the place chosen and the *regueifa* singers who will confront each other poetically. Sometimes they announce the contest by means of signs placed in public places. In Vimianzo, the Brotherhood of Farmers organizes and pays the costs of the *regueifa*.

When it is time for the *regueifa*, the people from nearby parishes begin to arrive. They surround the platform (musical enclosure, if it takes place during the parish festival) raised for this purpose on the dance ground. Recently, loudspeakers have been added, so the improvised poetic melody can be heard without difficulty by the large audience. Those who commissioned the event preside and present the *regueifa* singers to the public. There are usually four singers, divided into pairs, who place themselves facing each other on the platform. One intones an octosyllabic verse, which he improvises about any subject that occurs to him and flings it at his adversary. The latter, in turn, immediately sings another octosyllabic quatrain as a reply. The first replies, and so on. If one of the pair is slow or hesitates in his response, his companion intervenes and enters the proceedings by singing his verse. As the night advances, two of the singers may rest while the other two upbraid each other. When one tires and wants to cede the podium to his companion, he expresses his wish in a verse. Anyone may change the subject at any time. The reply may acknowledge the new line of attack, start a different one, or continue with the previous one. The *regueifa* singer must comply with the octosyllabic poetic form, but he remains free to create the content. Although it is not common, a five-line verse may be sung. The melody with which it is sung determines to a certain extent the octosyllabic verse.

Improvisation and gracefulness are highly valued at such gatherings. No sooner does one finish singing than the other starts to answer him. If one commits errors in his versifying, he loses points with the commission members who count and decide the winner. If a rival or his companion

---

[7]   Galicia has 315 municipalities or small political segments. The average regional size per municipality is 93 square kilometers, and the average number of inhabitants per municipality is 10,550 in Coruna province, 7,150 in Lugo, 11,150 in Pontevedra, and 4,850 in Orense. The municipalities are traditionally, though not officially, subdivided into parishes. There are 3,496 rural parishes, 11 per municipality on the average, with an area of 8.1 square kilometers; there is an average density of 600 inhabitants per parish. A number of hamlets, each with an average of 80 persons, form the parish. There are about 24,500 of these entities in Galicia.

delays in replying, the opponent, depending on his inspiration, may launch other verses, until one of the two contestants is in a position to attack. If one remains silent because he does not know what to answer or because he cannot say it in rhyme and has to refer to his resting companion, he has lost and the commission and the public will demand that he withdraw. The one remaining is naturally at the mercy of his two opponents, who speed up the rhythm of their versifying and allow him little time to counterattack. This can lead to defeat, but this kind of defeat rarely occurs. Most of the famous *regueifa* singers of the la Coruna area have an amazing capacity for improvisation. One has only to propose a word to them — horse, for example — and before ten seconds have passed, they have begun to versify. And they continue to do so easily, without preparation, for half an hour on the same subject. Then without transition, and in verse, they ask that another subject be suggested to them. One afternoon, I had a visit from one of the famous poets from another village who knew I was interested in picking up the music of the *regueifa*. At that time, I was with two informants, one of whom was a *partixeiro*, a local official who handles the division of inherited lands and goods. When the *regueifa* singer saw him, he sang, looking at me while pointing at him with his index finger:

Este fai moitas partixas	This man apportions a lot of land
o mundo vailo dicendo;	The world is wont to say;
a contadas trampas d'el	Through many of his deceits
o homo vai vivendo.	The man manages to live.

On hearing him sing, a passerby, the local electrician, entered. His greeting was a completion of the previous verse:

A luz xa estamos sin ela	It appears we are not free
e ven con moitas palabras,	And they go with many words,
e va cobrando os cartos;	And he goes to collect the maps;
a culpa teno Opalla.	*Opalla* [the factory] is to blame.*

This verse was accompanied by a gesture, the pointing of the finger. Afterward, he improvised on whatever I suggested to him. In my choice of subjects, I tried hard to find abstract and difficult ones.[8]

Improvisation is fast in the same *regueifa*. On one occasion, a contender greeted the arriving parish priest in this manner:

*This verse and most of the others in this article are in Galician dialect, which is quite different from Spanish. The translation is only approximate. — *Translator*.

[8] This *regueifa* singer lives in Muinoseco (Coristanco). Another, no less a star, is from the parish of Carnes (Vimianzo). The latter remains undefeated except for the occasion when his throat did not allow him to continue singing. "I never met anyone in the district who could humble me," he told me.

Buenas tardes Senor cura,	Good day, Father,
milagro usted por aqui,	What a miracle you're here,
me parece un diputado	You seem to me to be an MP
de la corte de Madrid.	From the court of Madrid.

It is not an original verse, but it provided an occasion his rival immediately took advantage of, in order to annoy him with another verse calling him by his nickname:

O caldereiro e bon home,	The boilermaker is a good man,
Solo que ten un defecto,	He only has one defect,
que hace mois d'un ano	That for more than a year
que no cumple co precepto.	He has not carried out his duties.

This was the immediate reply:

Si no cumpli co precepto	If I have not carried out my duties
podo cumplir este ano,	I can do so this year,
bien o sabe o senor cura	For the Father well knows
que en so bo cristiano.	That I am a good Christian.

Regueifas almost exclusively involve attack, insult, and aggression, the latter occasionally passing from verbal to real. A singer explained *regueifa* in this way: "It is counterpoint singing in which I shoot him and he shoots me." Another said: "In the *regueifa* we shoot each other as much as we can; we know each other personally and our families. We accuse each other of being bad people, thieves, fond of women. If you have a small blemish, that is where I attack." On one occasion, a poet saw his opponent's beloved in the crowd and immediately launched his darts. They were all designed to call the public's attention to the woman. This opponent became furious and versified:

He de maldecir a Dios	You may speak ill of God
y o Cristo da carretera,	And the Christ of the highway,
nombrame e mi e a familia	Name me and my family
mais no me nombres a ela.	But do not mention her name.

The immediate reply of the triumphant *regueifa* singer, who had touched a sore point, was as follows:

Aunque me avises de Dios	Although you advise me of God
e mais de Virxen Maria,	And even the Virgin Mary,
ei che de nombrar a ela,	I wish to name that woman,
e non a tua familia.	And not your family.

This time, instead of replying in poetry, the person alluded to jumped over a small barricade to reach his stubborn opponent; the public intervened and the contest had to be abandoned.

The audience hopes that when one of the singers finds a needle with which to prick and mortify his rival, he will exploit it to the maximum. When one accuses another of stealing, the accused defended himself by proclaiming this five-line verse:

Eu non preciso roubar	I do not have to steal
que so un gran carpinteiro	For I am a great carpenter
e maestro de albaniles;	And a master of masons;
a conta de dous oficios	As I have two trades
estou granando muitos miles.	I am earning many thousands.

While the second singer awaited the counterattack, someone from Castro approached the first singer and said: "Tell him that he stole a ram." A moment later, this verse was in the air:

Eu non vou roubar zabatos	I am not going to steal shoes
que os compro o zapaterio,	Which you bought from the cobbler,
no vous a robar a Castro	I am not going to steal in Castro,
como tu robas carneiros.	As you steal rams.

In the face of the first party's threats and to force him to change the subject, the second singer launched the following:

Os carneiros marchan, marchan,	The rams are marching, marching,
os carneiros van marchando,	The rams are marching on,
e a conta dos do Castro,	And I have two from Castro,
a vida te vas pasando.	And life is passing you by.

The people who knew of the matter of the ram gave the award to the challenger with long applause. The one accused took out a razor and headed towards the challenger. But he soon found himself facing the ram's owner, who was going to "give him a beating" with his cane. The first singer later commented to me:

He even told me about the trouble. He told me: "Since I am being threatened, you are going to pay. You have a new cane." He told me all this on an occasion when I invited him to sing. I told him that with a new razor I wasn't afraid of him, either, and nothing happened. But if I had humbled myself, he would have beaten me. At times the one making a fuss is the one who loses. The one provoked is the one who least needs to be provoked, because he comes out openly.

The listener does not play a passive role. People come in cars and buses to participate in a *regueifa*, just as they go to local fiestas and pilgrimages, where they are the main participants. The number of persons, the atmosphere, and the attitudes are similar. They surround the singers' platform; they listen carefully; and as they know the local geography and the allusions to persons and problems underlined in the verses, they communicate empathetically with the actors. They laugh, protest against bad rhyme, appreciate and applaud poetic quality, and reward mental agility, acumen, and forceful attack or defense with shouts. According to one *regueifa* singer known for his defensive skill: "When he shoots off a good shot, the public applauds a lot." Another experiences the audience's action in the following manner: "When someone is winning, and I had been picked on to lose, he goes up [in points] and is not allowed to seek the protection [of the opponents]; at each step [each point he wins] the public applauds more, and at each step, it gives more encouragement." At times, it is the public who decides to which poet victory shall be granted: "In Senande I sang for six and a half hours. I shortened it two or three times . . . the public interceded through its hands and said that he should be declared beaten." At times, the audience's emotive response reaches a climax. One group favors one of the poets, perhaps because he is a neighbor; another group favors another. The former applauds and the latter protests, and they become involved in heavy discussions. Being partially drunk, some of the audience come to blows.

It is unusual for the poetic competition to end before dawn. The capacity to make poetry is not extinguished, and those commissioned to do so enthusiastically follow the battle's sudden changes of fortune. When one singer or a pair decisively outdistances the other, the commission and public decide to award the victory, which is the *regueifa*. All the singers then choose two assistants, one male and one female, who cut up and apportion the loaf among all those who wish to try it. The assistants dance a *muneira* [a Galician dance] and *jota* [an Aragonese and Valencian dance]. The female dances with a portion or a small loaf on her head, while she touches the piper. "She would lose merit if it should fall from her head; therefore they choose those who know how to jump and to walk to and fro without letting it fall."

When daybreak comes, they all return home. For weeks, they discuss, comment on, and relive certain details and verses they learned by heart. Later the poet sees his verses pass from mouth to mouth in the district. One singer recalled:

I have sung verses which I no longer recall but the public recalls them and says them, and so when I hear them I remember them, I am going to improvise and who is going to remember afterward! I answer and [the verses] remain behind. Later on those who are watching and have a good memory say: "you told him this, and you answered in this manner."

Villagers continue to repeat quatrains improvised at *regueifas* years before, applying them to present persons, events, and situations. Those little poems become in time condensations of local values. They express with rhythm, rhyme, and music the conflicts and tensions inherent in the individual-community relations. The exegesis to follow of some aspects of the *carreto* and *regueifa* reveals this moral crystallization and something more.

Observing the march of the tumbrel drivers and their carts along the main street of the town, which is the capital of the district, was like witnessing a play or a theatrical act. The actors, although they are considered residents of the town, actually live in the surrounding hamlet. And the village inhabitants feel that they are away from home when they go to the town. On the whole, the hamlet dwellers see themselves in opposition to the town dwellers.

Thus, they are entering a foreign stage to present their pantomime. In addition, the players, wishing to be noticed, make a noisy entrance and exhibit arrogance and lack of courtesy. They do not even look at those who greeted them. Actually, not only is it unnecessary for them to pass through the town and its main street, but in fact, they have to deviate from the direct route to do so. There is significance in the slow passage of the small group of cart drivers along the most important street of a major town, the official and actual seat (with its municipal council) of authority and government. On the one hand, the act demonstrates a high degree of assertion and solidarity of one segment, the hamlet. On the other hand, and inherent in the assertion itself, it demonstrates its opposition to and power over what is external to it; that is, the town center. The *carreto* thus heightens the competition of opposed interests.

The *carreto* started with the ceremonializing of the tense, dialectic relationship between the hamlet and the town. It continues to be the vehicle that symbolically expresses the conflict, but this time on another level: between members of the group who displayed strong internal cohesion at a morning spectacle. Not all the residents of the village always participate in the *carreto*; only those who are linked to the host by a special bond of friendship join in. Generally, the first toasts (*brindis*) are simply ironic; they tell how some are now taking advantage of food and drink for which they have worked, of someone present who is getting on in years and yet is still a bachelor, of a boy who went out with a young girl and left her. Why? So that these situations may be explained by the *loia*. But soon the verbal interchanges become accusations with more profound allusions. Why are not the other members of the village present?[9] Has the person alluded to in the verse really gone to the *carreto* because he is a neighbor or because of other, less avowable reasons? Why is it that a particular family has sent the least responsible person to the *carreto*? The defenses and counterattacks soon take on a strictly personal color. People are faulted and insulted for things they said or did or should not

---

[9]   This problem arises in small hamlets where it is economically feasible to invite all the neighbors to the banquet. The absence of one or several of them indicates strained relations with the host or one of the other guests. The *loias* celebrated on the occasion of the slaughter of pigs and at carnivals are virtually identical to the one on which I am commenting.

have said or done, for omissions in points of neighborliness, for removing water from an irrigation ditch or pasturing one's cow in someone else's field, and so on. From time to time, two *loia* singers pass from insult or personal attack to a scuffle. Although the other guests try to calm them down, at times the verses give rise to resentments that may last for years. The contents of a number of *loia* evenings indicate that the verses paraphrase the Ten Commandments, or the sum total of norms for interpersonal relations in a local community, norms of neighborliness, from an individual point of view. Each *loia* singer constitutes himself a judge of his neighbors and strongly and bitterly lashes out at those actions and omissions of his fellow-creatures that have perpetrated crimes against his own rights, real or claimed.

As we have seen, *loias* at weddings dramatize another aspect of local conflict. In very small villages, all the residents participate in the nuptial banquet. When the number increases, it may not be economically feasible for some families to invite everyone from the community. But since everyone is equally a neighbor and ready to cooperate in case of crisis, why should any be excluded from participation in a celebration? Their rights appear to have been violated. Those left out turn poetically militant. They go to where the celebration is being held and with rhymed songs ask to be included in some way. Note the symmetry in the symbolic message communicated by the *carreto* and wedding *loia*, although they are played on two different stages. The cart drivers belong officially to the town, but they feel excluded in some way. The villagers, in spite of being residents, are discriminated against in a rite of transition that takes place in the village. Both are from within, and yet both are outside. Both are condemned to be passive members, but both groups show themselves to be active. They leave their internal boundaries to *chirriar* (those from the *carreto*) or "sing" their protest in verses in a foreign area (in the municipal center or at the house of one of the newlyweds). In both situations, the priority of the whole or the aggregate (the town and the hamlet) is affirmed over that of the parts.

From this perspective, the *loia* is a claiming of rights, a group reaffirmation in the face of temporary excision or continued partial exclusion. There is, however, structural inconsistency: two parts of the same ceremony (the *chirriar* of the *carreto*, the song at the wedding). Exclusion from municipal benefits is loudly criticized;[10] thus, in principle, effective inclusion should be approved. But at the same time, an affirmation is made of the differences between the rights of the villager and those living in other parts of the municipality. Only those coming from the village are entitled to participate in the wedding, not those from the town. In other words, the *loia* is a means of corroborating the validity of different and

---

[10]   There is neither doctor nor pharmacy nor school (at times) nor telephone nor shops in the villages; often there is not even a paved road leading to it.

even opposing principles of local organization. This being the case, it is not surprising that the poetic melody (*regueifa*) should confirm and affirm another geographic-moral unit: the parish. I have already indicated that the *regueifa* is basically parochial in its organization. Thus, I am going to limit myself to copying a quatrain sung at a poetic contest. One *regueifa* singer was flogging his opponent, criticizing him for having a lover; the accusation was not poetic fiction. The duel, based on this theme, went on for half an hour; on one occasion, the accuser vocalized this quatrain:

Vou a decille una cousa	I am going to tell you something
a mais no se si a diga;	But I do not know how to say it;
?como andas na parroquia	How can you walk in the parish
alo co a tu amiga?	As if she were your friend?

The *regueifa* singer believed it to be a matter of censure that the other bard had introduced a woman who was not his own into the parish boundaries.

Furthermore, poetic singing in the *regueifa* demonstrates another plan for the orientation and legitimizing of values. It is not merely a question of revealing in rhyme a subjective experience that violates the local moral code, as in the *carreto*. Neither does it consist of expressing within a poetic framework the collective complaint of the excluded segment, as at *loias* and *carreto*. In his versifying, the *regueifa* singer criticizes the transgressing of the general moral order as a whole. After all, the *regueifa* singers are never among the residents of their own locality or parish and on some occasions, they do not even know each other by sight or sound when the duel ceremoniously begins. The verses of the *regueifa* expound and attack common infractions of the moral code. They attack those who are presumptuous, vain, or proud and who think they are superior to everyone else because they have brought money from America. The adulterer is also a repeated target for attack. He is reminded of his obligation to look after any children that may result from an illicit union. The person who is a thief or lover of women, one who is unmerciful to his neighbors, selfish or a complainer, is the type of person who is described poetically and whom one seeks to confound and, as far as possible, to destroy.

Regueifa singers do not come to the platform as private persons. Instead, they come on the stage as actors in the sham battle of an allegorical play in which vices and evil are directly condemned and virtue and good (according to the common local conception of these) are indirectly extolled. First the actors are physically separated from the audience, raised to a height above the public. One *regueifa* singer recalls how, when he was twelve years old, he was placed on a tavern counter, in order to compete with someone else on a table. These informal contests include a separation and elevation of the actors. The singers also realize that they are not acting in their individual capacities. They know that they are occupying a special position with unusual roles, rights, and duties.

When two people face each other for the first time, they usually confirm that they "admit everything" the other may wish to tell them. On one occasion, a poet declared in his verse that he had seen the other with a woman in a meadow, which was tantamount to accusing him of adultery. Later, I asked him if he had been referring to something true, and he answered me: "No, no, I didn't see him in the meadow, but it doesn't matter." The concrete fact is the least important consideration. Nor is it important whether it was one or another person. Adultery in general is being condemned.

Second, the *regueifa* singer is not acting (as in the *loias*) by virtue of his appointment or membership in a local group, category or location.

Third, the *regueifa*'s disposition or attitude is different from the normal one. "I admit everything they say to me because that is why I go. In fact, I shoot out quite a number of verses against myself. When some [the other *regueifa* singer] insists [singing] that I give him a clue, I give him some against myself," a famous bard said. Attacks in *regueifas* are far from being personal.[11] Naturally they may be offensive at certain times, and a person may take it personally, but in these cases the committee and public withdraw the *regueifa* singer from the ceremonial area, and the latter is once again invested with his private capacity.

The *regueifa* singer in public accepts even the most venomous kinds of attacks against himself and those close to him. He has to tolerate attacks directed against his wife and family. His position on the platform is the opposite of the normal one. Everyone knows he is being accused of behavior or omissions that are imaginary; that is, ones he has not perpetrated and to which his reaction would be violent under ordinary circumstances. On being separated and raised to the ceremonial rectangle, the *regueifa* singer sheds his private person and takes on a symbolic collective representation. While he is acting, he takes the place of and represents factors and dimensions of the moral world. When he attacks and lashes out, he becomes the standard-bearer of moral order. On the other hand, when he is accused and reproached, he crystallizes or embodies immorality and evil. Thus the actors occupy double, ambiguous, and contradictory positions. In a word, they are and act as mediators between the antithetical forces of order and disorder, of good and evil.

THE EXPRESSION OF AGGRESSION

Although there are many similarities and differences between *regueifas*

---

[11]   There were and are some *regueifas* sung at weddings, but this kind is similar to *loias* on the same occasions.

and *loias*, there are also regularities in this apparent diversity that should be interpreted. From a repetitive linguistic viewpoint, one could count the number of times in which words connoting aggression are used to describe these forms. Galician rural poetry is a form of aggression. The aggressive note absolutely predominates in the content of all popular and collective poetic ceremonializations. Although this is obvious with respect to *loias* and *regueifas*, consider the other collective poetic forms.

Until very recently — in some districts the custom is still practiced — residents of the village used to meet in one or two houses, according to the number of residents, to enjoy winter social evenings. The women would spin and the men would chat around the fire. These were called *fiadeiros*. Once a week or more often, the *fiadeiro* ended in a dance and also quite frequently there was a contest. The word *desafio*, which is known and used throughout the whole rural area to refer to the same event, is very expressive. "The challenge (*desafio*) of singing," as it is known in the villages of Pinor, was used not only for *fiadeiros* but also for the slaughtering of pigs. In the localities of Cea at slaughters, after supper, they all sang — they still do at times — in chorus, such songs as this:

Si queres desafiar,	If you want to compete,
si queres lo desafio,	If you want a competition,
vamoslo a encomenzar.	We are going to begin it.

Anyone who is now forty years old in the villages and towns of Rubinia and Bollo has sung verses of challenge (or "disputes," as they are known by everyone) at these meetings. One of the features of these songs of challenge is their repetition; rarely are they improvised. Whole verses used to circulate in the communities. When the time came, they were sung in groups to each other in the guise of a challenge. In Villardevos and Cualedro, the opposition was between the sexes; the women placed themselves at one side at *fiadeiros* and carnivals and the men at the other, to sing the verses, that is, "to make a contest." That custom still continues today in some villages in Oya where men and women verbally whip each other with "verses of challenge." A villager, Campo Lameiro, told me that at feasts and weddings, "the contests were often too biting and insulting." In Rodeiro, such contests usually took place between groups from different villages. They often ended with the brandishing of sticks that the men always brought to these gatherings. In Freanes, a small group of people told me, "We used to sing each song, each verse at the song contest." The ones I was able to pick up were really cruel and biting. In almost all the towns I have mentioned and in many others — that is in the villages of which they are made up — they distinguish between those *desafios* that are appropriate to weddings, slaughtering, and *fiadeiros*, and the "verses of censure" and "satires," which go with the Carnival.

Fiadeiros are the imaginary product of a local poet who knows his neighbors well and whom he criticizes at a public and solemn recital on a Carnival afternoon.

One aspect of verses of *desafio* is shown by the "verses of strife" (*coplas de contestacion*) which I have collected in the villages of Cospeito but which are common to many other areas. At the usual gatherings for slaughterings, weddings, fiestas, and *fiadeiros*, the residents intone familiar verses in which they ironically narrate about the fragility of human love, the material interests that predominate at weddings, the difficulty of relations with one's mother-in-law (or daughter-in-law); the advantages of bachelorhood (from the mouths of those who are married); the superiority of marriage (according to spinsters); and so on. Verses of silent protest against the hardness of country or sea life because of extreme poverty, of the abuse and eviction of the "laborer" by authorities or political leaders and especially by the notary public, and of emigration are much fewer in number than the subjects previously mentioned.

Loias or *brindis* [toasts], *regueifas*, *desafios*, verses of criticism and dispute, sung or recited in groups, in public, following rules and performed ceremonially — all show a common denominator of aggressiveness. They are also developed within a common framework; that is, at feasts, weddings, slaughterings, and carnivals. Finally, the element of sharing a table completes the syndrome of this rural, verbal artistic phenomenon.

Are not some of these characteristic notes antithetical? After all, what in the last instance seems to be pursued is the maintaining of a moral order that is frequently broken, and can aggression be a suitable means of achieving it? How can one vent one's fury against someone who has just sat at one's table, or against a bride on the very day of her wedding? What sense is there in accusing the *regueifa* singer of common actions that he has not committed? Is the target or purpose of the poetic contest to bring neighbors together so that they may leave this love feast divided?

As the problem is exclusively structural, its interpretation requires the uncovering of the basic reasons that created it in the first place. The village resident is the head of his house. The house and his position in it are the fundamental structural basis of relationships. A village is made up of a number of households that coexist in opposition and cooperation. House and village are antithetical in more than one sense, just as are the individual and the community. To make the picture more complex, the village coincides with neither the smallest political unit nor with the minimum area for economic or legal relationships. It is also not equivalent to a small religious and moral world. It does not constitute the sole focus of loyalty, nor is it always the basis of individual identity. Finally, it does not offer an exclusive cognitive-symbolic subsystem.[12] The resident

---

[12] All this is a condensation of statements in Tolosana (1971; i.p.).

who sings the *loia* and the *desafio* or hears the *regueifa* is the subject or bearer of all these dimensions at all times and at the same time. In his verses, the singer affirms the separation of those levels, of division and rupture, of his individuality; he does this in a concrete situation and according to specific interests. Within minutes, he also exclaims poetically the claims and demands to which he is entitled as a member of a group or category (in which he has just placed himself in order to intone its obliged rhymed words). All this means that the variations of form and content that can be pointed out in *loias*, *regueifas* and *desafios* are only a representation at a poetic level of the many aspects of the social structure. The alternation of unity and harmony, division and opposition (that are legitimized in the verses), correspond to a number of real situations.

While geographical-political structure of habitat and resources creates many situations that provoke aggressive responses, surely a community where aggressiveness prevails over other harmonious formulas or rituals ends by destroying itself. As the group in question has been submitted to strong pressures that are basically antagonistic, it has to develop dikes to contain these pressures, to organize an attack against them. Thus, the Galician people have succeeded in creating a cultural standard of aggressiveness that is expressed in varying degrees by individuals. These actions are in fact compatible with a high degree of communal harmony.[13] For example, the atmosphere in which aggressiveness is permitted is revealing. Occasions preceding its manifestation are, as we know, an affirmation of group solidarity, occurring at the *carreto*, weddings, carnivals, the slaughter of a pig, or a festival gathering of neighbors. In other words, the opportunity for aggression occurs within a festal environment. Furthermore, the *regueifa* takes place after the meal of the festival day and the *loia* at the *carreto*, carnivals, and slaughtering immediately after supper has ended, during the eating of dessert and drinking of liquors that extend the table fellowship for hours. Cooperation, camaraderie, feasting, joy, and table fellowship form the framework in which aggressiveness is permitted. These are a splendid combination of opposites and a characteristic of the Galician ethos. Furthermore, accumulated aggressiveness is held back so that it may be expended publicly rather than privately, and it is subject to rules and conditions. Table fellowship and the observations of rituals hold down and master individual aggressiveness; at least, they condition its eruption. They avert dangerous outbursts and soften some of the edges. *Loias*, *desafios*, and *regueifas* act as mechanisms for the control of aggression.

But note the subtlety of that mechanism. The cultural standard seems to say to each resident: your aggressiveness may be unrestricted, you have no barriers in its expression, as long as you express it after eating, in public, by singing, and in verse. Show your irritation against whomever

---

[13]   That is, not necessarily *individual* harmony, which does not exist.

you choose, and as much as you want, so long as you do it by singing. Be stubbornly aggressive, but in verse. The concentration required by singing and versification will, because of the complexity of the form, distract much of the attention that would otherwise have been centered exclusively on the emotive charge. This, then, is the basis of Galician aesthetic aggression.

WHY POETRY?

The attempt was made above to show how, for the Galician, just as for Baudelaire, the human condition is the fundamental poetic dimension. Now, among other things the author wants to show how, for the Galician, as for Mallarmé, verses are not only words but also intentions. Why does the Galician choose to use poetry? What is he trying to do through versification?

A good *regueifa* singer once said while commenting on the public's attitude when listening to poetry: "The public's attention is called to observing the poetry; they are like a person listening to the holy mass, and when someone or other upsets the gathering — he loses the threads of it." Shortcomings of assonance are noticed immediately; the guffaws and shouts of protest that follow punish the versifier's lack of skill. On these occasions, the aggressive content of the verse tends to be diluted in the commotion. When a "well-compared" quatrain — one whose rhyme and form have given pleasure — ends, the audience applauds. The listeners move about in an emotive atmosphere that stimulates catharsis as well as *bonhomie* and resentment. They attain an intense experience of social reality in those village *loias*; there, and through poetry, they feel part of a whole, whether they have been invited or discriminated against, attacked, or honored. There, things appear as they are for everyone else, *in poese veritas*.

In fact, poetry appears to be endowed with a mystical power to uncover hidden things, truths that are not known by other means. People do not clearly understand its principles of organization and structure, its inconsistencies and contradictions, the dialectic between synchronism and diachronism. They perceive and express many things poetically rather than intellectually. However, what is expressed in verse is rarely equivalent to a cold description, an *ethics* of reality; stylization, exaggeration, feeling, and fantasy elaborate the fact with metaphysical repercussions. The verses speak passionately of rights, obligations, loyalties, virtue, immorality, ideas, and sentiments. Expressed in another manner, the verses poetize experience in its moral aspects; they present facts in their moral form. Furthermore, verses suggest and persuade, emotionally incite one to do his duty, to comply with correct behavior, with order and synchronism. Thus, poetry expresses a moral-philosophic world that would be difficult to perceive in any other manner. It is a way, *its* way, of seeing that world.

Therefore, Galician rural poetry is knowledge, morality, order, synchronism, and aesthetics. It is also magic and religion, power, action, and diachronism. I have indicated how reality is transformed by the magic wand of poetry. There is no doubt that euphony, meter, rhythm, song, rhyme, metaphor, bold analogies, affinities, audacious assimilations, style, concise inferences, excess, and confusion all contribute with their sensational possibilities of communicating the magical suggestion and hypnotic power of poetry. But this is only a part of the magic of poetry and not the most important part, at that. It would be useful to look at it again, this time using horizontal analysis and starting with such questions as: On what popular occasions does poetry thrive? What is its use, end, motive?

PRAYER-POEMS

Invocations and magical-ritualistic formulas with which the author is acquainted (and these are more than a few in number) are generally in verse: those addressed to the saints, the Virgin Mary, cosmic forces, principles, being, activities, and powers. The propitiatory forms for dealing with enchantments, spirits, and saints, and for confronting apparitions and ghosts, are always little poems or rhyming verses. Poetry is used as a means of securing a cure of the pains and illnesses, real and imaginary, of persons of both sexes and every age, and of domestic animals. The many blessings for the protection of children, adults, and animals lavishly imparted by women specializing in ritual are all in the form of poetry. Storms are quelled by a verse. Exorcists utter verses in rhyme, and demons and other spirits are cast out of bodies, punished by poetic anger. Quacks prescribe verses; that is, they prescribe their recitation so a sick person may destroy his illness. Poetic recitation is effective protection against possible supernatural harm, against the evil eye and the envy of neighbors. Poetic prayer also brings a blessing on fields, to produce a fruitful harvest; on ships to return loaded with fish. Such prayer brings affluence and wealth. There are demonic invocations in verse to call the Prince of Darkness and force him to present himself. Once he has appeared he is asked (not necessarily in rhyme) for whatever one wishes. Finally, the easiest way of ending one's days on earth and the best passport to the other life is the recitation of a very well-known long poem.

In conversations, people (women especially, but not exclusively) referred to all those magical-ritualistic formulas already outlined by the attribute of *prayers*. All spoken prayers — except the official ones recited in church — rhyme, and are poetry. The popular experience of prayer and the idea of prayer among women as a whole include rhyme as an inherent characteristic. Men know this poetry, too, but it is generally women who recite it. There is something else: if one is distracted during the narration of a poem-prayer, if he makes a mistake, alters the order, or omits or changes a word, he destroys the power and effectiveness of the poem-prayer and cannot hope to achieve anything by it. He has to begin again. If the poetic formula does not produce any result, the failure is imputed to an involuntary and inadvertent error in its reciting. The power resides in the words, in the order, in the whole. The poetic word is *vis sacra*.

Poetry is the instrument of contact with other worlds, with supernatural powers and forces, mysterious beings, the world beyond. Poetry shortens distances, reduces differences, makes communication possible between very different extremes — for example, between men and divinity, especially when mortals want to communicate a petition that may seem unsuitable or that they deem difficult to obtain. To address those strange spheres one must use a language of ritual: poetry. Messages may not be sent in any other way, in ordinary language. The same thing happens in the social sphere. Ceremonial contact between nations frequently starts with poetic recitation. One must address foreign groups in poetry; verse is the means of speaking that commands attention. Criticisms against persons or sections of the community and the censuring of immorality must be clothed in poetry. Distances and differences are reduced by making a ceremony of an occasion, communicating the message by appropriate language, making a sacred occasion of it.

If these magico-ritualistic little poems,[14] if these prayers (recited properly and with devotion and without mistakes), secure the health of children and adults, protect from the snares of the devil, if they guard the cattle, increase harvests on land and sea, and free humanity from the machinations of evil neighbors, then other poems, narrated in their proper context — that is, publicly and ceremonially — will also achieve what they claim. The intrinsic power and effectiveness of the former must also be inherent in the latter. It is already known that the latter claim to banish selfishness and immorality, to restore and consolidate harmonious relations among neighbors. The ritual expression desired is the same in both cases. An identical mystical causation is also presumed in both cases.

Finally, one can regard poetry as a mediation between persons who are opposed in some manner, between persons and superior powers, between what is and what ought to be. Poetry is a way of overcoming disorder. Short poems and quatrains exhort, incite, advise, entreat, and direct. All this implies action, process, reformulation of desires and relations. Expressed in another way, popular poetry implies change, the achieving of a new state or order of things. What exists does not satisfy. The repetition of conflicts, of numerous individual failures and prolonged antagonisms,

[14] Magical for the observer, but not necessarily for the actor.

of the continual flourishing of structural inconsistencies, provides an experience of disorder, a perceiving of diachronism. With the passage of time, there is an increase of tensions. Reconciliation may be achieved through stable principles that close the door to insecurity and uncertainty, that elevate fixed moral points or mainstays. Poetic narration tries to reduce diachronistic disorder to a moral synchronistic order of rules and precepts. That poetic effort is never in fact achieved: it adorns each popular recitation with a splendid and generous romantic tint. The existential contraditions that are theatrically performed and exorcized at night on a public stage are strongly revived at dawn.

CONCLUSION

This study has touched briefly on a few aspects of certain kinds of Galician rural poetry. It is a fruitful and fascinating subject, as are other aspects of Galicia's rich folklore. Therefore, in conclusion it is appropriate to ask: Does folklore's institutionalizing of verbal art have any influence on the development of poetic imagination? On rereading field notes, the author sees how impressive was the verse-making facility of those giving information. There are many local poets today. No doubt the ability to manipulate language, the enormous lexical variability, and the linguistic virtuosity of any villager are in correlation with the many ceremonies and rituals that are in verse. Both men and women have put them into poetry.[15] Finally, one must not forget that, seven centuries ago, Galicia, with its poetic songs of praise, friendship, and joy, and with its ancient Spanish songs and dances (*villanescas*), was the first poetic nation of Spain.

REFERENCES

TOLOSANA, CARMELO LISON
  1971   *Anthropologia cultural de Galicia* [*Cultural anthropology of Galicia*]. Madrid: Siglio Veintuna de Espana Editors.
  i.p.   *Some aspects of the moral structure in Galician hamlets.*

[15]   In public and ceremonial contexts, actors are almost invariably men. Rituals and poetic formulas that are of a healing or propitiatory nature are a basically feminine property and territory. I have not commented on the music accompanying the poetry because I feel the singers do not give any special significance to it.

Conceptions of Fate in Stories Told by Greeks

ROBERT A. GEORGES

To students of man familiar with first-hand stories communicated by the Greeks,[1] the tendency for the narrators to dwell at length on the plights and fortunes of human beings is both striking and noteworthy. Individuals whose experiences are dramatized are usually characterized initially in terms of conventional extremes such as rich or poor, successful or unsuccessful, virtuous or immoral; but Greek storytellers are seldom satisfied with the general categorical oppositions suggested by such imprecise linguistic designations. Instead, they tend to provide explicit descriptions of the states and statuses of those whose actions and interactions constitute the subjects for their narrations. A prosperous man, for example, is rarely described merely as being rich; rather, his wealth is characterized in terms of the number of acres of land in his possession or the quantities of grain that his fields produce. Conversely, a poor man is not depicted simply as a person who is deprived of material possessions but, instead, as one who is unable to obtain the barest necessities of life ("even a little crust of bread") for his family or himself, despite his repeated attempts to find employment or to improve his lot by making great personal sacrifices. Furthermore, people's conditions are seldom taken for granted or left unaccounted for. Whether a man is wealthy or destitute and whether he succeeds or fails in his endeavors, the Greek storyteller usually feels obliged to provide an explanation or to offer a personal judgment. Occasionally, the achievement of success or the attainment of earthly riches is attributed to the fact that an individual is industrious and generous to others, on the one hand, or selfish and exploitive of human beings, on the other, while failure may be said to

---

[1] The word *Greek*, as used in this paper, is regarded as an identifying, linguistic label only. The problems involved in regarding any identifying, linguistic label as a designator of cultural identity are discussed in some detail later in this presentation.

result from one's laziness, lack of initiative, or indifference toward the counsel and advice of parents or elders. More often, however, the states and statuses of individuals are accounted for not in terms of human attitudes or actions, but rather because of external forces beyond one's control. In these instances, people are depicted as being what they are because they are destined or fated to be so.

It is with the conceptions of destiny or fate that are implicit in and communicated through Greek stories that I will deal here. Three questions provide the basis for this discussion:* (1) when, how, and by what (or whom) are the fates or destinies of people controlled, according to the stories?; (2) can the fates or destinies of people ever be altered or changed once they have been determined, according to the stories?; and (3) how can one account for the seeming preoccupation of a statistically significant number of Greek narrators with fatalistic concepts, and for the means by which these concepts are characterized and communicated during narrations?

In many stories told by Greeks, characterizing the circumstances under which the destinies of individuals are determined and the ways in which fated events unfold seems to provide the sole objective of the narration.[2] Such tales often begin with a description of a visitation by the Fates — who are always personified as female and most often depicted as being three in number[3] — to a house in which a newborn child resides. The purpose of the visit, of course, is to enable the Fates to decree the infant's destiny. Since their decision is usually made only after they have viewed the child, observed its surroundings, and given some consideration to conditions at the time of their visit, the nature of the actual decree differs considerably from story to story. The pronouncements of the Fates invariably come to pass. And so, it is the attempts made by individuals to comprehend or alter the inevitable course of events that generate the dramatic tension that make the narrator's stories cognitively recognizable and classifiable as stories.

One story (Abbott 1903:128–129) tells of a young man who receives permission to spend the night in the house of a poor man whose wife has

---

* The first two questions will be dealt with largely through references to published records of the linguistic aspects of the firsthand narrations of Greeks (that is, to narrative texts of folktales, as they are commonly called). The word folktale has different meanings to different scholars and is sometimes used inconsistently by a given investigator. Therefore, the word folktale has been avoided in this paper and the words story and tale have been used instead.

[2]   One should not infer from this remark that tellers of such tales necessarily have as their objectives to characterize the circumstances under which the destinies of individuals are determined and the ways in which fated events unfold. This might or might not be the case. There is no way of knowing why individuals are motivated to tell such stories or what effect the narrating has upon listeners without much more data than the usual collections provide.

[3]   The "Greek belief in fate," as scholars have inferred it from both ancient literature and modern folklore, is discussed in numerous works, including Hyde (1963:193–221), Lawson (1964:121–130), Sanders (1962) *passim*.

recently given birth to a baby girl. As the youth lies on the floor of the common sleeping room, the Fates enter. After a hasty surveillance and short consultation, one announces that the child will one day become the wife of the visiting youth. Fearful that such a prediction will come true and determined that it must not, the boy steals the child from her cradle, throws her into a thorny hedge a short distance from her home, and journeys hurriedly to a distant region.

The next morning the abandoned infant is found by its anxious parents, who discover that she is unhurt except for a deep scratch across her breast. As time passes, the girl matures into a beautiful woman. One day, the youth once again visits the neighborhood, where he takes a room at an inn opposite the cottage where the girl and her parents reside. The man spies the young woman at her window, falls in love with her, and receives permission to make her his wife. It is only after the marriage has been consummated that the youth sees the scar on the woman's breast, inquires about it, and realizes that his wife is the girl who was destined to marry him and whom he had sought to destroy. What was fated, therefore, had indeed come to pass, and the power of the fates to determine people's destinies is depicted as being absolute in this story, as well as in a substantial number of others recorded and reported in print by researchers (Dawkins 1953:335–339, 340–343; 1955:112–114).[4]

Although the Fates are most often characterized as making their pronouncements over newborn children, usually on the third day after birth,[5] they may also influence human beings at other times during their lives. In a story recorded from a Messinian narrator, a poor boy and his sister live alone and seldom have enough to eat (Megas 1970:54–57). One day, the boy receives three sardines in payment for an errand he has run for a man whom he encounters along the road. The boy takes the fish home to his sister, instructs her to cook them for dinner, and hurries off to look for work.

During his absence, three old women — the Fates in disguise — appear at the door; and the girl, embarrassed because she has nothing to offer her guests, remembers the sardines, which she prepared and sets before them. So pleased are the three women with the hospitality provided by

---

[4] A number of researchers have succumbed to the temptation to utilize stories that stress the irreversibility of the decrees of the Fates as evidence of a continual and unbroken "tradition" from ancient to modern times, often ignoring in the process other readily available evidence that conflicts with such a notion. For a perceptive discussion of the search on the part of many scholars for evidence in folkloristic data that could support the notion of "cultural continuity" in Greece from earliest recorded times to the present, see Megas (1970:xi–xlii).

[5] Many scholars infer from available written literature and ethnographic records that the notion that the Fates visit all newborn children on the third day after birth has the cognitive status of a belief adhered to universally by Greeks in ancient times and widely (if not universally) accepted by their descendants as well. That such an inference may be rooted in the presuppositions and assumptions of investigators is suggested later in this presentation.

the girl that they decide to change her fortune. One tells her that pearls will fall from her hair when she combs it; another says that when she washes her face, the basin will be filled with fish; and the third states that when she dries herself, roses will fall from the towel that she uses. All that the Fates promise comes to pass, and it is because of their generosity that the girl's existence becomes known to a king to whom she is eventually wed. The decision of the three old women to alter the fortune of an ill-fated girl suggests that the fates of human beings need not be irrevocable, provided the determiners of destiny are motivated, for some reason, to change them.[6]

In still other stories, the Fates are depicted not only as visitors to people's homes but also as beings whom people can seek out and petition. Thus, in a tale recorded from a storyteller in Cephallonia in 1959, a queen who is the mother of three daughters laments the fact that none of her children can procure a husband (Megas 1970:144–148). One day a beggarwoman, sensing the queen's uneasiness, suggests that one of the girls must have been ill fated from birth and that her destiny is affecting those of her two sisters. The youngest girl, aware that it must be she who is responsible for the plight of her sisters, decides to leave the palace dressed in nun's garb.

As she journeys, the girl is granted lodging in the homes of a succession of craftsworkers; and on each of these nights, the Fate who is responsible for the girl's ill fortune enters the homes of the girl's hosts and destroys their wares. It is only with gold coins and apologies that the girl finds it possible to placate her angry hosts; and it is not until she arrives at the palace of a perceptive, understanding queen that she learns of a possible solution to her problem.

Following the queen's advice, the girl travels to the mountaintop home of the Fates, where she encounters the one among them who is responsible for her destiny. In accordance with the wise queen's instructions, the girl offers a piece of bread to the one of the four women who was the determiner of her fate. Reluctantly, and only after considerable urging by the other Fates, the woman finally accepts the bread. In exchange for it, she gives the girl a ball of silk thread, which provides the means by which the young princess is eventually able to alter her destiny. By contrast with the story characterized earlier, in this instance a human being initiates the action that leads to a change in status. Once again, however, the alterability of fate is shown to be possible only if the initial determiner of a person's destiny wills that it be so.[7]

---

[6] For other story texts that suggest similar notions, see Lawson (1964:123–124) and Megas (1970:81–83).

[7] Lawson (1964:121–123) mentions a practice of individuals' taking offerings of cakes and honey to caves that are presumed to be haunts of the Fates. Those who do so, according to Lawson, often recite invocations that "give clear expression to the hope that the Fates may revise the decrees which they have already pronounced on the fortunes of the suppliant."

While the fortunes of men described in stories told by Greeks are often attributed to the whims and fancies of the Fates, another figure that is frequently characterized as being accountable for human destiny is Lady Luck. Unlike the Fates, she is neither depicted as a visitor to the homes of the newly born nor can she alter the fortunes of men at will. Instead, it is she whom individuals seek out when they are dissatisfied with their lots in life and desire explanations or remedies for their misfortunes. When requests for such information are made, Luck is described as being ready and able to respond. She may, as she does in some stories, show a man a series of fountains or streams, some of which gush water in abundance and some of which are merely a trickle. Those born at the time that water was plentiful, prosper, while those born when water was scarce must live in poverty forever.[8] It is not within Luck's power to change what exists, according to the tales, for no one can alter a condition that existed at the time of an individual's birth. But Luck is sometimes described as having the ability to do more than simply provide explanations, for she can also offer advice that can result in a change in a person's fortune, as a lengthy story recorded from a narrator on the island of Kos clearly illustrates (Dawkins 1950:358–368).

The tale concerns a rich man who, just before his death, divides his wealth between his two sons and requests that they never separate. The elder son, however, decides to part company with his younger brother after their father's death. Consequently, the fortune of the younger son grows, while that of the elder son rapidly dwindles to nothing.

Convinced that Luck is responsible for his plight, the elder son sets out to find her. On his journey, he encounters others who also are suffering from misfortune, and he promises to seek explanations for them from Luck, once he has located her and is able to confront her.

After a long search, the elder brother encounters Luck, who requests that he remain in her house for four days in order to learn why his fortune has been so bad. Each morning, the souls of newborn babies appear outside Luck's door, clamoring for gifts, and each day Luck gives generously of her wealth. After the fourth day, however, Luck's store of riches has been depleted, much to her sorrow and to the surprise of the elder brother.

With nothing left to eat and nothing with which to purchase provisions,

---

Lawson asserts ". . . that such a hope should be fulfilled is contrary to the general beliefs of the people. The Fates, they know, are inexorable so far as concerns the changing of any of their purposes once set. . . ." Assuming that Lawson's report (that such a practice is, or at one time was, rather common) is accurate, it would seem to be questionable to suggest, as he does, that people do not believe that such an act can produce results. Without some anticipation of an expected result, it is unlikely that a human being would behave in such a way.

[8] Texts of such tales are printed or referred to in Dawkins (1953:460–462; 1955:119).

Luck suggests that she and the elder brother seek work. The two earn a scanty wage, but between them they manage to make enough to afford a simple meal. When the newborn souls arrive at Luck's door the next morning, there is nothing for them but a few crusts and crumbs. Again Luck and the elder brother attempt to find work, but this time without success. The souls of the newborn that appear the following morning get nothing at all, for there is nothing to give them.

The lesson for the elder brother is clear: his newborn soul, too, must have arrived at Luck's door on a day when she had nothing to give. He asks Luck if there is any way that he can change his fortune. She informs him that he can do so only if he marries the adopted daughter of his younger brother and remembers never to boast of any good fortune that might come to him. Before departing, the elder brother remembers those whom he had encountered on his journey, and he asks how each might alter his fortune. He conveys the advice Luck has given him to those for whom he acted as representative, returns to the home of his younger brother, and requests and is granted the hand of his brother's adopted daughter.

Following the wedding, the elder son's fortune begins to change. As he prospers, however, he forgets Luck's warning; and when he begins to boast to others of the vastness of his lands and the productivity of his fields, he also begins to receive reports of the imminent destruction of his property. It is only then that he recalls Luck's interdiction, repents for his boastfulness and learns that his lands have been among those spared from destruction. Never again does he boast, and for the rest of his life he prospers. He never separates from his wife or brother and never forgets Luck's advice.

In this story, as in many others recorded and reported by researchers from Greek narrators (Dawkins 1950:363–368; 1953:458–465), Luck is depicted as being accountable for men's destinies but powerless to determine fate on an individual basis or to alter the fortunes of specific persons as a result of her experiences with them. At the same time, however, Luck is often characterized as being understanding and know-ledgeable enough to propose solutions for human misfortunes. It is the actions of human beings, not of Luck, that lead to a change in state or status, but it is to Luck that an individual must appeal in order to discover the means of change.[9]

Other tales recorded from Greek narrators suggest that neither the Fates nor Lady Luck serves as the arbiter of human destiny; rather, it is with God that such powers rest. It is He alone who wills what men shall be and do; it is He who controls and manipulates the fate of every human

[9]   For discussions of the conceptions of Luck, as inferred by investigators from observa-tions and records of the behavior of Greeks, see such works as Dawkins (1950:363–368) and Sanders (1962:129–130, 181–185, 216–264 *passim*).

being. In such stories, it is indirectly through prophecies and signs that persons often learn what God has willed for them; what God wills must necessarily be so. But like the Fates and Luck in other tales, God is often depicted as being accessible to those who seek Him out and sympathetic to those who petition Him for explanations or intervention. A story communicated by a narrator from Kos reveals God's ability to manipulate people's destinies in subtle and ingenious ways in order to change human fortunes, on the one hand, and to insure that what is fated will come to pass, on the other.

In this story, a king and a vizier who have no heirs both long for children (Dawkins 1950:281–287). The king vows, in the name of God, that if only a son could be born to the wife of one of them and a daughter to the wife of the other, the two children would be wed one day and rule the kingdom together. It comes to pass that the wives of the two men soon discover that they are with child, but while the girl born to the queen is fair and beautiful, the boy to whom the vizier's wife gives birth is black.

Determined to get out of his agreement with the vizier when the children reach marriageable age, the king sends the black boy to find God and to ask Him whether what is written can be unwritten. Duty-bound to carry out the king's command, but perplexed by the nature and significance of the task, the boy begins his journey. As he travels aimlessly from place to place in search of God, he encounters, in turn, a blind man, a man who is submerged in water up to his neck, and a lonely exiled outlaw, each of whom asks the boy to entreat God to reverse his fortunes, should the youth succeed in finding Him. The boy promises to do so. When he meets an old, white-haired man and learns that He is God, he tells Him of the king's request and is told by Him that what is written is not to be unwritten.

God also responds to the boy's inquiries about the fates of those whom he had encountered on his journey. As he travels home, the boy informs the three petitioners of God's assessments of their conditions. The exiled outlaw is instructed to distribute among the poor all that he has stolen from others if he wishes to be accepted once again into the society from which he has been exiled. To the drowning man, the boy gives God's answer that there is no solution for his misfortune, for he cannot stop blaspheming. As he approaches the blind man, the boy discovers a hole from which he obtains wet clay, with which to anoint the blind man's eyes, as God instructed him to do. The man's sight is immediately restored and, at the same time, the hand with which the boy applies the clay turns white. Realizing for the first time that his own destiny is involved in the king's question and in God's answer, the boy disrobes and rolls in the clay until his entire body has been transformed from black to white.

Now both wealthy because of a reward given to him by the grateful exiled outlaw and white because of the miraculous change in skin color, the boy returns to the city. There he opens a shop and manages to attract the attention of the king by underselling the other merchants in the kingdom. Motivated by the merchants' complaints, the king goes to the shop to reprimand the boy, but he forgets the purpose of his mission when he sees the youth. He is so struck by the boy's wealth and appearance that he offers him his daughter's hand in marriage. Plans for the wedding are quickly completed, for the unsuspecting king is fearful that the black youth will return. Before the marriage ceremony takes place, however, the boy reveals his true identity. What was written is thus carried out, as God had asserted it must be.

The complex nature of the relationships between the actions of people and the fates that have been decreed for them are implicit throughout this tale, and the multiple means by which God can control and manipulate human destinies are clearly exemplified. That God is capable of changing people's fortunes at will does not insure those who petition Him for alternative destinies that He will necessarily grant their requests, however, for His decisions on such matters are shown to be determined by a number of factors, including His judgment as to whether or not an individual is morally deserving of such consideration. Thus, God refuses to alter the fortune of the drowning man, for blasphemy is characterized as unforgivable in His eyes, and those who blaspheme are destined to suffer punishment for their transgressions. The fortune of the exiled outlaw is shown to be readily changeable however, since the man who acquired his wealth by stealing from others can compensate for this deed by distributing the stolen goods among the poor (and thus enjoy a better fate for having acted in accordance with God's will). The birth of a black child to the vizier's wife and the transformation of the boy into a white youth are clearly acts for which God alone is responsible, according to the story. The words of the narrator reveal that it is the youth's obedience to his king, together with his concern for the plights of other suffering mortals, that motivate God to change the boy's appearance and status so that what is written can be carried out without difficulty or additional delay.

Implicit in these five stories — as well as in many other tales communicated by Greek narrators — are references to the notion that the fates or destinies of people are determined, enforced, and manipulated by abstract beings or extrahuman forces over which people have no direct control. The stories provide no consistent characterization of the nature of these forces or beings, however, nor do the tales reveal that the fortunes of all people are determined and controlled by a common being or force, or that any one given force or being behaves or operates in predictable ways. Moreover, arbitrarily selected stories recorded from Greeks stressing fatalistic themes frequently present concepts that are not only inconsistent, but even contradictory. The fates of human beings, once determined, are often characterized as irrevocable, for example, but they are also frequently depicted as alterable or even completely revers- ible, usually as a result of face-to-face interactions between mortals and the controllers of their destinies. Similarly, the extrahuman forces charac- terized in stories may be described as either accessible or inaccessible to human beings, sympathetic or unsympathetic to people's earthly plights, able or unable to offer advice or to alter human fortunes. How, then, can one account for the seeming preoccupation of a statistically significant number of Greek narrators with fatalistic concepts? How can one account for the means by which these concepts are characterized and communi- cated in the course of narrating?

CULTURAL IDENTIFICATION AND THE STUDY OF NARRATIVES

The kinds of answers that can be proposed to these questions are depen- dent upon the nature of the conceptual schemes to which individual investigators are committed and hence which serve as the intellectual foundations for the study of the kinds of phenomena of which the data under consideration are conceived to be records. On the basis of an analysis of published studies of such phenomena, one can infer that three conceptual schemes have gained widespread acceptance among folklor- ists. It is in terms of one of the three that most folklore scholars answer the questions just discussed.[10]

To some investigators, it is obvious that stories such as those character- ized earlier in this presentation are part of the Greek cultural heritage. These tales, together with the concepts that are implicit in and communi- cated through them, many researchers would insist, are clearly survivals from earlier eras in Greek cultural history — eras when Greeks could apparently account for inexplicable human states and unanticipated events in no other way than to attribute them to the machinations of imaginary supernatural beings or extrahuman forces. Stories that per- sonified fate and depicted the destinies of people as determined and controlled by personified abstractions offered one means by which the early Greeks both expressed and revealed beliefs to which they adhered. Moreover, once such tales were created and communicated, the stories were passed on from person to person and handed down from generation to generation through the process of oral tradition, thus accounting for

---

[10] The author feels it will be instructive, therefore, to characterize the nature of these three conceptual schemes and to consider, in the course of doing so, what kinds of notions seem to underlie, and to be implicit in, each of the schemes and what kinds of answers researchers who are committed to each of the schemes would be likely to propose to the questions posed above.

their perpetuation through time and their dissemination through space. Contemporary narrators who communicate such stories, then, are conceived to do so because they are both heirs to and preservers of tales that have become traditional in Greek culture. Whether those who tell and listen to such stories subscribe to the conceptions of fate that appear to be implicit in them is of little concern to researchers who are committed to this conceptual scheme. Since the tales and the concepts that they communicate are considered historical survivals, the principal scholarly motivation for recording and studying the stories is to gain insights into a way of life that apparently *was*, not one that necessarily *is*. Insight is gained into a set of beliefs presumed to have been prevalent at some time in the past and assumed to have been supplanted — either completely or for all but a small minority of Greeks — by a more logical or sophisticated cultural belief system.[11]

Other researchers would reject the notion that these stories are tales from past periods in Greek cultural history which have become traditional as a result of their having been repeated and thus perpetuated somewhat mechanically by generations of traditional bearers. Instead, these investigators view the tales as unique creations of individual narrators who are able to generate and communicate such stories as a result of their familiarity with story components and storytelling conventions that are assumed to be both culturally determined and culturally unique. In the course of time, proponents of this viewpoint insist, the Greeks — like members of other cultures — have developed a distinctive corpus of narrative structures, motifs, themes, and stylistic commonplaces that have become traditional through repeated use. The personifications of fate and characterizations of interactions between persons and extrahuman forces are included in this cultural stock of narrative devices and narrating techniques. Greek storytellers transmit tales that focus upon and include references to conceptions of fate because fatalistic motifs and themes are part of their cultural inventory of traditional story components and storytelling conventions. The selection and utilization of such motifs and themes are essentially creative acts, for linguistic characterizations of fatalistic notions are conceived to be culturally determined artistic symbols that the storytellers manipulate and exploit for dramatic effect in the course of narrating. Whether those who tell and listen to such tales believe that their lives are predestined, or whether they conceptualize fate as it is depicted in the stories, is of secondary concern to those

---

[11]   Implicit in such notions is the assumption that there are belief systems common to individual cultures and that aspects of a cultural belief system may persist among some individuals after others have developed more sophisticated alternatives. Primitives are often conceived to be adherents to outmoded belief systems by those segments of the human species who are civilized — a notion that is an obvious holdover from the days when the unilinear view of cultural evolution led to the ability to label persons differently on different "rungs of an evolutionary ladder."

researchers who use this framework; of primary interest are the artistic appropriateness and aesthetic functions of unique configurations of narrative components of which fatalistic motifs and themes are integral parts.[12]

To still other investigators, the apparent preoccupation with fatalistic notions is regarded as a meaningful manifestation of the Greek *Weltanschauung*. Fatalism, these researchers say, is an important part of the world view of the culture. Stories that depict human existence as fated or dramatize interactions between persons and the controllers of their destinies are both indexes and expressive manifestations of beliefs to which Greeks have apparently been conditioned culturally, and to which they presumably subscribe. The fact that fate is personified, or the nature of human destiny is characterized in multiple ways by Greek narrators, might be accounted for on the basis of past cultural contacts or normal culture change, on the one hand, or in terms of the abstract nature of the underlying concepts upon which such narrative motifs and themes are based, on the other. The apparent recurrence of fatalistic motifs and themes in stories communicated at first hand by and among Greeks, these investigators would insist, must reflect actual beliefs that are part of the overall cultural belief system, for narrators can characterize and dramatize only those concepts that are culturally learned and culturally significant. Storytelling, from the viewpoint of those who employ this conceptual scheme, is thus a means of both expressing and contributing to the perpetuation of the cultural world view. Stories are considered significant source data inasmuch as a people's *Weltanschauung* can presumably be inferred and comprehended. Since human behavior is conceived to be rooted in and determined by one's world view of the culture, then any aspect of human behavior is assumed to be reflective of the world view of which individual members of a given culture are considered collectively to be both heirs and perpetuators.[13]

Each of these three conceptual schemes is one to which substantial numbers of folklorists are committed and in terms of which questions such as those raised by the data under consideration in this paper have been, and are presently being, answered. The popularity of these three schemes is readily understandable, for the utilization of each can be justified by past scholarly precedent, and the seemingly inherent correctness of each can be demonstrated on the basis of available data. The investigator who sees these tales and their underlying conceptions as historical survivals is operating on the basis of an intellectual tradition

---

[12] Claude Lévi-Strauss (1966) characterizes such a conception by comparing it with the way in which a *bricoleur* manipulates and configures his *bricolage*.
[13] Studies which exemplify this theory are now common among anthropologists (at least in the United States) and seem to have their intellectual roots in the writings of Benjamin Lee Whorf and Robert Redfield. For one essay that champions such a conceptualization, see Hallowell (1964:49–82).

established by the Grimms and other early nineteenth-century scholars; he or she need only search through historical records about the Greeks to find analogous stories (the tale of Meleanger as reported by early mythographers, for instance) or linguistic characterizations of seemingly archaic or outmoded beliefs (in discussions of Greek pagan religions, for example) to support and exemplify his contention that stories recorded from Greeks which either focus upon, or include references to, the extrahuman control of human destinies, are "survivals" from earlier eras in Greek cultural history.

Similarly, the researcher who is convinced that fatalistic themes and motifs are artistic symbols that are traditional in Greek culture and that Greek storytellers utilize, manipulate, and exploit them for aesthetic purposes can trace his intellectual roots to Ruth Benedict's characterization (1935) of the narrating process as she inferred it from her study of Zuni storytellers, or to Albert B. Lord's conceptualization (1960) of the process of "creating within a tradition," which grew out of his and Milman Parry's studies of south Slavic epic singers. He can search through older literary documents (such as the plays of Sophocles) and past records of the expressive behavior of anonymous informants (including early anthologies of Greek folktales, such as the nineteenth-century collections of von Hahn (1864) or Schmidt (1877)) and discover that the same or comparable narrative elements have a long, recurrent use in Greek written and oral literatures. For the scholar who regards Greek tales about human fate as indexes of the Greek world view, the writings of such anthropologists as Radcliffe-Brown (1922) and Malinowski (1926) provide the intellectual precedent. The conceptions of fate can be correlated with actual beliefs about the extrahuman control of human destinies, as can be seen in a consideration of other Greek culture traits (the reported practice of setting out plates of sweets in the room of a newborn child on the third night after its birth for the Fates, for instance),[14] or from various combinations of selected ethnographic data reported by fieldworkers (the tendency of Greeks to preface discussions of future activities with the phrase, "If God wills," coupled with the reported practice among Greeks of accounting for human failure by asserting that "it was not fated to be," for example).[15]

The fact that each of these conceptual schemes can be used as a framework to answer the questions posed earlier does not mean that the investigator can arbitrarily select and employ any one of the three schemes or that the utilization of any of the schemes will necessarily enable one to propose intellectually defensible answers to the questions.

[14]   This practice is mentioned in works by Abbott (1903:125), Lawson (1964:125), and Megas (1970:liii).
[15]   Sanders (1962) and Lawson (1964) are among those researchers who, in passing, mention this practice.

A commitment to any one of the schemes, in fact, would seem to require or to imply rejection of the other two, for each involves a somewhat different set of assumptions about the nature and significance of the fatalistic concepts.

More important, a commitment to any of these conceptual schemes would seem to imply acceptance of the notion that Greeks tell stories that embody fatalistic concepts solely because they are identifiable as Greeks. Clearly, despite the obvious differences among them, the three conceptual schemes under consideration are all rooted in the common presupposition that human beings who tell stories that are based on abstract concepts do so because such concepts and stories are part of a historio-cultural tradition of which those individuals are conceived to be both "heirs" and "perpetuators." In order to determine whether it is intellectually defensible to propose answers to both the kinds of questions and the specific questions we have posed about cultural conceptual schemes, it is first necessary to determine whether it is intellectually defensible to conceptualize human narrative behavior as an expressive manifestation of a unique historio-cultural tradition.

To conceive of historio-cultural tradition as the basis for and the sole or principal means of explaining or accounting for human behavior is to presuppose that while every human being is identifiable, first and foremost, as a member of a common biological species (*Homo sapiens*), it is, in fact, his identity as a "cultural being" that determines most of his behavior (including any "phenomena" that are conceived to result from, or to be outputs or outcomes of, his behavior). Moreover, to conceive of one's cultural identity as the principal means of understanding any behavior or behavioral facet is to conceive of the process of identifying individuals "culturally" as a necessary prerequisite to the study of man. In order to be able to identify individuals culturally, however, one must first presuppose or assume that multiple human subpopulations exist, that every human being belongs to one of these "existing" subpopulations, that each of these subpopulations has evolved a distinctive culture, and that the behavior of every human being is in some way determined by (and a determinant of) the history and nature of the culture of the subpopulation in which he is classified. Furthermore, since the process of identifying human beings culturally is a process by means of which individuals are grouped together, on the one hand, and by means of which individuals who are "grouped together" on the basis of common cultural identities are differentiated collectively from each other, on the other hand, then the implications of this process would seem to be (1) that individuals who are identifiable culturally must necessarily behave in some strikingly similar ways for similar reasons and (2) that the behavior of individual human beings therefore, is comprehensible and explainable in collective and relativistic terms (that is, in terms of presumed or inferred behavioral *similarities* of their sub-populations). Because the concept of cultural identity is a concept fundamental to researchers committed to the "historio-culturally-oriented" conceptual schemes, and because one can defensibly explain or account for human behavior in terms of such schemes only if the concept of "cultural identity" can be shown to be intellectually defensible, it would seem essential to determine the nature of the process by which investigators ascribe cultural identities to human beings whose behavior they are trying to comprehend.

On the basis of any randomly-selected corpus of published works written by scholars who are committed to historio-culturally-oriented conceptual schemes, one can infer that diverse criteria serve as the basis for identifying human beings culturally. In some instances, the cultural identity that is ascribed to an individual seems to be based upon (or to be inferred) from the name(s) of the place(s) in which an individual lives (if alive), lived (when alive), or was born; an individual may also be identified culturally on the basis of the name(s) of the place(s) in which his progenitors live, lived, or were born.[16] In other cases, the way in which a person is identified culturally appears to be dependent upon (or to be inferred from) the name of the language of which he is (if living) or was (when living) a speaker or which the person learned first (and of which, therefore, he or she is or was what is conceived to be a "native speaker"); or an individual's "cultural identity" may be determined on the basis of the name of the language of which his or her progenitors are (if living) or were (when living) speakers or native speakers. An individual may also be identified culturally on the basis of the name of the race to which he or she is conceived to belong as a result of perceptible physical characteristics which he or she seemed "to possess"; or the cultural identity may be considered to be rooted in a self-proclaimed or inferred commitment to a set of concepts, assumptions, and actions evolved by a particular individual or individuals, named for or by an individual or individuals, and communicated and learned systematically as a set of beliefs and customs by and from its proponent(s).[17] In addition, an individual is sometimes identified "culturally" on the basis of the name(s) given to specific acts or activities in which he or she is conceived to engage on a regular or repetitive basis for purposes of accomplishing some seemingly readily

[16]   Such an assortment of placename-based identifying labels as "American," "Ozarker," "New Englander," "Texan," "New Yorker," "Illinois-Egyptian," and "urbanite" are frequently conceived to be designators of cultural or subcultural identity, as well as simply identifying linguistic labels. Other linguistic labels, which are based on conceptions of a combination of place of ancestry and place of residence — for example, "Irish-American," "Italian-American" — are also often considered to be designators of cultural identity.

[17]   Examples would include any identifying linguistic labels used to denote religious commitment or affiliation — for example, *Mormon, Jew, Catholic* — which are often also conceived to be designators of cultural identity.

obvious and/or specifiable objective(s). Finally, the cultural identity that is ascribed to an individual is often rooted in conceptual schemes that are themselves based upon human judgments concerning the relative degree to which human beings seem to be able to comprehend, explain, control, and exploit natural phenomena. Hence, investigators can and do identify human beings culturally on the basis of a wide range and variety of criteria; and this process of identifying human beings culturally seems to begin with, and to manifest itself overtly in, the assignment of identifying linguistic labels by means of which human beings can be grouped together and collectively differentiated, on the one hand, and on the basis of which the nature of the cultures of these human groups can be inferred and characterized following the discernment or discovery of apparent consistencies, both through time and at any given point in time, in the behavior of those who are identifiable culturally in the same way.

The fact that human beings can and do identify themselves and each other in diverse ways — and often in similar ways, but on the basis of differing and even inconsistently employed criteria or sets of criteria — is not surprising,[18] of course, for the process of comparing and contrasting phenomena of all kinds, assigning identifying linguistic labels to them, grouping them together, and differentiating among them (either as individual phenomena or as groups or classes of phenomena) are obviously fundamental, perceptual, and cognitive processes. The fact that human beings can and do identify themselves and each other culturally on the basis of differing and varying criteria and sets of criteria, however, suggests that there is no single set of criteria on the basis of which researchers can ascribe cultural identities, thus indicating that the process of identifying human beings culturally is in fact an arbitrary and subjective process, for any identifying linguistic label can be conceived to be a designator of cultural identity, and any individuals who can be grouped together on the basis of a common, identifying linguistic label can be conceived to share a common culture. This being the case, the concept "cultural identity" would seem to be of questionable usefulness to scholars. Hence the intellectual defensibility of employing any conceptual scheme which requires the *a priori* acceptance of the validity of the concept of "cultural identity" would seem to be questionable as well.

The relevance of these points to the specific questions that were raised earlier in this presentation on the basis of the examination of a particular corpus of data is easily demonstrable. To conceive of conceptions of fate that appear to be implicit in and communicated through stories told by

---

[18]   Individuals may be identified both linguistically and culturally as *Greeks* or *Germans* or *Poles*, for example, on the basis of the name of the place in which they reside, the language that they speak, the place in which either they or their progenitors were born, some perceptible physical characteristic(s), or some combination of these criteria (and perhaps on the basis of other criteria as well).

Greeks — and/or stories that are told by Greeks that appear to be based on or to have as one of their objectives to characterize and communicate fatalistic concepts — as either (1) survivals from earlier eras in Greek cultural history, (2) artistic symbols which are traditional in Greek culture, or (3) indexes of the cultural world view of Greeks is to presuppose that individuals who are identifiable as Greeks (regardless of what criterion or set of criteria serves as the basis for so identifying them linguistically) behave as they do when they function as narrators solely because they are identifiable as Greeks (for "Greek" is considered not only an identifying linguistic label, but a designator of cultural identity as well). This theory is untenable or at least highly questionable on the basis of our systematic analysis. If, for instance, the concept "cultural identity" cannot be defended intellectually (and analysis suggests that it cannot), then the concept of "historio-cultural tradition" would also seem to be intellectually indefensible; and there would appear to be no defensible intellectual basis or justification for explaining or accounting for any human phenomenon or aspect of human behavior in terms of the cultural identity of its human source or in terms of an historio-cultural tradition of which its human source is assumed to be both heir and perpetuator by virtue of the fact that individuals who are or were the human sources are identifiable by means of a particular linguistic label that is considered to be indicative of their cultural identities. Furthermore, to answer both the *kinds* of questions and the *specific* questions posed in this presentation in terms of any historio-culturally-oriented conceptual scheme is to reject — at least implicitly — a number of well-proven facts about the behavior of human beings: (1) that individuals who are identifiable by means of a common linguistic label exhibit a wide range and variety of behaviors, sometimes responding similarly and sometimes quite differently to specific sets of stimuli, and sometimes responding quite similarly to particular stimuli, but for different reasons; (2) that there are discernible similarities, as well as differences, in the behaviors of individual human beings who are identifiable by means of different linguistic labels, and those who are identifiable by means of different linguistic labels may respond to specific sets of stimuli in similar ways for similar, as well as for different, reasons (and vice versa); (3) that individuals who are identifiable by means of particular linguistic labels sometimes learn to behave as they do from human beings who *are* identifiable linguistically in the same way as they are, and they sometimes learn to behave as they do from individuals who are *not* identifiable linguistically in the same way as they; (4) that individual human beings sometimes behave as they do because the behaviors of others with whom they interact directly serve as models for their own behavior, and sometimes they behave as they do because they generate conceptual models of behavior of which their perceptible behavior is a manifestation; and (5) that learning is continual, and that because human beings can and do learn and their behavior is dynamic and ever-changing, not static and conventional.

The conceptions of fate that appear to be communicated through stories told by individuals who are identifiable (on the basis of any criterion or set of criteria) as Greeks, then, *cannot* be comprehended, explained, or accounted for, it would seem, in terms of any conceptual scheme on the basis of a concept of historio-cultural tradition (and the concept of cultural identity as well). Hence, such stories cannot be regarded defensibly as survivals from earlier eras in Greek cultural history, or as indexes of the cultural world view of Greeks. It would appear to be plausible to hypothesize, however, that some individuals who are identifiable as Greeks and who tell these stories might conceive of them as historical survivals, artistic symbols, or indexes of a *personal* world view.[19] Furthermore, one could speculate that a statistically significant number of Greek narrators appear to have been preoccupied with fatalistic concepts because of the nature of the existing data base, for fieldworkers who elicited stories from Greeks may either have asked their informants to tell them such stories or have selected for publication only stories that embodied unusual or folk notions because such tales conformed best to the researchers' conceptions of the nature of the folk mind, the nature of folktales, the nature of the thinking and behavior of Greeks, or the nature of Greek historio-cultural traditions.[20]

The limitations of historio-cultural-oriented conceptual schemes, as demonstrated in this presentation, reveal the need for an entirely different kind of framework — one that has its intellectual roots in behaviorally based and behaviorally oriented research. The generation of such a scheme, it seems clear, is the logical next step in folkloristics. Recent studies of narrating, such as those by Leach (1954), Crowley (1966), Toelken (1969), and Georges (1969), as well as recent research on learning, communicating, and interacting by Skinner (1957), Cherry (1957), Hall (1959), and Goodenough (1965), reveal that historio-cultural-oriented conceptual schemes can no longer serve the needs of the scholar in the modern world.

[19]   Evidence that serves as the basis for generating such hypotheses comes from observations of narrators and analysis of the circumstances of the storytelling. Some Greeks preface the telling of such tales with remarks that indicate their awareness that such conceptions are going to be characterized during the narrating, and they make explicit just how these conceptions are regarded. Narrators and listeners frequently discuss fatalistic concepts following the communication of stories that embody them, revealing through their remarks their conceptions of, and attitudes toward, such concepts. The range of behaviors, attitudes, and viewpoints is considerable.

[20]   That folklorists (and others) often conduct fieldwork with the explicit objective of obtaining certain kinds of data or information — and that they often fail to make records of, or to report in print, data or information that do not corroborate or exemplify their assumptions and assertions — is, of course, well known. Authors of fieldwork guides, such as Goldstein (1964) try to make their readers aware of the temptation to "seek particular data, to the exclusion of all else," and they emphasize the folly in doing so.

REFERENCES

ABBOTT, G. F.
  1903   *Macedonian folklore*. Cambridge: University Press.
BENEDICT, RUTH
  1935   Zuni mythology. *Anthropology* 21:xi–xliii.
CHERRY, COLIN
  1957   *On human communication*. Cambridge, Mass.: Technology Press of the Massachusetts Institute of Technology.
CROWLEY, DANIEL J.
  1966   *I could talk old-story good: creativity in Bahamian folklore*. University of California Folklore Studies 17.
DAWKINS, R. M.
  1950   *Forty-five stories from the Dodekanese*. Cambridge: University Press.
  1953   *Modern Greek folktales*. Oxford: Clarendon Press.
  1955   *More Greek folktales*. Oxford: Clarendon Press.
GEORGES, ROBERT A.
  1969   Toward an understanding of storytelling events. *Journal of American Folklore* 82:313–328.
GOLDSTEIN, KENNETH S.
  1964   *A guide for field workers in folklore*. Philadelphia: American Folklore Society Publication.
GOODENOUGH, WARD H.
  1965   "Rethinking 'status' and 'role': toward a general model of the cultural organization of social relationships," in *The relevance of models for social anthropology*. Edited by Max Gluckman and Fred Eggan, 1–24. London: Tavistock Publications.
HALL, EDWARD T.
  1959   *The silent language*. Greenwich, Conn.: Fawcett.
HALLOWELL, A. IRVING
  1964   "Ojibwa ontology, behavior, and world view," in *Primitive views of the world*. Edited by Stanley Diamand, 49–82. New York: Columbia University Press.
HYDE, WALTER W.
  1963   *Greek religion and its survivals*. New York: Cooper Square Publishers.
LAWSON, JOHN CUTHBERG
  1964   *Modern Greek folklore and ancient Greek religion*. New Hyde Park, N.Y.: University Books.
LEACH, EDMUND
  1954   *Political systems of highland Burma*. London: G. Bell and Sons.
LEVI-STRAUSS, CLAUDE
  1966   *The savage mind*. Chicago: University of Chicago Press.
LORD, ALBERT B.
  1960   *The singer of tales*. Cambridge: Harvard University Press.
MALINOWSKI, BRONISLAW
  1926   *Myth in primitive psychology*. London: Kegan Paul, Trench, Trubner.
MEGAS, GEORGIOS A., *editor*
  1970   *Folktales of Greece*. Chicago: University of Chicago Press.
RADCLIFFE-BROWN, A. R.
  1922   *The Andaman Islanders*. Cambridge: University Press.

SANDERS, IRWIN T.
1962   *Rainbow in the rock: the people of rural Greece.* Cambridge: Harvard University Press.
SCHMIDT, BERNARD
1877   *Griechische Märchen, Sagen, und Volkslieder.* Leipzig: B. G. Teubner.
SKINNER, B. F.
1957   *Verbal behavior.* New York: Appleton-Century-Crofts.
TOELKEN, J. BARRE
1969   The "pretty language" of yellowman: genre, mode, and texture in Navaho coyote narratives. *Genre* 2:211–235.
VON HAHN, JOHANN GEORG
1864   *Griechische und albanische Märchen.* Leipzig: Georg Müller.

The Pragmatism of Herat Folk Theater

HAFIZULLAH BAGHBAN

Folk theater is a living component of circumcision and wedding festivities in peasant villages and nomad camps in western Afghanistan. Traditionally preserved oral texts, traditional troupes of itinerant actors, and temporary stages characterize this form. Although no written evidence about native Afghan theater is at hand, studies of similar troupes in neighboring countries of the Middle East throw light on its past. In Iran Mejid Rezvani (1962:109) indicates that dramatic art had been known before the conquest of Alexander the Great, fourth century B.C. The Persian courts supported buffoons (*meskhere*) who are the precursors of the present clowns (*loutis*). Furthermore, Jiri Cejpek shows that the Sassanid kings had jesters and jugglers who were pushed into anonymity after the victory of Islam and who reappeared with the decline of the caliphs' power. According to Cejpek (1968:687), folk farce is a "late development of very old traditions common to all peoples of the Near East."

In the Arab countries, the existence of the Afghan and Iranian types of *meskhere* has also been confirmed. However, scholarship dealing with the Arab comedians is scarce in Western languages, especially in English and French. Only in passing does Jacob M. Landau (1965:4) mention an Ahmad Fahim al-Far (Ahmad Fahim the mouse), who headed a troupe of twelve male performers in Cairo before World War I and who was beloved by the Cairene population. He says, "In our days these performances are limited to the poorer not Europeanized population and their number gradually diminishes."

In Turkey, Nicholas Martinovich attributes the origin of *Karagoz* shadow plays to China and the origin of *Orta Oiunu* live comedies to Byzantium.[1] Nevertheless, there is evidence that the Turks, the Persians,

---

[1] *Karagoz* is the name of the main character of the shadow plays in Turkish and Arab countries. *Orta Oiunu* means "live comedies."

and the Arabs had their own puppetry and farces, and in the course of prolonged contact their theater traditions were reciprocated. The Seldjuk Turks (1077–1302) and the Ottoman Turks (1290–1908) were instrumental in bringing about this reciprocity of traditions (And 1963:9–10; Martinovich 1968:13). Faced with centuries of exchange and the absence of concrete documents, it is not easy to look for the exact location where these performances originated, but a comparison of the available materials shows that the form, content, and context of *Orta Oiunu* resemble those of the Afghan farce (*sayl*), the Iranian farce (*tamasha* or *namayish*), and the Arab farce.

From this background sketch it can be seen that secular folk theater is an old but poorly sponsored part of Middle Eastern culture. Whenever conditions were favorable, such theater flourished at courts and served as both a status symbol and an entertainment in the rituals of the nobility. In times of social, political, and religious oppression, folk theater sought sanctuary in the countryside among the peasants.

Under the influence of its rapidly changing cultural milieu, Herat folk theater reflects a pragmatic outlook toward life's events. The existence of such an outlook can be seen in the position folk theater holds in the conflict between the new and the old as Afghanistan moves into the twentieth century. The criterion for change is not "What is new is good" or "What is old is good" but, rather "What works is good."

Based on this world view, Herat folk theater serves several functions: (1) It reflects a negative attitude toward dysfunctional traditions and exerts sanctioned pressure on individuals and groups to abandon them; (2) It updates the functional traditions and helps accelerate the process of enculturation; (3) It examines the new traditions, absorbs those that serve the well-being of the society, and lures its audience into accepting them. In fulfilling these functions it depends on native aesthetics and symbolism as its media of transmission. Numerous examples illustrate the role of this art form in Afghan modernization.

Before the arrival of Islam as a religion, polygamy served social, political, and economic functions that bolstered the security of the individual and the solidarity of the group. To reconcile polygamy's pre-Islamic importance as a tradition with post-Islamic political demands, the Koran allowed the practice of polygamy (although it put restrictions upon it). According to the Koran, a Muslim may take more than one wife, if he can be just to them all (Koran-i Mejid 1967:452).

But now, with conditions changed due to the influence of industrialization and its accompaniments of mass communication, mass transportation, and mass education, polygamy has lost its primary economic and political function. Nevertheless, a rich, but uneducated, minority continues to practice polygamy, contrary to the philosophy of Islam. In the first half of the twentieth century, the exile of the late King Amanullah is partly attributed to the reaction of this Afghan minority to his policy against polygamy (Gregorian 1969:261).

Taking advantage of its impersonal nature and reflecting the attitude of the majority, folk theater holds a firm position against polygamy. *Mard-i Duzana*, a play from the repertoire of professional male actors, and *Ambaghbazi*, a play from the repertoire of nonprofessional, dilettante female actresses, deal exclusively with this topic. Both plays condense unpleasant realities about polygamy and in a comic manner present them to their audiences. Results of interviews show that these plays reinforce the existing negative concept of polygamy. Thus, the slow decline of polygamy can be accelerated by drama (Baer 1964:38).

The validity of the attitudes reflected in this drama and the pressure it exerts on the audience are also confirmed by other folklore genres. Proverbs, quatrains, songs, and tales collected from the Herat area show the same attitude toward polygamy. In addition, personal anecdotes related by men and women who have led polygamous lives support the drama's position. Therefore, it may be concluded that the attitude expressed by drama is true to life.

In the villages of Herat, the meaning and function of hospitality change according to whether it is bestowed on a kinsman, a friend, or a person whom the host does not know. Among kinsmen and friends, hospitality is a symbol of solidarity and is to be reciprocated. When the hospitality required by custom is not issued, not accepted, or not returned it leads to poor and sometimes hostile relations. On the other hand, adversity may end and friendship may begin with hospitality.

Unless a village functions as a stop for buses or caravans, it does not offer commercial food and lodging. Thus, strangers passing through a village stay in the mosque or are taken home by a villager. On the one hand, no immediate reciprocity is expected for this kind of hospitality. On the other hand, it is much easier for the traveler to depend on people's hospitality than on his own pocketbook.

If someone is not obligated to provide hospitality and he has no hope for immediate reciprocation, why should he be hospitable? Just as hospitality among kinsmen and friends has important functions, hospitality to unknown persons serves important social purposes. Hotels, motels, and restaurants do not exist in Afghan villages; and, in addition, persons cannot afford to pay for food and lodging. Therefore, hospitality functions as a substitute for services not available and as an aid to the limited resources of travelers. Furthermore, it is believed that God will repay the host in this world and in the world to come.

Thus hospitality has served the well-being of Afghans for generations and still has useful functions. Society has sensed the vital role of hospitality and, accordingly, has formed a positive attitude toward it. Folk drama reflects this attitude and through native aesthetics and symbolism helps to perpetuate hospitality as a tradition. Since the livelihood of the folk actors rests on the generosity of the villagers, they use the stage to condemn miserliness and praise generosity. For instance, in the repertoire of the Ghayzan and Jendakhan actors, there are twelve plays. The formulaic preludes of each play are applied to serve this function, and one of the plays, *Shakoorbazi*, is a satire both on taking advantage of hospitality and on poor hospitality. Shakoor and his children represent demanding guests, and the friend to whose house they have gone is a poor host. In this play, and spread throughout the whole repertoire of the Herat actors, hospitality is considered functional and therefore good.

Afghan peasants and nomads revere *'ilm* [scholarship] and *'uloma* [scholars] in their religious context. Village quarters (*mahals*), and nomad camps have mosques that, in addition to serving as places of worship, function as boarding schools to the *talibs* [students of religion]. Food and lodging are given to them by the members of the mosques free of charge, and even money for their books and clothes comes from the community. Although no formal degree is offered by the mosque, and neither is there a set limit to the mosque education, after a few years of study a *talib* becomes a *mullah* and helps perpetuate the line of village priesthood.

Under the indoctrination of the *mullahs*, their own conservatism, and their zealous religiosity, the peasantry and the nomads reflect a negative attitude toward secular education. Unless persons with Western education provide good models to show that learning is a step toward a better economic life and not a menace to local religious beliefs, they are not eager to send their children to school. Although the method of setting examples has proven effective, it is a slow and time-consuming process. Folk theater, as a secular art form looked upon with disapproval by the mosque, plays a dynamic role in spreading the message of education. By applying native aesthetics and symbolism, it mollifies the audience's antieducation attitudes.

As I pointed out in "An Overview of Herat Folk Literature," one play in the repertoire of the Dihtappa actors contrasts the behavior of two brothers (Baghban 1968:51–62, 81–88). One brother has gone to school, has married an educated woman, is respectful to his parents, relatives, and neighbors, and helps them in any way he can. The other brother has not gone to school, gambles for a living, keeps pigeons in the house, has no respect for his elders, and fights with his father for money to gamble. This plot then, reinforced with examples from real life, encourages the audience to cooperate with educational authorities. Twenty years ago, in a village where I later did research (1967), the people bribed the headmaster of their newly established school not to enroll their children. Today the same parents petition the headmaster to select their children for school. Although folk theater is not wholly responsible for this change in attitude, it was instrumental to some degree in bringing about the change.

Arnold Van Gennep's *The rites of passage* (1960) looks at circumcisions, weddings, and funerals as symbolic definitions of the individual's movement from one situation to another, from childhood to manhood, celibacy to marriage, life to death. In the tradition of Van Gennep, James L. Peacock (1968:6) entitles his study of Javanese *ludruk* drama, *Rites of modernization*. Peacock uses *ludruk* plays to see the way they help the Javanese "symbolically define their movements . . . from traditional to modern situations."

Herat folk drama is part of the wedding and circumcision festivities and reflects a pragmatic view of life. On the basis of context and outlook, this drama has definitive functions as Van Gennep and Peacock see them. In both types of transition — for example, childhood to manhood or traditional to modern — Herat theater has a balancing role that merits attention.

REFERENCES

AND, METIN
1963 *A history of theatre and popular entertainment in Turkey*. Ankara.
BAER, GABRIEL
1964 *Population and society in the Arab east*. New York: Frederick A. Praeger.
BAGHBAN, HAFIZULLAH
1968 An overview of Herat folk literature. *Afghanistan* 21.
CEJPEK, JIRI
1968 "Iranian folk-literature" in *History of Iranian literature*. Edited by Jan Rypka. Dordrecht, Holland.
GREGORIAN, VARTAN
1969 *The emergence of modern Afghanistan*. Stanford: Stanford University Press.
KORAN-I MEJID
1967 *Koran-i mejid*. Kabul: Government Printing House.
LANDAU, JACOB M.
1965 *Studies in Arab theater and cinema*. Philadelphia: University of Pennsylvania Press.
MARTINOVITCH, NICHOLAS
1968 *The Turkish theatre*, New York: B. Blom.
PEACOCK, JAMES L.
1968 *Rites of modernization*. Chicago: University of Chicago Press.
REZVANI, MEJID
1962 *Le théâtre et le dance en Iran* [Iranian theater and dance]. Paris.
VAN GENNEP, ARNOLD
1960 *The rites of passage*. Translated by M. B. Vizedom and G. L. Caffee. Chicago: University of Chicago Press.

The Modern Local Historian in Africa

DAN BEN-AMOS

The introduction of literacy into traditional African societies has added writing and printing as dimensions to the communication of historical knowledge. A by-product of this development is the availability of new information sources for historical-folkloristic research, namely, the works of local historians. In most cases these appear in thin pamphlets, published by local printers, and circulate among a local educated public; occasionally, their reading audience extends beyond the boundaries of the original indigenous community and reaches university historians, who treat these publications as if they were primary sources for historical reconstruction. They are thought to reflect the common view of the past that prevails in a given culture. They represent the folk history of the people or, if the term is used in a fashion that parallels the concept "ethnoscience" (Sturtevant 1968:462–464), their *ethnohistory*. Hence, the attribute of primacy relates to ideas about history and does not indicate the nature of the testimony.

Theoretically, such a view is justified since writers of these pamphlets obtained knowledge about the history of their society through the culturally established communication channels. They heard stories about the past in the context of storytelling occasions; they were able to infer the historicity of events and personalities from linguistic allusions and metaphors; they pondered the meanings of place names; and they attempted to reconstruct past episodes from the annual commemorative ceremonies in which they participated. When all these modes of learning proved insufficient and gaps in their knowledge of tradition remained,

This research project was conducted under the auspices of Midwestern Universities Consortium for International Activities during 1966 and received further support for its continuation from the National Institute of Mental Health.

they deliberately questioned specialists, who retained and recited historical narrations and genealogical lists.

The publication of such pamphlets has shifted the locus of authority
over historical traditions, transferring it from the elders in the community
to the printed word. The permanence of written accounts, coupled with
the prestige accorded modern forms of scholarship, has enhanced the
position of historical writings in the community. No doubt, such a shift is
not absolute and does not equally affect the entire community. Whenever
the printed account contradicts the knowledge gained from traditional
authorities, it is easier to blame the authors for inaccuracies and errors
than to find fault with oral history. After all, individual writers are more
vulnerable to criticism than is an anonymous tradition. Yet, in spite of the
potential criticism, the factors of stability and modernity weight the
balance in favor of print over oral transmission.

The works of the Bini local historian Chief Jacob Egharevba can
illustrate the position historical writings have attained in both traditional
and academic communities. The Bini people of Nigeria are proud of their
history. The Benin kingdom was one of the main western African
empires, and its traditional history abounds with tales of intra- and
intertribal warfare, conquests, and victories. The Benin empire reached
its political peak in the fifteenth and sixteenth centuries, during which
time the sovereignty of the *Oba*, the "king," was respected as far west as
Dahomey (Bradbury 1957, 1959, 1967). Egharevba took it upon himself
to unfold before the modern world the greatness that was Benin, recording the oral traditions and examining them critically.

Egharevba conducted his study of Benin history and culture in the
1920's and 1930's. During that period, the elders of the community were
people who had acquired their historical knowledge within the Bini
traditional framework, and their information was only slightly affected by
the impact of British influence following the punitive expedition of 1897,
which left Benin in ruins (Akenzua 1960; Boisnagen 1897; Bacon 1897;
Roth 1903:ii–xxi; Ryder 1969:277–294). Today this generation is virtually extinct and such knowledge is rarely available. Egharevba collected
from them narratives, testimonies, and historical explanations, matched
these with various fragments of information, smoothed away any conflicting views, and molded the materials into a composite version of the
traditional history of Benin. On the basis of his own knowledge and this
extensive research, Egharevba amassed a great deal of information that is
traditionally unavailable to any single person in Benin. Customarily, this
historical knowledge is distributed among various keepers of tradition:
priests, whose task it is to memorize the royal genealogy; ceremonial
singers, who incorporate historical information into their ritualistic
songs; and narrators, who entertain their audience with stories of Benin's
heroic past. No individual in Benin is completely familiar with all the

historical, religious, and social information that Egharevba accumulated through laborious research and synthesized in his works. The publications that resulted from his studies are numerous (P. Ben-Amos 1968a:6, 13–15).

Prominent among them is *A short history of Benin* (1960), a book that had a great impact on Benin society and has come to be known as the authoritative account of Benin past. Although some factions in Benin, because of their own social and personal interests, belittle the book and consider it full of inaccuracies, most people in the city regard it as the accurate rendition of Benin history. Bradbury (1959:267–268) cited an extreme case in which the then *Esekhurhe* [priest of the royal ancestors], whose duties include memorization of dynastic lists, resorted to Egharevba's work rather than relying on the information he had obtained orally from his father, who himself was Egharevba's informant. Thus, Egharevba's work has a confirmative function in the transmission of oral tradition in Benin.

For modern scholars this book represents the traditional and uncritical version of Benin history. As such, it often serves as a convenient starting point for the examination of the validity and accuracy of oral tradition in the light of documentary evidence. Researchers naturally find many cases in which traditional narrative history is incongruent with external testimonies, archival materials, or simple empirical logical reasoning, as Bradbury (1959:267–268), Ryder (1965:25), Wolf (1963:193–218), and Kalous (1970) illustrated on several occasions.

The scholarly acceptance of the written rendition of oral tradition as a true representation of the "historical beliefs" (Hudson 1966:53) and "the common view of the past" (Sturtevant 1968:463) ignores a basic aspect of culture change. Features do not simply replace each other. The introduction of a new element into a society involves a subsequent readjustment of the entire system. This is true of economic and social aspects of life and is equally applicable to the communication of historical knowledge. Thus, the writing of tradition also entails the incorporation of new attitudes toward the concepts of truth, historical fact, and causality. Local authors acquire their new ideas through formal Western education and extensive reading. Literacy enables them not only to write oral tradition but also to expose themselves to the influences of modern historical writings. Therefore, the transition from oral to written communication also involves a shift in the models for descriptive accuracy and explanatory adequacy in historical narration and a redefinition of the boundaries between possibility and probability in history. Local historian-writers do not accept the validity of an account merely on the basis of its verification by traditional authorities. They subject the narratives to critical logical examination in which belief alone is no longer a standard for inclusion or exclusion of facts in the description of the past. The narratives must meet the criteria of analysis and critical judgment.

Furthermore, by the very act of writing, the local historians address themselves to an audience that has nontraditional models for historical narration and explanation. In their own writings, the historians make a conscious attempt to approximate these new examples and to meet the expectations of logic and order with which they associate their potential readers. Consequently, the local historians could not possibly commit to print traditional ideas about history.

Through a partial misunderstanding on my part, a situation evolved in which it became possible for me to examine the modifications that Egharevba had introduced into the traditional Bini conception of historical accounts. While doing research in Benin on the communicative forms and techniques of oral tradition, I paid several visits to Egharevba. We conversed in English and I explained to him that my research required me to be present on occasions in which Bini people tell stories and sing songs. Egharevba understood correctly that my interest was directed not only at the formal aspects of entertainment but also at the content of the tales themselves. After several such visits, Egharevba seemed slightly offended at not having been asked to relate the history of Benin, since he rightly considered himself the most knowledgeable person on that subject. I tried to explain that my position as a folklorist, not a historian, necessitated that the present study be focused not on what really happened in the past, but only in the way people view it, regardless of truth. In fact, I expressed a readiness to listen to tales that the Bini considered fictional, tales they knew had no historical validity. In the course of that conversation, the discussion turned to various Bini terms for traditional narratives, and Egharevba offered to relate nonhistorical stories — that is, tales that he knew but that he had excluded from his book on the basis of relevancy. He considered them fictional narratives. Thus, by contrast, these tales provide some clues to Egharevba's conception of history, the range of realistic possibilities and probable causalities, which, in turn, one would be able to compare with Bini views of history.

THE TALES[1]

1. *Tortoise and the Devil*[2]

The tortoise was a student under the devil for years, and there he learned all the wisdom and the cunning [that] he usually applied all about. When he left the devil, when he finished his time and left the devil, some years it was after [that] he thought of going to Ife and made an elaborate preparation. Before going, anyway, he consulted from a seer, or the diviner of the *Ih'ominigbon*,[3] whether his journey to Ife would be prosperous. The diviner advised it, to send, to send . . . a she-goat, a fat she-goat, mashed yam, [a] knife and other necessary things to its master, the devil, before going.

The tortoise began grumbling that he ha[d] served the devil for many years, and there is no reason again that it should send him any things. When the diviner emphasized that [the tortoise] should do so, well, he promised to do so when he returned from Ife. He went, or [*sic*] when going, he knocked one of his feet to something, which — eh — foretold a good omen, that the journey would be very prosperous.

Accordingly the *Olofin*[4] of Ife, or the king of Ife, the old king of Ife, gave him as presents very many valuable things. On his return journey home, well, he ordered his followers to carry him so that his legs will not touch the ground, and that he might not get a wound at that time. When he was nearly home he asked them to put him down, that . . . he would not encounter any difficulty any more. Immediately he saw — an old man . . . He asked the tortoise . . . please to shave his head for him. Because they were cursing him, the head was cursing him, the ears. The tortoise began to shave. When he shaved [one] part and turned to the other part, before shaving, the other one [would] . . . grow again. He began to shave it. Before shaving the other part, the hair of the other part [would] grow again. He was surprised. He continued shaving, continued shaving. Consequently, all his followers deserted. All his followers ran away when they saw that the old man was no other man but the devil, the master of the tortoise. The tortoise took excuse from the master devil that he go to discharge urine in the bush, and from there he ran away, and hid himself under . . . dirt things, see, under a dung hill, just like a dung hill. Well, [when] the devil shouted for [the tortoise], he could not hear the voice. So he took all the property home, you see, he made use of all the property that the tortoise brought from Ife. Well, ever since the tortoise [is] to be found in a thick

---

[1] Chief Jacob Egharevba told me these tales in 1966 at his home. He spoke in English with occasional insertion of Bini terms. Although at times he searched for the correct word, corrected himself, or repeated himself, his English was fluent. The text is a transcription of his narration. I omitted only phrases that were repeated because of hesitation or external interruption. The most common self-correction in Egharevba's English narration was the substitution of *it* for *he* in reference to animals. The Bini language has a single pronoun for third person. (I would like to thank Rebecca Agheyisi for her assistance in the transcription of these texts.)

[2] Egharevba refers to *Esu* (a harmful messenger of the gods in Bini beliefs) (Melzian 1937:42).

[3] A diviner who used the seeds of the tree *Ogwega, detarium senegalense*, for making his predictions. The seed is broken into two parts, then tied together, four halves on each string. The diviner casts four such strings in front of him and informs the person of his future. Melzian states that the term *ominigbon* is synonymous with *ogwega*. The term is not in common usage and is preferred by the masters of this divining art (Melzian 1937:137, 145).

[4] Usually the title of the ruler of Ife is *Oni*. The *Olofin* is the title of rulers of other Yoruba cities like Oyo.

bush or under a dung hill. You see, ever since. So this lesson taught us that whatever may be the necessary advice given us, we must always, we must always act with it. You see, we must always, we must always act with it, accordingly, so that we might not meet any trouble or mishap.

2.   The Vulture and the Wise Man[5]

At one time in those days, the people wanted to kill a vulture and eat it. And before doing so they had a very good meeting over it, and they sent a wise man called Umewaen[6] to the next world to interview fathergod.[7] The wise man went to the next world, to the heaven, and when he got to the fathergod, he told him all the messages that were sent through him. Fathergod said: "All right." He sent him to a place to lodge and asked him to give him a few days to consider the matter. The wise man agreed. He did so.

On the very day that the wise man left for heaven, the vulture also went to a diviner and consulted what [it] should do, what it should do to escape the danger. The diviner advised it, to get a parcel of cola nuts, tie it and to put one at the top of it and put it in the square between the world and heaven[8] and then come back, and the third day to go to the heaven. The vulture did so accordingly. When he got to the fathergod, on the third day, he [was] received . . . very well.

On the third day, [the fathergod] sent the wise man to go and buy cola nuts for him from the world market. When he was coming, he saw the parcel of cola nuts which the vulture, he did not know, which the vulture sacrificed. He took it to the fathergod. The fathergod said: "Well, ah! you returned so quickly? He said: "Yes." He said: "Yes, sir." From these cola nuts, the fathergod offered or gave to the vulture, and the vulture told him that this is the cola nut that he sacrificed in the square between the world and the heaven.

Fathergod said: "No!" It was bought by [the man].

"No," he said. The vulture emphasized that it was the sacrifice cola nut that he sacrificed in the square between the heaven and the earth. Thereupon fathergod said to the wise man to testify to the fact, and he agreed that it was the very cola that he brought to fathergod. Fathergod, enraged, enraged he growled [at] him and said: "You are a liar! You told him[9] yesterday that it was, that you bought it from the market, on the world market. Now you confess that it was a sacrifice cola nut. Why did you bring a sacrifice cola nut to him?" So fathergod [was] vexed and chained the wise man in heaven forever and charged the vulture to go free, that whoever killed it and [ate] should die with it. The vulture returned to the world rejoicing all about. And ever since, well, it is rigidly forbidden to kill and eat vulture. Anybody that attempt[s] it will die immediately. So it is a parable among people then, that the wise man is in heaven and the vulture is in the world. If the wise man had returned from the heaven, well, the vulture would be eaten. So, they

5   For another version of this tale, see Egharevba (1950:52–53).
6   The word *ewaen* means "wisdom"; *um* is perhaps a variant of *omo*, or "child." Thus the name means "child of wisdom."
7   Egharevba's translation of the Binet epithet *erha n'osa*.
8   *Ada* means "junction" or "crossroads." According to the Bini world view, a hole in the ground leads to heaven. The road ends where heaven and earth meet. This is the crossroads of heaven and earth (*ad' agbon ad' erimwin*). According to Egharevba, any hidden place can be regarded as such a square.
9   Fathergod refers to himself.

say, well, a child said, or says, well, a vulture can be eaten. And they asked him: "Those who eat or have eaten the vulture, where are they?" He said: "They have gone to the heaven."

So this story, this imaginary story, teaches us that we must always tell the truth. That nothing but the truth will save us, as the truth saved the vulture. We must always avoid telling lies, but the truth, the perfect truth, the whole truth.

3. The Vulture and His Mother

In these days, the elders sent the vulture to Ife as an ambassador. Before going, he consulted the oracle, *ominigbon* oracle, whether or not his journey to Ife would be Prosperous. [He] was asked or was advised by the *ominigbon* diviner to get rotten things all rotten things, all kind[s] of rotten things and sacrifice to the square which leads to Ife. He said: "All right." [He] will do so. When he got home, he began to make preparation and promised to make the sacrifice when he returned from Ife. He went. [He] was warmly received in Ile-Ife. On [the] returning journey — or in those days, the journey to Ile-Ife always took a period of three years. About a week of his departure from home, his mother began to [become] sick, seriously sick. She was treated, but the treatment failed. At any rate, she died. The corpse was accordingly tied in a bamboo mat, *aghen*, we call it, *agen* bamboo mat, tied it and put in the square leading to Ile-Ife.

Of course, when the vulture was returning home, [he] was so hungry, [he] nearly died of starvation. When he got to [the] square, [he] did not know the corpse of his mother and [ate] a quantity, if not the whole, and then came home. When he got home, he went directly to the palace and delivered the message and gave account of his embassy to Ile-Ife. When he got home, well, he learned that his mother was dead. He asked the cocks. They told him: "The corpse has been sent to the square leading to Ile-Ife. And they learned that you have eaten a quantity of your mother's corpse or meat."

This is what the vulture could not, you see, stand. Immediately he ran to the heaven and gave the account to god and entreated him endlessly to be merciful on him, or on it, to make it possible that all people of the earth . . . [eat] their mothers as [he] has done, as [himself] has done. Oh, fathergod looked at him, he moved in mercy with him and said: "All right." So fathergod made something like breast in the breast of all women so that every child must suck the breast before growing up, if at all, a week or the very day. Ever since, everybody on earth ha[s] to eat his or her mother, as the vulture has done previously. This is the end of the story. It teaches us also that it is quite necessary for us to be doing according to the advice of the divination, *ominigbon* divination, or the advice of the seer or diviner to us, because if the vulture had taken the advice, the mother could not have [been] so seriously sick and died before his return from Ife.

4. The Olokun[10]

The Olokun in Benin was a man, or is a man and not goddess, it is a god not goddess, as always [has] been with the English people.

In those days, Olokun was a great god of the sea and the fountain of riches. He

[10] For another version of this tale, see Egharevba (1950:50–52).

was so rich that at one time he was boasting, bragging that his father the almighty god did not excel him in anything, or surpass him in anything, or surpass him in anything. The boasting was so awful that a special meeting was convened over it, and the people asked them to fix a day for a special exhibition to know who is the greatest, the most powerful, the most sensible and the most universal or popular. Accordingly seventh day was fixed for them to appear for the people to see. On the seventh day fixed, almighty god sent a chameleon and clad it with changeable colors to tell to the Olokun, to tell him to dress very well, because Olokun is his son; he did not like him to be exposed to a great shame before the people. When the chameleon reached the Olokun's palace, he asked the servant of Olokun, he sent a message through the servant of Olokun, that he was sent by almighty god, his father, to [give] him a special message. Olokun came out, with his hands supporters, his wives, his forward followers, in a gay dress to see the chameleon. When the chameleon was delivering the message, the Olokun, in a surprise, saw the same dress that he put on the chameleon. "Ah!" he [said] surprised, retired again, put on another gorgeous dress, appeared again. He saw the same with the chameleon, he retired again, put on more fine dress, more beautiful wives, fine-figures followers and hands supporters, with a brass chair *agba*, coral beads dress, coral crown, eeh, all over. Alas, he saw the same thing on the chameleon. "Ah!" he exclaimed, that if a chameleon, the messenger of his father, the almighty god, could put on the same dress as himself, how then the almighty himself will look like. He therefore sent a messenger, the chameleon, to the palace to tell his father, the almighty god, that he is the king of kings, lord of lords, and a man who is the choice of the people. On his part, that he Olokun submitted, submitted himself, to god today and forever, the Olokun. At this message, there was a shout, a shout of applause among the tongues of people, crowd of people surrounded almighty god. Then the meeting was dispersed.

This is the end of the story.

Before he started the narrative that follows, Egharevba commented that, unlike the other tales, the following is a true story, albeit surprising.

5.   *Ezalugha*

One man, named Ezalugha, he was a medical student under the *Ake*.[11] *Ake* was one of the famous heroes of Ewuare's reign. He was a student of, medical student under *Ake*. When *Ake* died, well, he began his master's work. According to custom, the people of that village Ilobi in Isi sent the young men to bring yams to the Oba at Benin City. And Ezalugha was numbered with the people. When they got to the palace, the yams were delivered and carried into the palace. Then they arranged a match, a wrestling match. They began to wrestle. Ezalugha came out. He knocked several people down, to the shame of the people of the city. And he could not be knocked down. At that time, there was a beautiful girl, called Ebhu, a daughter of the then Iyase.[12] Ebhu witnessed the wrestling match and concluded to marry Ezalugha. Without delay she followed him home, to his village home

[11]   According to Egharevba (1960:16), he was a hero who was deified by the Bini people. He is worshiped as the god of archery mainly in the Isi villages (Melzian 1937:6, 100).

[12]   One of the more important Bini chiefs, the head of the *Eghaebho n'Ore*, the town chiefs. He had the sole right to argue or censure the Oba in public (Bradbury 1957:25–28).

Ilobi. About a year of her arrival there, her father died at Benin City. So, well, they had to prepare for the burial and for the internment and burial ceremony. Well, Ezalugha did not come along with Ebhu his wife, but when she is ready to go, Ezalugha has a medical axe and an axehead; he placed it in the shrine of his goddess of medicine Osun. On the very day that Ebhu was leaving for Benin City, he took the axehead from the axe and put it on the ground for Ebhu to cross over. Ebhu did not know, she crossed it and came to Benin City. Well, the internment took place and so they began the burial ceremony. According to custom, after the completion of the burial ceremony, they have to give thanks to the people who came to help them and who helped them during the occasion. Well, they were thanking the then *Uwangue*[13] chief. Then *Unwague*, a great chief in Benin, pressed Ebhu to extend his love to her. Ebhu refused. He pressed her on and on. Well, Ebhu took leave of him to go home first and return. Well, Ebhu returned after the thanking. He forced Ebhu again. Well, when they were in the action, you understand me? When they were in the action, you see, when they were in sexual knowledge, you see, sexual intercourse, well, a cock feather from the axe in the shrine of his goddess of medicine Osun began to ring like this, to wave like this, wave like this, which tells Ezalugha that somebody was doing something to his wife. Immediately, he put the axehead to the axe and they were together. The man could not come down of the woman, and the woman got no place to escape. They were there until they called for the help of the householder, who tried and failed. The neighbors were invited, they tried and failed. They covered them with a cloth down. They invited all the medical people, all was a failure. Well, the incident was reported to the Oba, and immediately, the Oba invited his medicine people, the *ewaise*; they tried their skill but failed. Well, the diviner consulted the *ominigbon* divination, and it was advised to sen[d] for Ezalugha from Ilobi in Isi. The Oba sent two messengers. That very night they went there and returned the man.

When he was coming, he put the axe and the axehead in one of his bags. When he got to the palace, the Oba asked him whether he knew something about it.

He said: "Yes, he did it." Well, the Oba asked him to release the people immediately. He took the axe away from the axehead and they, the man and woman, the man now completely came out from the woman['s] breast. But they were fated and died. You understand. Ezalugha was arrested as a murderer. He was sent to the *ewedo*, prison. And then the decision was taken to send him to *osa*, to sacrifice him to the god of *osa*. Accordingly on the third day, *Unwague* arranged all the quarter people, himself dressed in a gorgeous attire he [stood] on a stool and ordered Ezalugha to be bound. He was bound and was ordered to be executed. Ezalugha shouted, shouted, to [evoke] the spirit of his goddess *Osun*, *nigiogio*, [and it was] this occasion that arranged to save him from this danger to the surprise of the people. He repeated again, again,

Okhuo (i) fu ohunmwun!
Emuen!
Igho igho gboo!
Igho igho gboo!
Igho igho gboo!
Emuen!
Okpolemu n kpol' emun!
Egbe ere o ro!

[13] The head of the Iwebo palace society. He supervised trade with European merchants (Bradbury 1957:39; Melzian 1937:207).

Okhuo ru ehunmwun!
Okhuo ru uhunmwun!
Okhuo ru uhunmwun!
Okhuo ru uhunmwun![14]

Surprisingly, when he was about to be executed, well, they find him sat on a chair, and the *Unwague* who was on the chair in a gorgeous attire was executed. The people trembled and trembled, trembled and trembled, feared and shouted, cried to the palace to tell the Oba. When the Oba heard the news he discharged the man to go home freely. Well, when he was about to go, all the physicians, the native doctors arranged themselves, had a meeting that the man had actually put them to shame . . . in the practice of their knowledge of their medicine.

When he was going, he transformed himself into a pregnant woman. The people lined, hid themselves in the bush all the way, about a mile long. He wonderfully passed away to his village Ilobi in Isi, safely, unhurt. Everybody was surprised at him. So he was ever since called and appel[l]ated Ezalugha *n'ebo ma hie*; that is Ezalugha whom medicine never failed. This is the end of the story. He was feared and respected throughout the history.

6.   The Calabash of Wisdom[15]

The tortoise was universally known to be the wisest of all beings. And accordingly, they used to boast and brag about their wisdom. On one occasion a tortoise, however, thought within himself, or within itself, that he will put all the wisdom of human beings or all the wisdom of the whole world in a calabash and cork it, so that nobody should get the sense again. Accordingly, one day he did so, corked it and [was] going to bury it in somewhere. When he was going, he met a very big fallen tree across the road. He put the calabash of wisdom on his breast, so that it may not be seized away in its back. Well, as it was attempting to cross the tree, it could not because of the calabash on its breast. He was patrolling here and there about the fallen tree, he could not cross it through on account of the calabash on its breast in the front. But when a man was coming, who did not know the intention of the tortoise, [he] said to it: "What are you doing, tortoise?" "Well, I wish," he said, "to cross this tree," but the calabash in [his] front, could not allow [him] to pass through. So the man laughed and laughed at him saying: "You the wisest of beast? You are so fool, to put the calabash of the wisdom on your breast. Can't you put it in the back and then pass all the same?" He did so, he passed away safely. So he was greatly ashamed that it had been boasted that tortoise was the wisest of all beings and now he was put to shame. So it broke the calabash of the wisdom into pieces and scattered everywhere. So, ever since it is not quite necessary for any man, he may be all wise, he may be master of knowledge, to be boasting that he was wiser than all the people in the world because a small boy, it was a small boy who put or killed the giant Arhuanran in Udo,[16] or David the

---

14   Probably *osun* incantations. I was unable to translate this text.
15   For another version of this tale, see Egharevba (1950:46–47).
16   In the tradition of Benin City, Arhuanran is known as a stupid giant, the son of Oba Ozolua and the brother of Oba Esigie (ca. fifteenth through sixteenth centuries). Arhuanran was born first, in the morning; Esigie was born on the evening of the same day. However, since the news about the birth of his sons reached the Oba in reverse order, Esigie was considered the legitimate heir to the throne. This situation, according to tradition, was the cause for the great animosity between the two brothers. In the many stories and proverbs about Arhuanran, he figures as a powerful giant whose strength exceeds his sense.

small child killed the Goliath. So, it is not necessary for anybody to boast of his wisdom or his power, or his knowledge, or anything that he would do. This is the end of the story.

CONTINUITY AND CHANGE IN ORAL HISTORY

These tales, together with Egharevba's *A short history of Benin*, make possible a close examination of his own adherence to and deviation from tradition. These modifications will be discussed in terms of (1) the performance of historical narratives, (2) the generic categorization of narratives, and (3) the actors in historical narratives.

The Performance of Narratives

The telling of history in Benin on traditional occasions involves both singing and speaking. The songs are interspersed between the narrative episodes and are often an integral part of the plot. They provide a respite in the flow of actions and enabled the audience to partake in the chorus and in this way actively to participate in the telling of tales. In that regard Bini storytelling hardly differs from the performance of narratives in other African societies. As a result of the performance situation of traditional narratives, songs become an integral part of the conception of history in Benin in direct contrast to Western narration of history, which focuses upon political, military, and economic affairs and excludes songs of kings, soldiers, and peasants as irrelevant. Curiously, while Egharevba does not replicate in his writing the stylistic features of oral narration — he omits repetition and opening and closing formulas — he retains some songs of narratives as an indispensable part of the historical account. Egharevba (1960:45) quotes a soldiers' song, a festive song of a royal wedding (1960:19–20), and a lyrical song of a suffering king (1960:39), and thus transforms entertaining elements of storytelling occasions into historical facts.

The Generic Categories of Narratives

The singing that is interspersed throughout the prose narration probably serves to relieve audience fatigue, actively to incorporate the listeners into the storytelling, and to recapitulate the actions told in prose (Innes 1965). In Benin, however, the mode of performance serves also as a taxonomic mark that differentiates between two genres of stories: *okha*, a tale with songs, and *umaṝanmwen*, a tale without songs. A third genre, *ere*, functions as a parable, a short narrative that the speakers may apply directly to particular conversational situations. Thus the very characteristics of the act of narrative performance serve for generic distinction in Benin. The criterion of truth, historical validity, which Bascom (1965) uses to construct an analytical system of prose narrative classification is hardly applicable for taxonomic purposes to Benin tradition. Depending on one's informants in Benin, truth is either a universal attribute of tales or it stands in free variation with fiction. Thus, both *okha* and *umařanmwen* could be either historical or fictional. *Ere*, however, is regarded as a true narrative, since its rhetorical effectiveness depends upon its validity. Consequently, the validity of narrative cannot serve as a distinctive feature of the different genres, and it is irrelevant to the native taxonomic system. This fact does not imply, by any means, the insignificance of truth in the evaluation of prose narratives. Rather, the faithful, detailed, and realistic description; the orthodox, though not necessarily verbatim, adherence to the traditional version of tales; and the constant verification of the historicity of events by reference to landmarks and distinct places are a few of the literary devices that are used to enforce the notion that the events in the story really happened. This is comparable to the aesthetics of visual arts (P. Ben-Amos 1968b). The *Märchen*-like anonymity of the characters and places is almost absent from any narrative genre in Benin.

It is with respect to this very basic cognition of tradition that Egharevba differs from his fellow Bini. Egharevba not only employs different terms to designate the narrative genres of oral tradition but also conceives of new features by which to distinguish them. It is hardly surprising to find out that, as a person with an acute sense of history, he could not be content with a communicative taxonomy of narratives and replaced the traditional system with an idiosyncratic classification in which truth is the distinctive criterion. According to Egharevba, the two polar narrative genres in Benin are *itan* and *umařanmwen*, which relate to each other as truth to fiction, history to nonhistory. *Okha* retains a middle position in this system as a story that could be but is not necessarily true. Most of the tales Egharevba told me were, accordingly, *umařanmwen*. Actually, his comprehension of this term is based on a literal-etymological interpretation of the word. *Umařanmwen* is a compound that consists of two components, *uma*, "council," and *ařanmwen*, "animal" and, literally, it means "council of animals" (Melzian 1937:12, 206). Hence, Egharevba's consideration of this genre as fictional is based on inference from the etymological-literal meaning of this compound.

The second major change in Egharevba's taxonomic system of oral tradition is the introduction of *itan* as a name for a prose narrative genre, a term that is borrowed directly from the Yoruba language, in which it means "myths, traditions or 'histories'" (Bascom 1943:129).[17] In Benin, the same word, *itan*, refers to another verbal genre altogether: that of the proverb.[18] This semantic change is an idiosyncratic innovation introduced by Egharevba himself. In fact, he rendered the title of his book, *A short history of Benin*, as *Ekhere vbe ebe itan Edo* (Melzian 1937:45). However, most Bini, I found, use the word *itan* in the sense of proverb, not of history. For example, it appears in that way in the title of the book, *Iyeva yan ariasen vbe itan edo na zedu ere ye Ẹbo* (Aigbe 1960). Thus Egharevba provided an existing Bini word with a new semantic meaning in order to be able to formulate his own taxonomic system of Bini oral tradition.

These cultural and personal conceptions of narrative categories that underlie Egharevba's attitude toward the content of the tales explain the principles of thematic inclusion and exclusion of incidents from the respective genres. By adopting new distinctive qualities for genres, Egharevba, as a local historian, sets his own rules of selectivity of topics for potential inclusion in the history of Benin. Still, his view of history only partially reflects the conception of historical facts, actions, and actors in Benin tradition.

The Actors in Historical Narratives

The fictional narratives that Egharevba told me share one main feature: their protagonists are animals. This characteristic seems to have been the principal criterion used by Egharevba for their exclusion from the category of historical narratives. After all, it is unreasonable to believe that the tortoise, the vulture, and the chameleon actually talked, interacted with people, and behaved as humans. Yet the nature of the *dramatis personae* constitutes a feature that distinguishes fiction from truth only in Egharevba's conception of oral tradition, and it does not correspond with the common Bini view of history.

[17] Although the term *itan* has an identical orthographic representation in both languages, it is pronounced *itan* and *itọn* in Bini and Yoruba, respectively. Thus Egharevba's usage of the term is phonetically similar to the Bini *itan* and semantically identical with the Yoruba *itọn*. (I would like to thank Rebecca Agheyisi for clarifying this point for me.) The fact that Egharevba makes use of Yoruba terms and narrative category can be explained by his own biography and does not reflect the influence of Yoruba culture on Benin. He was born in the western region and continued to have family relations there.

[18] Melzian (1937:102) provides four meanings for *itan*: "(1) proverb, (2) story (mainly exemplifying a proverb), (3) meaning or moral contained in a proverb: *itan re* 'its meaning,' (4) history (with an application for life) with a moral." Actually, this range of meanings in *A concise dictionary of the Bini language of southern Nigeria* would apparently constitute an additional difficulty since it contains both meanings of *itan*: the commonly accepted one of a proverb and Egharevba's own translation as history. If we take into consideration that Egharevba himself was one of Melzian's informants, however, it is possible to assume that some of these interpretations are his own contributions.

Unlike Egharevba and perhaps other educated people, traditional Bini tend to regard animal tales as truly historical narratives. The events related in these stories took place during the *Ogiso* period of the previous ruling dynasty. The animals were courtiers in the *Ogiso* palace in *Idumwan-Idu* (Bradbury 1957:19). They often breached accepted rules of conduct and, in many cases, their actions were plainly destructive. The attributes of the tortoise, for example, are not only cleverness and wisdom but also wickedness and malice, and his present-day nonhuman appearance is considered a punishment for this antisocial behavior.

This punitive transformation is compatible with Bini beliefs concerning death and afterlife. Accordingly, after the dead reaches the land of the spirits (*erinmwin*), he may be reincarnated in new living form, either human or animal. Thus present-day animals are degraded incarnations of previous human beings. Fourteen such reincarnations (*aria 'bhehe*) are possible. In other Benin narratives, as well as in the texts provided by Egharevba, there are often lapses from human to nonhuman references to these characters. The narrators may refer to them in terms of human attributes, the most distinguished of which is speech, while at the same time they continue to develop the plot on the basis of the animal features of the heroes. These narrative methods are not based on literary personification of the animals, rather, they draw on the assumption that the tortoise (*egwi*), the chameleon (*erokhin*), and the spider (*akpakpa*) were at one time human beings (Evans-Pritchard 1967:23–27). The narratives are mostly anchored in the *Ogiso* period and not in the present time. Yet the remoteness of that era does not invalidate its historicity in the Bini cognition. From the Bini viewpoint, the *Ogiso* period is neither mythical nor semimythical, as Bradbury (1957:19) has designated it. In spite of the political change and the dynastic shift, there is a sense of continuity in Benin history, and any imposition of dividing lines between one era and another will be in disregard of the Binis' own conception of their history.

In a similar manner, Egharevba modified traditions about human figures when they appear to contradict experience. For example, according to Benin indigenous history, Oba Ehengbuda lived 200 years as a prince, 200 years as the *Edaiken* [crown prince] of Uselu, and 200 years as an Oba. Egharevba modifies this tradition and states carefully that "it is said that Ehgenbuda lived thirty years as Oko [prince], thirty years as Edaiken of Uselu, and thirty years on the throne." Thus, while he preserved the formulistic structure of this biographical scheme, he cast it into terms that were more compatible with the experience of reality.

More significant than the occasional modifications of biographical details is the general focus of Egharevba's work, which by the very selectivity implied in the idea of "short history" actually alters the range of historical events and personality in Benin tradition. Egharevba's work centers around the royal family and, to a certain extent, is not so much the history of Benin at large as the chronology of its rulers. By choosing this framework for this account of the past, Egharevba followed not only traditional court genealogists but also European historical scholarship, which for years focused on the central political body and neglected to pay the political struggles at the sidelines the attention they deserve. However, without disregarding the central position of the Oba, the Bini people also tell about the battles between rural chiefs and their continual struggles for power. At the time of this research, the most popular tale among storytellers was the story of Agboghidi, a rural chief whom Egharevba (1960:34) mentioned only in passing. The information in this story, which the Bini regard as historically valid, may have as much relevance to the ethnohistory of Benin as the tales Egharevba included.

A FINAL WORD

No doubt, local historians such as Egharevba have contributed greatly to the process of recording African history. Even if their work is not considered at all times historically valid, at least it is assumed to provide a faithful account of the traditional views of the past. This brief discussion, illustrated by Egharevba's work and conversations, clearly demonstrates that it is necessary to exercise caution in this respect as well. The effects of literacy run deeper, in that case, than was previously suspected. The learning of writing and the commitment of local traditions to book form involve the incorporation of the values and conceptions of literate society, which are not necessarily related to the mechanics of writing. Moreover, the written local histories are geared to a new reading audience outside the traditional groups to which the oral narratives are intended. This change in audience involves further modifications in traditional views of history in terms of the selections of details and the explanation of historical causality. Consequently, the final result differs from the historical beliefs of the group. In order to examine the relationships of such writings to the common views of the past, it is necessary to seek corroborative evidence from a source that is both old and new, namely, the local traditions that are still available. Only a comparison with these sources enables one to evaluate the relationships between folk history and ethnohistory.

REFERENCES

AIGBE, EMMAN I.
    1960   *Iyeva yan ariasen vbe itan edo na zedu ere ye Ẹbo* [1040 Edo proverbs with their English translation]. Lagos.

AKENZUA, E.
1960   Benin — 1897: a Beni's view. *Nigeria Magazine* 65.
BACON, COMMANDER R. H.
1897   *Benin: the city of blood*. London: Edward Arnold.
BASCOM, WILLIAM
1943   The relationship of Yoruba folklore to divining. *Journal of American Folklore* 56:129.
1965   The forms of folklore: prose narratives. *Journal of American Folklore* 77:3–20.
BEN-AMOS, DAN
1967   Storytelling in Benin. *African Arts/Arts Afrique* 1(1):55.
BEN-AMOS, PAULA
1968a *Bibliography of Benin art*. New York: The Museum of Primitive Art.
1968b "The aesthetics of Bini tourist art." Paper presented at the African Studies Association Annual meeting, Los Angeles.
BOISNAGON, CAPTAIN A.
1897   *The Benin massacre*. London: Methuen.
BRADBURY, R. E.
1957   *The Benin kingdom and the Edo-speaking peoples of south-west Nigeria: Ethnographic survey of Africa, West Africa*. London: International African Institute.
1959   Chronological problems in the study of Benin history. *Journal of the Historical Society of Nigeria* 1.
1967   "The Benin kingdom," in *West African kingdoms in the nineteenth century*. Edited by Daryll Forde and P. M. Kaberry. London: Oxford University Press.
EGHAREVBA, JACOB U.
1950   *Some stories of ancient Benin*. Benin City, Nigeria: published by the author.
1960   *A short history of Benin* (third edition). Ibadan: Ibadan University Press. (First edition published in Lagos by C. M. S. Bookshop, 1934.)
EVANS-PRITCHARD, E. E.
1967   *The Zande trickster*. Oxford: The Clarendon Press.
FIKRY-ATALLAH, MONA
1972   "Tales collected from the Wala of Wa," in *African Folklore*. Edited by Richard M. Dorson, 397–400. Garden City, N.Y.: Doubleday.
FINNEGAN, RUTH
1970   *Oral literature in Africa*. Oxford: The Clarendon Press.
HUDSON, CHARLES
1966   Folk history and ethnohistory. *Ethnohistory* 13:53.
INNES, GORDON
1965   The function of the song in Mende folktales. *Sierra Leone Language Review* 4:54–63.
KALOUS, MILAN
1970   A contribution to some problems of Benin chronology. *Archiv Orientalni* 38:431–436.
KUBIK, GERHARD
1968   Alo-Yoruba story songs. *African Music Society Journal* 4:10–22.
MELZIAN, HANS
1937   *A concise dictionary of the Bini language of southern Nigeria*. London: Kegan Paul, Trench, Trubner.

NOSS, PHILIP A.
1972 "Description in Gbaya literary art," in *African folklore*. Edited by R. M. Dorson, 81–86. Garden City, N.Y.: Doubleday.

ROTH, H. LING
1903 *Great Benin: its customs, arts, and horrors*. London: F. King and Sons.

RYDER, A. F. C.
1965 A reconsideration of the Ife-Benin relationships. *Journal of African History* 6:25.
1969 *Benin and the Europeans 1485–1897*. Ibadan History Series. London: Longmans Green.

STURTEVANT, WILLIAM C.
1968 "Anthropology, history, and ethnohistory," in *Introduction to cultural anthropology: essays in the scope and method of the science of man*. Edited by James A. Clifton. Boston: Houghton Mifflin.

WOLF, S.
1963 Benin-Konigslisten. *Annals of the Naprstek Museum Praha* 2:193–218.

Biographical Notes

ROGER D. ABRAHAMS (1933–   ) is currently Professor of English and Anthropology at the University of Texas at Austin, serving his time as Chairman of the English Department. He has done a good deal of field work in Afro-American communities from which have emerged the books: *Deep down in the jungle* (1964 and 1970), *Deep the water, shallow the shore* (1966), *Positively black* (1970), *Talking black* (1977), as well as numerous books in the areas of American folksongs and children's games. Soon to appear is the monumental *Bibliography of Afro-American folklore and culture* (2 vols. ISHI, 1978) edited with John Szwed.

BOGUMIL W. ANDRZEJEWSKI (1922–   ) was born in Poland. He is currently Reader in Cushitic Languages at the School of Oriental and African Studies, University of London, and Co-Chairman of the African oral literature program for the M.A. degree in Area Studies. He was educated at the Universities of Oxford and London. Since 1950 he has spent several years in the Horn of Africa conducting linguistic and literary researches. Relevant publications include a collection of annotated Somali texts entitled *Hikmad Soomaali* (with Muuse H.I. Galaal, 1956), *Somali poetry: an introduction* (with I. M. Lewis, 1964), and the Somali play *Shabeelnaagood* (1974), which he transcribed from a taped performance and translated (as *Leopard among the women*), together with an essay on the Somali theater.

HIROYUKI ARAKI (1924–   ) is now Professor of Comparative Culture at the Hiroshima University. He was educated at the Kyoto University, and Indiana University and has done fieldwork in Japan and Korea. His publications include *Folktales of Koshiki-jima* (1970); *Behavior patterns of Japanese* (1973); *Logic of Japanese sentiment* (1976); *Earth-God Sutra of blind monks* (1978). He is also an editor of *Folktales of the World*, published by Miyaishoten in Japan (1974).

HAFIZULLAH BAGHBAN (1938–   ) is currently Visiting Assistant Professor of Folklore at the Folklore Department, Indiana University. He was educated at Kabul University in Afghanistan; Teachers College, Columbia University; and Folklore Institute, Indiana University. He has conducted folklore fieldwork in Afghanistan in 1961, 1967–1968, and 1972–1973. Among his publications are "An overview of Herat folk literature" *Adab* 16 (1968–1969; "The fable as a means of moral instruction" *Tarbiyat* 6 (1973); "A preliminary bibliography of Middle Eastern Folklore"; and *Folklore forum: bibliographic and special series* 9 (1972). Entitled "The context and concept of humor in Magadi Theater," his dissertation is currently under review by the Near East Center at the University of Texas.

DAN BEN-AMOS (1934–   ) is a Professor of Folklore at the University of Pennsylvania. He was educated at the Hebrew University of Jerusalem and Indiana University. His field research was among the Edo people of Nigeria. Among his publications are *Sweet words: storytelling events in Benin*, *Folklore genres* (editor), *Folklore: performance and communication* (editor with Kenneth S. Goldstein), *In praise of the Baal Shem Tov* (editor and translator with Jerome R. Mintz).

CARLA BIANCO (1931–   ), is currently Associate Professor of Cultural Anthropology at the "Istituto di Filosofia" of the University of Firenze and Lecturer in Urban Studies and Folklore at the Rome program of Temple University. She has a Doctorate from the University of Rome and a Ph.D. from Indiana University. She has done extensive field research in Italy, the United States, and Canada, receiving grants and fellowships from the Wenner-Gren Foundation, the A.C.L.S., the Museum of Man of Ottawa, and the Fulbright-Hays Program. She has concentrated on the subject of folklore and emigration (*The two Rosetos*, 1974), folk religion, folk narrative (*Discoteca di Stato Catalog*, 1970). Her recent publications and present work refer to the study of ethnicity and fieldwork methodology.

LINDA DÉGH (1920–   ) was educated at the University of Budapest, Hungary (Ph.D. 1943) where she taught till 1964. She moved to the U.S.A. in 1964 where she is now Professor of Folklore in the Folklore Department at Indiana University, Bloomington. Founder and Editor of the *Indiana Folklore*; Associate Editor of *Journal of American Folklore*; Pitré Prize winner, 1963; Gúggenheim Fellow, 1970/71; Fellow of the

American Folklore Society, Author of *Folktales of Hungary* (1975); *Folktales and society* (1969); *People in the tobacco belt: four lives* (1975), *Studies in East European folk narrative* (1978) and many articles. Her research interests include folk narrative genres, performers and performance, processes of narrative transmission, urban and regional ethnic folklore, symbols and emblems of ethnicity in the United States, Canada and Europe.

RICHARD M. DORSON (1916–   ) was born in New York City. He was educated at Exeter (1929–1933), and Harvard (A.B. 1937, M.A. 1940 in American History, Ph.D. 1943 in History of American Civilization). He taught in the history departments at Harvard, 1943–1944, Michigan State University, 1944–1956, and Indiana University, 1957 to present, where he holds the title Distinguished Professor of History and Folklore (conferred in 1971) and Director of the Folklore Institute (which he organized in 1963). He has held three Gúggenheim fellowships, two American Council of Learned Society Fellowships, a Library of Congress fellowship, and a Fulbright award as visiting professor of American Studies at Tokyo University, 1956–1957. His publications include twenty-three books written or edited, twelve books of which he is general editor in the series *Folktales of the World* (University of Chicago Press), and about 250 articles, essays, and book chapters.

JAMES W. FERNANDEZ (1930–   ) is Professor of Anthropology at Princeton University. Two of his publications are relevant to the study in this book: *The mission of metaphor in expressive culture* (1974) and *Poetry in motion: being moved by amusement, by mockery and by mortality in the Asturian Mountains* (1977).

MONA FIKRY-ATALLAH (1937–   ) was born in Cairo, Egypt. She was educated at Boston University and Indiana University where she obtained her Ph.D. in folklore, writing her dissertation on "Wa: A case study of social values and social tensions as reflected in the oral traditions of the Wala of northern Ghana". Her essay "Wala oral history and Wa's social realities" appeared in the book *African folklore* (1972). She has taught Afro-American Studies at Howard University.

ROBERT A. GEORGES (1933–   ) is Professor of English and Folklore at UCLA. He received his M.A. degree from the University of Pennsylvania and his Ph.D. from Indiana University, writing his dissertation on "Greek-American Folk Beliefs: Survivals and Living Tradition". He has carried out fieldwork in various Greek communities in the United States. Among his recent publications are *Stilpon P. Kyriakides: two studies in modern Greek folklore* (1968); *Studies in mythology* (1968); "Toward an understanding of storytelling events" (1969); and "The general concept of legend: some assumptions to be reexamined and reassessed" (1971).

SAYYID HURREIZ (1940–   ) was born in Budapest, Hungary but was raised in the Sudan. He took his Ph.D. in folklore from Indiana University, writing his dissertation on "Ja'aliyyin folktales: An interplay of African, Arabian, and Islamic elements". He is now Senior Lecturer at the Institute of African and Asian Studies at the University of Khartoum. His fieldwork in the Sudan has also resulted in the texts of Manasir and Ja'aliyyin tales and his article "Afro-Arab relations in the Sudanese folktale", which have been published in *African folklore*, edited by R. M. Dorson (1972). He has also coedited, with H. W. Bell, *Directions in Sudanese linguistics and folklore* (1974).

SUSAN KALČIK (1939–   ), who is of Slovak-American heritage, was born in Cleveland, Ohio. She received her M.A. from Miami University and is a Ph.D. candidate in folklore at the University of Texas. At present, she is a folklorist in the Smithsonian Folklife Program in Washington, D.C. Among her recent publications are "'Like Ann's gynecologist or the time I was raped'; personal narratives in women's rap groups" (1975) and "The performance of identity: music and musicians in the ethnic American community" (1978). She has also coauthored, with Bess Lomax Hawes, "In celebration of ethnicity" (1976) and "American folklore and American studies" (1976), with Roger Abrahams and Richard Bauman.

BARBARA KIRSHENBLATT-GIMBLETT (1942–   ) is Associate Professor of Folklore and Folklife at the University of Pennsylvania (Philadelphia) and Visiting Associate Professor of Yiddish Studies at Columbia University and the Max Weinreich Center for Advanced Jewish Studies (YIVO), both in New York City. She was educated at the University of Toronto, University of California (Berkeley), and Indiana University (Bloomington). She has conducted fieldwork among Jewish immigrants in Toronto, Ontario, and in New York City. She has authored, coauthored, and edited the following: *Speech play: research and resources for studying linguistic creativity* (1976); *Image before my eyes: A photographic history of Jewish life in Poland, 1864–1939* (1977); *Fabric of Jewish life: textiles from the Jewish Museum collection* (1977); "A parable in context: A social interactional analysis of a storytelling performance" (1975); and "The concept and varieties of narrative performance in East European Jewish Culture" (1974).

ROBERT B. KLYMASZ (1936–   ) is Executive Director of the Ukrainian Cultural and Educational Centre in Winnipeg, Canada, and served earlier as Folklorist and Senior Coordinator heading the Slavic and East European Programme, Canadian Centre for Folk Culture Studies, National Museum of Man, Ottawa, where he designed and implemented much of the Museum's first intensive investigations of minority nonaboriginal ethnic groups in Canada. He was educated at universities in Canada, the United States and Czechoslovakia, and has conducted fieldwork over a period of several years among Ukrainians in Western Canada and, more recently, in the Chicago area. He has taught at the Universities of Manitoba, Ottawa, Harvard, and St. Andrew's College in Winnipeg. Relevant publications include *An introduction to the Ukrainian–Canadian immigrant folksong cycle* (1970) and "From immigrant to ethnic folklore: A Canadian view of process and transition" (1973).

DEMETRIOS S. LOUKATOS (1908–   ) is Emeritus Professor of Ethnography and Folklore at the University of Ioannina (Greece). He was educated at the Universities of Athens and Paris (Philosophy and Ethnology). From 1938 until 1962 he worked at the Academy of Athens' Folklore Archives, and has conducted fieldwork in different parts of Greece. His publications have included studies on proverbs, riddles, folktales, and songs as well as on birth, marriage, death, and religion in Greece. He is the author of several books: *Popular religion in Cephalonia* (1946), translated into French (1950); *Popular maxims from Cephalonia* (1952); *Greek popular texts* (1957); *Folklorica contemporanea* (1963); *Proverbia e(x) Fabulis* (1972) and most recently: *Introduction to the Greek Folklore* (1977).

ELLI KÖNGÄS MARANDA (1932–   ) was born in Tervola, Finland. She received her M.A. from the University of Helsinki and her Ph.D. in folklore from Indiana University, writing her dissertation on "Finnish-American folklore: quantitative and qualitative analysis", and is currently a member of the faculty at Laval University, Canada. Among her recent publications are *Finnish folklore reader and glossary* (1968) and "Theory and practice of riddle analysis" in *Towards new perspectives in folklore* (1972). She has also coedited, with Pierre Maranda, *Structural analysis of oral tradition* (1971) and *Structural models in folklore and transformational essays* (1972).

RUTH I. MESERVE (1944–   ) was educated at the University of Kansas where she concentrated on Asian studies; she has taken graduate work at the University of Kansas and Indiana University. As a husband and wife team Ruth and Walter Meserve have completed fieldwork in Hong Kong and Taiwan (1970) and in Chinese communities in Penang, Malaysia, and Singapore (1976). Their research interests include a history of modern Chinese drama and theater and the role of drama and theater in both problem solving and social change. Their joint publications include two collections — *Modern drama from communist China* (1970) and *Modern literature from China* (1974) — and several articles of which the following are representative: "China's children's theatre: education and propaganda" (1973), "Communist China's war theatre" (1972), "Lao Sheh: from people's artist to 'An enemy of the people'" (1974), and "*The white-haired girl:* a model for continuing revolution" (1976).

WALTER J. MESERVE (1923–   ) holds degrees from Bates College, Boston University and the University of Washington (Ph.D.). He is a professor in the Department of Theater and Drama at Indiana University where he is also affiliated with the Department of East Asian Languages and Cultures; he is currently External Examiner in Theater and Drama for the Universiti Sains Malaysia (Penang).

VENETIA NEWALL (1935–   ) is an Honorary Research Fellow in Folklore at University College London. She has been Honorary Secretary of the Folklore Society since 1967. She was educated at St. Andrews University, Scotland, and at the Sorbonne. Her publications include: *An egg at Easter: A folklore study* (awarded the 1971 Chicago International Folklore Prize by the University of Chicago). Relevant articles include: "Black Britain: the Jamaicans and their folklore" (1975), "Selected Jamaican foodways in the homeland and in England" (1976), "Ghost lore of the Jamaican ethnic community in Britain" (1976), "Some examples of the practice of Obeah by West Indian immigrants in London" (forthcoming), "Love and marriage customs of the Jamaican community in Britain" (forthcoming).

JUHA PENTIKÄINEN (1940–   ) is Professor of Comparative Religion at the University of Helsinki. He received his M.A. from the University of Helsinki in 1963, a Phil.Lic. from Turku 1966, and a Ph.D. from Turku in 1968 with a dissertation on Nordic and North Eurasian folk belief. He has been Visiting Professor of Anthropology at the University of California, Berkeley, and Visiting Professor of Folklore at the University of Indiana, Bloomington. He has been the Chief Editor of *Temenos* since 1967, the Chairman of the Nordic Council of the Humanities since 1974, and Member of the Finnish UNESCO Council. His special interests include methodology of anthropological research, Arctic cultures, and religious and psychological anthropology.

DUNJA RIHTMAN-AUGUŠTIN (1926–   ) is currently Director of the Institute for Folklore Research in Zagreb and Editor of the yearbook *Narodna umjetnost* (Folk art). She attended the University of Zagreb where she received her first degree in Ethnology (Ph.D. in Sociology).

She has published about 30 papers (articles and studies in books and reviews) dealing with cultural change, cultural and social values, transition of folk culture, interaction of peasant and urban folklore, problems of contemporary folklore and its second existence. Relevant recent articles include "Traditional thinking" (1974), "Transition of folk culture in Yugoslavia" (1976), and "Assumptions for modern ethnological research" (1976).

AHMED RUSHDI SALEH (1920–   ) received his B.A. from Cairo University and M.A. from the Higher Institute of Journalism. Since 1941 he has worked as announcer, journalist, Visiting Professor of Cultural Anthropology (Folklore) at Alexandria University, Director of Cairo Center of Folklore, and Director of the National Folkloric Ensemble. From 1962 to 1965 he presented a weekly television program on folklore. He has published many books, theses, and articles on folklore including folk literature, prose folk sayings, folk poetry of folk songs, folk arts, and folklore in the Arab world. He has also written many books on dramatic criticism and history and a collection of short stories (*The second wife*) which was filmed in 1966. In 1978 his fifth and sixth novels were published entitled *Who has ever seen my love* and *The lady of the hotel*.

CARMELO LISON TOLOSANA (1929–   ) is currently Professor and Director of the Department of Social Anthropology and Vice Dean of the Faculty of Politics and Sociology at the Universidad Complutense de Madrid. Educated at the Universities of Zaragoza and Oxford, he has carried out anthropological fieldwork in Aragon and in Galicia. He has taught at the University of Sessex in the department of Social Anthropology and also in Campinas, Sao Paulo. His publications include *Belmonte de los Caballeros: A sociological study of a Spanish town* (1966); *Antropología Cultural de Galicia* (1971); *Perfiles Símbolico-Morales de la Cultura Gallega* (1974); and *Invitación a la Antropología de Espana* (1977).

ANDREW VÁZSONYI (1906–   ) was born in Hungary and educated at the Pázmány Péter University in Budapest (B.A. and LL.D.). He is currently Research Associate of the Indiana University Research Center for Language and Semiotic Studies after having retired as Associate Chairman of the same center. His recent publications concern mostly life and culture of immigrants, theory of folklore transmission, modern legends and problems of mass communication.

Index of Names

Index of Subjects